OPRAH WINFREY

AND THE GLAMOUR OF MISERY

OPRAH WINFREY
AND THE GLAMOUR OF MISERY

An Essay on Popular Culture

EVA ILLOUZ

COLUMBIA UNIVERSITY PRESS
NEW YORK

COLUMBIA UNIVERSITY PRESS

Publishers Since 1893
New York   Chichester, West Sussex
Copyright © 2003 Columbia University Press

Library of Congress Cataloging-in-Publication Data
Illouz, Eva, 1961–
Oprah Winfrey and the glamour of misery : an essay on popular culture /
Eva Illouz.
p. cm.
Includes bibliographical references and index.
ISBN 0–231–11812–0 (cloth : alk. paper) — ISBN 0–231–11813–9 (paper :
alk. paper)
1. Winfrey, Oprah. 2. Oprah Winfrey show. I. Title.
PN 1992.4.W56 I55 2003
791.45′028′092—dc21   2002034782

Columbia University Press books are printed on permanent
and durable acid-free paper.
Printed in the United States of America
c 10 9 8 7 6 5 4 3 2 1
p 10 9 8 7 6 5 4 3 2 1

To Elchanan, Nathanel, and Immanuel

Bombastic manifestoes
Civil warfare
Pitched battles
campaigns
filled Mr. Cogito
with boredom
in every generation
appear those who wish
to snatch poetry
from the claws
of everydayness
with stubbornness worthy of a better cause
already in their youth
they enter the orders
of Most Holy Subtlety
and Ascension
they strain the mind and body
to express what is
beyond
what is
above
they don't even suspect
how many promises
enchantments
surprises
are concealed in the language spoken by all of us
tinker tailor and Horace.

—Zbigniew Herbert

CONTENTS

Acknowledgments   xi

1 Introduction: Oprah Winfrey and the Study of Culture   1

2 The Success of a Self-Failed Woman   16

3 Everyday Life as the Uncanny:
The Oprah Winfrey Show as a New Cultural Genre   47

4 Pain and Circuses   77

5 The Hypertext of Identity   120

6 Suffering and Self-Help as Global Forms of Identity   156

7 The Sources and Resources of *The Oprah Winfrey Show*   178

8 Toward an Impure Critique of Popular Culture   206

9 Conclusion: Ordinary People, Extraordinary Television   236

Notes   243

Biblography   263

Subject Index   293

Name Index   297

ACKNOWLEDGMENTS

If it takes a village to raise a child, at times, it seems it takes an even bigger village to produce a book. Amy Jordan, Susan Neiman, and Beatrice Smedley have provided invaluable comments during the gestation of the book. Carol Kidron's relentless rigor made this birth far less painful and far more pleasurable. Elizabeth Long's acumen and generosity provided a tremendous help in giving birth by pointing to important flaws and emphasizing strengths.

Larry Gross believed in this project when it was only an idea: my gratitude goes to him.

Yoram Bilu, Carola Hilfrich, Eppie Kreitner, Michele Lamont, Boaz Shamir, Eitan Wilf, and Louise Woodstock generously gave of their time, encouragement, critiques, and insights. I especially want to thank Michele Lamont for her enduring trust. Janice Fisher and Leslie Kriesel at Columbia University Press expertly turned a disheveled baby into a tidy one.

The Shain Center and the Research and Development Authority at the Hebrew University of Jerusalem provided much-needed financial help. I have been lucky to benefit from Ran Carmeli's assistance and expertise.

This book is dedicated to Nathanel and Immanuel, who never fail to remind me of the glamour and miseries of daily life, and to Elchanan, a full partner in the ideas and the housecleaning without which this book could not have seen the light.

OPRAH WINFREY

AND THE GLAMOUR OF MISERY

1

INTRODUCTION: OPRAH WINFREY AND
THE SOCIOLOGY OF CULTURE

To our scholars, strangely enough, even the most pressing question does not occur: to what end is their work . . . useful? Surely not to earn a living or hunt for positions of honor? No, truly not. . . . What good at all is science if it has no time for culture? . . . whence, whither, wherefore is all science, if it is not meant to lead to culture?
           —Friedrich Nietzsche

Oprah Winfrey is the protagonist of the story to be told here, but this book has broader intentions: to reflect on the meaning of popular culture and to offer new strategies for interpreting that meaning. In that respect, this book is a long rumination on the current state of cultural studies, with two distinct purposes. The first is to move the study of popular culture away from the power-pleasure-resistance conceptual trio that has dominated it and to bring it within the fold of "moral sociology," which has traditionally explored the role that culture plays in making sense of our lives and in binding us to a realm of values. The second purpose is to explore the methodological difficulties involved in capturing the "meaning" of a cultural enterprise as complex as that of Oprah Winfrey. In this sense, this study can be read as an exercise in cultural interpretation and, more specifically, in the interpretation of popular culture.

Oprah Winfrey is a particularly apt subject for these multiple tasks, for she offers a spectacular example of the ways in which a cultural form—the Oprah Winfrey persona—has assumed an almost unprecedented role in the American cultural scene. Oprah embodies not only quintessentially

American values but also an American way of using and making culture. Oprah Winfrey has risen in only one decade to the status of richest woman in the media world—accumulating wealth equivalent to that of the GNP of a small country[1]—and her fame and her cultural role are unprecedented in television. An excerpt from the biography on her Web site makes this clear:

> Oprah Winfrey has already left an indelible mark on the face of television. From her humble beginnings in rural Mississippi, Oprah's legacy has established her as one of the most important figures in popular culture. Her contributions can be felt beyond the world of television and into areas such as publishing, music, film, philanthropy, education, health and fitness as well as social awareness. As supervising producer and host of *The Oprah Winfrey Show*, Oprah entertains, enlightens, and empowers millions of viewers around the world.
>
> Oprah has been honored with the most prestigious awards in broadcasting, including the George Foster Peabody Individual Achievement Award (1996) and the IRTS Gold Medal Award (1996). In 1997, Oprah was named *Newsweek*'s most important person in books and media and *TV Guide*'s "Television Performer of the Year." The following year, Oprah received The National Academy of Television Arts & Sciences' Lifetime Achievement Award. Also in 1998, she was named one of the 100 most influential people of the 20th Century by *Time* magazine. In November 1999, Oprah received one of the publishing industry's top honors, the National Book Foundation's 50th Anniversary Gold Medal, for her influential contribution to reading and books. She has also received seven Emmy Awards for Outstanding Talk Show Host and nine Emmy Awards for Outstanding Talk Show. In September 2002, Oprah was honored with the first-ever Bob Hope Humanitarian Award at the 54th Annual Prime-Time Emmy Awards. (http://www.oprah.com/about/press/about_press_bio.jhtml)

Oprah Winfrey is not only a famous character—a condition shared by many others. She is a cultural phenomenon. As an article published in *Ebony* put it: "From the beginning, her show has captured the American television psyche like nothing the industry has seen before or since. The fact is, since her show went national in 1986, it has remained head and shoulders above the others. All of them."[2]

Her talk show has won thirty Daytime Emmy Awards, and, at the rather young age of 44, Oprah garnered the Lifetime Achievement Award. In 1994, she was named by *Forbes* as the highest paid entertainer (winning over such male media figures as Bill Cosby and Steven Spielberg). Oprah Winfrey is more than a taste maker; she not only embodies values that many Americans revere but also has invented a cultural form that has changed television and American culture. In 2000, anyone logging in at the world-famous Amazon.com bookstore could find a rubric entitled "Oprah Winfrey Books," along with such general rubrics as "Fiction" and "Nonfiction." These books were the novels chosen by Oprah Winfrey to appear in her famous monthly Book Club. Her choices alone have been decisive for the careers of numerous authors and publishing houses. Why? Because Oprah Winfrey has been one of the most important commercial forces in the U.S. publishing industry. In April 2000, Oprah even established a new magazine, O Magazine, which Newsweek called "the most successful magazine start-up in history."[3]

An article in Vanity Fair put the point aptly: "Oprah Winfrey arguably has more influence on the culture than any university president, politician, or religious leader, except perhaps the Pope."[4] Or, as writer Fran Lebowitz put it, "Oprah is probably the greatest media influence on the adult population. She is almost a religion."[5] I would even go a step further. In the realm of popular culture, Oprah Winfrey is one of the most important American cultural phenomena of the second half of the twentieth century, if we measure "importance" by her visibility,[6] the size of the fortune she has managed to amass in one decade, the size of her daily audience,[7] the number of imitations she has generated, the innovativeness of her show, and her impact on various aspects of American culture—an effect that some have called, somewhat derogatively, the "Oprahization of culture." In 2001, the "Top Ten Words of 2001 Announced by Your Dictionary.Com" defined "Oprahization" facetiously but tellingly as follows: "Describes the litmus test of political utterances: if it doesn't play on Oprah, it doesn't play at all."

The obvious cultural visibility and economic size of the Oprah phenomenon should provide a good enough reason to undertake a study of its meaning. Indeed, Oprah has such influence that she is an ideal example of those collective "big" cultural phenomena that sociologists of culture love to analyze because they reveal a society's mindset.

But there is another reason why Oprah Winfrey is a compelling object of study. In spite of her popularity, or perhaps because of it, Oprah Winfrey has been the object of disdain on part of the "old" intellectual and cultural elites. In a 1993 Chicago Magazine article, Ms. Harrison, an essayist and fiction writer who in 1989 had written an in-depth profile of Oprah, was quoted as saying: "Her show . . . I just can't watch it. You will forgive me, but it's white trailer trash. It debases language, it debases emotion. It provides everyone with glib psychological formulas. These people go around talking like a fortune cookie. And I think she is in very large part responsible for that."[8]

This echoes a more general disparaging view, aptly represented by Robert Thompson, director of Syracuse University's Center for the Study of Popular Television, who said that talk shows exemplify the fact that "TV has so much on it that's so stupid."[9] Like so many other elements of popular culture, Oprah Winfrey and her talk show have generated ritual declarations of disdain from public intellectuals, political activists, feminists, and conservative moral crusaders. Precisely for this reason, Oprah is of great value to the student of culture. The cultural objects that irritate tastes and habits are the very ones that shed the brightest light on the hidden moral assumptions of the guardians of taste.[10] Such cultural objects make explicit the tacit divisions and boundaries through which culture is classified and thrown into either the trash bin or the treasure chest.[11] Indeed, the criticisms of Oprah Winfrey offer a convenient compendium of the very critiques that are ritually targeted at popular culture. If talk shows systematically blur boundaries constitutive of middle-class taste, Oprah offers a privileged point from which to examine such boundaries, partly because she herself manipulates them in a virtuoso fashion.

With regard to the traditional corpus of studies in the sociology of culture, these are sufficient and even compelling reasons for studying Oprah Winfrey. Yet there is a last and perhaps most consequential reason why Oprah Winfrey is of such burning interest to the student of culture: she demands a drastic reconceptualization of popular culture. Indeed, "pleasure," "power," and "resistance"—the main concepts of cultural studies in the 1980s and 1990s—are inadequate in helping us to gain a deep understanding of her phenomenon.

Show after show, I was struck by the fact that Winfrey seems to bring us back to the question of the ethical force of cultural meanings, which has haunted sociology since the turn of the twentieth century. Oprah's use of culture invites us to go back to Max Weber's view that culture is a way to respond to chaos and to meaninglessness by offering rational systems of explanations of the world.[12] Weber's view, which was mostly applied to religious systems, should be extended to popular culture. Popular culture is not only about entertainment. It is also, more often than is acknowledged in cultural studies, about moral dilemmas: how to cope with a world that consistently fails us and how to make sense of the minor and major forms of suffering that plague ordinary lives. In this book I argue that Oprah Winfrey has become an international and a mighty (western) symbol, because she offers a new cultural form through which to present and process suffering generated by the "chaos" of intimate social relationships, one of the major cultural features of the late modern era.[13] Oprah Winfrey shows us how to cope with chaos by offering a rationalized view of the self, inspired by the language of therapy, to manage and change the self. *The Oprah Winfrey Show* is a popular cultural form that makes sense of suffering at a time when psychic pain has become a permanent feature of our polities and when, simultaneously, so much in our culture presumes that well-being and happiness depend on successful self-management.

However, this "old-fashioned" approach to popular culture—viewing it as an arena in which the ethical orientation of the self is addressed—must be framed in radically new terms. For this "old" vocation of culture has been recast by Oprah Winfrey in an unprecedented new form. Oprah points to the fact that cultural objects are no longer defined by space, territory, nation, or technology. She is better understood as a criss-crossing of expert knowledge, multiple media technologies, and orality intertwined with multiple forms of literacy, overlapping media industries, cyberspace, support groups, and traditional charismatic authority. *The Oprah Winfrey Show* has a tentacular structure that defies boundaries and definitions of what constitutes a text. Its format and topic areas reach into the domains of the family (which includes topics such as intimacy, parenthood, divorce, and siblings), the publishing industry, various experts (psychologists, doctors, lawyers, financial consultants, et cetera), stars of the music and cinema industries, volunteer organizations, the legal and political systems, and, finally and most importantly, the singular, particular, and ordinary biography of the common man and woman.

Because this tentacular cultural structure stretches from the biographical to the transnational, from the personal life story to the economic empire, traditional models of cultural analysis fail, as they conceive of culture as bound by territory and nation or circumscribed within one social sphere (e.g., "family," "mass media," or "the state"). While these are still relevant dimensions of much of our cultural material, they cannot account for a form as meandering as that of Oprah Winfrey. While my previous book, *Consuming the Romantic Utopia*, examined the process by which a private practice—courtship—went to the public sphere of consumption and was commodified within and through icons of consumption, here I examine how the public sphere implodes from the multiplicity of private worlds it stages and how it builds new and unprecedented connections between the individual biography and the intensely commodified medium of television.

IN SEARCH OF MEANING

In the last decade, talk shows have come to occupy a central place in American television, a fact that has elicited public outcry over the vulgarization of culture as well as a flurry of studies on their meaning and impact. Because the topic has been so controversial, most studies have been preoccupied with the question of whether talk shows debase cultural standards and political consciousness. For example, for Heaton and Wilson (1995), talk shows crudely manipulate their guests; betray the basic moral code of truthfulness; are "voyeuristic," "sensationalist," and "sleazy"; encourage stereotyping; and debase standards of public debate.[14] For many such commentators, the intense revealing of private life in public that is the distinctive mark of talk shows threatens a genuine public sphere, stereotypes women, encourages a culture of victimhood, and commercializes private life.

Other analysts beg for us to understand talk shows as a phenomenon that throws into question our conventional definitions of "public sphere." In their excellent study of audiences' responses to talk shows, Livingstone and Lunt have argued that talk shows in fact expand the scope of the public sphere.[15] If classical liberalism holds that that sphere should include a homogeneous public whose members hold and discuss well-formed opinions, talk shows construct viewers as a fragmented plurality of publics, members of which enter the public sphere with half-formed opinions, life stories, and even emotions. This suggests that what counts as a public discussion has been enlarged to include topics not dreamed of by the theorists of liberalism.

In an even more pointed way, Shattuc has argued that, far from subduing women, talk shows engage them in a complex and fragile dynamic of empowerment, providing an arena in which to discuss "women's issues" and giving voice to the voiceless. Such conclusions, in turn, suggest that we should revise our presumably gender-blind notions of "public sphere."[16] Finally, in his excellent study, Joshua Gamson (1998) has argued that talk shows deconstruct notions of gender and sexuality, thereby transforming our representations of sexual minorities and opening up the possibility for a more egalitarian politics of representation of these minorities.

In contradistinction to these studies, I focus on the Oprah Winfrey talk show first and foremost as the product of a set of intentions deployed by a cultural agent (see chapter 2). Thus, my interpretation of the Oprah Winfrey show is less interested in the politics of representation of her texts than in the moral positions she takes and makes manifest through her intentional manipulation of cultural codes (see chapters 4 and 5). I argue that, more than many televisual texts, as a text *The Oprah Winfrey Show* is inseparable from the set of intentions Oprah Winfrey tries to deliver to her viewers.

A COMPREHENSIVE APPROACH TO CULTURE

Broadly, the analysis of culture can be approached along three paths. The first is concerned with what we may call the realm of the "ethical": that is, the ways in which culture bestows on our actions a sense of "purpose" and "meaning" through a realm of values or through powerful symbols that motivate and guide our action "from within." This perspective approaches culture as the force that binds us to the social body through values, rituals, or morality plays.[17] "Meaning" implies here a kind of energetic engagement of the self in a social and cultural community through the upholding, defense, and performance of those values, core symbols, and morality plays.

The second approach is indifferent to the ways culture informs our moral choices. It approaches culture as an arena in which different groups struggle to define what is worthy and legitimate and that establishes mechanisms of exclusion and inclusion to institutionalize such definitions. Popular culture is viewed as a terrain in which strategies of resistance, empowerment, and symbolic violence are exerted. In this view, meaning is a resource mobilized by actors to bestow legitimacy on their actions or to deny the legitimacy of others' culture.[18]

Finally, a third approach views "meaning" as the outcome of social forces mirrored and/or distorted in a text. These forces can be institutional, economic, legal, social, or organizational. They "explain" meaning in the sense that the text is examined in terms of its context of production. By whom, how, and for whom a text is produced constitute the main parameters of a text's production and will be used to explicate its "meaning."[19]

This book offers a comprehensive strategy for studying popular culture, a strategy that holds together the ethical dimension (the ways in which a particular cultural meaning shapes and enhances the meaning of our lives), the critical dimension (how culture exists in the context of power relations that it helps to maintain or twist), and the institutional dimension (which organizational and institutional parameters shape the production and reception of a text). To be precise, I argue for an approach to culture that follows the lines of what Georges Marcus calls "pragmatic holism." Pragmatic holism moves between different levels of analysis, recognizing the limitations and the "intractability" of each level. In Marcus's words, this method "juxtaposes several alternative accounts of the same subject or phenomenon. It is pragmatic in that it recognizes that you can't *really* say it all; all analyses, no matter how totalistic their rhetorics, are partial. Rather, you can try for a comprehensive display of levels of analysis, of epistemological angles, so to speak."[20]

These three approaches to culture—the ethical, the critical, and the institutional—should be juxtaposed and articulated with, rather than opposed to, one another. For example, as I shall show, we cannot wage an adequate critique of popular culture unless we have devised strategies to find out just what the text intends to perform. Moreover, the critiques that have been proferred about and against Oprah Winfrey have become incorporated in Oprah's textual strategies, in such a way that it becomes difficult to disentangle the moral critiques of the text from the text itself. Analytically, then, I have three broad intents. One is to clarify the historical and cultural meanings that the persona of Oprah Winfrey and her show incarnate, articulate, stage, and perform. The second is to understand the moral enterprise of Oprah Winfrey in the context of a social order that severely strains the capacity of the self to make sense of its social environment; in that respect, my analysis takes very seriously Oprah's therapeutic vocation. The third is a critique of the moral and therapeutic role that Oprah Winfrey has assumed.

INTERPRETATION

Oprah Winfrey's popularity and success are so spectacular that they compel us to ask, with anthropologist Dan Sperber, a simple question: "Why are some representations more catching than others?"[21] To address this question, we must have a robust method of interpreting texts. But when the sociologist inquires about the meaning of a contemporary text, she is likely to be as perplexed as the historian of the remote past. Both scholars are left with the unnerving job of trying to explicate why certain cultural objects are more efficient and efficacious than others in capturing the social imagination[22] while using tools that make their results too often resemble guesswork. The study of meaning should produce more than an educated guess. No matter how "thick" our study is, it does not excuse us from the methodological obligations to weigh our interpretations against those of others and to ground them as best we can in the social context that has given rise to them.

If the interpretation of a Balinese cockfight was to show how a small incident branches out to "the enormous complexities of social experience,"[23] in the case of Oprah, the challenge is the opposite: she contains and addresses such a wide variety of experiences, stories, and institutions that it is difficult to simplify this labyrinthic cultural form without sacrificing depth and complexity. Indeed, Oprah Winfrey and her show belong to the category of texts that are much "thicker than others."[24] The phenomenon contains multiple cultural forms that demand a variety of tools and sites of study: Oprah's biography, the autobiographical discourse of her guests, the codes of speech used by the talk show to produce an ephemeral but nonetheless powerful reality, the prescriptive speech of the experts invited on her show, the literary formula of the novels she chooses for her readers monthly, the critical articles written about Oprah in the popular press, her Web site, O Magazine. These form a complex and overlapping, mixed-media structure that poses a formidable challenge to textual analysis. Thus the first methodological difficulty is to draw the boundaries of the text(s) we are studying. Where does the talk show text start and end? If "O Magazine is an Oprah Winfrey show that one can hold in one's hand"—as the initiators of the concept claimed—then there is at least contiguity, if not continuity, between the electronic and print versions of The Oprah Winfrey Show, and our analysis cannot be based on the technological differences between the two.

The second difficulty is to figure out the best strategy for analyzing the megatextual structure of The Oprah Winfrey Show. Indeed, if "the study of television is the study of effects,"[25] then focusing on "texts" would seem either injudicious or lazy unless one is hoping, ultimately, to extrapolate to effects. Textual analysis is notoriously problematic, for it is vulnerable to the hermeneutic fallacy of "discovering" in texts the meanings that researchers brought with them. Moreover, the study of reception seems to have marked such a breakthrough in our understanding of the impact of the media that the study of texts has come to seem an imperfect substitute.[26] In the context of the preeminence of audience ethnographies, "textual analysis" seems a flawed method through which to grasp the ways meanings are incorporated into daily life. Because audience analysis seems to have become the royal road to study the meaning of media, a word of explanation on my choice is appropriate. A basic justification for a study of texts is offered by Liebes and Katz: "Content analysis is clearly an essential prerequisite for defining what's on television."[27] To study reception, one needs a frame of reference, which is best provided by the rigorous analysis of the content of television. But this justification is not a real one, for it makes the study of texts ancillary to the study of reception.

The study of texts as texts is all the more warranted in Oprah's case, because the very distinction between texts and users is so blurred that it calls into question the distinction between "author" and "reader" that is at the core of traditional literary and communication theory. Ironically and paradoxically, because we have become the uninterrupted "audiences" of various cultural institutions (advertising, marketing, art, television, radio, newspapers, popular psychology, best-selling books, street posters, fashion designers, and body shapes), the distinction between texts and their interpretation has become somewhat artificial and problematic.[28] As historian of the book Roger Chartier has argued, there is actually a continuity between the mental or cultural schemata that structure a text and the mental or cultural categories through which viewers grasp the world of a text. If this was true in the history of sixteenth-century books, it is all the more pertinent in an era where creators of texts are themselves audiences of other texts, and where media technologies and texts have become so closely intertwined. For example, the code of "family communication," so pervasive in talk shows, is the joint product of the publishing industry's self-help manuals and the psychological professions that have elaborated throughout the twentieth century such descriptive and prescriptive models of family relations.[29] This code also structures the cultural world of talk show guests, producers, and viewers, as well as the narratives of family situation comedies and dramas that populate prime-time TV—often centered around disruptions in family communication (*Thirtysomething, All in the Family*), satires of family communication (*The Simpsons*), and idealized versions of family communication (*The Brady Bunch, The Cosby Show*).

This does not mean that the two kinds of schemata—that of the text and that of its reader—are similar or reducible to each other. (Indeed, texts are usually self-contained within space and time and have a stylistic structure, whereas experience flows in an unstructured way.) But it does mean that we can—if provided with the adequate tools—learn a great deal about the mental and cultural worlds of their users through texts and that the relationship between texts and audiences is both circuitous and circular.

There is a final reason talk shows do not lend themselves well to the traditional division between "texts" and their "audiences." The very format of the talk show mixes in a highly perplexing fashion an authorial design with the oral testimonies and stories of the show's numerous and varied guests. In this respect, talk shows make the dichotomy between texts and their "reception" crumble, for the raw material of the show's text is made of the live and natural discourse of "real" actors.[30] Indeed, a main characteristic of *The Oprah Winfrey Show* is that it telescopes the production of the text and the response to it. Audience and guest reactions to the show before, during, and after are intrinsic to the genre (see chapter 3 for a fuller analysis of this). The genre itself incorporates the response to it, forcing us to move away from the classical production/reception dichotomy.

Reception study is not a more sophisticated and exhaustive way to grasp the meaning of a text. Instead, the study of reception has altogether another project in mind: it is preoccupied with understanding how texts are made present in people's lives, that is, how they are incorporated in an economy of needs and social relations. By contrast, the study of texts is the study, to use Paul Ricoeur's expression, of "communication in and through distance."[31] Both spatial and temporal distance formalize communication, best captured through the notion of "genre,"[32] which in turn informs us about conventions of discourse and expression (see chapter 3). In fact, I would argue that we can grasp the shape, volume, and structure of a cultural lexicon better through "texts" than through interviews.

While it does not undertake a systematic analysis of viewer responses to Oprah Winfrey, this study nonetheless incorporates analyses of cultural responses to the show through two main bodies of data. One is her Web site, which contains thousands of messages that provide extensive information on the cultural frameworks within which her show and persona are interpreted. The second comes from an extensive (albeit not exhaustive) search of responses to the show by commentators and journalists in popular magazines. If the Web site provides information on the schemata and cultural frameworks of women from working-class to middle-class backgrounds, the popular and highbrow magazines provide extensive information on the reception of Oprah Winfrey by "cultural specialists" such as journalists, essayists, and academics.

These two forms of reception differ in many obvious ways. While journalists, commentators, and academics attend to a cultural object by self-consciously using formal principles of classification (aesthetic or moral), viewers visiting the Oprah Web site are more immediately implicated in the meaning of the show and are less often in a position to examine the principles that animate their stories, commentaries, and responses to it. In other words, cultural commentators of all persuasions attend to the normative fabric of a text—i.e., which values it conveys, which norms it breaks—much better than viewers or Web site users, who are more attentive to their involvement in the economy of personal meanings enacted by the text. Thus, my hermeneutic strategy pays a great deal of attention to the reception of Oprah Winfrey, but in a different way from what is conventionally dubbed "reception analysis": it is not the readers' way of making sense of *The Oprah Winfrey Show* that interests me as much as the ways in which readers and viewers—who are located at different points of the cultural hierarchy and who approach cultural material with different forms of reflexivity—activate norms, values, and aesthetic criteria to approach cultural material. When examining the readers' and viewers' responses on the Web site, I am less interested in their literal interpretations of any specific show than in the ways in which the show—as a genre—generates discussion, prayer groups, and reflexive self-management. Similarly, my study of the reception of Oprah Winfrey by cultural specialists focuses on the normative and aesthetic criteria underlying the critique and on the ways it is used to defend a certain conception of culture (chapter 8).

This study, then, is based on a mass of texts in which I almost sank: close to one hundred transcripts of shows made available by a commercial company (Burelles); a year and a half of watching the show regularly; some twenty books from the Oprah Winfrey Book Club; a dozen self-help guides discussed during her show; a critical mass of articles about Oprah from the popular press; a number of biographies of Oprah Winfrey; fifteen issues of *O Magazine*; and, finally, several hundred messages responding and reacting to the show on the Oprah Winfrey Web site (in the Book Club rubric, "Heal your spirit," and "Angel Network").

To analyze this mass of texts, I have followed three criteria, essential to make the analysis more than guesswork. First, in order to avoid the famous problem of circularity of interpretation, I incorporate whenever possible the intentions of Oprah Winfrey, a strategy I explain and justify in chapter 2 and chapter 3. Second, I attempt to make my interpretation answer to the criterion of plenitude, which suggests that interpretation should explain as many different aspects of the text as possible. Third, I attempt to keep my interpretation parsimonious. We should try to reduce as much as possible the distance between the interpretation of the text, the social conditions that are supposed to explain it, and the text itself. We should prefer interpretations in which the link between the text and the social conditions is direct (see chapters 6 and 7).[33]

CRITIQUE AND UNDERSTANDING

A cultural object such as Oprah, both popular and offensive to highbrow taste, presents a conundrum for sociological analysis. If sociologists do not want to condemn themselves to reconfirming their own (usually highbrow) tastes or to promoting their own (usually progressive) political agendas, they will want to understand this text from "within," without condescension and without a merely patronizing tolerance for whatever pleasures its audience finds in it. But in adopting this democratic stance, the sociologist becomes ill-equipped to criticize the politics of pleasure. Indeed, endorsing the "pleasure" generated by certain texts leaves us unable to probe further and question the nature of that pleasure. On the other hand, when the sociologist turns to the tradition of critical theory, which has mustered a formidable arsenal of critiques of the culture industries, she seems also condemned to a certain intellectual paralysis that derives from the unswerving assumption that culture and commodity ought to remain in irrevocably separate realms.

I wrestle precisely with the antinomy between understanding and critique in the context of the intensely commodified "political economy" of sentiments offered by Oprah Winfrey (see chapter 8). As I understand it, the task of cultural critique is to enhance human practices by treading a fine line between the "real" and the "ideal," the "is" and the "ought to be." Indicting the critical evaluation of popular culture as "elitist" is theoretically and politically disempowering, as it does not enable us to discuss and distinguish between regressive and emancipatory trends in popular culture.[34] A critical evaluation of popular culture can properly take place only after we have elucidated its meanings.

The task of analyzing the Oprah Winfrey phenomenon must be done within the tension between understanding and critique, because she contains highly perplexing contradictions. There is no doubt that Oprah has perfected with an uncanny talent the exploitation of private sorrow for television profits, and there is no doubt that she blatantly flouts the prohibition against mixing the private realm of sentiments with the market. But she also represents one of the most decisively democratic cultural forms to date in the medium of television.

Understanding and critique need not be in conflict.[35] For powerful critiques derive from an intimate understanding of their object and appeal to its very moral code. This book relies on this simple insight. I am as skeptical of the Olympian critique of the Frankfurt School as I am of the glib postmodernist endorsement of "carnivalesque" consumerism. An Olympian critique will not do because it does not articulate critique from an intimate understanding of the object of critique. I am equally wary of postmodern sociology, which views popular culture as either meaningless background noise or a carnivalesque mockery of hierarchy; in both cases, mass media, and television in particular, are viewed as "sensory machines" with little or no cognitive content. Yet Oprah Winfrey is a powerful example of the resources of ordinary language when it is engaged in the activities of "meaning making" and reflecting on our condition. She is a blatant counterexample to the postmodern view that popular culture is benign, meaningless, or cacophonic.

Thus, if I take popular culture seriously, it is not for the same reasons or in the same ways as postmoderns do. It is less the "transgressive" or "playful" character of popular culture that makes it valuable than the ways in which it connects to the activities of "ordinary language," particularly to the ways in which it discusses our obligations to others, dilemmas, and ordinary moral commitments.

Such an approach to popular culture draws on philosophical claims by Wittgenstein, Stanley Cavell, Martha Nussbaum, Alexander Nehemas, Robert Pippin, and Richard Rorty. These philosophers claim in various ways that ordinary language, stories, morality plays, literature, and metaphors are powerful ways of interrogating reality. These philosophers have claimed that literature and art articulate and even clarify important philosophical questions; I would like to extend this view to popular culture. Indeed, in her exceptional ability to depict and reflect on the predicaments of the self, Oprah Winfrey, no less than tragic plays, novels, or movies, compels us to ask questions fundamental to modern and postmodern existence: How is autonomy to be reached? What is and what ought to be the relationship between individuals and institutions? What is the meaning of marriage and sexuality for men and women in the contemporary era? These and other such questions structure the symbolic world of the text of Oprah Winfrey. As I show in this book, the persona of Oprah Winfrey and her show are symbolic devices no less powerful than works of art that ask what it means to have a self in an era where having an "authentic" self (her term) has become a highly elusive project. This approach will not only give us a richer understanding of popular culture but also make us better equipped to simultaneously understand and criticize it.

Following Wayne Booth and Martha Nussbaum, I call the kind of critique I apply to texts "ethical criticism." Ethical criticism tries to understand how texts enhance our "general aim to live well"[36] and interrogates the text from the standpoint of values and the moral fabric of our lives. It tries to understand what kinds of deliberations are involved in a text, what terms it uses to define a problem, and how a text contributes to practical dilemmas and orientations. The practice of ethical criticism demands that we think differently about the distinction between the "highbrow thought" embodied in philosophy and the realm of unreflective entertainment embodied in popular culture. Oprah Winfrey has placed herself at the heart of the most pressing moral questions of our lives. Indeed, Oprah Winfrey and her show comment on what have become the "hard conditions" of personal life in the late modern era and provide "moral maps" for orientation in such "hard conditions." Broadly, my argument is that her cultural enterprise—ranging from her talk show to her book club and magazine—is both a rumination about and a set of tools for coping with the "new and normal chaos" of personal relationships in the era of reflexive modernity.[37] In this sense they demand that we move away from an idea of culture as simply a mirror of or commentary on the world; talk shows are an ongoing cultural resource for the self to manage itself and to develop "strategies of action." We need, therefore, to understand language in the television genre as a species of action that takes place in and affects the world.[38]

THE SUCCESS OF A SELF-FAILED WOMAN

> Every age has a keyhole to which its eye is pasted.
> —Mary McCarthy, "My Confession"

In the early twentieth century, "stars" were synonymous with glamour, happiness, romance, exoticism, and luxury. For example, the greatest movie stars of the 1920s, Mary Pickford and Douglas Fairbanks, were characterized by *Photoplay*, a 1920s magazine specializing in the life and careers of movie stars, as follows: "They are living a great love poem in the practical, difficult, much discussed relation of modern marriage."[1] These celebrities seemed to harmoniously reconcile the contradictory requirements of conjugal bliss, hard work, extravagant wealth, beauty, and youth.

A reader of *Photoplay* would be startled by the ways in which Oprah Winfrey's success story has been told in the media and by her path to stardom. Indeed, if transported to the present, such a reader would be surprised by the self-presentation of one of the most famous personas of contemporary American culture, as reported in an early article on her rise:

> She also confesses her own personal tragedies. In the past, she has recounted her failed relationships, a childhood episode of sexual abuse, and her constant battle to lose weight. These insights have endeared her to America, making her one of

the most sought-after speakers in the country. . . . Oprah Winfrey says she still has trouble thinking of herself as a celebrity. . . . As successful as she is at present, Oprah admits that the going has not always been smooth, particularly in her personal life. In her less confident days, she says that she relinquished her self-respect to men. "The relationships I had were totally detrimental," she says. "I was a doormat. But the thing about it is, you realize that there is a doormat overload out there because everybody's been one. Now, I say, 'I will never give up my power to another person.'"[2]

What marks the stardom of Oprah Winfrey is one salient fact: it is the outcome not of her beauty or performance in famous movies but rather of the relentless public telling and marketing of her own and others' personal biographies. As J. L. Decker put it in his study of American narratives of success, a major difference between nineteenth- and early twentieth-century models of success and those of the late twentieth century is that while in the former the "story" was an afterthought to the accumulation of riches, in the late twentieth century it is the story that enables success. If indeed modern "celebrity is the self that sells,"[3] then Oprah embodies the prominence of the self more than any other famous character of the contemporary American cultural scene. At the same time that she established her show in that scene, Oprah Winfrey packaged and commodified her own life in a way that resonated with the construction and packaging of her guests' lives. As one of her biographers accurately put it, "much is known about Oprah's personal life, perhaps more than any other celebrity in our time."[4] If Oprah has blurred her private and public life with the same virtuosity she has used with her guests, it is because there is an intimate mirroring between Oprah's biography and her talk show. Having commodified her own and others' biographies, she has turned herself into a "talk show guest" par excellence.

Oprah's biography is thus illuminating in two ways: as a text that provides insights into the meanings with which she has imbued her vast cultural enterprise and as a cultural product she has intentionally and artfully packaged for public consumption. As a story shaped by events Oprah had no control over, her biography gives us access to the social conditions and cultural resources from which she has drawn to create her cultural enterprise.[5] But, like the myriad stories told on the show, her biography is a cultural commodity produced and packaged through the collaborative efforts of the guests, the host, and the producers. In this chapter, I analyze Oprah's biography both as a social fact that can help us understand the meaning of her enterprise and as a text that sheds light on the meaning Oprah Winfrey wants to bestow on that enterprise.

As I hope to show, Oprah's biography is the place to start analyzing her cultural enterprise, for two reasons: biographical narratives are a privileged category to gather information on cultural actors' "intentions," for, more than many forms of speech, autobiographical discourse expresses one's sense of self, identity, and motivation for acting in the world. Therefore, Oprah Winfrey's autobiographical discourse is very useful for understanding the intentions and meaning with which she has imbued her show. What someone intends to say and how they mobilize rhetorical devices and cultural resources to present a convincing story of themselves cannot be extraneous to the meaning of that persona.

The second reason has to do with the fact that Oprah's biography is permeated with the very meanings that are central to her show, because both cultural forms are motivated by the same set of intentions and form a single cultural project. More than any other public persona, Oprah has used her own life to shape the meaning of her performance, and, in turn, has used the format and formula of her show to shape and make sense of her biography. Thus a remarkable element of Oprah's public biography is that its extraordinary dynamism depends on and is generated by the very organizational apparatus she has created.

INTENTION AND INTERPRETATION

Meaning has two facets. One is a structure of codes that precedes the concrete empirical act of speaking and is formed of binary oppositions, icons, stereotypes, and conventional meanings of words and symbols (for example, the stereotype of the *femme fatale* makes sense only in opposition to the icon of the pure and innocent woman). The second dimension of meaning is an "event"—a unique empirical utterance, which depends on particular contextual cues (e.g., a particular type of "femininity" is enacted in practice in a myriad of context-dependent ways). What makes meaning shift is, among other factors, the fact that concrete situations are imbued with the actors' "intentions," interpretations, and strategies.

The problem of cultural interpretation is to account for both the stable and the shifting features of meaning. To recover the meaning of a text is thus to recover both the *structure of the code*—which makes an utterance meaningful because it is shared by a community of people—and the *concrete intention*—which makes an utterance bound to the particular strategies, values, interests, and goals pursued by actors. Especially when it concerns a cultural form totally dependent on a charismatic character—that is, organized by and around one central figure—the study of meaning must recover the intentions of that actor. To use Walter Benjamin's words, like that of the translator, our task "consists in finding that intended effect [*Intention*] upon the language into which he is translating which holds in it the echo of the original."[6]

Focusing on Oprah's "intentions" to understand the meaning of her text provides two significant advantages. It can help us avoid the problem of circularity of interpretation, that is, the tautological character of interpretation in which one "finds" the very meanings one assumed were there from the start (e.g., "stereotyping of women," or "reproduction of status quo"). Identifying intentions can help us attend to and identify the most *salient* patterns of meaning of a very dense and multilayered text without making our interpretation circular. We will be in a better position to establish which meanings are more salient, in a way that is not predicated on our own a priori decision about the important meanings of a text. Moreover, the use of "intentionality" can provide us with a more convincing interpretation of culture, because it allows us to better understand how culture is actively and willfully created by agents. As anthropologist Lila Abu-Lughod has aptly put it, "the cultural forms transmitted by television . . . are produced *deliberately* for people."[7] If a text can be convincingly linked to the set of intentions encoded in it, we can in turn use these intentions as "keys" to interpret the text, that is, to understand which meanings in it are more salient than others, and how they connect to the social experience of their producer.

Such a strategy is all the more relevant because Oprah Winfrey has stated her views and intentions in endless interviews to the press and on her show, thus providing us with a rare opportunity to reconstruct Benjamin's "echo of the original." Moreover, inasmuch as she has relentlessly explained the rationale behind her initiatives, making bold moves to change and rejuvenate her show, over which she has had total control (she owns her own studio), the analysis of her intentions seems particularly relevant for understanding the meanings with which her persona and program are imbued.

To be sure, by referring to intention I do not mean to suggest that a text is a psychological event or that our interpretation should be identical to the actor's own self-perceptions. Although they emanate from an agent's deliberate use of symbols, intentions are constrained by social structure. Nor does the notion of intentionality presuppose sincerity or perfect knowledge of one's motives. I suspect that Oprah Winfrey, like other cultural entrepreneurs, manipulates her audience and uses her high moral ground to gain more respectability and market profits. But when using the notion of intentionality, the sociologist does not have to adjudicate about the sincerity of motives. Whether manipulative or sincere, it is Oprah's *deliberate* use of symbols to produce a given reality that should interest us and that constitutes the raw material from which we can reconstruct the meaning of her text. For example, when, in 1995, Oprah decided to upgrade the format of her show because it was increasingly attacked, she manipulated cultural codes so that the show would become more palatable to middle-class taste. Whether she was "sincerely" appalled by the direction taken by (her own and other) shows or acted as a shrewd, self-interested entrepreneur is of interest to the psychologist or to the moralist, not the sociologist. What is interesting sociologically is the way in which she consciously upgraded the format of her show by using certain cultural and social codes so as to gain greater "respectability."

Moreover, the notion of intentionality does not presuppose that the actor has perfect knowledge of the causes that have shaped her intentions (I may know what I want, but not know why I want what I want), or an understanding of the antecedents of the meanings she utters. Because intentions activate structures of meaning,[8] they help us identify which of these structures might have been encoded in a text, without presuming that the actor necessarily comprehends their organization or origin. For example, when discussing her own life or that of her guests, Oprah Winfrey frequently uses the language of suffering and pain. This alerts us that "suffering" is a central cultural code we can use to probe the meaning of her cultural enterprise. But this does not mean that Oprah is aware of the relation that the contemporary language of suffering may (or may not) bear to the cultural tradition of Christianity, the political lexicon of rights, or therapeutic discourse.[9] Thus, by using intention as a crucial interpretive tool, I do not intend to reduce Oprah's text to a psychological event or even to suggest that an understanding of her "intentions" exhausts our interpretation of her text. My point, rather, is that intentions point to approximations of meaning, to the general "problem" raised by a text. Intentions are not "hidden away" in someone's head, but rather are the patterned ways in which a member of a group responds to problems raised by particular situations, these patterns being shaped in turn by various situational and structural constraints.[10]

My point thus is a double one: inasmuch as a cultural text (or performance) is "about" a problem in the world, it has a unity that can be, if only partially, grasped by actors engaged in the process of making sense of a situation and acting within it. Additionally, far from being psychological or subjective, intentions are the outcome of the choices made within a set of social constraints. They might transform these constraints, but they cannot be understood without them. Thus, perhaps paradoxically, intentions always point to the social constraints that bind them. It follows that they do not determine outcomes mechanically, but rather refer to what Clifford Geertz suggests are "liabilities to perform particular classes of acts or have particular classes of feeling."[11] In that sense, intentions do not provide the "exact" and "precise" meaning of a text, only an imprecise and approximate "class" of feeling and meaning encoded in it. If interpretation is, in Frederic Jameson's famous words, an "allegorical act," a master code for interpreting layers of text, the main characters and plot lines of my "allegory" will resonate with the characters and plot lines through which Oprah has shaped her biography, publicly discussed the motivations for her cultural enterprise, and systematically blended her private self with her public persona.[12]

AN AFRICAN AMERICAN HABITUS

Intentions are to be identified in the ways in which people play with and transform the social and cultural resources at their disposal. In that sense, intentions include "habits, styles, and skills (the 'habitus') that allow agents to continually produce innovative actions that are nonetheless meaningful to others around them."[13] The habitus guides someone's view of the social world and ways of acting within it, yet allows a great deal of flexibility according to desire, creativity, and strategies. Habitus is thus a crucial mechanism both shaping and constraining intentions. What are the "skills and resources" that have shaped Oprah's "liability to perform particular classes of act"? How has she used them to construct her biography? How does her biography display the interplay between "creativity" and "constraint"? Because this question is central to this book, it resurfaces in chapter 7, which focuses on the interplay between Oprah's cultural style and the broader patterns of African American culture. The present chapter is devoted more specifically to an understanding of the ways in which her biography has been shaped and, conversely, the ways in which she has made sense of this biography.

A BLACK LEGACY

In the myriad of social forces likely to have shaped Oprah's biography, one seems to stand out: her membership in the AfricancAmerican community. For example, in a 1995 article, Oprah Winfrey declared: "The fact that I was created a Black woman in this lifetime, everything in my life is built around honoring that. I feel a sense of reverence to that. I hold it sacred. And I am always asking myself the question, 'What do I owe in service of having been created a Black woman?'"[14] Oprah's repeatedly proclaimed membership in the black community as well as her self-proclaimed commitment to the advancement of women are key to understand the meaning of her cultural enterprise. Her gender and connection to the African American community are key components of the skills and dispositions (the habitus) that have shaped Oprah's biography and her cultural creations.[15]

Indeed, a formative element of Oprah's biography is that she was steeped in the southern black values and culture, which revolved around the church and the then-still-recent history of slavery. As one of her biographers put it: "Rejoicing in her black ancestry and delving into the heroes and heroines—particularly the heroines—of American blacks' struggles for freedom, she learned all she could about her people's experiences in slavery."[16] Oprah has repeatedly avowed a direct continuity between herself and black female characters such as Maya Angelou, Sojourner Truth, and Madame C. J. Walker, about whom she has said that they "are [her] legacy."[17] A cover article about Oprah Winfrey in *Time Magazine*, offering a brief account of her life, put the point aptly: "Winfrey has been drawing on that [slavery's] legacy for support since childhood. Throughout the years of being shuttled between her mother's apartment in Milwaukee, Wisconsin, and her maternal grandmother's farm in the segregated town of Kosciusko, Mississippi, young Oprah maintained a fascination for black history and with slavery in particular."[18] Oprah has repeatedly professed a strong identification with the suffering of her ancestors as well as with the affirmative aspects of black culture. In fact, her understanding of her own biography as a story of fortitude in the face of adversity is deeply anchored in African American culture (see chapter 7).

THE ROLE OF THE BLACK CHURCH

The black culture in which Oprah was immersed was deeply religious. Oprah Winfrey's socialization within the Southern Baptist black church offers additional clues about those aspects of African American culture likely to have been important elements shaping her biography. Sociologist of black social movements Aldon Morris summarizes aptly: "The African-American Church has been an agency-laden institution for centuries. Its transcendent belief system stresses that all people are equal before God because God is the parent of humanity. For centuries, the African-American Church has condemned racial inequality because it is inconsistent with ultimate religious values. These beliefs are ingrained in the cultural fabric of the Church and given repeated expression through religious sermons, writings, music, testimonies, prayers, rituals, and emotional interactions."[19] The black church was thus a unique cultural matrix that emphasized emotionality, orality, and oratorial skills as well as the demand for justice, based not on abstract notions or systematic political ideologies but rather on moral action geared to the relief of the tangible suffering of black people. As will become obvious, these elements pervade *The Oprah Winfrey Show*, which has taken on the vocation of relieving a multiplicity of forms of suffering through the use of speech infused with the rhetorical style of black preachers. Oprah said, "I have been an orator, really, all my life. Since I was three and a half, I've been coming up in the church speaking. I did all of the James Weldon Johnson sermons. He has a series of seven sermons beginning with the 'Creation' and ending with 'Judgment.' I used to do them for churches all over the city of Nashville."[20]

Oprah's immersion in black culture did not take the form of a political commitment, at least not as we conventionally understand this term. Recalling her college years, she says: "I felt that most of the kids hated and resented me. They were into black power and anger. I was not."[21] In a later interview she gave to *People Weekly*, she confirmed that her position within the field of black politics did not change: "She identifies herself first as a woman, next as a black woman, not at all as black spokesperson, although she is in tremendous demand to be one. 'Whenever I hear the words "community organization" or "task force," I know I'm in deep trouble,' she says, adding, 'People feel you have to lead a civil rights movement every day of your life, that you have to be a spokeswoman and represent *the race*. I understand what they're talking about, but you don't have to do what other people want you to do. Blackness is something I just am. I'm black. I'm a woman. I wear a size 10 shoe. It's all the same to me."[22] Oprah's refusal to frame her commitment in (radical) political terms is undoubtedly a key element making her commitment to black people palatable to middle-class America. By framing that commitment in cultural and moral rather than political or ideological terms, she has been able to mobilize cultural themes and values that have a broad universal appeal. Thus Oprah begs to be interpreted as a moral entrepreneur who by this very fact amplifies an important aspect of African American culture that forged tight connections among politics, religion, morality, and spirituality.

Indeed, throughout the nineteenth century, the only legitimate political outlet for black organization was the church, with the result that it produced a "spiritualized" version of political action. This aspect of African American culture is constitutive of Oprah's cultural habitus and of her show. The originality Oprah has brought to the small screen is precisely rooted in African American culture. It imbues her show and enterprise with a *moral* meaning, that is, with a systematic interrogation of commitments and values and with the injunction that we reform our ways. As will become even more obvious in subsequent chapters, Oprah consistently twists political categories and transforms them into ethical and spiritual ones. "I look on the show as my own *ministry*," she says. "I want it to free people from their fears and constraints. I want it to teach them."[23] Black politics—or at least one strand of it—is anchored in a view that is far more moral and spiritual than conventional (white) western politics, which since Machiavelli has identified politics with instrumental action. Oprah is located at the interface between stardom and spiritual/moral leadership, and this intertwining is one of the characteristics that both sets her apart from other television talk shows hosts and defines her persona. "I believe people must grow and change; they must, or they will shrivel up. Their souls will shrink," Oprah Winfrey repeatedly says. Her words have the cadence of a southern minister's. "I hope always to be expanding my life, always to be expanding my thinking."[24] As journalist Gretchen Reynolds puts it, "She wants her show to be more than good entertainment: She wants it to be edifying. She wants it, she says, to reflect her own growth."[25]

FRAIL FAMILIES

Before divorce and single-parent families became staples of sociology and of public discourse, Oprah Winfrey experienced them firsthand. She was born out of wedlock and spent her childhood and her adolescence shifting among her grandmother's, her mother's, and her father's homes, located in three different states (Mississippi, Wisconsin, Tennessee). Precisely because, like many other members of the African American community, she never experienced family as a single and bounded territorial and emotional

unit, I argue that she is particularly apt at viewing it as an arbitrary and shifting entity. As she herself said, "We [her mother and Oprah] have never
hugged, we have never said, 'I love you.' And yet we are both at peace with
that. On the other hand, I think that Maya Angelou was my mother in another life. I love her deeply. Something is there between us. *So fallopian
tubes and ovaries do not a mother make*" (emphasis added).[26] What Oprah
suggests here is that a family can be self-created rather than imposed by biology and that there is a disjuncture among biology, social conventions, and
personal choice. Such a decoupling of biology, institutions, emotions, and
individual choice, a cultural trait of the African American community, is a
cornerstone of the genre of talk shows, and at the very heart of the personal
and institutional dilemmas addressed by the Oprah Winfrey talk show. This
cultural characteristic was accentuated in Oprah's life by her different
homes and the fact that she was far more influenced by nonbiological mother figures such as her grandmother and her stepmother than by her biological mother, which is likely to have made her particularly skilled at understanding family relationships as "chosen" rather than ascribed.

DOMESTIC VIOLENCE

As numerous interviews and reports have chronicled, Oprah has had
firsthand experience of violent patriarchy inside the family. From the age of
twelve, she was repeatedly sexually abused by various male members of her
family, which partly explains why she has relentlessly pursued this topic on
her show. "By the time she was fourteen, she had been raped by a teenage
cousin, sexually abused by an uncle, and had run away from home."[27] But
what is interesting is that Oprah Winfrey reported on these events in contradictory ways: she felt that the assaults had left an indelible mark on her
psyche, yet, like other victims of incest, she also mentioned that she experienced them with a mixture of shame and pleasure. Like many women who
were sexually assaulted at a young age, Oprah felt a great deal of emotional
confusion and difficulty in distinguishing between aggressiveness and caring. "She says she allowed the fondling to continue because she liked the
attention and didn't want to get anyone in trouble," and "I think a lot of the
confusion and guilt comes to the child because it does feel good."[28] This
particular structure of experience, mixing violence, shame, and pleasure,
plays a central part in Oprah's cultural habitus and is constitutive of her talk
show, exemplar of a genre that has mixed narrative pleasure with the narration of domestic violence.

When Oprah told her father she was being abused, he carefully pushed the stories under the familial rug and refused to confront his own brother. Oprah has continuously claimed that this response left her profoundly scarred. From her accounts, it in fact appears that she experienced the secrecy and privacy as violent aggression on the integrity and autonomy of her person. I infer that because of and through this experience, the sanctuary of privacy in which family secrets are so often carefully sealed became a *problematic* feature of her family life as well as a norm against which she consciously and explicitly rebelled. This leads me to the following suggestion: *The Oprah Winfrey Show* is a cultural response to (and against) the politics of secrecy that is fundamental to the middle-class nuclear family, the violent side of which Oprah experienced directly. While the institution of the family is maintained by imposing a strong ideological separation between secrecy and exposure, private and public life, Oprah's response to her childhood experience has been that there is virtually no dispute or suffering that ought to remain outside the reach and the eye of public exposure.

CROSSING SOCIAL WORLDS

Oprah Winfrey was born in Mississippi in 1954, the same year school segregation was ruled unconstitutional by the Supreme Court. It was a time when equality was publicly debated and discussed in American society, and she grew up with a powerful awareness of the barriers and discrimination that separated blacks from whites. Yet this was also a time when these barriers could be crossed.

As noted above, Oprah moved numerous times back and forth between her mother's household and her father's. The two homes were dramatically different: while her mother was laissez-faire (according to Oprah's accounts, her mother was unable to control her as a child), her father was strongly disciplinarian. Oprah was also the first black student to attend an all-white school as part of a 1960s experiment in desegregation in which children from black neighborhoods attended a white suburban school. She attended an affluent school while living with her mother, who was cleaning the apartments of the white families whose children were Oprah's classmates. Some time later, she was also raped and abused. So from an early age, she learned the difficult skill of navigating within and between worlds, internalizing their different rules. This ability to move swiftly between social and moral settings has had three major implications in the formation of her habitus. The first is that she became a virtuoso in the management of self, developing the formal skills needed to understand and function in vastly different moral and social environments. For example, when the field of talk shows became crowded and when critiques directed to her show and others grew vehement, she reacted by uplifting and innovating her format. Exposing her strategic moves to the public, she declared, as a journalist reports it, that she had been motivated by a desire to "distance herself from the obnoxious talk shows that had burgeoned across the television landscape. She shifted her show's focus away from the degrading and the confrontational toward spiritual and substantive issues."[29] In this and in many other ways, Oprah has shown an uncanny versatility and an ability to respond to the demands of new situations by changing her cultural identity.

Her virtuosity in crossing social boundaries is apparent in another respect. As she herself has relentlessly claimed, "Because of the various environments I was exposed to, I am better able to understand what others have gone through."[30] In other words, she is expert at adopting shifting points of view and at identifying and understanding different ways of life. Interestingly enough, it is this compassionate and empathic temperament—which, as I have stated and will fully argue later, is strongly grounded in the emotional and moral culture of the African American community—that has made her unfit for the traditional format of television with which she began her career. For example, at the age of twenty-two, Oprah was assigned to anchor a news program on a Baltimore TV station. She failed at this task because she could not bring to her work the objectivity and neutrality required. When assigned to report on a fire that had broken out in a Baltimore neighborhood, she burst into tears onscreen, pouring out her compassion to the victims. This exemplifies the notion of habitus, which simultaneously orients perceptions and actions and disqualifies us for certain tasks.

Oprah's exposure to various environments made her particularly apt at evaluating and comparing ethical habits and styles that characterize individuals and families. She thus became committed to a particular ethical style, that of her father. Early on, that commitment was self-generated rather than passively accepted. Becoming quickly aware of the fact that her father's ethos was far more adapted to the requirements of the surrounding society, she espoused his Puritanism. Indeed, Vernon Winfrey's disciplinary style has been strongly internalized and has become an intrinsic element of her cultural enterprise. "When my father took me, it changed the course of my life. He saved me."[31] This style pervades her wholesale adoption of the self-ethos of therapeutic culture.

I have argued that four elements are central to Oprah's habitus: her membership in the African American community; the rhetoric and moral outlook of the African American church, in which she was socialized; the experience of the family as an arbitrary, secretive, and violent institution; and finally, the multiplicity of social worlds in which she has lived. These elements have made her a rare virtuoso at crossing social worlds with an exceptional commitment to the disciplinarian ethos that was far more adaptive to enabling her to conform to the requirements of a mobile, capitalist, and middle-class dominated culture.

A THERAPEUTIC BIOGRAPHY

How did Oprah transform the elements that make up her habitus into a biography to be watched and consumed? How has Oprah transformed life experiences into a marketable self? If, as Joshua Gamson suggests, "stars have a privileged position in the definition of social roles and types,"[32] then the study of the transformation of life experiences into a famous biography ought to provide an important insight into a social "type."

On the face of it, Oprah Winfrey is to be ranked alongside the great businessmen of this and the previous century: John Jacob Astor, Cornelius Vanderbilt, and Bill Gates are names that have appeared along with hers as the embodiment of the spectacular worldly success of people with determination, talent, and ambition.[33] Oprah has attained all forms of success: she was awarded the coveted Emmy; she received the Peabody Award for Lifetime Achievement; she has amassed phenomenal wealth; she is internationally known and mingles with political figures, Hollywood stars, and singers as well as with highbrow literary figures across the globe. But Oprah Winfrey's success story differs significantly from that of most other famous figures, both because of the way she has enlisted the media in the process of constructing her biography and because of its very content. The mass media do not simply "report" on (or amplify) her success but play an active part in determining the decisive moments of her biography. Oprah has "written" her biography and transformed it into a public text, both through her self-revelations on her show and through collaboration with journalists, who have participated willingly or reluctantly.

When writing a story or a biography, journalists operate with implicit symbolic codes about what makes a story worthwhile, conventions that specify what is intelligible, worthy of our interest, and believable in a life.[34]

They use codes about what in a life is worth taking notice of and admiring. The following is a comprehensive list of what, according to journalists, are the remarkable features of Oprah's life as they have appeared in a sample of more than 200 articles published from 1986 to 2001 about her in a wide variety of popular magazines:

- Oprah had a difficult childhood. Elements of that difficult childhood include poverty, but even more importantly, her broken home, her hostile mother, and her disciplinarian father as well as the sexual abuse she suffered. All the biographies mention her early hardships and story of sexual abuse.
- She has risen from utter poverty and a neglected childhood to worldwide fame. Here also, almost all stories stress that she has become the head of a media empire despite her many self-doubts and hardships. Her incessant hard work is also almost always mentioned, thus suggesting strongly that her success is perceived as entirely legitimate and even deserved.
- Her struggle with her weight played a key role in her personal and professional development. A large quantity of articles report on the fluctuations of her weight and body shape.
- Her philanthropy is abundantly noticed and reported on. As she herself and the journalists reporting on her life like to repeat, she regularly showers family and friends with presents. Her generosity extends from her private circle to the outer realm of society, as when, for example, she endowed her alma mater with large scholarships; she gave away her $500,000 acting fee to help the children of Henry Horner Homes, a misery-ridden Chicago housing project about which a movie was made and in which she starred; and she gave $200 to a poor woman when she visited the slums of Johannesburg.
- Finally, her relationship with her fiancé, close friends, and family are also abundantly commented upon. Especially discussed are her close relationships with Gayle King, her best friend, and Graham Stedman, her eternal fiancé, as well as her numerous hesitations regarding marriage and her ultimate decision not to marry.

But what this list does not show is that Oprah's biography differs from that of other stars because it has radically transformed the ways in which her "authenticity" is constructed and managed. Stars—Hollywoodian and others—have always handled the relationship between the stage and the backstage of their lives in a complex fashion, trying to keep their private failings away from the public eye yet reveal enough of them to turn the reader/viewer into a confidant.[35] Modern stars are thus experts at the subtle art of manipulating distance and intimacy. Such artistry has generally been consciously exploited by the movie industry, which casts stars in such a way that their private and screen lives echo and mirror each other.[36] Indeed, the problem of stardom is to create authenticity, that is, to make sure that celebrities appear to us as more than an image, that they seem real, at once intimate and distant. But a close look at Oprah's biography shows that she has entirely recast the meaning of "authenticity."

One of the central differences between Oprah and other stars is that while most media stars are visual icons—of beauty and youth—Oprah Winfrey is first and foremost *a biographical icon*, a persona we know not for her beauty or singing or acting talents but rather for the ways in which she has staged her own and others' personal lives. As an article analyzing the source of her fortune put it: "Oprah's life is the essence of her brand, and her willingness to open up about it on daytime TV helped win the enduring trust of her audience."[37] In contrast to cinema celebrities, based on an aura of distance, television celebrities are based on familiarity.[38] Because we see some of them every day and in our domestic environment, television stars are not endowed with an aura of distance and glamour. This familiarity is all the more pronounced in Oprah's case, as she quickly stepped out of the boundaries of her role as TV host and publicized the most intimate aspects of her personal life. The familiarity she maintains is based on a symbolic work of self-presentation in which she shows her self as embattled in the problems of everyday life (and ultimately victorious over them) through two main techniques. One is her construction of the studio as an extension of her private life and as a continuation of her true self. The other is her way of interviewing her guests, which blurs the distinction between their lives and her own.

Using the confusion between stage and backstage that is integral to talk shows, Oprah has made her TV program into an intimate space designed to display her private self. For example, she has occasionally invited her life companion Stedman to the studio, and some of her "friends in real life" as participants on the show. She frequently begins a show by telling the audience where she spent the weekend, how thrilled she felt about meeting another celebrity, why she wears glasses and not her usual contact lenses, or that her shoes "are killing [her]," etc. Just as the show purports to display everyday problems of its guests, it is continuous with Oprah's everyday life. This suggests that Oprah Winfrey does not represent simply another version of the American Dream.[39] Her persona is articulated at the juncture of "stardom" and the "ordinary," the charismatic and the quotidian. When Oprah Winfrey tells us how scared she was when she received the Emmy or how difficult it was to lose weight, she is casting stardom and success into entirely new codes: stardom is constructed as contiguous with rather than extraneous to the murky zone of everyday life. Oprah's widely publicized struggle with her weight is located precisely at this juncture: as she makes sure to insist, her weight loss and physical exercise show her "strength of will," endurance, and sheer ambition; yet, by revealing her painful effort to fashion her body, she also defetishizes what is otherwise the most revered ideal of media culture: the thin and flawless body. Quite unlike other women stars, such as Madonna, who seems to be a remote plastic image playing with mass media icons and displaying clean images of sheer power, Oprah Winfrey appears as someone we have come to know intimately in the corners of our kitchen and who addresses us in our daily—rather than cer-emonial—identity.

This systematic defetishization of her persona (or at least the appearance thereof) is in fact one of her central techniques to address her viewers and readers. For example, in the March 2001 issue of O Magazine, the feature article, "Self-Esteem: The 'O' Guide to Getting It," is accompanied by an-other called "Blowing Our Cover" that discusses Oprah's explicit intent to deconstruct the process of her own image building as well as the magazine artifact as a whole. This is how the article is summarized in the front pages of the magazine: "'O' writer at large Lisa Kogan traveled with Oprah to Charleston, South Carolina, to take a peek behind the scenes of our cover shoot; her experience is chronicled in 'Blowing Our Cover.' 'So many women pass newsstands and wonder why they can't achieve the kind of glamour they see on magazines,' Kogan says. 'Oprah wanted to show that it actually takes a village to pull it off.'"[40] "'So many women, myself included, see a magazine and think, Now, why don't I look like that?' she says one day during an ideas meeting. 'Let's show everybody what being a cover girl re-ally takes.'"[41] This article was enormously successful, as evidenced by the amount of mail O Magazine subsequently received as well as the testi-monies of many women who claimed that since the article they now "dare to leave the house without make-up."[42]

The second technique of defetishization consists in building continuities between her own and her guests' revelations. To give an example, inter-viewing Tipper Gore, former Vice President Al Gore's wife, she subtly trans-forms herself into the one delivering the information.

WINFREY: What about the rap about him [Vice-President Al Gore] being boring. . . I have to say this because when I first got—Stedman . . .

MRS. GORE: Yeah.

WINFREY: . . . and I have been together now so many years, but anyway, when I
first . . .

MRS. GORE: It's not boring, is it?

WINFREY: No. No. But I was just gonna say this . . .

MRS. GORE: Right.

WINFREY: . . . when I was first introduced to him . . . somebody said to me, "Oh,
Stedman, he is so boring," and what they meant was he has integrity.

MRS. GORE: Right.

WINFREY: He's gonna be monogamous, he has character, he stands up for what
he believes in.[43]

Oprah very frequently uses this technique of interviewing, in which she in-
terjects episodes and emotions from her own life to the point where it becomes unclear who the "real interviewee" is or whether Oprah's confessions
only aim to probe her guests to reveal themselves. One of Oprah's most
memorable shows, on Trudi Chase (see chapter 4), a young woman who had
been violently abused from early childhood, illustrates this subtle confusion
of roles and identities. In Oprah's words: "I did a show last year with Trudi
Chase, who was a victim of just severe sexual and child abuse, and in the
midst of telling her story, I started crying uncontrollably. I could not stop. *It
was all of my own stuff coming out. It was my own stuff coming out on national
television*" (emphasis added).[44] In this example, it is clear that Oprah Winfrey has created two intertwined, closely mirroring stories. Although it is not
quite clear what Oprah is revealing to us, what is important in this sentence
is that it is encoded as a confession in response to her guest's confession.

Such defetishization of her persona is all the more interesting when we
take a second look: it appears that it is a technique in the process of constructing her celebrity. Oprah's persona seems to have emerged not in spite
of but *precisely thanks to* her failures. This is how her biography is typically
written.

At 9, she was raped by a teenage cousin who was baby-sitting. He took her to the
zoo and bought her ice cream so she wouldn't tell. That year, in the playground, a
schoolmate told her how babies were made, and she says the worst horror of the
rape was going through the entire fifth grade believing she was pregnant. . . .
Throughout the next five years she was repeatedly abused by three other men, trust-

ed family friends. Growing up in Milwaukee, she lied, broke curfew, stole from her mother's purse, ran away from home and tried to date everything "with pants on." . . . At home she is one of those anxious women who cleans before the housekeeper arrives, just to make sure the housekeeper doesn't get a bad impression.[45]

If her life story has captured the American imagination, it is because she is a female response to Horatio Alger, offering a feminine parody of the masculine myth of self-help. She has regularly revealed "secrets" that had all one thing in common: they bore the mark of a failed psyche and failed relationships. Oprah's celebrity derives, to a great extent, from the public uses she has made of the privately "failed" parts of her biography. Although she grew up in utter poverty and deprivation, this material adversity is always mentioned in passing by journalists, as if it was uninteresting or insignificant. Rather, as Oprah incessantly stresses, psychological obstacles were the more significant hurdles she overcame, and in that respect her biography of success differs significantly from that of the great (male) success stories we are familiar with. Far from boasting an ineffable quality of power or talent, Oprah Winfrey casts herself as the condensed version of the problems that plague the most ordinary of women: lack of self-esteem, sexual abuse, overweight, failed romantic relations. She became famous not *in spite of* having been abused but *because* she was abused and because she publicized that fact. Her success is cast as a therapeutic victory over the extraordinary shortcomings of a difficult life. Thus an astonishing aspect of Oprah's celebrity is that the *construction* of her self as a star is closely intertwined with the *deconstruction* of her self as a star (deconstruction being understood here as a *rhetorical gesture* of deconstruction). Her celebrity was established by holding to the male world of success an inverted mirror of the forms of misery that world has generated in women's lives. One in a myriad of examples is the column she regularly authors in O *Magazine*, "What I Know for Sure," which delivers a series of psychological inner understandings in the form of a revelation of her tribulations: "As a girl growing up shuffled between Mississipi, Nashville, and Milwaukee, I didn't feel loved. I thought I could make people approve of me by becoming an achiever."[46] In contradiction with "male success stories," the story is not about the success but about a failed self—which is what brings success.

But what is exactly the cultural mechanism through which failure is converted into success? Why are the revelations of those failed parts of her life and psyche so captivating? The story of failures could not produce celebrity if American culture did not have a cultural mechanism to transform failure into a positive experience. Oprah Winfrey's failures have become success because she has cast her shortcomings in the cultural code of what we may call *a therapeutic biography*: what is being exposed are not "events" that occur in the "real" world, as much as the plots and subplots of her psychological struggle with herself. The therapeutic biography in turn enables Oprah to capitalize on her failures by recycling them into a narrative of victory and self-overcoming. An example of this can be found in the way in which she revealed her past use of heroin.

In July 1995, Oprah made a confession. "When Oprah heard one say that she was 'more addicted to the man than to the drugs,' something shifted in her. She thought, 'Oh, that's my story,' she recalls. 'That's how I felt.' . . . The moment she [Oprah] confessed it, all hell broke loose at HARPO [her production company]. But even as the panic swirled around her, Oprah felt an inner peace rising to envelope her. . . ."[47]

The "event" that is produced here is a "recognition" that she was equally "addicted" to men and to drugs. Oprah is thus able to make this "newsworthy," and by "confessing" this newfound revelation, she is able to break the conventions of the public sphere, once again turning television into the arena for her psychological self-understandings. Even more interesting is the fact that there are two events reported here: one is the confession and the other is the "inner reconciliation" brought about by the public confession. This liberation and peace come about through the televised confession and can in turn be recycled for the newspapers, as another newsworthy event. Thus the confession is a pretext for an interview to the press because of the impact it had on her psyche. For example:

> The revelation has actually been a lot more than okay. For Oprah it has been liberating. "What I learned from it," she explains, "is that the thing that you fear the most truly has no power. Your fear of it is what has the power. But the thing itself cannot touch you. What I learned that day is that the truth will set you free."[48]

This is typical of Oprah Winfrey's construction of her persona on and through television, for this event is capitalized on twice: once as a confession that produces a minijournalistic sensation and therefore becomes a "story" ready to be consumed; a second time as a tale of "liberation." Telling the story in public becomes one more segment in Oprah's biography, bringing a psychic closure to an element of her life. The example illustrates how she uses television appearances to experience (psychic) events she considers crucial to her own (private?) life.

Here is another example of the ways in which Oprah manufactures a "psychic event" that comes into existence by virtue of being told in the media and that straddles and blurs entirely the boundaries between her television life and her private life. Oprah Winfrey has been promising a book about her life, but one day she drops what the journalist calls the "bombshell": the book will not be written. This becomes an event worth reporting as well as an event of biographical significance because, once again, Oprah constructs it as a "psychic" event:

Emerging from the buzz, the banter, the brouhaha caused by Oprah Winfrey's bombshell announcement that she would not release her eagerly awaited book this fall was one simple missed the real story (sic). This book—unfinished, unpublished, unseen by the public—this book changed her life. . . . Writing her life story forced her to confront all her demons, to, as she puts it, "stand and look at myself naked." What she saw staring back at her stunned her. And then it freed her. "As I peeled away the layers of my life, I realized that all my craziness, all my pain and difficulties, stemmed from me not valuing myself," she says. "And what I now know is that every single bit of pain I have experienced in my life was a result of me worrying about what another person was going to think of me." What other people were going to think of her if she stopped The Book almost made Oprah go through with it even though for months, her inner voice had been telling her it was not the story she wanted to release.[49]

What makes the nonwriting of the book a piece of news—in fact, a scoop—is that it is immediately transformed into a psychic "event": namely, the fact that she overcame her "fear of the opinion that others have of her" and that she has now attained a "new freedom." In another article reporting on the same event, this is how it is incorporated in her biography:

Before the Book, she was emotionally adrift in the murky and suffocating waters of self-doubt. . . . What matters is how she felt inside, in the deepest corridors of her soul. And there she never felt good enough. Everything flows from that: her perpetual struggle with obesity ("The Pounds represented the weight of my life"), her sexually active adolescence ("It wasn't because I liked running around having sex. It was because once I started I didn't want the other boys to be mad at me"), her willingness to make a fool of herself for a man in the name of love ("I was in relationship after relationship where I was mistreated because I felt that was what I deserved"). "I know it appears I have everything," Oprah says, glancing around her $20 million, 88,000-square-foot film and TV complex just west of downtown Chicago. "And people think because you're on TV you have the world by a string. But I have struggled with my own self-value for many, many years. And I am just now coming to terms with it."[50]

This is a very interesting way to construct her biography, for the significant episodes of her life are the landmarks of a failed psyche: obesity, compulsion to please, lack of self-esteen, struggle with her own self. We may characterize the story composed of these main sequences as a therapeutic narrative.

To take another well-known example, Oprah's struggles with weight occupy a large share of all of her biographical portraits. But what has made her struggle function as a "story"—that is, a symbolic structure with narrative tension and development—is the fact that it has been cast by Oprah Winfrey, and subsequently by the journalists who report on her life, as a *psychological* struggle. Thus, as she put it in numerous interviews, her ongoing dieting and failures to diet were due to her lingering "guilt." Her weight problem was causally related to a problem of self-esteem. In the same vein, when she succeeded at maintaining her diet, she claimed that her success was the result of a deep "psychological inner understanding," not the effect of hiring a private trainer and a private cook.

A therapeutic narrative is a story *about* the self, and about the events that have helped the self achieve health, or, more frequently, that have caused it to fail. Like all narratives, the therapeutic narrative is structured by the tension between a goal, psychic well-being or "health," and obstacles to that well-being—pathologies or dysfunctions that constitute what narratologists call a complication, what gets the action going. Complications can be traumatic events, wounds to the self inflicted by other people, or self-defeating beliefs and behavior. The emotions (shame, guilt, insecurity, self-hatred, etc.) become, as is the case here, the characters of the inner story that unfolds within the subject; that is, the story told is *about* such entities as "shame" or "guilt," which acquire a narrative autonomy in the larger story of the self. Thus, Oprah Winfrey's biography may be said to be radically therapeutic. As it is set on proving, happiness and success depend on the understanding of one's past, on being aware of and overcoming one's fears and anxieties, and on realizing one's "true self."

The therapeutic narrative of her life is induced performatively by her interviews with the press and confessions on TV. By learning about her self and by claiming that such self-knowledge—acquired under and for the camera—can in turn transform her, she creates numerous simultaneous speech acts that form the main narrative segments of her life: confessing in public she was raped is the narrative sequence that completes the narrative sequence about the real fact of being raped and brings it to closure. This enactment of her life story is an apt illustration for Toni Morrison's claim that "Narrative is radical, creating at the very moment it is being created."[51] Oprah Winfrey has created such "radical autobiography" at the same time as it has created her through the cultural code of therapy.

THE HEALING POWER OF TV

Oprah's biography has been uncannily connected to television not only in the sense that TV has been the immediate outlet through which she has constructed it but in the sense that her biography has *evolved through television*: the main psychic milestones of her life were not only experienced on but were created by and for television. What turns out to be the most striking aspect of her "biography"—the events through which a coherent narrative of her life is shaped—is that it is thoroughly intertwined with her televisual life. For example, the first show that electrified the nation was in 1986, a memorable performance in which she turned herself into one of her confessing guests by revealing, in what seemed to be a spontaneous and unprepared act of self-exposure, that she had been sexually abused.

> On one recent program, about battered women and incest, when a middle-aged woman said she had been sexually abused, Miss Winfrey began to cry. Miss Winfrey called for a station break and put her arms around the woman. She knew the anguish all too well, she said: not only had she been raped by a cousin when she was 9, she had also been sexually abused by her mother's boyfriend.[52]

Oprah's career has been punctuated by these milestone revelations of her family secrets, which have boosted her audience significantly, imparting to *The Oprah Winfrey Show* a style characterized by the mutual disclosures of guests and host. More than ten years after the 1986 show, *Salon Magazine's* Mary Elizabeth Williams wrote "Today, in a climate of rampant celebrity oversharing, Oprah's initial revelations may not seem particularly unusual or gutsy. At the time, they were electrifying."[53]

To put things slightly differently: Oprah packaged her own biography on her own show in a way that followed the format of the show but also mirrored her guests' stories closely, and showed by her own example *the healing power of* TV. Using her talk show as a way to fashion the narrative of her life and as a tool to shape it reflexively and to "change" her self, she also uses her own life to structure her talk show, which frames a larger psychological narrative of self-understanding and emancipation.

For example, in one of her first shows on the agonies of being overweight, she discussed her own—then heavy—weight, explaining it as a result of her anxieties and lack of self-esteem, themselves the results of a dysfunctional childhood. In fact, the three or four milestones of Oprah's career took place through revelations that she made about herself—her difficulties going on a diet, her history of sexual abuse, her miscarriage at the age of fourteen, and her problems with self-esteem—that have had a tremendous impact on the popularity of her show. But what is even more interesting is that after these revelations, Oprah's life *really changed* as she grew ever more thin, success-ful, glamorous, and self-confident. She thus became her own ideal typical guest in that she showed repeatedly on her body and psyche that television can and does change lives. The medium thus provided her with an extraor-dinary platform on which to enact her therapeutic narrative— not only telling a story, but changing it through the act of telling it. What is thus so peculiar about Oprah Winfrey's biography is that it not only performs the form and content of her guests' stories but also enacts the self-proclaimed vocation of the show to change lives. Oprah Winfrey offers us the unprece-dented spectacle of a biography in the making: a biographical narrative that unfolds in "real time" and develops through the various changes undergone by her body and psyche. She has done this by casting her life as a thera-peutic biography, written and narrated around psychic events.

Let me offer the most famous example of this: in 1984, at the very begin-ning of her career, Oprah was described by a *Newsweek* article according to the script of the "black mammy": "nearly 200 pounds of Mississippi-bred black womanhood, brassy, earthy, street-smart and soulful."[54] Five years later she would be described by a *New York Times* article as "slim and aw-fully glamorous."[55] Clearly this is a spectacular transformation, relentlessly documented by TV and the popular press. And in the interval of those five years, Oprah made the viewer the direct witness of her ongoing and pro-gressive transformation. For example, in November 1988 Oprah Winfrey rolled on the stage with a little wagon containing 67 pounds of beef fat; this was the exact amount of weight she had managed to shed. Displaying her new slim body in her new Calvin Klein jeans, she made the show a personal platform for the display of her own self-transformation. What she paraded was not only her slim body, but more crucially a new segment of her autobiography, soon to be converted into a sequence of a larger therapeutic narrative, itself liable to be recycled and commodified by the diet industry. In 1989 the story took a new turn: Oprah confessed she had gained back 17 of the 67 pounds she had lost, thus bringing a new twist to the narrative plot of her weight loss. As she said: "the battle only begins with losing the weight . . . keeping it off is really the true challenge."[56] What enables such narratives to develop under our own eyes is the use of a therapeutic language in which talking about one's problems constitutes an event in and of itself. What makes the narrative of her weight loss worthy of the viewer's attention is the fact that it is cast as a spiritual and psychic struggle. As one of her biographers, Georges Mair, writes wryly, "her medically supervised diet had been discussed almost daily on her show."[57] This story came to a stunning narrative resolution, once again witnessed by the whole nation, when in 1998 she appeared on the cover of *Vogue* magazine, a position coveted by the most glamorous Hollywood stars. The story of her diet thus offers a *narrative spectacle*, evolving within the "real" time of "real" life. It interwines psyche and body, and in fact makes them mirrors of each other, one being alternatively the "narrative complication" of the other.

One of the most interesting formal features of the therapeutic narrative is that it can be indefinitely prolonged in numerous subplots. For example: "That was the Oprah we first got to know: strong, confident, unswayed by the pain of her past. But more recently, she has admitted that she has been forever scarred by her experiences. 'I was, and am, severely damaged by the experience [of abuse]. All the years that I convinced myself I was healed, I wasn't. I still carried the shame, and I unconsciously blamed myself for those men's acts.'"[58] This 1993 interview recycles the earlier narrative of sexual abuse by creating a new narrative subunit, based on the fact that she still "carried the shame." In 1993, a journalist gave a glimpse of Oprah's life in an article tellingly titled: "Oprah Opens Up About Her Weight, Her Wedding, and Why She Withheld the Book."[59] Anyone familiar with Oprah knows that like the book, the much-awaited wedding never took place. But although in 1993 she had already taken control of her weight, it was still a worthy story to tell publicly because, as she put it, "the pounds represented the weight of [her] life." By making her real weight into a metaphor for a psychological process, she could extend, once again, her narrative of weight loss, and thus with the participation of the journalist. Not only has Oprah packaged her life on and for television, but the medium also has espoused the "real" time of her life, almost taking the highly naturalistic style of documentaries (started on British TV) that followed individuals through the course of their lives.

When she did manage to keep her weight down, thanks to a private train-er, she then wrote a book, which, thanks to her show, became an instant best-seller. Here again, her commercial venture takes the form of a thera-peutic event. In the book we find practical advice on aerobic exercises, a de-tailed account of Oprah's ongoing struggles with weight, the psychological interpretation of such struggles, and finally, an extract of her "weight" diary. To give an example:

> March 9th: This is what I wish for, to absolutely eliminate weight as an issue for myself. That I will not eat, drink, or consume anything that will prevent me from reaching my goal. That is what I wish for, the determination and will to do it, just do it no matter what. It is possible and I will.
>
> November 14th, 1989: Anniversary of the diet show, 168 pounds. I'm thorough-ly disgusted with myself. I couldn't even get thin for the anniversary show. Where is my resolve? Every day I awaken with good intentions and then I fail.
>
> February 20th, 1991: . . . Sometimes I can feel the connection between my own fears and the weight. So what am I afraid of? That's the question. The answer can set me free.[60]

Again, in this diary Oprah transforms with great skill an inner dialogue into a public performance aimed at an audience. The diary shows a process of psychological self-transformation slowly unfolding with the collaboration of her TV talk show. But it is also yet another medium and platform through which Oprah rewrites, yet once more, her diet narrative as an inner psychic narrative. Weight loss, a narrative thread through which we can follow the psychic events of her psyche, is in turn translated in commercial ventures performed by a variety of social actors in a variety of cultural media.

Let me provide a final example of the ways in which television is ap-pended to Oprah's private life through a therapeutic narrative. In 1996, Oprah devoted an entire show to mad cow disease. The show caused meat sales to plummet nationwide, and, as a result, she was taken to court by the "Texas cattlemen." When she faced a trial in Amarillo, she moved her pro-duction team to that city and continued to produce her show, thus making her trial an event known and anxiously followed by her viewers. She also hired Dr. Phil McGraw, the president of Courtroom Sciences, a firm spe-cializing in preparing lawyers for trial. McGraw helped her win, and she in turn transformed McGraw's life as well. "Since then, she has invited her favourite tough guy to join her Change Your Life Team. She also urged him to write a book, and this time, he listened to her."[61] Phil McGraw became one of her regular experts and wrote a book, *Life Strategies*, that became an instant best-seller.[62] Once again, she manipulated the boundary between her private and public self in such a way that there was a continuity and transparency between the two. What was, after all, a civil lawsuit became a public debate followed by the nation. A personal friend, McGraw, became, through her show, a public figure as well. Although nothing in *Life Strategies* distinguishes it from a plethora of popular guides to self-styled success, it became an instant blockbuster (selling over a million copies) through the association with Oprah. However, what is particularly noteworthy about this whole episode is that the trial with Texas cattlemen was framed as a therapeutic victory and that this construction was, as in Bob Greene's case with the diet, the result of McGraw's retrospective account in the form of a book that uses the same therapeutic language as in the talk show. He recounts the following dialogue with Oprah when they were in Amarillo, at midnight:

"Oprah, look at me, right now. You'd better wake up, girl, and wake up now. . . . You'd better get over it and get in the game, or these good ol' boys are going to hand you your ass on a platter." . . . I saw of flash of anger in her eyes as she instinctively recoiled. But I recognized that her anger had nothing to do with me. . . . She looked at me in the eye . . . and said: "*No they will not.*" I truly believe that at that precise moment, the cattlemen lost their case.[63]

The book is then set on helping its readers create such moments of intense focus and determination. In this exchange, Oprah Winfrey again constructs her public self through an exposition of the private agonies of her soul. And again, what justifies the writing of the book, the publicizing of Oprah's states of mind, is the fact that she won her case when something "inside her" shifted, that is, when she gained a new psychological understanding. Another of Oprah's private epiphanies is converted into a cultural commodity to be "shared" with (that is, sold to) the audience.

Therapeutic narratives thus offer the spectacle of a biography in the making and perfectly fit the postmodern pattern of recycling cultural material. Healing is never quite what it seems; new forms of suffering can always pop up, inviting further healing and thereby generating new stories—and new media interviews, shows, self-revelations, and therefore psychological developments. Moreover, this therapeutic narrative can be stretched to various media. Oprah's weight battle becomes an ongoing, unfinished story, progressively inscribed in various texts: her show, her best-seller with Greene on physical fitness, her diary, her interviews to the press about her weight

struggle, her interviews to the press about her best-seller. "Few public figures have discussed their weight so publicly—or have been so willing to
admit the fears and insecurities and anger a woman can experience when
her body feels out of control . . . after showing off her new body in skin-tight
jeans and a cosmetics ad celebrating 'The Most Unforgettable Women in
the World,' Oprah sank steadily into despair as the pounds crept back in the
months and years that followed her public unveiling. 'I've lost my resolve,'
she wrote a year later in her journal."[64] This journalist continues writing a
weight narrative that by now has become a multisited story with multiple
platforms.

> INTERVIEWER: Speaking of being your best, you've lost lot of weight again. How
> did you do it this time?
> . . . I gained about 22 pounds last winter during the trial in Texas, when I was
> being sued by the beef industry. . . . The pay was hard. Tough hiking every day
> for a month in Telluride. . . .
> INTERVIEWER: How much did you lose?
> WINFREY: About 20 pounds. . . .
> INTERVIEWER: Did you work out with Bob [Greene]?
> WINFREY: Yes, to get in shape for the *Vogue* cover.
> WINFREY: I went through this period when—when it was about 1980 and 1983—
> and I look at it now as my period of mental illness. I mean, I know. I mean, I
> know I was sick. So I say it was a time in my life when I was ill, I really look at it.
> My best friend Gayle helped me through it, was very, you know, comforting me,
> and everything. I say I was ill, and that was then, and I've recovered now.[65]

Here again, Oprah "proves" that she has healed herself. But what is healed
is not a visible bodily sign; by re-narrating her own story of romantic de-
spondency as a story of "mental illness," she can capitalize on the "event"
twice: once by making herself a part of a vast community of "mentally ill"
women; and a second time by being able to claim that she has healed herself, thus serving as an example for the rest of the ill women.

Because the reality Oprah talks about is psychic or therapeutic, it is very
easy to create—the only "trophy" to display is her self-proclaimed (and forever intangible) health, which in turn can be easily recycled, that is, worked
on to produce new and expandable stories. This is why her close friend and
strategist advisor, Phil McGraw, and many journalists have claimed that
"the private Oprah and the television Oprah are about as close to the same
as anyone might imagine."[66] The events she refers to as being of a higher

spiritual value or as being the most painful all have to do with television (for example, she stated that a painful event was when the rumor that Stedman was gay circulated in the tabloids); her confessions are regularly presented as crucial events that "liberate" something and make her surmount her inner fears. This tactic has been imitated by many talk show hosts, who have tried to also appear "vulnerable" and to abolish the barrier between themselves and their guests (as, for example Ricky Lake, who avows a struggle with weight).

What is remarkable about Oprah's autobiography is that it is in constant motion, under the watchful eye of the camera: her (non)marriage, her weight fluctuations, her decision to change her program, her revelations about her sexual abuse, her subsequent and consequent feelings, her ruminations, hesitations, and decisions are made for the media and with their full collaboration.

THE DIETER AS THE CHARISMATIC LEADER

In a seminal article in 1944, Leo Lowenthal analyzed biographies published over a period of thirty years and showed, rather successfully, that biographies of "great men" recorded fairly accurately the massive economic and social changes that had occurred.[67] However, biographies written during the 1930s significantly differed from those written at the beginning of the century. While the latter primarily covered industrial or political men, the former chronicled the lives of glamorous and carefree stars. Lowenthal's view was that these new biographies were artificial and disingenuous portrayals of public figures, who could no longer serve as moral guides.

Oprah Winfrey largely disproves Lowenthal's assessment, for her celebrity is characterized by a mixture of stardom and moral guidance. Like those of the early businessmen and politicians Lowenthal praised, her biography is oriented toward edification and moral uplift. Perhaps even more than the traditional success stories, Oprah's success story combines the virtues of the entrepreneur (hard work, discipline, innovativeness) as well as the qualities of the spiritual guide, if by "spiritual guide" we mean a person endowed with the authority to proffer what best suits a "soul" or "psyche." In fact, her expert use of television to expose her biography and to show us a life in the making enacts and embodies charismatic leadership. More exactly, Oprah's biography offers a postmodern therapeutic version of what Max Weber calls "charismatic leadership."

According to Weber, charismatic power—contrary to rational or traditional authority—derives from extraordinary personal powers, such as endurance, strength of will, and dedication to the welfare of others: "Charisma knows only inner determination and inner restraint."[68] A charismatic leader must show ability both to endure suffering and to care for the salvation of others. "The Charismatic leader gains and maintains authority solely by proving his strength in life. . . . Above all . . . his divine mission must 'prove' itself in that those who faithfully surrender to him must fare well."[69]

Oprah's biography displays attributes of charismatic leadership, for she not only offers a narrative of past suffering but also prolongs this narrative within the present, by constantly creating and exposing a long series of psychic obstacles to be overcome and converting her triumphs over herself into an altruistic desire to help others—most often on her show. What makes Oprah's charisma unique is her outstanding telegenic ability to present herself as suffering even in the midst of extravagant wealth and glamour, as displaying self-control and discipline (in the form of her diet and spectacular physical transformation) as well as an ethic of care in the form of televisual empathy for a variety of ills and forms of distress. These are the essential attributes of spiritual leaders. For example, in a 1993 show on overweight people, a woman recounted her agonies in trying to lose weight; at the end of the show Oprah hugged this woman and told her how much she [the guest] "just reminds [her] of [herself]," thus creating an empathic relation of care in which Oprah was simultaneously suffering and victorious over her sufferings.

This is why Oprah's staging of her diet as an important part of her life story is so important to her persona. The body, as has now become commonly accepted, stands as a metaphor for the social order. "The social construction of the female body is based on a thin ideal, which has become the symbol of youth, beauty, vitality, success, and health."[70] The ideal to which Oprah Winfrey has conformed after painful work is the ideal achieved by 5 to 10 percent of the population and corresponds to the most stringent standards of femininity.[71] In this respect, dieting has become a powerful metaphor for the "chosen" few of the feminine group. Norms about thinness have intensified since women have made gains in advanced industrial society. When women attain position of power, expectations regarding their thinness grow, which, according to some, represent "an attempt to neutralize these gains."[72] But this interpretation of dieting is insufficient, for diet, as Oprah insists, is accompanied by a great deal of suffering and agony. Hers seems to be close to the ascetic practices of self-mortification by which a leader shows and displays body control, which signifies self-mastery, which in turn functions as a signal that one is entitled to exert (spiritual) authority over others. Oprah's dieting demands sacrifice, self-discipline, and suffering; most of all, it signifies a spiritual journey. Because Oprah has cast her physical transformation in psychological terms, she thus offers a postmodern version of a narrative of spiritual growth, akin to the stories of the saints, who have "grown" from their psychic and physical trials and are entitled to their spiritual status by virtue of the knowledge they have gained and their desire to share this knowledge with others to help them.

The therapeutic biography as performed by Oprah displays the qualities that help assert charismatic leadership and authority: endurance and self-control; spiritual or moral equality with those the charismatic leader wants to save or lead (for example, in the fact that the leader has experienced the same kinds of ills and misfortunes); the capacity to "care" for others and to stimulate them with the energy the leader has accumulated from "saving" himself.[73] Oprah subtly invites viewers and guests to imitate her own life, thus creating a powerful charismatic relationship based on the fact that she indeed performs the goods she promises to deliver: namely, the symbolic tools to reform one's life and get better. The therapeutic narrative in which she has cast her biography is thus mobilized to assert a form of charismatic power that is able to create new sources of legitimacy as it performs, induces, and displays the very change it promises.

Charisma also contains liminal elements. Some charismatic characters, including Oprah, address the changeability and indeterminacy of social order; they are "fluid, shifting, solvent, vital, and full of energy without the capacity to stabilize [themselves]."[74] In her capacity to move swiftly from "black mammy" to Vogue cover star, from a battered woman to the most powerful black woman in American history, from an ordinary woman to a global icon, Oprah Winfrey offers an unstable persona that fascinates because of its dynamism. Moreover, what makes her form of charisma liminal is that she addresses the social order precisely at its limits and that she plays with the dissolution and reassembling of social interactions.

In that sense, Oprah Winfrey is not only a charismatic leader with liminal symbolic power to dissolve the contours of normal social order but also what anthropologists Richard Grathoff[75] and Don Handelman[76] have dubbed a "symbolic type," a social character "consistently and wholly true to the logic of its own internal composition" (an example is the clown).[77] A symbolic type can be, as in Oprah's case, profoundly inconsistent, paradoxical, and heterogenous (like tricksters or fools). A symbolic type embodies both a culture and its negation. This is why, according to Handelman, such types are "larger than life." They have another characteristic: they stand above context, are endowed with the almost unique capacity to "mold context to the logic of its own composition."[78] This capacity is key to understanding the cultural power of Oprah Winfrey, for she has indeed created a persona that is reflected in, shaped by, and in turn constitutive of the talk show, as the social context in which the contradictions of her persona are deployed.

CONCLUSION

The meanings with which Oprah has imbued her biography display what Ann Swidler has called "a long-term strategy of action,"[79] a way of acting consistently throughout various situations and across time by mobilizing a given set of resources and skills. This strategy is characterized by the double use of the meanings of suffering and self-transformation, which have been particularly stylized in African American culture. The meanings Oprah Winfrey manipulates, quite intentionally, to establish her life story—psychic suffering and self-change—emerge as the primary constituents of what she perceives as her identity and moral mission.

3

EVERYDAY LIFE AS THE UNCANNY: *THE OPRAH WINFREY SHOW* AS A NEW CULTURAL GENRE

> It is self-evident how greatly fidelity in reproducing the form impedes the rendering of the sense. Thus no case for literalness can be based on a desire to retain the meaning. Meaning is served far better—and literature and language far worse—by the unrestrained licence of bad translators.
>
> —Walter Benjamin, *Illuminations*, 78

The Oprah Winfrey Show has become a text of breathtaking proportions, stretching from the United States to India, Europe, Africa, and Asia. It is remarkable not only for the variety of issues it addresses, the scope of its influence, and the size of its audience, but also because few global media empires are the outcome of one person's single-handed enterprise. This is not to deny that the shrewd and aggressive marketing strategies of the King Corporation—which has syndicated Oprah's show since 1986—have played an important role in helping Oprah gain the upper hand in the market. But her success has been so swift, significant, and durable that the economic explanation alone will not do. Marketing aggressiveness cannot explain why Oprah Winfrey's notoriety and sheer impact have by far surpassed that of her predecessor, Phil Donahue,[1] why the scope of her cultural production has steadily increased, and why her moral status and stature have become—and spectacularly so—akin to that of spiritual leaders. After all, Oprah Winfrey started her career with a type of show close to the carnivalesque vulgarity of Jerry Springer, but a decade later invited and interviewed Toni Morrison, Nelson Mandela, and Tipper Gore, and in the aftermath of the

September 11 attacks was chosen to conduct a national memorial ceremony. This chapter explores how Oprah manipulated the codes of the already existing genre of talk shows in such a way that she became the most popular talk show host in America as well as a cultural and moral icon.

A genre can be defined as a way in which meanings are systematically organized in symbolic forms that are patterned and that consequently generate expectations that guide the interpretation of a text. Through genre, the meaning of symbolic forms is "stabilized," that is, invested with the very codes by which they will be interpreted. A new cultural genre is a response to a social situation. "It singles out a pattern of experience that is sufficiently representative of our social structure, that recurs sufficiently often *mutandis mutatis*, for people to 'need a word for it' and to adopt an attitude towards it. Each work of art is the addition of a word to an informal dictionary."[2] If a cultural genre emerges from certain social conditions, we can define our approach to genres as the attempt to understand which social conditions are addressed by a patterned set of meanings and how.[3] The confessional talk show is to the late twentieth century what the novel was to the eighteenth century: a new and powerful cultural form that captures the central problems posed to identity in the contemporary era and resolves them with a particular narrative formula (see chapters 4 and 5). In the same way that the eighteenth-century novel emerged from and in turn codified bourgeois domesticity, ideals of love, and market mobility, twentieth-century talk shows have captured and codified the postmodern collapse of selfhood, identity, and family in the framework of daily life. While the novel presupposed a coherent self that could struggle against and triumph over society (embodied in families, communities, and social norms), the Oprah Winfrey show's core "fiction" is that of an individual whose moral foundations have collapsed (or are threatening to collapse) and who struggles with herself to regain functionality in the basic institutions of society (most notably, the market and the family).

Since this text is created by and centered on one particular individual, it is reasonable to assume that Oprah's intentions have been encoded in it so that, across time, they generate patterned expectations and responses both from her guests and from her viewers. Because the notion of genre traditionally does not make room for the intentions of the actor creating culture, I will refer to the systematic encoding of intentions in cultural forms as "style." In using the notion of style, I want to underscore the fact that "genre" can be a strategic response to a given situation, here the decomposition of the self in conditions of late or reflexive modernity (see chapter 7 for a fuller account of this idea). "Style" makes a statement in reference to problems that arise in people's daily lives, to practical dilemmas.[4] For example, to say that "bad things happen to good people" is very different from actually watching this take place in the format and genre of tragedy. To understand a style (or genre) means to understand the devices that have been deliberately chosen to say something, as well as the impact of the cultural form on what is said. What defines "style" is that it shows and performs what it says. Thus style engages a reader concretely in a practical interrogation. For example, in her study of Aeschylian tragedy, Martha Nussbaum has suggested that the tragedy articulates our practical intuitions about moral conflict better than theoretical discussion.[5] In this approach, "tragedy" is a form that *performs* meaning and makes us ask such questions as: Why are good and meritorious people punished? Can we avert our destiny? As I will demonstrate, *The Oprah Winfrey Show* displays a definite style that engages us in moral interrogations. This style is first and foremost ethical; that is, it addresses and raises moral dilemmas that pertain to the definition of the good life and good selves.

To a certain extent, this style is not entirely Oprah's, for it was "invented" by Donahue. However, Oprah Winfrey uses new stylistic devices to stage her guests. In this chapter, I focus on the innovations she has introduced to the talk show genre and offer hypotheses about what has made her show into such a popular and successful cultural form. For this reason, this chapter pertains mostly to the first decade during which *The Oprah Winfrey Show* was produced. This focus on her early years may help us understand what initially made her show so popular.

THE OPRAH WINFREY TALK SHOW: A NEW GENRE?

It has frequently been observed that talk shows are a populistic genre, in the sense that they give voice to people who are normally silenced in the public sphere: deviants, minorities, women, and working-class people constitute the bulk of talk show audiences. To a certain extent this was even more true of *The Oprah Winfrey Show*: when she first appeared on national television in 1986, a black overweight woman significantly altered the white male, glamour-dominated format of such shows. Elaborating on this idea, Joshua Gamson and K. S. Lowney[6] have suggested in separate studies that the cultural roots of the talk show are to be found in "deviant" cultural forms such as the freak show and the circus, respectively. Indeed, as I and others have suggested,[7] through its systematic inversion of social hierarchies and moral codes and its privileging of the aesthetic of the grotesque, the talk show is carnivalesque in spirit. Lowney goes a step further and argues that talk shows mix the aesthetic of the circus and the morality of the Revivalist movement, whose public rituals were full of emotionality and drama and demanded that each individual "take control of her or his salvation."[8] Others, like Shattuck, locate the origin of the talk show in the "baby sobbers" and the *True Confessions* genre, that is, in "true" stories of misfortune that were primarily geared to working-class women. The Oprah Winfrey talk show draws from religious revivalism, the *True Confessions* literary genre, early radio and contemporary TV talk shows, and the freak tradition, but has creatively combined them into a cultural genre that was new by virtue of the fact that it addressed a distinctively new social reality using a unique style.

In trying to understand the specificity of *The Oprah Winfrey Show*, I will identify the ways in which it differed from *The Phil Donahue Show*, which, despite its wide popularity, was supplanted and surpassed by Oprah's show in the late 1980s.[9] This comparison may yield insights into why Oprah's cultural style gained a popularity and cultural significance that Phil Donahue and his program did not and perhaps could not achieve.

Before Winfrey redefined the field of talk shows, Donahue was perceived to be "serious, thoughtful, and sensitive about momentous national and international issues of politics, economics, and medecine."[10] If the Donahue and the Oprah Winfrey shows slowly but surely came to look similar, this was because Donahue succumbed to economic and competitive pressures forcing him to invite "transvestites, dwarf tossing, and sexual dysfunction to hold his audience, which had found out about sex, fat, and love from Oprah and Geraldo."[11] This was a style he readily adopted but that was not his initially. If we compare *The Phil Donahue Show* and *The Oprah Winfrey Show* before Donahue started to imitate his own imitators, we may find some interesting ways to characterize Oprah's genre.

A CACOPHONOUS NARRATIVE GENRE

One difference between the two shows is the emphasis each put on "issues" versus "stories." *The Phil Donahue Show* was "issue" or "content" oriented. In contrast, what defines *The Oprah Winfrey Show* is a specific story. Her talk show was more decisively situated in the genre and tradition of storytelling, which Walter Benjamin defines as "experience which is passed from mouth to mouth."[12] Benjamin suggests that the born storyteller—and

Oprah Winfrey undoubtedly is one—has an orientation toward practical in-terests. The story she tells or elicits is geared to produce an effect on the life of its narrator and that of its listener. Her talk show is thus heir to the oral form in that it aims to give shape to her own experience and to feed and nur-ture others' experience. Moreover, like Donahue, Oprah Winfrey intro-duced to television a far more cacophonous style than most other programs had: one show could denounce child abuse, while another would explore and try to understand why people engage in incestuous relations. One show could deal with the inability of men and women to be in "control of their lives," while another would address people who are unable to "just let go" and enjoy life. One show could deplore controlling and authoritative par-ents, yet another would lament the problem of "rebellious children." From the start, her show offered a cacophony of moral dilemmas rather than a fixed and predictable set of moral messages to which it was committed. But the cacophony was far more accentuated in Oprah's case, for it resulted not only from thematic variety but also from the fact that her show itself was more centered on the conflicting points of view of the participants. What defines an Oprah show is a guest and the particular story he or she is telling, or more precisely, his or her point of view on a particular story. The indi-viduals we encounter bear their own interpretation or version of reality, often staged as opposed to others' interpretation. This is why I suggest that the Oprah talk show was from the start more committed to a planned and controlled "cacophony" than Donahue's show was.

The very "mood" of the stories told on *The Phil Donahue Show* and *The Oprah Winfrey Show* also differed. Although Donahue was definitely at-tuned to the problems women and men faced in their daily lives, Oprah rad-icalized this orientation and elicited topics that, with regard to the defini-tion of the public sphere, fall into the category of "the trivial." More than Donahue, she addressed problems related to the microscopic texture of everyday life. Losing weight, learning how to say no, using one's good china, and going out without make-up are topics as classic to *The Oprah Winfrey Show* as her "sensationalist" focus on deviant behavior. Oprah understood better than Donahue the minute and trivial problems that plague women's everyday life and staged them, focusing on the myriad ways and processes through which identity is formed and malformed. Episode titles like "How Far Would You Go to Protect Your Child?," "Stuck in a Traditional Mar-riage," "Women Confront Men to Find Out Why They Were Dumped," "School for Husbands," "Ten Stupid Things Women Do," "Should You Be Ashamed?," "Can't Get Over Your Ex," and "Friendship on Trial" indicate that her show was about the collapse of interpersonal relations that form the basis of everyday life.

A DRAMATURGIC GENRE

Oprah Winfrey used many of Donahue's innovations, but twisted them in such a way that her genre bore the distinctive mark of her authorship. Where Phil Donahue initially presented himself in front of a relatively undifferentiated audience, Oprah Winfrey split her guests and her audience in a more clear, formal way, thus making the show less centered on "issues" and more centered on particular individuals telling their life story. Making her studio audience take a significant role was one of Winfrey's major innovations.[13] Some have argued that this move marked the demise of the "serious content" that characterized the Donahue show. But from a formal standpoint, this demarcation of the audience from the guests resembles the structure of early Greek tragedies, in which a chorus addressed the audience and interacted with a set of characters engaged in a passionate conflict (e.g., Medea or Electra) or in a heart-rending reunion (Iphigenia at Centaurus; Alceste). As in Greek theater, Oprah split the stage between the actors (the guests coming to tell an emotionally powerful story) and the chorus (studio audience), whose function is to comment on the main action, that is, on the guests' stories and on the interactions between them. Thus the Oprah Winfrey talk show had a far more dramaturgic structure than the Donahue show: it staged intense emotional conflicts and isolated more clearly the singular speech of particular individuals, and it included a more formal device to comment on the actions and sentiments of the protagonists. This formula has of course been widely imitated. A clear division between guests and studio audience meant that the viewers could project themselves onto two different "units," the guests' particular autobiographical stories and the studio's "second-degree" audience, whose function is to react to the topic of the show and to the guests' stories.

The division between audience and guests is redoubled by another division, between experts and guests, which in turn mimics a division between two forms of speech—the singular narrative and the general-normative one. The tension between these two forms of speech signifies that the viewer is drawn within a variety of points of view that coexist with rather than conflict with one another. This in turn opens up the structure of the story told by the guest, providing multiple points of view from which to examine it. Like the ancient tragedy, *The Oprah Winfrey Show* is thus a *moral* genre, where the morality is generated by the conflicts of points of view staged by the show.

THE HOST

Of the talk show hosts I am aware of (Sally Jessy Raphael, Ricky Lake, Rolonda, Montel Williams, Jerry Springer, and, of course, Donahue himself as well as Oprah), Oprah Winfrey is indubitably the most charismatic and the most personally involved in her show. As argued in chapter 2, she has used her talk show as an autobiographical platform, which is a dramatic difference from Donahue. To the best of my knowledge, while Donahue was familiar and democratic, he never transformed himself into a confessing subject, never became one of his own guests. Winfrey, on the other hand, has used her show to expose and shape her biography, thus blurring the boundary between host and guests.

Thus *The Oprah Winfrey Show* differs in two important respects from *The Phil Donahue Show*: it has a far more dramaturgic structure in the sense that it stresses the dramatic and emotional components of guests' stories, yet, at the same time, it uses Oprah's persona and biography to blur the boundary between audience, guests, and host, thus creating a form of intimacy that is both highly structured and highly egalitarian. This feature has been imitated by such latecomers to the field as Ricky Lake and Montel Williams.

Oprah's manipulation of her public and private persona, as well as the ways in which she has positioned herself as similar and even equivalent to her own guests, have made her into a new brand of charismatic leader, a subject already touched upon in the previous chapter. Her distinctiveness resides in the fact that of all talk show hosts, she is both the most similar to and the most distant from her guests: similar because her biography mimics the dysfunctions of her guests; distant because the commodification of her biography has helped her amass phenomenal wealth and reach a form of stardom unrivaled by any other television (and other media) celebrity. This mix of ordinariness and outstanding charisma sets her apart from Donahue. For example, Donahue could have never have participated in the kind of banter Oprah is known to have with her guests (both because of his gender and because of the ways in which he played the role of talk show host): "a pretty shoe does not mean you can wear it. So these are like [pointing at her shoes], stand up for 10 minutes and then sit down shoes."[14]

The persona of Oprah Winfrey is articulated at the juncture of stardom and the ordinary, the charismatic and the daily, to the point where one cannot tell who addresses her audience: a crafted television personality or a "real" woman. Quite unlike other female stars such as Madonna (a remote image, a mass media icon displaying clean images of sheer power), Oprah Winfrey appears as someone intimate and familiar. We have come to know her in our kitchens and through her everyday, rather than ceremonial, identity. Mixing attributes of televisual and spiritual leadership with the defetishization of her stardom, she has assumed a *liminal* status, crossing a symbolic threshold past which stardom is inverted and reduced to the most ordinary status, while ordinary lives are propelled to the status of (ephemeral) stardom and glamour. The more Oprah Winfrey became famous and powerful, the more intimate and familiar she became with her audience.

AN ETHIC OF CARE

The mirroring of the host's, the guests', and the audience's life stories Winfrey practices is reminiscent of the structure of support groups, especially with regard to the role of "leaders." Like a support group, *The Oprah Winfrey Show* is structured by the triadic relationship among the host (leader), the individual (telling the story), and the group (whose boundaries are always diffuse, since it includes the audience as well as viewers). At the center of the support group, sociologist Robert Wuthnow suggests, is the leader, who is at once "one of the group" in that she or he knows intimately the problems discussed by members, and "more than the run-of-the-mill member of the group," because he or she has charismatic qualities, most notably expressed in sincere care for others.[15] The leader of the support group displays an "ethic of care" and plays with the boundary between hosting and confessing, leading and being one of "the people in need." This description corresponds closely to Winfrey's mode of interaction with her audience, but not to Donahue's. While Donohue adopted a tone of conversational familiarity, he never made himself interchangeable with his audience; he never cried while listening to a story, while Oprah periodically did, nor did he hug audience members to show his support. Oprah staged an immediate and embodied relationship with her audience by offering "tears and hugs"—the ethic of care—while Donahue hosted his show from a more remote position, maintaining an emotional distance between him and his audience.

In the same vein, Oprah has used and endorsed an openly moral language in an effort to uplift lives, while Donahue has shied away from assuming the role of spiritual leader. The best example of this is when he and Oprah were accused of doing "trash TV": he justified himself by stating that he was doing what he was getting paid to do. Winfrey, on the other hand, chose to acknowledge the morally dubious direction her show was taking, and changed its format in such a way that it addressed these moral critiques (see chapter 5 for further discussion).

AN UNSTABLE STABILITY

Not only did Oprah display a concrete relation with her guests, she also used several devices to make the audience a structural component of the genre. That is, she has made the audience the main trope of her show, which thus became more populist and more interactive than Donahue's. First, many of her topics, as well as her guests, are selected by the production team from the thousands of letters audience members send in each month. In this respect, the show functions as a natural and immediate conduit for the audience's biographical experiences. Donahue's topics were more likely to have been devised by him or his team. Second, although Oprah clearly differentiates between her guests and her audience, she nonetheless stages the audience as a central participant by regularly soliciting comments from members, thus adding their subplots to guests' narratives. The audience is thus given a narrative and structural role in the very format of the show. Third, because the show necessitates very little technological preparation and few expenses, it can react and respond to the audience very swiftly. For example, after a show where Gary Zukav—an expert in advice on happiness and spiritual renewal—was the star guest, distilling his wisdom to the studio audience, Oprah received so much e-mail that she decided to devote another full hour to him, this time inviting viewers to tell how his book, Seat of the Soul, had changed their lives. Thus the audience feedback is staged and made into a dynamic component of the show as well as the very object of our gaze. Fourth, the show often follows up on its own effects within the homes and lives of guests, creating a "pseudo-private sphere" so that guests' ordinary lives become closely linked with the show, which actively helps and acts on the guests' lives after their appearance (see chapter 5). This, in turn, suggests that The Oprah Winfrey Show functions by endlessly recycling the very audiences it has created; Oprah's cultural formula reduces the distance between agency and spectatorship, the television studio and the home, guests and viewers, host and audience. The show embodies what, according to philosopher

Arthur Danto, characterizes the literary work: the fact that it exists for the reader and not "on its own account."[16]

When Oprah appeared on the American television scene, no other cultural genre had integrated and interwoven the audience so systematically into its design, content, and structure. Oprah Winfrey has thoroughly blurred commercial and grassroots television, making it impossible to distinguish between the responsiveness of television to ordinary lives and the use of those lives to further the interests of Harpo Productions (Oprah Winfrey's company). I would even go a step further and suggest that what is so unique about this narrative genre is the fact that ultimately viewers, guests, and hosts are all *interchangeable*.

A SELF-REFERENTIAL GENRE

Another difference separating *The Oprah Winfrey Show* from *The Phil Donahue Show* is that where the latter was referential (discussing issues in the "real" world), the former was far more self-referential. Donahue's talk show referred to a reality "out there" (covering topics such as sexual abuse, pedophiles, unfaithful husbands, etc.) that was discussed by Donahue and the audience. Oprah Winfrey used this formula but added a crucial element to it, making her show markedly self-referential: it discussed an issue by staging it as a discursive event, which became the proper object of the show: a confrontation, a confession, or a reconciliation (a formula that has since been widely imitated by other popular shows). Oprah's show produces the very event it reports on, a linguistic one. Indeed, confessions, reconciliations, and disputes are speech acts that point to themselves and not to an order of truthfulness or reality beyond. The guests have become defined by the speech act they perform for the camera. This is a supreme example of what John Austin called illocutionary speech acts, wherein by saying something, we also do it.[17]

The epithets of "trash" and "voyeurism" that have been frequently used in describing her show refer to the fact that it does not as much discuss intimate relationships themselves as show them; that is, that *The Oprah Winfrey Show* is a performative genre. Rather than documenting an event that has taken place in the past, it has made the viewer participate more often in an event that is created at the very time that it is "documented" by the camera and told by the protagonists.

In Northrop Frye's terms,[18] the mythopoetic theme of the genre elaborated by Oprah Winfrey, its leading and organizing motive, is language, and more specifically, the various forms taken by verbal interactions, from informal conversations to highly structured debates. The show organizes the flow of conversation—natural discourse—within three main categories of speech codes:[19] autobiographical stories (of participants); analytical and prescriptive speech (of the expert and occasionally of an "experienced" layperson); and interrogative speech (of the host and the studio audience). The intertwining of these forms of speech unfolds like a a story superimposed on the concrete stories told by participants. Her show proceeds according to a standard structure: a person or a couple are introduced (exposition); a problem or conflict between them or between the participant and an absent other is raised (complication); the conflict is intensified (by the host's staging of the antagonism and/or the public's partisan participation); and a quasi-resolution (or more frequently, the promise of a resolution) is reached, usually through the deus ex machina-like intervention of an expert.

However, in contradistinction to the traditional story plot, the narrative structure does not proceed from characters' actions but from the structured exchange of disputes, arguments, and dialogue. The craft of Oprah Winfrey resides precisely in knowing how to interweave different modes of speech into a coherent structure in which the interrogative, prescriptive, and autobiographical forms expose, complicate, and resolve the issue at hand. For example, when the audience asks participants vituperative questions, this creates a "complication" in the narrative that is resolved not through a change in people's state and actions but rather through language (expert's advice, host's admonition, participants' confessions). The result is that Oprah Winfrey's shows provide weak narrative closures. In the genre of the realist novel, the end usually illuminates and gives meaning to the whole structure, but on her show, it is the *process* of talking that is of interest, because linguistic exchange is the paramount reality. Language, or, more exactly, an implicit model of "communicative action," is the central motive of talk shows, which are paradigmatic exemplars of Kenneth Burke's claim that "Language is primarily a species of action . . . rather than an instrument of definition."[20]

THE COMMODIFICATION OF BIOGRAPHY

Like *The Phil Donahue Show*, *The Oprah Winfrey Show* not only produces stories but also converts them into commodities. Talk shows are contained in the larger economic order of commercial TV, but they differ from the rest of commercial television because they transform the participants' own life stories and biographies into commodities and circulate them in global markets, a process that differs from other kinds of commodification by the media. A comparison with a writer invited on any television program clarifies the difference. After an appearance on a popular program, the writer will sell between 10,000 and 50,000 more books. In this case, the media function as amplifiers of the market mechanism and benefit "everyone": the television program, the writer, the book industry, and the audience. This mechanism is obvious in Oprah Winfrey's case, as her Book Club has had profound effects on the book industry as a whole.

But talk shows in which ordinary actors expose their life stories are different: they do not publicize or advertise a commodity already circulating on the market. Instead, they create commodities—a biographical story converted into TV time sold to advertisers—from the raw material of participants' stories of pain, deprivation, and conflict. In that respect, talk shows represent the ultimate penetration of global capitalism into the innermost fabric of our lives.

These created commodities are unpaid for and represent a pure surplus value. A quick look at the Oprah Winfrey Web site suggests that a "story" is perceived as the main commodity to be traded, but it is never "remunerated." For example, Oprah's site offers a series of forthcoming subjects with short descriptions, and an electronic form for visitors to fill out that includes several boxes, the most prominent of which reads: "Your story." While famous people invited to talk shows only enhance their commodity value by a media appearance, talk shows inviting "ordinary" actors twist the rationality of classical economic exchange and even the postmodern rationality of an image-based economics. Life stories are collected and traded for the guests' ephemeral appearance in the public sphere , but this appearance has no economic returns, or symbolic value, for it ultimately returns to the non-remunerated realm of private life. This dynamic points to a new face of global capitalism: it is not people's flesh, blood, and bones that are mobilized for the engine of capitalist profit, but their life stories and family secrets. *The Oprah Winfrey Show* and *The Phil Donahue Show* can be said to be characterized by "person" and not by "commodity" fetishism: it is not commodities that seem divorced from those who produced them, but people and life stories that seem divorced from the commodity logic that produced them.

However, there is an important difference between the two shows. Donahue did not have any qualms paying two of the policemen who were accused of beating Rodney King $25,000 to appear on his show. As George Mair summarizes it: "Donahue declares: 'Why should multinational corporations like Time Warner and General Electric get their software [i.e., their guests] for free when the money they make on the ratings generated by these interviews certainly benefits their stockholders? I don't see the great moral agony here.'"[21]

In contrast, Winfrey has always refused to pay her guests and in certain cases has preferred to lose the exclusivity of high-profile interviews (like with Monica Lewinski) rather than engage in a monetary exchange. This suggests that the commodification of ordinary lives she practices is different from Donahue's in that she has made the symbolic character of her show (and the plane tickets and hotel rooms) the only commodity she is willing to exchange for stories. In fact, one of the chief characteristics of Oprah Winfrey, and an essential key to her success, is the fact that she has cast herself as a moral entrepreneur, less interested in profits than in spiritual growth. For example, unlike Martha Stewart, who sold her name to companies (such as Kmart for housewares) and whose own company became public, Oprah says that selling her name—or any part of her business—is akin to selling herself. "If I lost control of the business," she says, "I'd lose myself—or at least the ability to be myself. Owning myself is a way to be myself."[22] This quote, from an in-depth review of Oprah's economic assets and strategies published in *Fortune* magazine, illustrates how Winfrey systematically casts herself as a moral rather than economic or media entrepreneur. For example, in April 2002 Oprah Winfrey decided to stop producing her famous and highly successful Book Club because she did not feel inspired by the books she was reading anymore. This suggests again the extent to which Winfrey frames her enterprise in moral rather than economic and instrumental terms. This in turn precisely explains Oprah's wealth, for the success of her enterprise has derived from the trust she generates, which is in turn a direct outcome of the moral framing of her enterprise.

To conclude this section: *The Oprah Winfrey Show* differs from *The Phil Donahue Show* in that it is more centered on both the host and the audience and creates a symbiotic relation between them. The mirroring structure between Oprah's own biography and her guests' stories (discussed in the previous chapter) is key to understanding what sets her apart from Donahue. I will now offer a hypothesis that connects this chapter with the previous one: the difference between Donahue and Winfrey—and one of the probable explanations for her extraordinary popularity—is the fact that Winfrey is a "symbolic type," a social figure that embodies the group in its ability to play with contradictory symbols and merge them. Her persona includes care and self-reliance, glamour and familiarity, power and ordinariness, and she has used it to create a deeply contradictory genre capable of addressing both deviance and daily life, norm breaking and morality, individual and intimate relations. Because she has cast herself as a symbolic type, Winfrey has explored and used the possibilities of the medium of television to a far greater extent than Donahue. Indeed, television has five formal characteristics: it is familiar, it is interactive, it is routinized, it inserts itself in everyday life, and it is "live," that is, it creates an illusion of simultaneity between the moment of watching and the moment of diffusion.[23] Winfrey combines and embodies each of these features in the ways she has constructed her persona, her rhetorical mode of address, her routinization and dramatization of stories, and the performativity of the show. The quintessential characteristic of Winfrey is thus that both her show and her persona have made far greater and more exhaustive use of the medium of television than Donahue did.

THE UNCANNY GLAMOUR OF EVERYDAY LIFE

When thinking about what makes any cultural creation "popular," we cannot offer a rule of thumb or formula. Indeed, since popularity in late capitalist cultures results from finding the right balance between innovation and convention, the attempt to find easy recipes for it is doomed to failure. However, by examining some of the studies of contemporary and premodern popular texts, we can identify a number of recurrent elements that may help us understand some of the cultural mechanisms likely to make a text popular.[24]

In his study of traditional folktales, Robert Darnton has shown that they consistently addressed the difficult social and economic conditions of peasant life in premodern Europe.[25] The plots and narrative structures of these tales, he argues, can be readily explained by the demography and economy of that era: the frequency of stepparents can be interpreted as emanating from the high proportion of remarriages due to spouses' deaths; the frequent theme of magic tables filling with delicious foods can be explained by the pervasiveness of hunger and famines; the prevalence of tricksters indicates that feudal regulations were often evaded and manipulated. In short, Darnton suggests that the social and physical environment of premodern European peasants is both the background and the content of these folktales and that, far from expressing universal psychic structures, the tales incorporated and mirrored the social and economic conditions of their audience. Darnton speculates that these tales served ascognitive maps to help peasants make sense of the harsh and arbitrary conditions of their lives. According to this analysis, popular texts are likely to be those texts that encode problematic and demanding social conditions.[26]

One of the characteristics of modern polities is that they are saturated with contradictions (between social spheres, norms, roles, and values), and that these contradictions in turn produce disorientation and difficulties for the self. From this it follows that popular texts are likely to be precisely those texts that encode and address social contradictions, and that those cultural enterpreneurs who, for biographical and structural reasons, stand at the meeting point of contradictions central to modern polities are likely to produce powerful symbolic forms. For example, in her study of widely popular guidebooks to child rearing (such as Dr. Spock's and Terry Brazelton's), Sharon Hayes suggests that these books have been immensely successful because they address women in their dual role as both experts and traditional caregivers—positions usually experienced as mutually exclusive.[27] Moreover, these books demand from women that they apply to child rearing both a romantic ethic of unconditional love and a rational form of nurturance based on scientific-therapeutic views. In a similar vein, in her path-breaking study of romance novels, Janice Radway shows that what she dubs the "successful romance" addresses women in their conflicted desire to be autonomous yet connected to others.[28]

A second hypothesis regarding the popularity of texts follows from the first: texts are likely to be popular when they offer symbolic resolutions to social contradictions, in the form of characters (for example, the trickster) who reconcile incompatible attributes (the weak triumphs over the strong) or in the form of particular narrative closures (the death of lovers reconciles the affirmation of love and obligations to family and society, which cannot allow love as a basis for marriage).

Finally, precisely because popular texts often address social contradictions, they are likely to provide a sense of guidance in a difficult and chaotic social order. Geertz suggests that when there is a shift in social structure or a period of transition accompanied by social struggles, culture becomes a resource actors draw upon to orient themselves. "It is a loss of orientation that most directly gives rise to ideological activity, an inability, for lack of usable models, to comprehend the universe of civic rights and responsibilities in which one finds oneself located. The development of a differentiated polity . . . may and commonly does bring with it severe social dislocation and psychological tension."[29] Indeed, Darnton, Hayes, and Radway suggest very clearly that various forms of popular culture provide a sense of direction for the self in the midst of difficult conditions and social contradictions. Oprah Winfrey accomplishes exactly this function as she addresses forms of suffering caused by the contradictions of modernity and provides symbolic frameworks to help the self cope with that suffering. As will become clearer in the following chapters, *The Oprah Winfrey Show* stages the central contradictions of identity and offers symbolic recipes to resolve them.

THE UNEVENTFUL

As already mentioned, when examining the themes of the Oprah Winfrey show we are struck by two facts: how trivial and prosaic many of her topics are (does makeup improve your appearance? why don't you use your best china?) and the great interest in deviance within the framework of family (fathers who raped their daughters; women who have split personalities). Lowney and Gamson have focused on the latter aspect of talk shows, viewing them as contemporary versions of the freak show. But this interpretation is not adequate in Oprah Winfrey's case, for it misses the extent to which her show combines in a very perplexing way the deviant and the mundane in single episodes and across different programs.

One of the striking features of the show is its magnification of the routine and the ordinary. Television—particularly daytime television—is a notoriously parasocial medium.[30] It invites and solicits viewers in their daily lives and settings. *The Oprah Winfrey Show* represents a deepening of the parasocial aesthetic. Oprah outdid Donahue, among other reasons, because she was the master of parasocial interaction and knew, like no other television host, how to insert herself into the most domestic aspects of women's lives, making her particularly familiar and intimate to the women who were home during the airing of her program. Her technique makes abundant use of the conative function of language, in which one addresses another directly in the mode of interpellation.[31] For example:

> I know right now children are running around the house, that—I know you know, not to be thawing the chicken out, that you're thawing it in the microwave. Hit pause on that right now. Call your friends, tell them if they can't watch right now, you should really tape this, 'cause this is really important—important for you and even more important if you could share this with your children . . . if you want to have a more meaningful, fulfilled, deeper, richer existence.[32]

It is well known that television has been particularly apt at grasping women's experiences in the home and family,[33] but few persona have so manifestly turned to women in their most uncompromised domestic identity, which explains, partly, why close to 80 percent of Oprah's audience is women.[34] In the same vein, we may recall that one of the sentences she pronounces most often is, "I'm not a mother, but I think it's the most important job in the world," by which she intends to convey a sense of respect—bordering on awe—for the mundane tasks of child rearing and housekeeping. Oprah Winfrey directly and unapologetically addresses women's lives inside the home, the daily tasks performed for and within the family, and aims at bestowing glory on these tasks. Recalling what Ian Ang and others have said about melodrama, we may say that even if all issues do not pertain to the interpersonal, everything is told or envisioned from that perspective.[35]

Let us look at a series of shows that were listed as "upcoming" in September 1999 on the Oprah Web site, to which viewers were invited to submit their stories: "How Do You Deal with Temptation?," "Have You Had Plastic Surgery, But Are Still Unhappy with Your Looks?," "Is Your Recent Weight Gain Making You Insecure?," "Do You Feel That You Can't Be Seen in Public Without Make-Up?," "Do You Have a Difficult Time Being Friends with Other Women?," "Are You Fighting with Your Relatives?," "Are You Unhappy with Your Looks?." All of these topics are located in the category of the "trivial" as they pertain to the invisible work of having and maintaining a self in the domain of everyday life. However, when foregrounded and aggrandized, they take on a new and almost strange character. Indeed, one of the remarkable innovations of *The Oprah Winfrey Show* consists precisely in distorting the scale of ordinary problems by overemphasizing the trivial and normalizing the extraordinary. I surmise that this is one of the reasons Oprah's show was initially reviled: instead of accomplishing the function of discrimination and moral elevation that ought to underlie culture, it scrambled the "high" and the "low," the mundane and the deviant, by altering the conventions of representation that regulate the visible to the invisible, the collective to the particular, the public to the domestic. This technique resembles that of the painter Botero, who distorts the proportion of different parts of the body, for example, by drawing gigantic buttocks on small legs. Although both Botero and Oprah are realistic, their play with scale creates a new object from an ordinary one and shifts our understanding of the relationship between what is ordinary and what deserves public attention. This technique is a dominant characteristic of Oprah's style.

In her relentless way of addressing domesticity, social problems, and self-improvement, Oprah Winfrey undoubtedly taps into a middle-class ethos that might be characterized, briefly, by the values of domesticity, family, work, and a model of selfhood oriented toward action, success, and a belief in meritocracy. Middle-class identity is deployed in what philosopher Charles Taylor has called the realm of "everyday life," a cultural site resulting from a transformation of selfhood. As Taylor[36] and sociologist Anthony Giddens[37] have suggested, modernity has shifted the locus of morality and selfhood to the quotidian, characterized by the affirmation of work and family for the formation of identity. Everyday life has become the site within which personal identity is articulated and different conceptions of the good are elaborated. Stanley Cavell's characterization is even more apt in the case that occupies us here. He characterizes the ordinary as the realm of the uneventful, "an interpretation of the everyday, the common, the low, the near."[38] Indeed, Oprah's genre knows how to dramatize the uneventful, or to find within it its own drama. By magnifying the everyday, the common, the low, and the near, Oprah bestows upon them a dramatic element.

A DEVIANT MIDDLE CLASS

The emphasis on daily life places the show squarely in the historical tradition of middle-class taste, which has affirmed and cultivated daily life as the site for the positive affirmation of identity.[39] The notion of middle-class culture is hopelessly fuzzy, but it can be broadly characterized by its belief in the value of success, the necessity to adapt the self to social institutions, the intrinsic worthiness of marriage, the fear of marginality, the orientation of identity to production and reproduction, and perhaps most of all, the view that identity and morality are to be formed and exercised within the realm of daily life. Yet, if there is one single fact that Oprah Winfrey clearly demonstrates, it is that the middle-class ethos is also riddled with contradictions and saturated with the presence of the "others" it has tried to exclude. One of Oprah Winfrey's most distinctive techniques is to frame and present her topics in a way that systematically blurs boundaries, bringing the margins to the center and forcing the center to gaze at the margins. As Daniel Keyes put it, the daytime talk show is a "latter-day reworking of Ancient Greek Tragedy which typically focused the audience's attention on cultural others who violate customs and taboos."[40] Indeed, at face value, the typical guest of the American talk show is an ironic counterpoint to the American dream. More often than not, this guest offers a story of failure or pain and, unlike the mythical figures of Robinson Crusoe and Horatio Alger, is hardly self-reliant, solitary, or triumphant. The participants in talk shows are almost always people who struggle with the murky problems of identity, relations with others, abuse, and self-control (or lack of it). Mothers, daughters, and their ongoing conflicts; women and their ex-fiancées; divorced couples fighting over child custody; women confronting past lovers who extorted money from them; people who have experienced emotional or sexual abuse; mothers who have been physically injured by their sons; people lacking self-assertion—all these have one thing in common: they illustrate the difficulty of monitoring the self in everyday life and of maintaining relations with others. What fascinates the viewer of *The Oprah Winfrey Show* is the fact that she or he is witnessing the reverse of an ideal self. We rarely see people in control, in happy or harmonious relations; rather, we see a self in a situation of ordinary failure. Oprah Winfrey has threaded a subtle line between eliciting compassion—toward someone who is more miserable than we are—and identification with the plight of others—who could be us. Whereas talk show hosts like Jerry Springer and Ricky Lake trot out guests who are so deviant that they make viewers feel superior and more positive about their own modest lives, Oprah works at finding guests that have lives, problems, struggles with which ordinary viewers can easily identify. This constant and central technique is illustrated by the fact that when she turned to interviewing traditional Hollywood stars, she highlighted in them what makes them "ordinary" and "down to earth": top fashion models were shown cleaning and cooking, movie actresses in their motherly roles, etc. "Everyday life" and "ordinariness" is thus a chief code organizing the choice of topic and the ways in which it is framed.

If the bread and butter of the news is the problematic relations between institutions (the state, political parties, the economy) and individuals, the bread and butter of the Oprah Winfrey talk show is the problematic relation of the self to its significant others: children, mothers, friends, husbands, wives, fathers, lovers. Oprah Winfrey is far less interested in documenting natural disasters or denouncing economic injustices than in exploring the ways that the self can be symbolically injured in the dense web of intimate relations. In that respect, at least at the beginning, *The Oprah Winfrey Show* drew from and radicalized a long-time American theme, that of the falsely happy family. This theme can be found in best-selling American novels, such as *Peyton Place*, which unmasked the tangled and violent relations behind the ordinary and harmonious façade of American suburbia. Even more famous is the long-standing best-seller *The Valley of the Dolls*, which shattered the ideal of the happy housewife. *The Oprah Winfrey Show* continues the tradition of melodrama and soap opera, playing on the same cultural repertoire of disturbed or strained family relations. Like the genre of melodrama, it stages individuals in problematic families or intimate relationships. This is a pervasive theme of daytime television programs (usually geared to women). For example, the Latin American formula of the melodrama bears affinities with *The Oprah Winfrey Show*: "the family context tends to be riddled hapharzadly with social pathology and individual problems—unhappy homes, incurable diseases, illegitimate children, alcoholism, incestuous or quasi-incestuous cohabitation. The variations run the whole gamut from romantic adventures to social dramas."[41] In the soap opera, another feminine genre par excellence, "Such a state of crisis is not at all exceptional or uncommon. . . . On the contrary, crisis can be said to be endemic to it."[42] Like the melodrama and the soap opera, the talk show addresses situations of crisis located in the realm of daily life. *The Oprah Winfrey Show* repeatedly exposes the family as the arena wherein the self is both formed and malformed, constructed and destroyed.

To conclude, I suggest that the main subject of *The Oprah Winfrey Show* is not the life of freaks but rather "the struggles of everyday life." Recalling Peter Gay's work on Freud, we may say that the normal routine or ordinary life is presented as an achievement difficult to reach—the exception and therefore the implicit ideal posited by her show.[43]

THE QUEERING OF EVERYDAY LIFE

Oprah Winfrey focuses on domestic and everyday life from the perspective of women. But what makes her representation original is the fact that she systematically *queers* the realm of domesticity. I will explain this with one example. Early during the AIDS crisis, Oprah devoted a day to the epidemic and dubbed it "Compassion Day." This was her opener:

> If you've watched this show in the past 9′ years, you know there's no AIDS type. We've had doctors and writers, teens, housewives, children and senior citizens, in every imaginable size, age, color.[44]

Here Oprah Winfrey empties AIDS of its connotations and normalizes what had been constructed as a morally "polluting" disease.[45] To take another example, pertaining to alcoholism:

It's amazing. It's wonderful because—it's amazing and wonderful too, because people watching the show today, I'm sure, when they hear the word "alcoholics," they think of what Bill was describing earlier as bums on the street. They don't think of nice-looking, healthy-looking, well-dressed, coming-from-nice-homes people like yourselves.[46]

In the same way that Oprah renders normal what is constructed as marginal and threatening to the middle-class ethos, makes what is normal—conventional domesticity—foreign and strange:

My guests today lead double lives. During the day they are homemakers and devoted mothers, but after they tuck their children into bed at night their secret lives begin. They leave their homes each night to work as prostitutes. [Turning to one of her guests:] So by day you lead this wonderful life, and you bake cookies and you go to Girl Scout meetings, and you do all this stuff. Mom. You make the lunches and you're the mom. And then when do you change?[47]

This way of presenting her guests clearly plays on the contrast between middle-class respectability and an underground deviant identity. In fact, Oprah aims at nothing less than making "home" into a foreign place, that is, at rendering it strange by presenting ordinary mothers as prostitutes in the closet. Another example will clarify that technique:

Hello everybody. I'm Oprah Winfrey. Our show today confronts a problem that is so widespread that chances are it is happening right now in your very home, and you may not even know it. It is a frightening problem because once it happens to you it will more than likely happen to your children, too. I speak from personal experience, because I was raped by a relative. At the time he was 14 years old.

To introduce her topic, Oprah explicitly sets the story within the setting of the home, placing the viewer in the most mundane surroundings, and emphasizes the ordinariness of her guests. Then, in an about face, she projects upon this ordinary background disturbing and unsettling events. Her technique is similar to Magritte's surrealism, which presents attributes of conventionality (e.g., a man in a conventional dark suit) in an unfamiliar and even disturbing environment. This technique is again apparent in a show on homelessness. What interests Oprah is not so much the problem of homelessness itself (as a social or economic problem), but rather the fact that the homeless people invited on her show are in fact ordinary people, working at ordinary jobs. Again, it is the fact that they simultaneously display attributes of conventionality and marginality that makes them interesting. Oprah undermines the representation of respectability and normality by showing us that the normal and the destitute overlap and substitute for each other:

> 'My name is Josephine Roth. And two weeks before I became homeless, I would have never known. I came from an uppermiddle-class background. I have an honorary doctorate. I'm a painter. I have children. And I should say that I did not become homeless the way most women do, and it's not like somebody did me in or I got taken in a divorce. I had an unfortunate investment and lost all my money. My children do not know I am homeless. . . . I've been without a home for seven years. . . . When we use the word homeless, people think of those people who are so visible on the street, whose spirits are so wounded, who don't care for themselves, who probably drink a lot. I've never identified with that description of homeless.[48]

Here again, Oprah undermines the representation of respectability and normality by showing us that the normal and the destitute overlap and substitute for each other. Oprah's technique consists of a systematic undermining of ordinary representations both of normality and of deviance.

There is a deeper cultural mode of representation behind Oprah's inversion of normality and deviance, which we may characterize, following Freud's notion, as being the mode of representation of the uncanny—*das unheimliche*.[49] In order to clarify the meaning of the "uncanny," Freud refers to its opposite, *Heimlich*, which has two meanings: the first is something that is familiar, that belongs to the house, that is intimate and friendly; the other is that which is "concealed, kept from sight, withheld from others." As Freud tells us, there are situations where *Heimlich* becomes *Unheimliche*. The uncanny thus is not exactly the opposite of the familiar, but rather a subcategory of it. I submit that the fascination of Oprah's talk show stems from the fact that she undermines the conventional image of the family and interpersonal relationships by making them "uncanny," perhaps in a more literal sense than that meant by Freud. The uncanny, according to Freud, is a property of the familiar world: something that is very familiar loses its familiarity. It is this loss that is disturbing. The uncanny—*Unheimliche*—is thus something that was familiar but that we can no longer recognize properly. In the context of Oprah Winfrey's show, what makes everyday life lose its familiarity is precisely the fact that it *loses its secretive character*. Here, the second meaning of *Heimlich* comes into play: when so much light is thrown into its dark and secret corners, daily life becomes strange and foreign, *Unheimliche*, uncanny. I would like to illustrate this by further quoting from the show mentioned above:

My first guests are very courageous people. They are victims of sexual abuse who have agreed to appear here with their molesters. Ben began to sexually fondle his daughter Donna when Donna was just a child. It ripped their family apart, almost ruined a marriage and turned Donna's childhood into memories of painful touches. They've been through extensive counseling and are now living together as a family in the same home.

The concept of family is telescoped here with the most serious taboo of our culture, incest. The viewer witnesses a variation of what classics scholar Ann Carson calls "aischrologia," "saying ugly things" in Greek. In ancient Greece, certain women's festivals included an interval "in which women shouted abusive remarks or obscenities or dirty jokes at one another. . . . Men were not welcome at these rituals and Greek legend contains more than a few cautionary tales of men castrated, dismembered or killed when they blundered into them. These stories suggest a backlog of sexual anger. . . . Ancient society was happy to have women drain off such unpleasant tendencies and raw emotion into a leakproof ritual container."[50] This form of speech, Carson suggests, was perfected and institutionalized by psychoanalysis. Both Freud and Breuer used the term "katharsis" and a "talking cure" for their therapy. In Freud's theory, the female patient knows something that is trapped inside, that pollutes the soul, and is cleansed when she is induced to talk about "unspeakable things." *The Oprah Winfrey Show* operates as aischrologia, a site at which "ugly words" are proferred. But in the above example, what makes this speech even more unspeakable is the fact that it brings what psychoanalysis considers the dark secrets of the psyche to the light and showmanship of public television. Thus Oprah performs something like the ancient ritual of and offers a form of catharsis.

The juxtaposition of daily life with acts and facts that stand at the margins of conventional speech has the effect of queering the representation of the middle-class family. Indeed, sociologist Steven Seidman's definition of "queering" is very reminiscent of Oprah's own technique: "I view queering as deconstructive—that is, as a discursive strategy involving the displacement or the placing into doubt of foundational assumptions (e.g., about the subject, knowledge, society, and history) for the purpose of opening up critical social analysis and political practice. . . . I call this deconstructive move 'queering' because I intend to make *strange or 'queer' what is considered known, familiar, and commonplace, what is assumed to be the order or things, the natural way, the normal, the healthy and so on*"[51] (emphasis added). At this, Oprah is a virtuoso: by aggrandizing daily life in its most trivial aspects and simultaneously defamiliarizing it, she is able to show the arbitrary character of its normative underpinnings. The deviant is made normal and the everyday is made to look unfamiliar.

In the early years of her show, everyday life was a terrain saturated with the voice of the "other," the marginal, the destitute, the diseased. To be sure, Oprah progressively moved away from this technique and has increasingly focused on the ordinary and the mundane as such. But queering was one of the techniques that made her show initially so innovative and arresting. Therefore, I argue that she has radicalized the cultural tropes offered by Freud.

By queering her representation of the family, Oprah Winfrey shakes also the foundations of the moral point of view with which her show is approached. Let me illustrate how Oprah unsettles familiar and almost unquestioned norms, by pursuing the example quoted above once again:

WINFREY: I applaud your courage in coming on the show. I'll start with you, Tom. It started when your daughter was seven?

TOM [WHO MOLESTED HIS DAUGHTER]: Right.

WINFREY: Do you remember the first time?

TOM: Well, the first time was when I went in to dry her off after she was taking a bath.

WINFREY: Was this on your mind? Had you been thinking about it, planning on it?

TOM: No, no, not at first. Just, I did feel attraction and a friendship towards Shawn.

WINFREY: Attraction and friendship.

TOM: Right.

WINFREY: Because Shawn is technically a stepdaughter.

TOM: Right.

WINFREY: A stepdaughter, But you were really the only father she knows, right?

TOM: Yeah.

WINFREY: So you came to live in the house and become her stepfather when she was how old?

TOM: Seven.

WINFREY: Seven years old. So you felt friendship and then attraction, sexual attraction?

TOM: Later on, sexual attraction.

WINFREY: Later. So the night you go in to dry her off, you did what, Tom?

TOM: I dried her off between the legs—now I see it as the first time that had happened.

WINFREY: And you thought what, when you dried her off between the legs?

TOM: Different—it was a different experience for me, because my family wasn't free with nudity and whatnot, like that.

WINFREY: When you were drying your daughter off between the legs, did you feel sexually aroused, then?

TOM: Not at that time.

WINFREY: So that's the first time sort of something entered your mind?

TOM: Yeah.

WINFREY: When did that something go on to something else?

TOM: Later on, when I, oh, four-six months later, when I was in bed with her and fondled her.

WINFREY: How did she end up in bed with you?

TOM: I just went up to her room and entered her room and laid on the bed with her.

WINFREY: She was still seven at the time?

TOM: She was eight, eight now.

WINFREY: Shawn, do you remember the first time?

SHAWN [ABUSED AS CHILD]: No, no, because there were so many times, I don't remember.

WINFREY: So many times, you don't remember.

SHAWN: Yes.

WINFREY: When is the first time you do remember?

SHAWN: I don't know.

WINFREY: You don't.

SHAWN: No.

WINFREY: When do you recall this happening to you and you knowing that something was wrong, that this was not what you were supposed to be doing? Or maybe you didn't for a while, even know?

SHAWN: Well, I didn't really know that it was wrong. I just knew that I didn't really want to get out of the situation, because he would, like, buy me anything I wanted, and I was, just getting anything I wanted, and I thought that was great. But I didn't like the sexual part.

WINFREY: So you would be nice to her and give her things, and . . .

TOM: Treated her as an equal and communicated with her.

WINFREY: As though she were.

TOM: She had her problems with her mother in communication, there was almost no communication, a lot of anger between her and her mother. I took advantadge of that, treated her as an equal and also as an adult.

WINFREY: When did the fondling move on to something else?

TOM: It stayed mainly fondling.

WINFREY: Did you ever try to actually have sexual intercourse with Shawn?

TOM: Once, yes.

WINFREY: And what happened?

TOM: It didn't work.

WINFREY: It didn't work, right. You were too large for her, is that true?

TOM: Yeah.

WINFREY: Do you remember that?

SHAWN: Yeah, I do. . . .

[LATER, WINFREY IS TALKING TO SHAWN, THE DAUGHTER WHO WAS SEXUALLY ABUSED]: Why did you not tell someone else?

SHAWN: Because he had told me that my mom wasn't to know, and we had such a bad relationship at that time.

WINFREY: You and your mother. . . . When you were eight years old, nine years old?

SHAWN: Yeah. Through the whole time we were having a really bad relationship. And it's like I was afraid of her just really blowing up at me and stuff, getting really mad. I didn't know what to expect.

WINFREY: Why did you think that this was happening? Why did you think this was . . .

SHAWN: I didn't know.

WINFREY [TURNING TO TOM, THE FATHER]: You didn't know. So did you feel good about it? After a while, did you convince yourself that this was something that Shawn wanted?

TOM: Yeah, I wanted her acceptance of the relationship also. . . . I felt acceptance and sexual pleasure from the situation, and it was also, I was having friction with my wife so I turned to Shawn for acceptance.

WINFREY: And what would you get from an eight-year-old that you couldn't get from your wife?

TOM: An eight-year-old is—like Shawn—easier to communicate with me at the time. I had more difficulty communicating with my wife and other adults, and a child is more—they haven't experienced things, so you know, she had a tendency to accept whatever I said.

In this sequence, the uncanny has erupted. The viewer is invited to observe a scenario that is simultaneously banal and domestic (a father and his stepdaughter), but that challenges one of most entranched moral taboos, that of incest. The family is recognizable as ordinary, yet it is made into a strange and foreign institution. What makes the image "uncanny" is the fact that this family has entered the zone of taboo, yet behaves as a typical family. Moreover, we cannot assign a fixed moral meaning to these characters. Is Shawn Tom's daughter or is she not? Does the fact that she communicated with her surrogate father better than her own mother did make her an adult? Does the fact that she did not object to the sexual relation make her "consenting"? Does Tom's estrangement from his wife provide an extenuating circumstance? If many narrative forms offer pleasure through the closure they provide, here the reverse is true: pleasure results from the ways in which Oprah opens up and scrambles moral categories and makes it difficult to inscribe moral certainty and closure in the narrative. It is this unceratinty that in turn creates the feeling that the "uncanny" pervades this dialogue.

I submit that the main pleasure of such shows derives from the fact that they undermine clear moral categories: when we hear the justifications of the father and the daughter, it becomes more difficult to distinguish between victim and perpetrator and to adjudicate between them. More precisely, both father and daughter somehow appear to be victims of their own self (or of their childhood). This specificity of the genre of talk shows become obvious when we compare it to the soap opera, in which "suffering is often the fault of the villainess who tries to make things happen and control events better than the subject/spectator can."[52] In contrast, *The Oprah Winfrey Show* presents very few villains, and they are always villains we are willing to listen to and understand. It does overlap with the genre of the soap opera in that it undermines the possibility of forming a single moral point of view "by constantly presenting her [the viewer] with the many-sidedness of any question, by never-reaching a permanent conclusion."[53] As illustrated above, Oprah Winfrey radicalizes ambiguity by destabilizing the moral ground for even a universal and deeply rooted taboo such as incest. The show does not, of course, make us willing to accept Tom's behavior, but it forces us to confront the subjectivity of his actions, to ask ourselves whether we can understand him and whether we are convinced by his voice. The show thus engages us in an exercise in which the boundaries of our moral imagination get stretched; we watch deviants, delinquents, and other norm-breakers explain and justify their acts in their own voices, and this makes it more difficult to hold on to our moral classifications. Oprah's show, like others, was deemed to be vulgar precisely because it did not simply invert or subvert boundaries between the moral and the immoral, but rather incessantly engaged us in a debate about the contextual validity of the norms and values we hold. The desecration of the boundary between pure and impure, silence and talk, moral and immoral is achieved by engaging in a public discussion about this boundary and by conjuring up the reasons people engage in "immoral" or "deviant" actions. Even if the host and/or the public or the experts often act as the representatives of middle-class morality, the very format of talk shows deconstructs human relationships, in the very sense that Derrida has given to the word "deconstruction": by showing that the signified of intimate relationships—their normative grounding—is empty, shifting, and unstable. Talk shows suggest that our actions are constantly shifting under a multiplicity of signifiers.

By making it possible for people to be held accountable through discussion and argumentation, Oprah's show implicitly endorses the idea that all norms, classifications, and definitions are up for grabs, and that we can question and discuss their foundations in terms of individuals and the choices they make. Ironically, the show's endless staging of the fact that no norm can be taken for granted is what makes it into a moral genre that foregrounds reflexively the normative and moral underpinnings of our actions.

Oprah Winfrey is a deconstructive text par excellence in yet another respect. Deconstruction, as Derrida has argued, is characterized by the view that language contains the trace of that which it excludes: to speak of incest is to speak about normative family relations, and vice versa; to speak about the healthy family is to speak about what characterizes pathology. This is why, according to Derrida, language is forever shifting, unstable, unattached to what it refers to. The domestic realm of everyday life staged so abundantly by Oprah contains the "trace" of the many "others" it has tried to exclude. Oprah's show implodes all binary distinctions, to the point where the middle-class ethos can no longer hold on to a simple dichotomy of us and them, white and black, female and male. The effect is to queer middle-class culture: to decenter it and to bring the margin inside.

Indeed, the middle-class subject posited by television appears to be riddled with that which it has tried to negate. As Peter Stallybrass and A. White eloquently put it: "whilst the 'free' democratic individual appeared to be contentless, a point of judgement and rational evaluation which was purely formal and perspectival, in fact it was constituted through and through by the the clamour of particular voices to which it tried to be universally superior. It is on this account that the very blandness and transparency of bourgeois reason is in fact nothing other than the critical negation of a social 'colourfulness,' of a heterogeneous diversity of specific contents, upon which it is, nonetheless, completely dependent."[54] Oprah's show is indeed diverse, even messy, in that it both celebrates ordinary normality and gives voice to what the democratic, middle-class subject cannot contain: emotions, the grotesque, sexuality, the violence of nuclear families and of repressed desire. It offers a "vertiginous and disorienting calling of voices from above and below."[55]

THE NEW AND NORMAL CHAOS OF RELATIONSHIPS

Popular cultural forms contain the social conditions from which they emerge. I submit that *The Oprah Winfrey Show* functions as a symbolic device to explore the collapse of "moral foundations" and homelessness in search of norms to ground and justify individuals' claims and grievances about close others. The show's open-ended moral structure captured the American mind because it gives form to the collapse of foundations, the notorious hallmark of late (or post)modernity. Should we stay together for the children? Should we leave an abusive relationship? Should we forgive the daughter who has slept with her mother's boyfriend?—all these are questions about the norms that ought to guide our actions in an era where normative guidance is no longer readily available. Contemporary democratic cultures have a fragmented and pluralistic normative order, which invites perspective-taking and role reversals rather than adhesion to a single set of norms and values; this is clearly what the Oprah Winfrey talk show stages better than any other cultural form. As anthropologist Don Handelman put it, "Symbolic types arise in situations of social inconsistency, where routine typifications of reality become discrete, contradictory, anomalous, and paradoxical."[56] Oprah Winfrey is a moral entrepreneur and symbolic type who has cast the contradictions and tensions of contemporary selfhood in the format of television. Her queering of daily life resonates with the estrangement and homelessness that have issued from the cracks and fissures in the ordinary, what Beck and Gernsheim-Beck have dubbed the "de-routinization of the mundane."[57] It is the very grantedness of daily life, of its routines and rules, that is breaking down under the plurality of normative discourses available. By making her guests the bearers of contested normative structures, Oprah mimics the contested and unstable character of close interpersonal relationships in middle-class family life—in other words, the kinds of experiences her viewers have but do not ordinarily give voice to.

The Oprah Winfrey Show stages the fact that in modernity individuals need to choose and fashion their own morality, to redefine for themselves social categories such as motherhood, to discuss their definition of the good life, and to weigh values such as equality and self-realization against other values such as marital stability. Late modernity poses formidable challenges to identity because "everything seems to conspire against . . . lifelong projects, permanent bonds, eternal alliances, immutable identities."[58] While many view the early Oprah as trashy because she focused on sensationalist and intimate stories,[59] I argue that deviants populate the world of talk shows because chaos has become, in the Becks' words, the normal condition of late modernity. If identity is chosen rather than given, and if all identities are equally protected by constitutional rights, then what really distinguishes a transvestite from a born-again Christian? Nothing, because across the sexual and political spectrum, identity has become radically *constructed*—that is, tailored to fit one's definition of the good life, deliberately chosen and deliberately exited. So-called deviance and normality then become somewhat interchangeable because both turn out to be coded in the master code of "choice."[60] I would simply add that this code is a great cultural leveler: any choice is worth another. It is this normative equality that for many makes talk shows a "tasteless" genre, devoid of a priori commitment to the art of making distinctions and hierarchies. If the world of talk shows is amoral, it is not because it has forsaken morality but, to the contrary, because it contains *all* moralities and does not offer a "higher" (foundational) principle to order them. (In chapter 5, however, I will show that on Oprah Winfrey's show, this scrambling and inversion of moral categories is manipulated so as to lead her guests and viewers to reorder the categories through a higher principle.)

This is also the reason why *The Oprah Winfrey Show* stages the emotions so profusely. If no public language is available to hierarchize chosen biographies, and if biographies themselves are frequently torn between competing norms (Should we or should we not stay together for the children?), then emotions, the spectacle of suffering, and the solicitation of the viewer's immediate sympathy become the only means of gazing at these life stories. This is what I explore in the next two chapters.

PAIN AND CIRCUSES

The sensibility we have inherited identifies spirituality and seriousness with turbulence, suffering, passion.
—Susan Sontag, "The Artist as Exemplary Sufferer," *Against Interpretation*

It is quite likely, as Homer has said, that the Gods send disasters to men so that they can tell of them, and that in this possibility speech finds its infinite resourcefulness. —Michel Foucault, *Aesthetics: Essential Works*

And for years, when people would say to me, "Why do you think people come on TV and tell the most unbelievable"—it's because nobody ever listened to them. —Oprah Winfrey, *Working with Emotional Intelligence*

While the bourgeois novel coincided with and addressed the emergence of the private sphere as a realm detached from the public sphere, *The Oprah Winfrey Show* gives form and meaning to a private sphere that is increasingly encroached upon and defined by the public sphere. But what makes the genre of the Oprah Winfrey talk show different from the novel is its self-proclaimed vocation to transform private experience through the deployment of public speech in the form of " debate," "dispute," "confession," and "therapeutic dialogue." Oprah's show can be said to be a performative genre par excellence—it performs and transforms private life at the same time that it names and stages it.

By viewing the show as a performative genre, we can reconnect to the problem of intentionality, for words and symbols can have pragmatic effects only when they are endowed with an intention. To christen a boat, to make a promise, or to proffer a curse "creates" the reality it names only by virtue of the *intentionality* of the person who utters it. The meaning of the show is thus the simultaneous enactment of an intention and the effect of that intention (to bring about "reconciliation," to "be a better person," etc.). This position may seem to endorse the naïve view that meaning is an intention that has produced its desired effect, which would bring us back to the prehistory of theories of meaning and interpretation. In fact, the whole discipline of cultural studies emerged from the assumption that the author's intentions are irrelevant to understanding the meaning of the text she has created, and that the form of the text, the intention of the text's producer, and the text's reception are structurally incongruent with one another. Indeed, the task of cultural studies is to analyze the gaps among these various sites of meaning. However, the various responses to and interpretations of *The Oprah Winfrey Show* display a surprising degree of congruence and stability. Journalists in the popular press, media scholars, the show's viewers, its guests, and visitors to Oprah's Web site deploy interpretive frames that closely overlap precisely because they all take as their point of departure their perception and understanding of Oprah's *intent*: to provide a stage for victims of various sorts and to empower them.

There is a compelling reason actors located at various positions of the cultural field are receptive to Oprah's intent and use it to frame their understanding of the show: both through the popular press and through her show, Oprah has created a powerful metatext, a text about her intentions and the worldview that guides her enterprise. The metatext is, in turn, able to produce a great deal of interpretive closure, that is, to frame the interpretation of the show. Because Oprah controls so many different cultural arenas, she has been able to mobilize a variety of technologies, actors, and sites to impress on the cultural field her skills, views, and style. This by no means suggests that she has rallied everybody to her cause or that she controls the spectrum of interpretations of her show. Rather, it simply means that Oprah Winfrey commands such power and control over a variety of resources that she is able to provide the "frame" within which her cultural project is interpreted by a variety of actors.

The "meaning" of her talk show is not as elusive or slippery as contemporary theories of meaning might sometimes suggest: it is located at the point of intersection between Oprah's intentions, the guests' motivations for telling their stories, and the viewers' (probable) motivations for listening. While the different actors may—and do—interpret these stories according to different values and cultural repertoires, they nonetheless operate within a common frame of reference shaped by Oprah's intent to, for example, "empower the self" and help others who are suffering. By discovering this point of intersection, we can link intentions with their reception and be in a better position to enter a text as complex as Oprah's through its "thickest" point—the point best able to tell us where and how this text connects to the nerve center of American culture. At this point of entry, we will be better able to find and select those "thick" meanings that make Oprah Winfrey a performance of values, symbols, ideas, fantasies, and fears central to American culture.

This strategy may appear to have a fundamental flaw: it negates the plurality of meanings that, since poststructuralism and postmodernism, we have come to take for granted in our analysis of culture.[1] Indeed, nobody could reasonably argue with the claim that the same text can be and actually is interpreted in a multiplicity of ways and that a text contains a multiplicity of voices that seem to defeat the attempt to make them the product of a unified, coherent, all-knowing agent. My point here is a modest one: some texts are more manifestly intentional than others, and this intentionality can in turn contain and constrain multiple interpretations within a common broad frame of reference. Beyond the extraordinarily heterogeneous cacophony of themes and interpretations of The Oprah Winfrey Show lie a basic project and intent, which is where our interpretation of her cultural enterprise must start. Thus, we may perhaps offset the problem that plagues cultural analysis, that of "arbitrary connectedness," and find useful points of intersection between texts and society that do not depend on the arbitrary decisions of the cultural analyst.[2]

I am not claiming that intentions and reception always and necessarily overlap, but that cultural exchange involves an implicit understanding of and response to a perceived intention, and that when a cultural actor like Oprah commands and wields a great deal of power and resources, her intentions are likely to constitute the broad frame of reference within which her project is interpreted.[3] Reinserting "intentions" is here all the more warranted because we are not dealing with a text detached from its context of production but rather with a text that is structurally centered on a powerful cultural character who acts in an authorial way vis-á-vis her various cultural entereprises. More than most texts, hers is highly interactive, incessantly communicating its intentions, incorporating the viewers' own interpretations of these intentions, and responding to them.

To unravel the points at which the different acts of meaning of the producer, the participants, and the viewers intersect, I have used four bodies of data, located in four textual fields. The first is Oprah Winfrey's self-proclaimed intentions, that is, the meanings she willfully imparts to her show as they appear in interviews with the press. The second is the guests' motivations for telling a story on the show as inferred from the thematic focus of that story. The third is the viewers' responses to the show as they appear both on the air and on Oprah's Web site. Last is the response to the show by cultural specialists, ranging from journalists in the popular press to authoritative cultural commentators. Instead of focusing on the gaps and breaks of meaning among these four sites, I am interested in the ways they resonate with one another and operate within a common broad frame of interpretation.

I suggest that one "thick" point at which to enter Oprah's labyrinthine text is the theme and performance of suffering selves. Suffering is indeed the broad cultural frame within which Oprah Winfrey's intentions are interpreted by various cultural specialists. Moreover, this theme is embedded in the very format of the show itself and may account for the probable motivations of a large number of guests to willingly participate in it. Finally, and perhaps most critically, this theme also offers the most convincing way of linking the talk show to the social conditions that have given rise to it. That is, "suffering" best explains the relationship of Oprah to her guests, the style within which she relates to them, and the relationship of this style with contemporary American society. When an interpretive key can account for the broad frame within which the intentions, style, and motivations for using a text are organized, we should prefer it because it is exhaustive and has a greater face-value validity.

The obvious and immediate meaning of the talk show as derived from the intentions of its producers is to give voice to a variety of ills, to have people talk about the ways in which they make themselves and others miserable. As the protagonist of a best-selling novel—ironically promoted by the Oprah Winfrey Book Club—put it:

> I'm sitting at the bar in the airport, minding my own business, trying to get psyched up for my flight, and I made the mistake of listening to one of those TV talk shows. They were interviewing some women with what the host kept calling *full-blown AIDS*, I guess. There they were, *weeping and wailing and wringing* their hands, wearing their prissy little Laura Ashley dresses and telling their edited-for-TV life stories[4] (emphasis added).

In her parodic tone, the heroine of this novel—*What Looks Like Crazy on an Ordinary Day*—has captured the frame of reference within which *The Oprah Winfrey Show* has been understood. "Weeping and wailing" are indeed what the show is about. This meaning is largely confirmed by the perception of numerous other cultural commentators. Barbara Ehrenreich, for example, suggests that "What the talk shows are about, in large part, is poverty and the distortions it visits on the human spirit."[5] Or, as a *Time* magazine article on Oprah put it: "The program . . . has won a huge following by focusing . . . on the often bizarre nooks and crannies of human misfortune."[6] Indeed, it is perplexing that students of talk shows and of *The Oprah Winfrey Show*, while noticing the prominence of the theme of suffering, have not undertaken a systematic investigation of it. Perhaps this is because suffering has been frequently dismissed as the sign of a culture of victimhood, i.e., a culture in which the victim enjoys a privileged status. Legal scholar Alan Dershowitz expressed this position most forcefully when he claimed that "it is virtually impossible to flip the TV channels during the daytime hours without seeing a bevy of sobbing women and men justifying their failed lives by reference to some past abuse, real or imagined."[7] Similarly, for Apt and Seezsold, the predilection of talk shows—including *The Oprah Winfrey Show*—for pain is obvious but at the same time "hideous."[8] The problem, according to them, is not only voyeurism and exploitation but also that, in making us see perpetrators as victims, talk shows in general reinforce an ethic of irresponsibility.

In a similar vein, the art critic Robert Hughes suggests that "talk shows are only the most prominent symptom of an increasingly confessional culture, one in which the *democracy of pain* reigns supreme. Everyone may not be rich and famous but everyone has suffered. . . . The world of talk shows frightens the horses because it is a world of feeling, disclosure, excess, purging"[9] (emphasis added). His view derives from intellectuals' distaste for emotional pathos, which in turn explains the lack of serious attention given to the performance of suffering on Oprah Winfrey's show.[10]

Thus, while commentators agree on Oprah's predilection for the image of the suffering self, by equating suffering with victimhood, they have failed to take that theme seriously. Self-disclosure and self-flagellation might be unseemly for public consumption, but the fascination they exert must be explained. This omission is all the more surprising given that suffering is an intrinsic element of Oprah's biography and her public persona as well as of her show. In a *Newsweek* article, a journalist commenting on her latest cultural enterprise writes:

Winfrey's new magazine marks the next step in her own, personal journey. She has always made private pain—from childhood sexual abuse to a now epic struggle with her weight—part of her public persona. With her TV show in the 1980s, she tapped into people's obsessions with themselves and made them feel it was okay to unearth their personal tragedies. By sharing her own setbacks, like her confidence-busting weight gain after a drastic liquid diet in 1988, she also signaled that it was all right to fail.[11]

Even if the barely veiled irony of this description indicates the author's disdain for the recycling of "tragedies" and "failures," the condensed summary invokes the very categories Oprah has used to fashion her self-made biography. Failure and suffering are the essential ingredients of her life narrative, the main symbolic tools through which she communicates with her audience. Similarly, writing in the mid-1990s, Elaine Rapping suggested in her study of the recovery movement that Oprah Winfrey and Geraldo Rivera are the most popular TV talk show hosts because they are "two people whose past experiences as victims, sufferers, and perpetrators of abuse are widely known and often invoked on their shows."[12] An understanding of the quasi-obsessive prominence of suffering will give us insight into why Oprah Winfrey articulates one of the most important discourses of identity currently available in the American polity.

A DEMOCRACY OF SUFFERERS

A great proportion of the stories on *The Oprah Winfrey Show* cover the range of problems normally addressed by a variety of experts and professionals. Divorce lawyers, psychologists, marriage counselors, social workers, doctors, judges, and nutritionists are the social figures deemed exclusively equipped and authorized to approach such problems as divorce, sexual abuse, self-destructiveness, anorexia, and deadly diseases. The genre that Oprah Winfrey has elaborated thus inverts the "normal" allocation and distribution of forms of social suffering and functions as an inverted mirror of the professions: the litany of problems that normally fills the professionals' private offices and is confined to their technical expertise now invades our screens. But instead of being compartmentalized in the technical language and practice of the professions, these problems all rush in at once, in the single space of television, as "life stories." Instead of showing suffering through the mediation of the rational, standardized, and technical language of experts, *The Oprah Winfrey Show* shows only the multiplicity of particular stories with which people normally solicit the experts' professional and technical intervention.

A quick tour of the themes of these stories suggests the following categories:

The Failed Self. The pervasive theme of the failed self deals with the ways in which people are unable to achieve happiness, mental health, or self-realization, because they themselves are not competent or functional. Examples are the show episodes titled "Tracey Gold: I Almost Starved to Death,"[13] "Too Ugly to Leave the House,"[14] "When You Just Can't Stop,"[15] "Anorexia Follow-Up,"[16] "Male Eating Disorders,"[17] "Ten Stupid Things Women Do: Part 2,"[18] and "You Are Not Who You Think You Are."[19]

The Assaulted Self. These shows address the variety of ways in which people's health or happiness has been impaired by somebody else's negligence or violence. Examples are "Road Map to Abuse,"[20] "Oprah's Child Alert: Domestic Violence Through the Eyes of a Child,"[21] "Child Alert: Pedophiles,"[22] "Athletes Who Abuse Women,"[23] "Did She Feed Her Daughter to Death?"[24] "Women Abused During Pregnancy,"[25] "Prison Rape Scandals,"[26] "Lives Shattered by Crime,"[27] "Unsolved Crimes on Oprah Stations,"[28] "Confrontation Between Convict and Victim,"[29] "My Wife Was Raped,"[30] "Married to a Molester,"[31] "Sexual Abuse in Families,"[32] and "Men Who Rape and Treatment for Rapists."[33]

Broken Relations. This category hinges upon the conflicts and difficulties that arise from broken or contested close relationships. Examples are "Broken Promises That Made Headlines,"[34] "Women Confront Men to Find Out Why They Were Dumped,"[35] "John Gray on Loving Again,"[36] "Forced to Give the Kids Away,"[37] "Runaway Parents Headed for Jail,"[38] "Bride Who Couldn't Remember Her Husband,"[39] "How to Forgive When You Can't Forget,"[40] "Can't Get Over Your Ex,"[41] "Stuck in a Traditional Marriage,"[42] "I Am Afraid to Hug Your Child,"[43] "People Who Sold Their Souls to the Devil,"[44] "My Teenager Daughter Is Driving Me Crazy,"[45] "Broken Engagements,"[46] "Do You Really Know Your Family?"[47] "Marital Problems,"[48] "Reuniting Families,"[49] "Children of Divorce,"[50] "Husbands with Double Lives,"[51] and "Absent Fathers 3."[52]

Misfortunes Caused by Blind Fate. This category deals with misfortunes caused not by malevolent design but by circumstances. Examples are "Deadly Diseases Where You Live,"[53] "Day of Compassion 1995,"[54] "AIDS Day of Compassion,"[55] and "The Day of Compassion."[56]

Social Problems. Examples are "Social Workers: Guilty?"[57] "Oprah's Child Alert: Children and Guns Part 1,"[58] "Pros and Cons of Welfare,"[59]

"Teen Mothers,"[60] "Confronting Racial Prejudice,"[61] "Profiling Prostitutes,"[62] and "Adult Children of Alcoholics."[63]

If classical liberalism identified a finite and well-known catalogue of victims (e.g., "the working class," "women," "minorities"), *The Oprah Winfrey Show* proposed from the start quite literally a carnival of victims, with anyone and everyone invited to join the parade. Yet it is not just anyone who actually gets on TV, for as has often been remarked, talk shows in general and *The Oprah Winfrey Show* in particular have a predilection for the socially destitute. Even if the ethos and the values promoted on the show are squarely located in the middle class, the population of talk shows is an inverted mirror of the successful or even simply "solid" middle class, as most of its population is composed of women, minorities, the young, and the deviant. As Barbara Ehrenreich put it: "You'll never find investment bankers bickering on *Rolonda,* or the host of *Gabrielle* recommending therapy to sobbing professors. With few exceptions the guests are drawn from trailer parks and tenements, from bleak streets and narrow, crowded rooms. Listen long enough, and you hear references to unpaid bills, to welfare, to 12-hour workdays and double shifts."[64] I agree, but only partially. Although one may occasionally find talk of bills and long work hours, we mostly hear about broken families, disappointed love, and failed selves, all of which might be related to unpaid bills but are certainly not equivalent to them.

In analyzing the speech of guests on *The Oprah Winfrey Show,* I move away from the knee-jerk assumption that the guests speak a language they neither understand nor control. I instead view them as "persons,"[65] able to make choices and evaluate their own lives, in the sense given to that word by philosopher Charles Taylor: namely, agents "who have a sense of self, of their own life, who can evaluate it, and make choices about it. . . . Even those who through some accident or misfortune are deprived of the ability to exercise these capacities are still understood as belonging to the species defined by this potentiality."[66]

When analyzing the guests' speech, I refer to them as agents endowed with the capacity to make such evaluations and to proffer the reasons for them. This strategy differs from the analysis of "discourse" or "ideology" that has characterized media studies in that it is interested in the moral frameworks and cultural repertoires that the guests actively and willfully use. Although the talk show format constrains the guests' speech, their moral intentions and evaluations influence the format of the show. My question here is: What are the cultural codes and cultural resources mobilized by

Oprah and her guests to make sense of the experience the guests came to talk about on the show? What makes particular stories interesting and fit for public speech?

THE NARRATIVE STRUCTURE OF FAILURE

Radio and television hosts use linguistic practices that serve to organize and routinize the particular discourse of their programs (news, talk shows, etc.).[67] Oprah Winfrey's discourse and the stories told on her show are the result of careful institutional practices that preassemble stories, guests, experts, and the discursive relations among them. The main discursive practice routinized both before and during the show is that of storytelling, particularly autobiographical storytelling, which revolves around key themes, such as the assaulted self or misfortune, which in turn are organized in various narrative frames that determine how elements follow each other and the overall meaning. Framing is a cultural device that gives the listener the particular social meaning of the theme of a story. For example, a story of incest can be framed as a social problem that plagues women, a story of family violence, or the psychological cause for the compulsion to choose one's own children as sexual victims. Moreover, framing constrains the emotion(s) the story should elicit.[68] For example, incest framed as a survival story will elicit mostly compassion, but framed as a social problem, it will elicit indignation. In the following sections, I examine how the narrative format of the stories told on *The Oprah Winfrey Show* cues the listener to cultural themes and emotions.

A biographical narrative selects and connects the "significant events" in a life, thus giving that life a meaning, direction, and purpose. Students of autobiographical discourse have argued that narratives shape our self-understandings and the ways we interact with others. Indeed, how we grasp our lives and communicate them to others depends on the narrative form we choose.[69] We recognize "the forms of our life stories . . . a comedy, a tragedy, a romance, a satire. We know them as they are told. Their plots are implicated in their structures."[70] Paul Ricoeur dubs this "emplotment of the self," or the integration of various events in one's life within an overall narrative framework—a story—that carries a general theme. Narratives of self draw upon broader, collective narratives, values, scripts that imbue these personal stories with socially significant meanings. Personal narratives can be linked to "cultural key scenarios," which give them a collective dimension as well.[71]

Cultural key scenarios are connected to "the structural values which endow social action with meaning and legitimacy."[72]

What then is the structure of the life stories Oprah Winfrey both solicits and constructs? These stories not only pertain to and enact larger and broader cultural narratives but also are tools used actively to assess lives, character, and experiences. They correspond to a large pool of cultural codes from which Oprah and her guests draw to narrate and re-narrate their experience. The narratives performed by, for, and with Oprah Winfrey are symbolic tools for staging and performing the self; but they also help the self cope with crisis and confusion and search meaningfully for identity.

Let me begin examining the patterns of autobiographical discourse with a simple question: What needs to happen in someone's life in order for the talk show guest, viewers, and visitors to the Web site to feel that the story is a "worthy" one to tell? How do these stories in turn point to key scenarios of our culture?

An Oprah Winfrey story starts with the violation of a norm—legal, moral, or pertaining to the integrity of the self. The stories told on *The Oprah Winfrey Show* are intelligible to us—and worthy of being listened to—in reference to a fabric of moral codes that have been violated and not, for example, in reference to a narrative code in which the main interest of the story resides in what will happen to the protagonists. Here is an example, of a mother whose daughter has betrayed her by having a prolonged affair with the mother's boyfriend:

[WINFREY:] I think that's a very interesting thing because you are betrayed by somebody who you really trusted, whether it is because the person slept with your friend, your mate, your husband, or just a devastating betrayal. I would think that's an interesting, that you said that you don't even know who you are. Because what you once believed to be true is no longer true, is that what you're saying to us, Fay?

[FAY CUNNINGHAM:] Yeah. Yeah. I am.

[WINFREY:] So you don't even trust yourself anymore because the person you believed you could trust you can't trust anymore.

[CUNNINGHAM:] I'm afraid to trust in myself; I'm afraid to trust in my judgment.

[WINFREY:] Mmm. . . .

[CUNNINGHAM:] Because I don't get it.

[WINFREY:] Because?

[CUNNINGHAM:] It still hurts like it was yesterday. . . . It just hurts. And you can't fix the hurt and you can't take your heart out and fix that.

Later on, on the same show, another guest explains why she has so many difficulties "letting go of her pain": "there's so much pain. It goes so deep. You
just can't let it go."[73]

This narrative has a retrospective structure, that is, it is about the relationship that the present self entertains vis-á-vis a past event, here a violation
of a moral code and an emotional relationship. The structure of the plot is
not engaged forward, looking to what will happen next, but rather backward, in a movement back and forth between past and present. Thus this
narrative does not have the structure of the quest narrative, in which the
protagonists are to find something they do not yet own, be it love, worldly
success, or the name of a murderer. Rather, this story is about the violation
of a normative code specifying the obligations binding daughter to mother,
a violation that threatens the self of the storyteller. We thus have here two
intertwined narrative themes: one is (the violation of) a normative, or moral,
code (daughter has sexual relations with a man already claimed by her
mother's sexuality) and the other is a therapeutic code (this event threatens
her psychological health). The intertwining of that which is normative behavior and that which pertains to the self is a distinctive mark of the stories
told on *The Oprah Winfrey Show*. While the moral code refers to the norms
and obligations that bind us to others, the therapeutic code points to the
ways in which one's life story differs from (or corresponds to) a model of psychological "health." For example, the betrayal event can become a "story"
because of a moral code regulating the relationship of daughters to mothers
and the (normative) prohibition against their exchanging sexual partners.
But it can become an Oprah Winfrey story because the violation of a moral
code leads us to the story of the ways the self becomes a problem for itself
(the mother can neither forgive nor be happy). The moral code thus generates a therapeutic code when the violation of norms implicates the self that
has been injured either by others or by itself (which constitutes the therapeutic story par excellence). Oprah Winfrey tries to shift the retrospective
structure of the story to a prospective one by raising the question of whether
the self can extricate itself and recover from its injuries.

It is the therapeutic code that opens up the structure of a story and engages the viewer in the question of what will happen to this person, whether
she will behave in a healthy way or not. For example:

At 25 years of age, my first guest gave up a zooming modeling career because, she
says, her boyfriend thought it was an indecent way to make a living. So, she says,
for the next three years she lived with him, doing nothing night and day except

waiting for his hourly phone calls. She says she did everything to please him, lost family and friends over her total devotion to him. It got to be too much, she says, when he didn't even trust her to walk the dog by herself. She says he would sneak home during the day and watch her in the park through a telescope. Welcome, Peggy Wilkins, to the show.[74]

Without a doubt, the story of Peggy Wilkins could be framed in a number of ways: one could admire her devotion and make her an exemplary model of self-sacrifice; view this story as an example of a violent male culture of possessiveness; or see this as a interesting story in which erotic pleasure is intertwined with the masochistic desire to be possessed, as well as with the sadistic desire to annihilate the will of another. Yet the story is not framed from any of those standpoints. Rather, it is told from the perspective of the kind of self required in and by liberal polities, that is, a self able to achieve "health," understood as the ability to combine autonomy with equality and intimacy. Oprah's framing of this woman's story is motivated by the assumption that intimate relations ought to be held to such norms as freedom, autonomy, and dignity. We may observe that this story is worthwhile because it rests on a set of normative assumptions that are at once moral and therapeutic: moral because they are predicated on the view that men and women are equal and that all social arrangements should preserve their dignity, and therapeutic because these assumptions are contained within a larger vision of the healthy self. Ms. Cunningham's and Ms. Wilkins's stories make sense to us because we assume that the violation of a moral code jeopardizes the self and its health: self-esteem, emotional reciprocity, and the preservation of one's best interests are the predicates that, when violated, motivate a therapeutic story, i.e., about a self unable to achieve self-mastery and well-being.

Therapeutic narratives are used to construct both what is important to the self and what is problematic to it. One of the ways in which they shape the biographical narratives of the self is through their capacity to *name* forms of psychic suffering that pertain to the ill-formation of the self. For example:

> [WINFREY:] . . . our true intention [on today's show] is to find out why so many of us hold back when it comes to indulging ourselves. For instance, when was the last time you ate on your good china? . . . We're talking about being afraid of using your good stuff.

Toward the end of the show, after Oprah has reviewed the many ways in which people obsessively preserve their furniture, she and her invited expert provide the following advice:

[WINFREY]: Are you living every day with passion—every other day, two days a week, with passion?. . . It means letting go of your fears that you allow to hold you back every day from experiencing the pleasures in life, like worrying you'll ruin the couch if you sit on it. . . .

[MS. LINN (A PASSION EXPERT):] So many times, when you don't want to wear something, like a dress, it's almost a way of saying that I don't deserve this now.

[WINFREY:] Yeah.

[LINN:] And to the extent that you just wear it, even if you're going, you know, out for dinner with the kids, it's a message to your inner self that says, "Yeah I deserve this. I deserve to be pretty. I deserve to feel good about myself."[75]

In this example, the trivial—whether or not to wear the pretty dress—has become a trigger for a larger narrative framed as a "therapeutic biographical narrative," possible because it names a dysfunction of the self—something that makes the self a problem to itself. This implies that *any topic belonging to the realm of everyday life* can become an interesting story if it is framed as a dysfunction and is translated in a narrative in which the self faces a predicament that it must simultaneously recognize, manage, and surmount. The upshot is that an almost infinite number of issues can become candidates for being "problems" or what narratologists call "complications," thus generating an endless pool of therapeutic stories. Therapeutic stories come "attached," so to speak, to their own set of experts, who contribute to institutionalizing this narrative discourse by providing causal frames, etiology, and plans of action. To say it differently, the therapeutic narrative code can make any problem function as the departure point for a narrative in which the self becomes a (specific) problem to itself, and is the pretext for mobilizing an "expert" who specializes in one particular form of dysfunction. A particular form of discourse—the therapeutic—generates and mobilizes an array of institutional, organizational, and professional resources.

It is easy to see how therapeutic biographies become centered on "suffering": it is the central "knot" of the narrative, what motivates it, helps it unfold, and makes it work. To better explain this, let me use an example:

[WINFREY:] Meet Scott. He's here out of love and concern for his father, Kit. Now, Kit's a prominent attorney in his community. He achieved most of his success with his wife at his side. But after thirty years of marriage, they separated just a few years ago. Their divorce was final just seven months ago. Now Scott worries about his father. Scott says his dad is really not over his mother and he's closing himself off from future happiness. And Pauline is also the girlfriend here— she is Kit's girlfriend—for the past few years. She says that Kit is so in love with his ex-wife that it's caused problems in their relationship. [Addressing her audience] Kit even wonders if he's obsessed with his ex. Are you?[76]

What makes Kit an interesting guest? After all, he is successful and wealthy, and his only claim to "suffering" is the banal and widespread experience of divorce. But he is perfect for the talk show because his story is about a failed self. In the therapeutic code, it is about his "refusal" to be happy, about the way his failure is self-generated. Clearly, what interests the viewer is the fact that this man's rather ordinary life has turned out to be a failed one, and that his misery is in fact voluntary—a fact that points to a disease of the self and of the will. Therapeutic storytelling is thus inherently circular: to tell a story is to tell a story about a diseased self (in this case, it is the son who frames his father's story in this way). As Michel Foucault laconically remarks in his *History of Sexuality*, the care of the self, cast in medical metaphors of health, paradoxically encourages a view of a "sick" self in need of correction and transformation.[77]

The therapeutic framing of biographical stories similarly narrates the self in terms of its "diseases." It is this assumption, central to *The Oprah Winfrey Show*, that makes it (like the therapeutic institution) "work": if failure is the result of a disease of the will, then it is self-made, and if it is self-made, it can also be unmade, which legitimates and perpetuates the very existence of the show and of the therapeutic institution that feeds it. Indeed, what is particularly interesting about therapeutic narratives is the fact that the narrative about the self quickly becomes a "narrative in action"—a story about the very process of understanding, working at, and overcoming (or not overcoming) one's problems.

The therapeutic code that constitutes these biographical narratives cuts through two cultural spheres: the normative-ethical and the scientific-professional. Therapeutic narratives became privileged narratives of modern identity when discourses on the psyche were modeled on the discourse of medicine and of the law, circumscribing health from pathology, normality from deviance. As Foucault showed so well in his 1974–75 lectures at the College de France, the motif of "health" was mobilized by the legal apparatus to legislate over the mad, the monster, and the perverse,[78] with the result that the therapeutic notion of "health" draws from the normative descriptions of the "average" citizen as well as from the medical discourse of pathology and normality. To be "psychologically healthy" then means being a competent member of a liberal society whose "autonomy," "self-determination," and "self-control" have currency in the public realm as well as in the private sphere of domesticity. In the therapeutic code, to willingly give up one's own freedom, equality, dignity, or well-being in the private sphere can become a "story" because it means betraying one's own "health" and one's competent membership in the liberal polity.

The therapeutic cultural scenario is pinioned between the normative-scientific and the narrative-biographical, the lawlike and the emotional. Because these biographical narratives simultaneously draw from norms such as "fairness," "justice," and "autonomy of the person," as well as from medical models of health, I submit that Oprah Winfrey solicits a dual mode of watching that taps into normativity and emotionality, discourse and biography, the general and the particular.

THE NARRATIVE STRUCTURE OF BAD LUCK

Stories not only inform the listener of a particular theme or cultural scenario but also demonstrate that it is infused with particular emotions, which give the story what Geertz calls a "mood" or "feeling." To be meaningful speech acts, stories must mobilize cultural codes, which in turn elicit particular emotions in the listener. Stories thus have both a structure and an emotional mood. They are told to produce effects on their listeners, to persuade, move, or incite; in that sense, they have a pragmatic intent. Oprah Winfrey's main pragmatic use of stories is to evoke particular emotions.

Narrative analysis has paid insufficient attention to the emotional dynamic contained in and generated by narrative discourse. This emotional dynamic establishes a strong relationship between listener and teller, receiver and producer of stories. Contrary to the ritual indictment of popular culture as kitsch because it is emotional, I argue, based on the now-abundant work in the sociology of emotions, that, to the extent that emotions contain and point to norms, values, and symbols, they can help us clarify the moral meaning of stories.[79] To the extent that emotions are crucial symbolic tools for expressing to ourselves and others who we are and what are our moral commitments, the emotions of these Oprah Winfrey stories can in turn provide indications about their moral fabric.

The viewer is drawn into a particular biographical story by the activation of particular kinds of emotions, which we may call "moral emotions," that bind the listener to the storyteller through a set of assumptions about worthy or reprehensible behavior. Oprah makes most frequent use of the emotions of indignation and compassion. These two emotions are moral in the sense that when activated, they always implicitly refer to a set of norms about the rights and duties that regulate social relations. While indignation is activated by the perception that collective norms of justice have been violated, compassion is evoked by the suffering of a particular person, which may or may not have been the result of a breach in ethical norms. Thus, the narrative form expresses and gives a form to the guests' own emotions and uses rhetorical devices to generate particular emotions in the viewer.

ASSAULTED SELVES: INDIGNATION

The emotion of indignation is elicited when the self is presented as the victim of outside circumstances she cannot control. Here is an example of the ways in which Oprah Winfrey frames a story so as to elicit our moral indignation. In a show on handguns and children, the following text runs on the screen: "A toy ball must pass 4 consumer safety standards before it is sold. There are no consumer safety standards for handguns."[80] This story clearly solicits indignation, which, like guilt, is a supremely moral emotion. More than our own status or honor, what is at stake in indignation is the sense that a moral feature of the world has been violated. It is a sentiment exercised mostly on behalf of others (when we ourselves are concerned, indignation becomes anger). Indignation may contain compassion, but differs from it in that while the latter is geared to a suffering person, the former need not be motivated by suffering, only by the infraction of a moral code (I might be indignant that X tried to hurt Y, even if Y never actually got hurt). While mass media usually elicit indignation in the context of public institutions, Oprah Winfrey frequently appeals to moral indignation in the context of domestic relations. For example:

[WINFREY:] We had really, really, really, big problems in getting people to come on and talk about this because it seems to be a secret boy's club, because athletes are so adored in this country that we set them up as heroes and a lot of them, perhaps, deserve to be heroes, they're sex symbols and role models. But when they become abusive in their relationships, everybody gets quiet. In recent years, hardly a week has passed without an athlete being accused of raping or beating some woman.[81]

As on so many other occasions, Oprah contrasts her show with the silence of society and institutions. She thus situates these stories in the practice—

routinized since the emergence of the public sphere — of denunciation. The denunciation is a double one: of the act itself, and of the silence that surrounds it. This category of speech is possible only if the person who denounces and her listeners share a common set of moral assumptions.[82] The same show continues as follows:

> [WINFREY:] He was slapping and choking his wife Felicia. Their seven-year-old son called 911 pleading for help.
>
> [JEFFREY MOON, WARREN MOON'S SON, IN EXCERPT FROM HIS CALL TO 911:] My daddy's going to hurt my mommy. And please hurry.
>
> [UNIDENTIFIED 911 OPERATOR:] OK.
>
> [MR. MOON:] I made a tremendous mistake. I take full responsibility for it.
>
> [WINFREY:] However, Warren Moon was recently acquitted of assault charges.

At this point, Oprah Winfrey is able to accomplish simultaneously four forms of denunciation. These concern (1) the particular story of a particular family; (2) the silence with which we excuse athletes' violence; (3) the mistreatment of women by men; and (4) a "metastory" illustrating the indifference of legal and social institutions to this form of violence. This denunciation thus intertwines the particular and the general, the normative and the emotional, the public debate and the identification with the plight of particular people.

Using feminist scholar Sara Ruddick's words, we may say that by framing domesticity in the category of speech of denunciation, Oprah aims to raise from within the family issues of fairness "that ha[ve] little to do with redistribution."[83] This in turn suggests that the modern family Oprah scrutinizes and exposes to denunciation is hardly a "private" haven anymore. Instead, it has increasingly become a micropublic sphere shaped and governed by the norms and procedural rules of the public sphere: reciprocity, equality, and autonomy have become the yardstick by which families are held accountable.[84] Such intertwining of the particular plight of a person and the invocation of a general normative order is at the heart of the construction of indignation as a public sentiment. This is precisely the way in which Voltaire and Zola constructed, rhetorically, an "*affaire,*" that is, a sense of public outrage geared to the defense of a particular individual ("Callas" and "Dreyfus" respectively) in order to defend a higher collective norm and good. However, while in the traditional public sphere, the "*affaire*" reverberates in the various sites of the public domain (the political sphere most notably), Oprah's cases do *not* affect other spheres or media.

Her denunciations reverberate only in the private lives of her guests, studio audience, TV viewers, and Web site visitors through a mechanism that, albeit public, still confines the story to the private sphere.

TRAGIC STORIES: COMPASSION

The solicitation of indignation is frequently mixed with the direct invocation of compassion—also a moral sentiment, provoked not by the violation of norms but rather by attending to particular people and to their plight. Compassion is often viewed as a secularized equivalent of the Christian ethic of brotherly love. However, while the Christian *agape* is directed indifferently toward villains and saints, rich and poor, compassion is a morally more differentiated sentiment, normally directed only to the sufferer, who is not identified as a villain. While indignation requires a clear distinction between victims and perpetrators, compassion demands only that a person be the object of undeserved suffering. A prime story type eliciting compassion is that of cruel malevolence:

[WINFREY:] When she graduated from high school, she was voted the most likely to succeed. Lisa Bryant was captain of the cheerleading squad and class vice president.

[COLONEL BRYANT:] She was always thinking, always trying to make life better.

[MRS. BRYANT:] For my 50th birthday, she came all the way from Princeton with 50 roses. I'm not going to have that anymore.

[WINFREY:] She graduated from Princeton with honors and planned on going to Harvard Law School.

[MRS. BRYANT:] The sky was the limit for her.

[WINFREY:] But just a month after these pictures were taken, 21-year-old Lisa was murdered. This man, a decorated member of the army's prestigious Old Guard, was convicted for her murder.[85]

Oprah Winfrey frames her guests' stories to emphasize the merit and virtue of victims, thus eliciting simultaneous indignation on behalf of the victim of the crime and compassion for her parents (the guests of the show). This framing makes sense because in our moral lexicon, victims call for our indignation and compassion especially if they have meritorious lives—their misfortune is all the more tragic because it is undeserved. I suggest that the emotional power of these stories derives from an essential attribute of our moral culture: what political philosopher Judith Shklar has dubbed the abhorrence for cruelty,[86] which she maintains is the cornerstone of the institutions of liberalism.

Another story structure in which compassion is an essential ingredient resembles tragedy in the sense that it is less concerned with malevolence per se and more preoccupied with the suprahuman forces that destroy lives. As in the structure of tragedy, this story format shows actors struggling with forces they do not and cannot control. For example:

> [WINFREY:] My next guest never dreamt he might be at risk for homelessness. He once lived in one of the most affluent neighborhoods in Los Angeles, but one day found himself penniless and living by an old beach pier. Brian Zukor was a successful architect making over $15,000 a month. Brian never thought his world would come to an end. . . .The road from riches to rags finally brought him here.[87]

By framing this man's story as one "from riches to rags" and by building his narrative around his abrupt destitution, Oprah presents it as a tragedy and mobilizes empathy and compassion. What she emphasizes in this story is precisely the lack of control of people over their destiny, as well as the arbitrariness of their tragic fate. Another example:

> [WINFREY:] It began like a Hollywood fairy tale. Handsome actor Paul Michael Glaser shot to fame in the hit series, "Starsky and Hutch." Elisabeth Meyer was a pretty schoolteacher whose smile just won his heart. They had two children, Ariel and Jake. But the fairy tale began to tragically unravel when Ariel turned four and came down with a mysterious illness. It was discovered that Elisabeth had received AIDS-tainted blood from the hospital, and had unknowingly passed it on to both of her babies.

This story illustrates what we may call the eruption of moral chaos in good lives, that is, the utter lack of correspondence between one's fate and one's moral worth. In the cultural history of narratives, such a story structure is very similar to the biblical story of Job, which is shaped around the incomprehensibility of Job's repeated misfortunes (his wife and children die; his fortune is taken away from him; he is the victim of diseases) in the face of both his (previous) happiness and his impeccable righteousness. What is emphasized in Job's story is a reversal of fortune that is all the more incomprehensible and unacceptable because he is righteous. Similarly, Oprah highlights the moral incoherence embedded in such stories by stressing the meritorious character of these lives. Such stories have the structure of tragedy as defined by George Steiner:

> Tragic drama tells us that the spheres of reason, order, and justice are terribly limited and that no progress in our science or technical resources will enlarge their relevance. . . . Call it what you will: a hidden or malevolent God, blind fate, the solicitations of hell, or the brute fury of our animal blood. It waits for us in ambush at the cross-roads. It mocks and destroys us.[88]

Compassion here thus addresses not only arbitrary twists of fate but also the basic premise of our moral universe: that virtue and merit ought to meet with an adequate reward. For example, in the aforementioned "fairy tale that unravels as a gruesome AIDS tragedy":

> [OPRAH:] The worst has been what?
> [GLASER:] The worst is, I think, what we're going through now—is dealing with the illness, waiting to see what happens medically with the children, hoping for a cure—if not, what's coming—waiting—waiting for a death. And see—I mean, it's, it's kind of hard. People—like my wife said one time: "Most people plan college for their children. We have to plan funerals."[89]

In contradistinction to, say, the eighteenth-century literature in which a heroine's misery was "sweet" and indicated a virtuous soul, this story format presents pain as neither gentle nor sweet. Instead of referring to a civilized, refined, gentle self, it refers to those experiences that exemplify the collapse of ordinary moral frames of reference.

These repeated and forceful techniques to elicit compassion could be— and have been—interpreted by cultural commentators as cheap manipulation for maximum pathos. However, I suggest that Oprah is here articulating in ordinary language the moral problem of "luck," a problem that is at the heart of the genre of tragedy and that has baffled ordinary people as well as professional philosophers. Philosopher Bernard Williams defines it as the problem[90] of coming to grips with the fact that some people enjoy privileges or are deprived of basic goods not because of any intrinsic merit or fault, but rather because of a set of circumstances they have no control over. The story of the destitution of powerful or successful characters by (what seems to be) the forces of blind fate has accompanied western culture since the Greek tragedy. It fascinates us still, because it seems to contradict and mock the aspiration to self-mastery and meritocracy that undergirds the legitimacy of contemporary polities.

NARRATIVE OF TRAUMA

Precisely because the show has the vocation of providing a platform for suffering, its privileged guests embody modern prototypes: they are the victims and bearers of "trauma." The trauma narrative seems to best embody modern tragic narratives of the suffering self because it condenses the family narrative, the abhorence for cruelty, and the moral demand that people be given a chance to develop unhindered.

To introduce this narrative, let me again offer a comparison with the story of Job, which provides two competing interpretations of the moral chaos entailed by Job's undeserved suffering. One interpretation—that of Job's friends—tries to find a hidden rationality explaining how and why his virtue is mocked by fate. The second—Job's strategy—consists of refusing to assign a hidden meaning (and therefore reason) to the unbearable moral and theological chaos signified by his misfortune.

Oprah Winfrey offers a third strategy to make sense of chaos, one that is properly modern. Oprah's main narrative technique makes both guest and viewer rehearse as intensely and vividly as possible the very moment during which the guest's life veered toward disaster, the moment when the guest's and viewers' ontological trust in the world collapsed. For example, Oprah interviewed Magic Johnson's wife about the day she learned that her husband was infected with HIV:

[MS. JOHNSON:] . . . the way he walked in the door, it just—I could tell, because I know him so well. I could tell just by the look on his face that something was wrong. And he was like, "Oh nothing. I'm fine. I'm fine.

[WINFREY:] So where were you when he told you? Where were you? Were you sitting down, standing up?

[JOHNSON:] In—yeah. Yeah, I was sitting in the TV room. . . .

[WINFREY:] Mmmmm.

[JOHNSON:] In our TV room.

[WINFREY:] What did you think?

[JOHNSON:] I had no idea.

[WINFREY:] Did you think somebody died?

[JOHNSON:] Yeah. That's what, I think, that was the first thing I asked. I'm like, "Did something happen to somebody in the family?"

[WINFREY:] Uh-huh.

[JOHNSON:] And he's like "no." And then he just told me, and I was totally shocked.

[WINFREY:] What did he say?

[JOHNSON:] "I just found out that I tested positive for the HIV virus."[91]

Oprah makes numerous efforts to take Ms. Johnson back to the discrete moment when her husband's revelation abruptly and radically transformed her life. The narrative is at once located in the past—in the moment when one's reality abruptly shifts—and in the present—as the mode of narration tries to make the viewers witnesses to a drama unfolding before their eyes. Through the telescoping of past and present, the "self" becomes the main protagonist of this narrative. The trauma narrative does not only relate a past event; it also reenacts the past in the present. It is a narrative about what a past event means for a present self.

For example, in a show on middle-class people who have become homeless, Oprah asked a woman, "Tell me about your mental anguish. In the videotape of you, we saw when you were looking at your scrapbook of your voluntary work, you started to cry. Why?"[92] Here again, Oprah Winfrey co-writes this guest's story in such a way that we can telescope past and present, see her tears being provoked by her memories of her previous middle-class life and by the remembered pain of becoming homeless. This narrative has the structure of trauma narrative—and not, for example, the structure of a political narrative denouncing poverty—because it is focused on *reliving* the very moment during which one's life and one's self split into two parts and the problem of the self becomes to know how to "stitch" the two parts together. Contrary to human rights organizations that are often interested in the physical damage done to individuals by representatives of institutions, *The Oprah Winfrey Show* enacts psychic damage in story form. The culture of recovery has contributed to a deep narrativization of the self through suffering. The trauma narrative is a powerful identity narrative that provides a "center" to the self by stitching together past and present in a narrative of self-knowledge. Indeed, trauma has become a main trope of modern identity.[93] In that sense, *The Oprah Winfrey Show* is part and parcel of what Ian Hacking calls the "arts of memory" through which the modern self has come to define itself by discovering, searching for its genesis and roots in the past. I would add that central to these "arts of memory" is the metaphor of pain, a metaphor through which Oprah emplots the self.

The ideal Oprah Winfrey story combines the four key cultural scenarios previously mentioned: the healthy self; the violation of norms as framed by the emotion of indignation; the victim of misfortune, malevolence, or forces beyond human control (whom we approach through compassion); and the temporal structure of trauma. The ideal/typical guests are those whose biography combines all four cultural scenarios. In the following illustration, a woman whose story has been abundantly recycled by the media, who has written an autobiography recounting her trials, and who has been the subject of a nationally aired documentary is presented by Oprah Winfrey as follows:

> [WINFREY:] This small baby girl was born whole, but was not allowed to remain safe for very long . . . because at the age of two, Trudi Chase was brutally raped by her stepfather and was continually abused until she ran away at the age of 16. But her nightmare did not end there because, as a result of the most horrific abuse, the most horrific things you can ever in your consciousness imagine, Trudi Chase dealt with her pain by splitting into several personalities. Eventually all those personalities—which has been documented—totaled 92 distinct people living in one mind. She calls them her troops. . . . Where is she now? Trudi Chase—the real Trudi Chase underwent years of therapy and most of the therapy—stop [Winfrey cries] was videotaped because Trudi says that she wanted others to someday be able to understand that they are not alone in their abuse. And that is why we are doing this show. . . . Now Trudi first told her story in this book, *When Rabbit Howls*. And last night ABC aired the first part of a made-for-television movie about Trudi's life and lives. . . . It all started when you were two.
>
> [MS. CHASE:] Two.
>
> [WINFREY:] Hmm. . . Hmm. . .
>
> [CHASE:] It was so hard to dredge up those memories, you know. I guess when we started out with Dr. Phillips, each one of us would have little. . . . Some of us [the troops] had to dig pretty deep just to get even the tiniest flicks.[94]

This woman's special status is signaled by the fact that, like presidents or movie stars, she occupies alone and for a whole hour the space of the show. Her voice is not complemented or contested by anyone else's. The woman's story is so gruesome and her suffering so overwhelming that it does not admit any contestation, for Trudi Chase is in many ways a super-victim, 92 times a victim of sexual abuse. Indeed, as the detractors of talk shows have relentlessly pointed out, the victims of abuse and traumas have become the heroes of our culture because, like war combatants, they have cast themselves in the role of "survivors." What makes this victim an ideal type is that her self has been fractured and destroyed in an extreme way, and that it has been recomposed and reconstructed from the debris of its past; she has, phoenixlike, reassembled herself from her own fragments and managed to piece together a functional self. Oprah's compassion for the teller of this story is made manifest by her tears. What is culturally specific about the trauma narrative is that it does not admit contestation. In the 1970s, under the influence of both feminists and therapists, the notion of trauma was applied to children who had been victims of abuse. Because this narrative intertwines children, as the most sacred characters of our culture, and sex, a social practice carefully contained by moral categories — the trauma narrative of abused children became to the family what the Holocaust is to political history: a form of uncontested and unrivaled evil, which bestows on its victims a special status, simply by virtue of "having been there" and having survived it. When someone uses such a narrative to account for their life, it becomes a total narrative, accounting for all aspects of their life, and it demands from society a total recognition and acknowledgment.

To take another significant example, the author of a best-selling autobiography and best-selling inspirational books, Iyanla Vanzant, came to the show with a similar identity and story as a survivor of trauma—child abuse, rape, domestic violence—and, by virtue of having survived it, became a "star" guest. What is particularly interesting is the fact that her life story very closely resembles Oprah's own (despite some superficial differences). In her book *Yesterday, I Cried*, Vanzant recounts the abuse she suffered at the hands of her grandmother, her sexual abuse as a child, being a victim of domestic violence, her two failed marriages, the births of her four children, her divorce, and how she put herself through college and became a lawyer, to eventually become the author of best-selling inspirational books. Like Trudi Chase and Oprah Winfrey herself, Iyanla Vanzant has recycled her life story in the publishing industry and on the Oprah Winfrey talk show, becoming a regular guest who, by virtue of her own example, quickly acquired the status of advisor/expert/co-host and taught other guests to acknowledge and overcome their own traumas. Mirroring Oprah's own story, Vanzant offers the spectacle of a biography in which the self has been assaulted, destroyed, and reconstructed, only to be recycled by various media industries. Vanzant's story reached a somewhat ironic closure when she herself became a talk show host, thus illustrating the way in which biography, suffering inflicted by and within the family, self-overcoming, and the story of that overcoming have become recyclable commodities, which respond to and create their cultural demand. It also illustrates the ultimate interchangeability of positions between guests and hosts.

"Pain" thus serves as a root metaphor to generate narratives of identity. Displacing traditional political metaphors to discuss forms of social evil, it privileges the biographical and locates suffering inside, rather than outside, the psyche. For example, discussing black history, Oprah says,

> If you don't acknowledge the pain in truth, then you carry forward the pain in distortion. It's no different from your own personal history and wounds. If you don't heal your personal wounds, they continue to bleed. And so we have a country of people who have continued to bleed.[95]

Here I would like to make a number of observations. Despite the great variety of stories and guests, there is a definite cultural style and intent behind Oprah's talk shows, which can be described, in shorthand, as the desire to expose and heal a disrupted biography in which the self's autonomy and dignity have been damaged. *The Oprah Winfrey Show* is such a powerful cultural form because it provides a forum in which to expose and discuss disrupted lives and various forms of suffering, from terminal disease to a variety of neuroses and childhood traumas to such life-disrupting events as divorce or bereavement. Moreover, this style can be defined as one that systematically performs the self through a biographical narrative that exposes the history of an individual psyche and its emotional components—lack of self-esteem, fear, jealousy, etc. To that extent, *The Oprah Winfrey Show* can be said to be a live archive of "failed lives."

Finally, the format of the talk show enables a close mirroring of host's and guest's biographies, to the point where their positions can become interchangeable, thus suggesting that suffering is framed in a biographical structure that can be easily applied to a variety of social experiences (see chapter 6 for a development of this idea).

At face value, Oprah would seem to be only one of many representatives of a broader cultural trend that has depoliticized a variety of problems previously defined as social or political by psychologizing them and subsuming them under the heading of "trauma" or "pain." Earthquakes, political massacres, abusive childhood, divorce, terrorism, and rape all turn out to belong to the same biographical structure under the same heading. However, the concept of a culture of recovery—which has lately generated a flurry of critiques—does not account well for the sociological complexity of the biographical narrative of a recovered self. What makes this narrative complex is that it is located at the threshold between the therapeutic and individualized discourses on the self, the various forms of denunciation that pervade civil society (of which feminism is the most visible and obvious example), and moral assumptions pertaining to the relationship between self and institutions. I suggest that the biographical narratives of recovery are more adequately characterized as an offshoot of the "politics of pity."[96]

Luc Boltanski suggests that in one of her less well-known books, *On Revolution,* Hannah Arendt makes a distinction between the "politics of pity" and the "politics of justice."[97] In the politics of pity, it is not institutions and abstract rules of justice that are invoked but the singular plight of a singular person. The sufferer cannot be reduced to a quantity (while poor people can, for example) or to another person (in contrast again to such a category as "poor," in which people are interchangeable). A suffering person makes a claim to uniqueness. Finally, the relation to the suffering person is mediated by the gaze. This is inherently a politics based on spectacle because it is about creating a relationship between the self and a *distant* stranger. I argue that, continuing the politics of pity as it emerged in the eighteenth century, Oprah mobilizes the same categories and types but telescopes them with the therapeutic discourse.

The Oprah Winfrey Show is paradigmatic of Arendt's politics of pity, with two important qualifications: while the sufferers evoked by Arendt are victims of earthquakes or political upheavals, the kind of pain the show gives voice to and performs for us primarily derives from the entanglement of the self in personal relationships. The traditional politics of pity has a predilection for documenting pain that derives from the relation between institutions and individuals; in contrast, Oprah Winfrey has a predilection for documenting the pain that derives from the difficulty of being a self and of entertaining a relation with others.

Moreover, the traditional politics of pity distinguishes between those who suffer and those who don't. To pity someone else is to pity them for pain in which, by definition, we are not directly implicated (thus a mother does not have pity for her dead child, because she herself is implicated in this tragedy). In contrast, Oprah tries to reduce to the minimum the distance separating sufferers and nonsufferers. In her version of the politics of pity, they are interchangeable because of the ways in which she makes suffering work in an overall and general narrative of identity. I examine this narrative in one of the most influential platforms of the show, her Book Club.

SUFFERING AS A TROPE OF IDENTITY: THE BOOK CLUB

In 1995, Oprah Winfrey launched her now-famous Book Club. The enterprise seemed to veer from the talk show's initial vocation. If Oprah's show had had until then a sensationalist flavor, the Book Club gave it a definite aura of respectability and even gentility. But while it unquestionably changed her status from simple entertainer to moral entrepreneur, I argue and show that most of her book selections have in fact only amplified and resonated with many of her show's existing themes and narrative formats, especially the theme of suffering biographies. The Book Club has made this theme far more salient and illustrates the cultural continuity among "middle," "high," and "low" aspects of Oprah's cultural enterprise. For the Book Club is a continuation and even a radicalization of the biographical project of suffering.

The Book Club's main innovation was to focus on novels, and to bring readers and authors together to discuss the book chosen by Oprah once a month. Considering the club's breathtaking success—an Oprah Winfrey Book Club choice is a guaranteed financial success[98]—we can assume that her choices express or at least resonate with an important discourse of selfhood currently available in American society. Her selection of books seems to be a potpourri in which the highbrow freely mixes with the lowbrow. The Book Club includes literary authors like Toni Morrison and Joyce Carol Oates as well as foreign authors reviewed at length by elite literary magazines (as Bernhard Schlink's *The Reader* was in *The New York Review of Books*). Yet, as numerous sociologists of culture have argued, people who work in market-oriented organizations act as cultural gatekeepers and mobilize cultural schemes that at once express their own cultural taste and calibrate it to meet the audience's expectations.

On the surface, no common thread unites the books chosen by Oprah Winfrey; each novel has a unique and distinctive plot line:[99] how a woman escapes an abusive marriage; a woman's grief at her husband's death in the crash of a plane he was piloting; the downfall of two twin brothers, one of whom becomes schizophrenic; the ordeals of a mother whose child is born mentally retarded; a young woman living with the memory of her drowned sister;a young woman who tests positive to HIV and finds meaning in helping others; and on and on. Such a variety of plots is not surprising, since Oprah consciously diversifies the choice of novels so as to maintain innovativeness and keep viewer interest high. But because Oprah Winfrey has a distinct habitus (see chapter 7) and is finely attuned to the needs and tastes of her audience, we can safely assume that she operates according to a definite style and worldview. Indeed, her choices contain striking recurrences. As literary scholar J. Hillis Miller remarks: "A long work like a novel is interpreted, by whatever sort of reader, in part through the identification of recurrences and of meanings generated through recurrences."[100] This observation can equally be applied to a series of novels, which generate meaning and point to the "taste" and habitus that guide Oprah's choices. Half a dozen common characteristics are clear.

First, with the exception of Wally Lamb's *I Know This Much Is True* and Schlink's *The Reader*, all the Book Club novels I read for this study have as their heroine a woman. None of these heroines has any glamorous attribute: they are never rich; only rarely are they explicitly beautiful; and they do not belong to the upper classes. The only novel where the protagonists manage through their hard work to be accepted by the respectable circles of their town is the story of the moral and social downfall of this same family (*We Were the Mulvaneys* by Joyce Carol Oates). All the heroines distinctly belong to the middle or lower-middle class and are afflicted with the chronic plagues of the powerless: diseases, poverty, mental illness, and psychological distress. Thus Oprah's Book Club's novels elicit identification with characters who could be Oprah's audience.

Second, these novels also represent a significant twist on traditional women's literature, which focused on the goals of matrimony and love. As a bourgeois genre, the sentimental novel dealt profusely with domesticity and love and, to that extent, can be said to have been a "feminine" genre. Oprah's book selections radicalize the "feminine" character of the novel, but with one important twist. The plot of all these stories never revolves around "finding" love; instead, the woman protagonist almost always already belongs to a dense network of commitments and social relations. In fact, most of the heroines are already married, as the plot focuses on a cluster of complications pertaining to the nature of the woman's commitment to her family.

When the novels include a love story as a subplot (e.g., Janet Fitch's *White Oleander* or Anna Quindlen's *Black and Blue*) the story is so marginal to the main narrative, which remains centered on the woman and her relationships to other women, that romantic love can be said to be extraneous. *All* the women in these novels are primarily defined as mothers, sisters, daughters, or wives, and not, as in the classical romance formula, as (actual or potential) lovers. We come to know and grasp these women only in the context of already constituted families, and through the prism of their roles and sentiments within a dense network of family relations. They are presented with copious details about their domesticity. To give only one example:

> Corrine was so amusing! Like a mom on T.V. she'd tell stories on herself, to the family, or relatives, or friends, or people she hardly knew but has just met, how she'd have loved to be a housewife, a normal American housewife, crazy about her kids, in her heart she loved housewifely chores like ironing, "calming and steadying on the nerves—isn't it?" Yet in the midst of ironing she'd get distracted by a telephone call, or a dog or cat wanting attention, or one of the kids, or something going on outside, she'd drift off from the ironing board only to be rudely recalled by the terrible smell of *scorch*. "It's my daughter who's the real homemaker: Button loves to iron."[101]

Although this excerpt bears the mark of Joyce Carol Oates's style, it is representative of the profusion of details and pleasure with which many of the novels chosen by Winfrey describe and locate women in their daily domestic setting.

A third recurring element throughout most of these novels is that they present women's position in the family and their relations to their children and husbands as problematic. In a way, they are an almost exact counterpart to traditional romance novels, which present women in search of love and matrimony and only rarely the story of a woman within an institutionalized family and her role as a spouse or mother. The Book Club novels explore the characters' movements within the boundaries of the family and the implosion of the family, whether it precedes the story or unfolds for the reader. Although none of these novels is properly "feminist" (certainly not in line with what Erica Jong or Adrienne Rich would write), they present a perspective on the family that derives, undoubtedly, from the feminist revolution in the sense that they almost all problematize the role and position of the woman within the family, and, by extension, the family itself.

Fourth, although most of the novels present women in the framework of their commitment and loyalty to their family, their motherhood is very often troubled and uncertain. For example, numerous heroines are mothers who betray their traditional duties: in *Midwives*, we are told that the heroine—a midwife accused of criminal negligence in a case of natural childbirth—works very long and unpredictable hours, thus leaving her daughter to the almost exclusive care of her father. In the first novel selected by Oprah, *The Deep End of the Ocean*, the son is kidnapped because of the mother's neglect during a high school class reunion; after the kidnapping the mother collapses into depression and leaves her two other children to drift into despair. *Breath, Eyes, Memory* is about the difficult estrangement of a daughter from her mother, who has left her to the care of her own mother (the daughter's grandmother) for many years. *Here on Earth* shows a woman so absorbed in her destructive relationship with an abusive lover that she neglects her daughter and "abandons" her to the care of her loving father. *White Oleander* stages a mother who is so possessive of her lover and so oblivious to her daughter's needs that in order to get revenge on a former lover she kills him and is imprisoned, which throws her daughter into a downward spiral through various foster families. *We Were the Mulvaneys* describes how a family decomposes when a mother sends her daughter to live with a distant relative in order to save her husband from his sense of shame at the fact that the daughter was raped. Conversely, and symmetrically, such novels as *Jewel* and *Black and Blue* portray women whose sole and exclusive motivation derives from their preoccupation with and commitment to the well-being of their child. These heroines' entire identity is summed up in their motherhood, to the point that we can say these two novels expand motherhood to quasi-mythical proportions.

Fifth, all women protagonists in these novels are very close to other women (sisters, mothers, friends, grandmothers), even if some of these relationships are defined as problematic and painful. In fact, over and over again, from one novel to the next, we are told by the narrator that women friends are the most important figures in these women's lives. Heroines always live in a dense web of feminine friendships. Male characters often do not feature as glamorous, romantic, or powerful, but rather as violent, abusive, or disloyal toward women (e.g., *Black and Blue*; *Breath, Eyes, Memory*; *The Pilot's Wife*; *We Were the Mulvaneys*; *I Know This Much Is True*; *Here on Earth*). While the Gothic genre and many romance novels present men who are aloof, distant, and cruel but are eventually revealed to be loving, caring, and nurturing,[102] the formula here is distinctly one where men *are* what they seem: either the passive onlookers of women's dramas or no longer able to protect and nurture; when they do wear a cruel or indifferent mask, they never shed it. In all the novels read for this study, heterosexual relations fare poorly. When a male character is counterposed to an abusive one, he is always protective and nurturing but utterly lacking in power or glamour, and is marginal to the main plot (for example, *Black and Blue*, *Here on Earth*, *The Deep End of the Ocean*). In fact, male nurturance is intimately associated with narrative passivity, in the sense that these male characters do not intervene in the story, shape the women's actions, or influence the main narrative thread. They are in the background and usually wait for the woman to overcome her crisis (*Here on Earth*; *Breath, Eyes, Memory*; *Midwives*; *Jewel*). In other words, what is conspicuously absent from these novels are two elements that characterized the traditional sentimental novel: the strong, protective, and omnipotent man, and the stage of "falling in love." Women in these novels almost never turn to men for help; instead, as if they were enacting Nancy Chodorow's theory, both men and women characters turn to other women for nurturance. We may take as an example Oprah's first Book Club selection, Jacquelyn Mitchard's *The Deep End of the Ocean*. In this book, the heroine undergoes a severe crisis when her son is kidnapped, and is eventually "saved" by her women friends. The same holds true for *Black and Blue*, another early selection: it is her friendship with a woman that makes the heroine able to readapt to the exigencies of life, trust others, and reassemble the shattered fragments of her identity.

Another distinctive element of these novels is that they present women who are distinctly *not* in the process of falling in love. Rather, what motivates the plot is that the heroine is searching for an identity to replace the current one, which is almost always in the process of disintegrating. In contrast to nineteenth-century novels, where the protagonist's social and personal identity is naturally embedded in the narrative, here the heroine struggles with the threat of a disintegrating self. *I Know This Much Is True*, *The Deep End of the Ocean*, *Black and Blue*, *The Pilot's Wife*, and *Here on Earth* all have in common a narrative interwoven with flashbacks to and fragments from the past that intrude in the consciousness of the heroine in the present. This retrospective narrative almost always serves to point to the difficulty of building a coherent sense of self from these fragments. With very few exceptions, all the novels contain protagonists—women especially—searching for their identity, what they owe to others, and how they should realize their self within relationships.

These novels do not provide any formula according to which the heroines are supposed to obtain success, love, or glamour. Rather, they deal with the question of how a self should cope with the trials of family relations, abuse, fatal disease, death, mental retardation or breakdowns, acute poverty, racism, pain, and loss. The single most distinctive element is their basic plot line: living through and making sense of loss, suffering, evil, and the disintegration of the self that ensues. To be more precise: in contradistinction to the genre of tragedy, the plot of these novels does not progress toward the final ghastly misfortune of the heroine. In all the novels of the Book Club selected for this study, the "tragedy" happens at the very beginning of the novel or is known to the *narrator*. The reader is not drawn into the narrative through such questions as "What will happen next?" "Which misfortune will occur?" or "How will the heroine's choices lead her to an awful end?" Rather, the awful end is always at the beginning, which suggests that what draws the reader in is the question of how a character will cope with something already known to be awful.

Here again a comparison with the story of Job may be useful because this story offers a similar narrative structure, in which the disaster occurs at the very beginning, thus making the plot revolve around the question of watching the protagonist's soul battling the forces of evil and suffering. In Oprah's novels also, the misfortune happens at the beginning of the narrative and the reader is made the witness of the heroine's inner struggle with her misfortune. There are crucial differences, however. Job has lost everything: his property, his wealth, his wife, and his dear children. But in the Book of Job, suffering is presented as a trial, as a test Job must pass or fail in order to prove his fortitude. His suffering points to an inscrutable theological order to which he must resign himself. The story is not about empathy with or compassion for his private plight but about the cosmic forces that are battling around Job's soul. When Job passes his trial, he (almost cheerfully) marries again and has other children. New family, new children, new cattle—all of these suggest that his losses are not unbearably irreplaceable, but quite the opposite. What interests us in Job's story is whether he will withstand the temptation of blasphemy (accusing God of being unjust or inexistent). To pass the test positively means precisely *not to change*. What marks his victory is the fact that he has remained, after all, the same Job. If he can cheerfully take a new wife and have new children, this signals to the reader his moral fortitude and righteousness.

This is what is utterly different from Oprah's Book Club novels and from *The Oprah Winfrey Show* itself. These novels make readers witnesses of the psychic experience of suffering and witnesses of the kind of transformations the heroine undergoes as a result of that ex‍preience. While in Job's story suffering has no psychologically transformative or educative function, in these novels it is the emotional and narrative vector through which women make their lives into a story and claim an identity. While in Job's story, suffering does not serve the project of self-discovery, in these novels suffering is close-ly intertwined with a discourse about the search for the authentic self. What makes the characters of these novels heroines is not that they are looking for love or success or sexual liberation, but simply and almost exclusively the fact that they face a severe threat to their identity caused by the plagues pub-licized in the present time (AIDS, domestic violence, mental retardation, abuse, rape, divorce, betrayal, etc.) and that, as a consequence, they reex-amine the meaning of their self and usually find a new one. In this respect, it is important to note that, with a few exceptions, these novels are always written in the first person, thus reconfirming Oprah's predilection for high-ly subjective modes of narration. Even more interesting, these stories are, like Oprah's guests' testimonies, always retrospective: most of the novels are not told in the "present of narration" (that is, unfolding for the reader and the protagonists at once), but rather as accounts of past events told by a nar-rative voice that looks back on them. Many stories are told from the stand-point of an adult looking back at his or her childhood (*Midwives*; *We Were the Mulvaneys*; *Breath, Eyes, Memory*). In a few cases, the retrospective nar-rative is structured in such a way that, while we know that characters hide ominous secrets and have experienced suffering, we only discover this late in the narrative. For example, *Breath, Eyes, Memory*; *Jewel*; *Midwives*; *Black and Blue*; *We Were the Mulvaneys*; *White Oleander*; and *I Know This Much Is True* have the same narrative *form*—interweaving flashbacks and frag-ments from the past with a description of the protagonist's present situa-tion—and the same confessional structure that characterize the talk show, thus suggesting a great continuity and cultural affinity between the show and the novels.

These novels are different from Georges Steiner's definition of the tradi-tional tragedy because they do not offer the spectacle of an individual being cursed by mysterious laws or destiny and implacably running to her self-destruction. What is distinctive about these misfortunes is that they always demand that the heroine rethink her identity and the nature of her relation to her close family. "My mother was like that woman who could never bleed and then could never stop bleeding, the one who gave in to her pain, to live as a butterfly. Yes, my mother was like me,"[103] says the heroine at the end of *Breath, Eyes, Memory*, understanding the secret affinity of pain binding her to her mother. Here the heroine's self-knowledge can be obtained only at the price of losing her mother and living through that painful loss. So suf-fering entails a reevaluation of the meaning of motherhood, love, or mar-riage. These novels are thus about women who try to rewrite the narrative of their lives through the experience of suffering. Suffering is presented as central to the formation of identity because it is the departure point for a process of self-reflection and self-understanding.

This interpretation is warranted not only by the structure of the narrative itself but also by the ways in which Oprah frames the novels discussed on her show. Oprah Winfrey does more than select books; she actively shapes their meaning by interpreting them for and with her readers. Here are only a few examples. About the novel *I Know This Much Is True*:

> Books connect us and bring us all closer. That's what many family members of the mentally ill wrote to us about Wally Lamb's book *I Know This Much Is True*. They had no idea, some of them, that so many other people shared the same kind of *loss, the same kind of pain and frustration* 104 (emphasis added).

About the novel *Black and Blue*:

> The details of *Black and Blue* came alive in that dinner. We felt a lot of the *fear and the pain* and some of the agony that these women felt when they eventually got out of their abusive marriage[105] (emphasis added).

About *Here on Earth*:

> Our author this month is Alice Hoffman. She's written 12 books, and she says she writes about women *getting lost* and finding their way back[106] (emphasis added).

Explaining the intent of the Book Club, Oprah draws a straight line between book reading and pain:

> It still amazes me that people *who are suffering* feel that they are alone in the world and no one else has ever experienced *whatever pain* it is they're feeling at the time. Our dinner guests admitted that they felt that way, too, until they sat down and realized that though their incomes and their hometowns and their clothes were all different, that they all shared a common bond. That's what books do, I'm telling you[107] (emphasis added).

This short analysis of the main narrative plots of novels selected for the Book Club indicates that there is a great deal of narrative unity between *The Oprah Winfrey Show* and the novels. This unity is apparent in the fact that the experience of suffering is the nodal point around which narratives of self are written, and constitutes the departure point of a narrative about a search for identity. Autobiography, storytelling, and suffering converge in a cultural matrix that performs the self in a powerful way.

THE MEANING OF PAIN AND SUFFERING

If the spectacle of "pain" is central to the meaning of Oprah Winfrey, its meaning remains to be clarified. Why is suffering such a rich way to talk about the self? To claim that Oprah Winfrey privileges a culture of victimhood will not do, for it does not explain to what social experience and cultural categories the "culture of the victim" refers. Which meanings are contained in the idiom of suffering, and how do these meanings make it such a powerful narrative of the self?

Some will argue that the spectacle of suffering is powerful because it subtly reminds us of our good fortune. For others, the spectacle of suffering is a morality play that liberates us from our anxieties about our own suffering, real or imagined. Finally, others might explain our attraction to the spectacle of suffering as an expression of displaced aggressiveness or as a socially induced form of perverted voyeurism. But none of these explanations examines "suffering" as a cultural category in its own right, as a text rich in meanings. In the final section of this chapter, I approach the question of why suffering is such a powerful category by viewing it as a "thick" cultural text, perhaps one of the thickest texts of contemporary American society.

THE CULTURE OF SUFFERING

Against what horizons of cultural assumptions does the representation of suffering make sense to us? If, as Christopher Lasch put it, "The victim has come to enjoy a certain moral superiority in our society,"[108] the question is from what this superiority derives and what makes it possible.

Looking back to history, we may observe somewhat of a paradox: while Christianity magnified and sacralized pain and suffering—both as an imitation of Christ's sacrifice and as a way to expiate sins—believers in the Christian faith did not define their identity in terms of suffering, either physical or psychic. Suffering was a curse one had to bear or a trade-off for access to Paradise, an imitation of Christ's life but not the epicenter of what constituted a self. On the other hand, while contemporary secular culture has put at its center self-made men and celebrities who incarnate beauty, power, glamour, and happiness, it has made suffering a mark and center of personal identity.[109] It would seem that suffering has become central to how we tell our life stories to ourselves and to others, because it condenses what it means to have a self in the late modern era. I suggest that suffering (or stories about it) is one of the thickest texts in contemporary culture because it contains and condenses stories about the self *that at once reflect the "objective" difficult conditions of selfhood and bestow meaning on these conditions.* If, as Barrington Moore eloquently put it, "Though some portion of personal unhappiness is probably an inevitable part of human fate, a very large portion is due to institutional causes,"[110] then we should find some correspondence between Oprah's predilection for the theme of suffering and the institutions that have produced the forms of suffering she stages. Thus, while most analysts studying therapeutic discourse and the recovery movement have viewed these cultural formations as the expression of a distorted and exaggerated cult of the self, I suggest they have been oblivious to the fact that modern polities produce *real* suffering mostly located in the self, and that this is what the recovery movement addresses. If meanings are strategies to cope with social situations and problems, then we should not dismiss the recovery movement as yet another attempt to defuse the gains of feminism; rather, we should understand which problems it confronts and how it organizes the self strategically within particular frames of meaning.

In his seminal book *Rethinking Psychiatry,* anthropologist Arthur Kleinman suggests, on the basis of the example of such countries as Taiwan, that major social changes bring about large increasea in the rates of neurotic disorders.[111] Modernization and the collapse of traditional communities seem to be accompanied by alcoholism and an increase in mental distress:

> the data argue for a significant role of unemployment, problematic work relationships, and stressful work conditions in the development of mental health problems. Life event changes perceived as stressful—bereavement, divorce, other key losses and threats—have been repeatedly shown to precede the onset of mental illness, whereas adequate social support and coping resources have been found to protect individuals from these problems.[112]

Kleinman concurs with other studies that have proved that social class, the economy, and social institutions are chief determinants of health and mental well-being and suggests that modernity produces real and powerful forms of suffering. Moreover, as many have observed, modern institutions exert contradictory demands on the self, burdening it with a multiplicity of roles and a lack of cultural coherence. The self thus is saddled with the task of managing itself in a Sisyphean way: without the cultural and moral resources that could provide a strong sense of direction, the self is doomed to endlessly improvise and invent the rules. But the rules that are valid and functional in one sphere (e.g., the market) are detrimental in another sphere (e.g., the family). One never finishes rolling the stone of identity making. Biography has become—in Ulrich Beck's words—a self-made project to be achieved reflexively, through self-observation, self-analysis, and self-understanding, an endless project to achieve and manage. While premodern Europe struggled with scarcity and generated such forms of suffering as chronic hunger and disease, late modern western societies simultaneously make massive demands on the self and starve it of the moral resources required to meet those demands, thus generating multiple forms of psychic suffering. Selves that fail to accomplish the many tasks required to manage and orchestrate the complicated score of work and family in the late modern era are likely to experience real social suffering, the infamous marks of modernity: loneliness, stress, depression, anxiety, feelings of worthlessness and meaninglessness. As Kleinman usefully reminds us, these are outcomes of the modernization process and are particularly prevalent among the resourceless: "Human misery of all kinds is greater among the poor, the oppressed, the helpless. . . . Most disorders . . . have their highest prevalence rate among the poor and disavantaged."[113]

Indeed, the stories of suffering told on *The Oprah Winfrey Show* reflect the particular condition of women, who are not only likely to be victimized in and by the family but also more likely to turn against themselves and to suffer from self-inflicted pain.[114] This suggests therefore that the cult of victimhood is not, as so many cultural commentators have argued, the result of the fickle imagination of a nation of whiners who have opted for narcissism.[115] Rather, the cult of victimhood has become prevalent first and foremost because late modern society produces real and powerful forms of distress. In this respect, my approach to the recovery movement differs from the scholars of Foucauldian inspiration for whom the language of psychic suffering shapes identity through networks of discourses. Language is a tool to make sense of social conditions, and the language of recovery points directly to the real and powerful assaults on the self by the institutions of modernity.

But these observations still do not explain why Oprah Winfrey's staging of suffering has become such a powerful, visible, and popular text. The

conditions of late modernity provide a facilitating context for the emergence of a language addressing the difficulties and aporias of the self, but
not an explanation for the extraordinary success of Oprah's cultural
idiom. Chapter 7 provides part of the answer to this question, but let me
meanwhile offer the following hypothesis: what has made Oprah Winfrey
into such a powerful text is the fact that she performs what is, according
to Max Weber and Clifford Geertz, one of the most basic and profound
functions of religion, namely, to account for unexplained suffering. To explain this, interestingly enough, Geertz uses the same category I have
identified in chapter 3 as central to the genre of Oprah Winfrey, namely
"the uncanny." He suggests that "under mental stress even perfectly familiar things may become suddenly disorganized and give us the hor-
rors."[116] And

> the odd, strange, uncanny must simply be accounted for . . . it is a persistent, con-
> stantly reexperienced difficultly in grasping certain aspects of nature, self, and so-
> ciety, in bringing certain elusive phenomena within the sphere of culturally for-
> mulatable fact, which renders man chronically uneasy and toward which a more
> equable flow of diagnostic symbols is consequently directed.[117]

This unease can be said to characterize the condition of modernity as a
whole. Karl Marx, Max Weber, and Freud himself viewed modernity as
characterized by this process of becoming increasingly estranged from one
own's self and by the perception that the social world did not provide a
home anymore, that it was becoming *unheimlich*. What Marx has called
"alienation" and Weber "disenchantment" are processes by which daily life
and close relationships have become "uncanny," at once familiar and foreign, intimate and threatening. Our sense of order is threatened most by, as
Geertz put it, the absurd that looms "as a constant background to the daily
round of practical life."[118] Similar to the property of the uncanny described
by Freud, everyday life has become both familiar and strange. The realm of
personal relations has become riddled with agonizing uncertainties, with no
normative rules and recipes to guide and ground people. Yet the realm of
the domestic—love, sexuality, parenthood—has assumed a far more crucial
role for the cultural reproduction of selfhood and identity.[119] The result is
that the same social forces that make the realm of close relations so central
and important to the self are those that undermine that realm. Precisely because modern lives have become saturated with risks (e.g., divorce, unemployment, political persecution), the need to fall on secure relations is

greater. At the same time, these relations are themselves ridden with risks. Thus, the difficulties experienced inside the family and the sphere of close relations become all the more difficult because they often are unexplained and unaccounted for. Moreover, modernity does not (and cannot) provide what religions are able to, namely, theodicies—accounts of and justifications for suffering.[120] If, following Geertz, a central function of culture is to explain why evil or baffling events plague our lives and how we can reconcile these to our conception of morality, then contemporary American (secular) culture lacks a cultural arena that has the capacity to address the question of suffering.

I submit that a symbolic arena in which the "uncanniness" of everyday life is addressed, made sense of, and most of all alleviated through performative speech and public rituals is likely to be of critical importance. In his study of conversion narrative, the anthropologist Peter Stromberg has argued that

> in any society it is precisely those activities in which social actors face the greatest uncertainty that tend to take the form of ritual. . . . In junctures of uncertainty, the formulas of ritual offer reassurance and a feeling of certainty. . . . Ritual may be constructed as an attempt to extend control beyond those boundaries, to establish certainty precisely where life seems least certain.[121]

My claim here is a simple one: Oprah addresses those arenas that are most ridden with uncertainties and offers powerful symbolic tools and rituals to alleviate those uncertainties. She stages in an unsurpassed way the profound disarray in which the late modern self is caught and offers resources to cope with it. Indeed, as Hoover and Lundby put it, "there are aspects of modern social and cultural embedment in the media that necessarily imbue the media's powerful symbols, icons, values, and functions with religious significance."[122] If we enlarge the definition of religion to a symbolic system that can synthesize contradictory and powerful symbols and generate strong beliefs, then we may suggest that Oprah accomplishes a religious symbolic performance. That is, she offers a "plausible myth of the ordering of existence,"[123] a theme explored in the next chapter.

This dimension is confirmed by an analysis of visitors to her Web site. These users unequivocally express the need to make sense of and reorder a disrupted experience. In the *Heal Your Spirit* section of the Oprah.com site, we find the following stories written by anonymous viewers of her show and site visitors:

i am having a problem finding my spirit because i can't find god. my mother died of a slow degenerative brain disease 6 years ago and since her death i am having a problem believing in god. it's not a god that is merciful, not a god that watches over you, not a god that will ease suffering. i've started to ask the hard questions about children dying, the holocost,[sic] evil in the world and trying to reconcile that with my concept of god. where do i go from here? i've been told to just "have faith" but that sound so hollow. i need to have some way of coming to terms with this in order to move forward. anyone found any answers out there? thanks, wendy.

Or to give another example:

[Divorce] is probably the hardest thing to do. . . . Going through a divorce is sad and painful. . . . It hurts from your heart and soul. . . . It almost can destroy you if you don't go through some kind of despair. . . . It does get better with time and healing if we do something everyday that will help us understand ourselves again. (Gemini9, Jan. 8, 2000)

Or still another testimony:

I am a single mother of two teenagers. In December, 1996 I was diagnosed with an inoperable brain tumor. I have since then received radiation and chemotherapy. I now go to the doctor every three months for an MRI. My problem is that I have spent the last three years in a depressed state and I sleep a lot and have gained about 80 pounds. If that wasn't enough I went through a divorce this year. I would like to change and make this a productive year. Any suggestions as to live my life as if there was not a cloud above it? My vision has been impacted so my appearance also has taken a change, I would like to get beyond that also. Any comments would be helpful. (Ljmsteph, Dec. 29, 1999)

As these three visitors to the Oprah Winfrey Web site suggest, *The Oprah Winfrey Show* (understood as the televised show and its Internet extension) is used as a conduit for the public communication of a self struggling with suffering and with the meaninglessness of that suffering. In that sense, Oprah's texts offer themselves as cultural strategies to cope with chaos and meaninglessness.[124]

The Book Club novels selected for this study have a similar structure in the sense that they present characters who struggle with the question of how to make sense of their unsettled lives and who look for resources to transform those lives. For example, in *I Know This Much Is True*, the narrator summarizes his failed marriage and his struggle to detach himself from his twin schizophrenic brother as follows:

> We held on for a little over a year, Dessa and me. We never really fought. Fighting took too much energy. Fighting would have ripped the scab right off the raw truth—that either God *was* so hateful that He'd singled us out for this (Dessa's theory) or that there was no God (mine). Life didn't *have* to make sense, I'd concluded: that was the big joke. Get it? You could have a brother who stuck metal clips in his hair to deflect enemy signals from Cuba, and a biological father who, in thirty-three years, had never shown his face, and a baby dead in her bassinet . . . and none of it meant a fucking thing. Life was a whoopee cushion, a chair yanked away just as you were having a seat.[125]

Paul Willis has offered the notion of grounded aesthetics to suggest that popular culture offers a form of aesthetics based in and entangled with problems of daily life.[126] Echoing him, I offer the idea of *grounded ethics*, which suggests that popular culture is used to articulate problems and dilemmas that arise from and take place within the very fabric of daily life. But we still lack a response to a last question: Why is the narrative of suffering such a compelling narrative of selfhood?

To respond adequately, we must remember that the project of modernity has been inextricably linked to the desire to eradicate suffering, which in turn was one of the main cultural rationales behind the deployment of scientific and state rationality. The promise of eradicating suffering was constitutive of the American modern liberal polity, faith in reason, and the deployment of expert knowledge. Such knowledge—medical, psychological, and sexual—has thus assumed the vocation of explaining, soothing, relieving, and removing all forms of pain from the social body.[127] Liberal culture is premised on the idea that suffering is curable by adequate and rational institutional organization. If suffering is a matter of social design rather than an incurable disease of the human condition, then it is central to liberal culture (because it is its removal that implicitly justifies the liberal project) yet intolerable because it points to the failure of our institutions to prevent or combat suffering. Concurrently, liberal polities presuppose that, if unfettered, individuality will turn into a beautiful life. In this way, the problem of happiness and suffering stipulates that now we are all, by virtue of our humanity, entitled, if not to happiness, at least to an absence of suffering. This assumption holds particularly true for the post–1960s generation. As Amato suggests in his study *Victims and Values,* "[the protesters of the 1960s] believed in a world without suffering."[128] I thus argue that the institutions of modernity produce a formidable contradiction: they inflict on the self a wide variety of forms of suffering, but they accentuate the individual's claim and right to a life devoid of suffering. To use an example close to Oprah Winfrey's preoccupation, we may say that at same time that the family has become the site of intense conflicts between the sexes and the generations, generating new forms of suffering, it has come to be the repository of ideals of self-realization, quiet harmony, and happiness, the objects of utopian longing. It is within this contradiction—between objective forms of psychic suffering produced by modern institutions and the subjective feeling of entitlement to happiness—that psychologists of all persuasions have come to play such a massive cultural role, in the culture at large and on Oprah's show in particular.

The therapeutic persuasion and the profession of psychology in particular have drawn their power precisely from this massive cultural contradiction. The cultural assumptions that make up the powerful and pervasive therapeutic discourse contribute to make suffering an anomaly to be not only accounted for but also disposed of. In fact, the therapeutic discourse entraps the self with the same paradox that is at the heart of modern identities: to lead pain-free lives, we are summoned to understand ourselves through the categories of pain and biographical trauma. At the same time that it enjoins us to excise suffering from our lives, the therapeutic discourse uses the category of "psychic pain" as the key narrative device to make sense of the self.[129] By hammering down models of normality and healthy psyches, the therapeutic hegemony makes psychic pain a sign of undeveloped or immature identity, thus making suffering the nodal point around which psyches, families, and social relations revolve and that they must resolve. The paradox, however, is that the therapeutic ethos encourages one to conceive of life in terms of suffering because pain provides the base around which psychologists can legitimate their knowledge and build narratives of selfhood. As anthropologist Richard Schweder puts so sharply: "A people's causal ontology for suffering plays a part in causing the suffering it explains, just as people's representations of a form of suffering may be part of the suffering it represents."[130] The more the causes for suffering are situated in the self, the more the self is understood in terms of its predicaments, and the more "real" diseases of the self will be produced.

The conjunction of the therapeutic, humanistic, and liberal discourses makes pain—or more exactly, the management of pain—the crucial dimension along which identity is formed, and along which the individual builds his or her relations to social institutions and make claims on them, the state being the obvious example. For our law, morality, and polity are widely premised on the assumption that absence of pain is not a reward but a *right*, which should be secured by our institutional arrangements. In the therapeutic and meritocratic worldviews, a good self manages to overcome the myriad inner obstacles that obstruct its way to self-fulfillment and to live its own definition of the good life. Thus, we are summoned to remove all sources of suffering, thus making suffering, ironically, a focal point of our identity. How we should remove it is what keeps the autobiographical narrative going. Because we are now all entitled at least to a life free of misery, suffering is to us what sex was to Victorians, something that becomes constitutive of our identity at the very moment we pronounce it taboo by expelling it and excising it from our ideal self.

But while this might explain how suffering can occupy such a central place in discourses of identity, it still does not explain why suffering people enjoy "special" moral privileges. Indeed, as some have remarked, "We live in a period in which victims are idealized."[131] When so much of our cultural ideals emphasize self-reliance, why has pain come to acquire a hidden glow?

The anthropologist Veena Das offers a compelling clue: suffering "mould[s] human beings into moral members of a society." At the same time that it signals the failure of social and cultural systems to alleviate or explain it, it also marks us as "social/moral subjects."[132] This is because suffering marks our acceptance of disciplinary procedures and of the society in which (bodily) suffering occurs. Pain located in the body marks "the consubstantiation between the social and the individual."[133] Das further argues that the individual is linked to the society through initiation rituals that inflict pain in order to mark access to a moral community. It is through pain that a society's claim to its members is clearest. This is apparent in (religious) self-mortificatory and ascetic practices that simultaneously make the believer's body obedient and docile and confer moral status upon him or her. As I show in the following chapter, through the experience of pain, people can become full moral agents, because suffering puts into motion some of the central moral competencies required of social agents in contemporary polities.

THE HYPERTEXT OF IDENTITY

Each life converges to some center expressed or still;
exists in every human nature a goal.

—Emily Dickinson, *Selected Poems*

The prominence of the image of suffering on commercial television has led many cultural scholars to the conclusion that talk shows are a cynical enterprise exploiting and manipulating human distress for the sake of profit. This view argues that the guests' and hosts' interaction is nothing more than manipulation of the former by the latter. The guest's desire to speak and to be seen on television is motivated by the distorted desire to have the requisite fifteen minutes of fame, to achieve the (false) promise of self-change, or simply to experience the cheap thrill of a television appearance. Such a distorted relationship between media organizations and their audience has frequently been classed under the heading of "ideology."

The concept of ideology and its many (close and distant) cousins has successfully explained how people make mistakes about their own needs and interests, which are usually known by the social analyst but not by the person herself. "Hegemony," "symbolic violence," and "surveillance" all explain how we are acted upon in a social order that is fundamentally violent. Although there are many fine and deep differences among these concepts, all three work similarly in defining the social analyst as one who unmasks the ploy of power and the mystification of consciousness, thereby making a simultaneous claim to political liberation and to truth.[1] This role has had a new lease on life through the discovery of "resistance." In fact, "resistance studies" can be seen as a variation on the theme of ideological domination, the problem of resistance being to find out how people evade, twist, or re-confirm ideology. The analyst observes and represents the strategies of re-sistance against the symbolic domination of the powerful.

The movement of the pendulum between "ideology" and "resistance" has been one of the central issues of the intellectual project of cultural stud-ies. While the power-resistance paradigm, which emerged in the late 1970s, has marked a fundamental renewal of the study of culture, it now threatens, in a number of ways, to paralyze the field in a mechanistic and dichotomous view of meaning. The assumption that cultural practices are determined by an all-encompassing ideology constitutes a serious impoverishment of our description of cultural action, even when it is mitigated by an account of "resistant meanings." Indeed, notions such as "power" and "ideology" are "bulldozer" concepts:[2] they reduce the complexity of situations and spheres of meaning to one single principle that purports to explain and describe the entire range of social action. Power-driven studies of culture produce a cu-riously flattened vision of social life, as they level various social situations and cultural meanings to the same determining principle: power (or resist-ance to power). For Foucault, "sexual liberation" is as suspect as sexual re-pression, corporal punishment or public executions as coercive as the man-agement of the prisoner through expert knowledge. Similarly, for the proponents of Gramsci or the Frankfurt School, a journalistic coverage of war biased toward American interests becomes equivalent to total ideologi-cal control and repression. When power covers and explains such an all-encompassing range of social phenomena, it prevents the making of useful distinctions. To push the point: because power-driven studies obliterate ac-tors' self-perceptions and even suspect "pleasure" to be contaminated by the same oppressive mechanism that operates in violent situations, the power-driven paradigm is ill-equipped to explain the difference between, for ex-ample, a concentration camp and a summer camp, since both can be in-dicted for issuing orders, disciplining bodies, and rigidly structuring time.[3]

This is emphatically *not* to deny the extraordinary contribution of the power paradigm to the study of culture; nor is it to say that power does not take many cunning forms and strategies. But curiously, the very same schol-ars who make power the motor of the social world end up denying in the so-cial world the very impulse that makes them want to study power, namely the desire to denounce injustices, to hold individuals and institutions accountable for failing to promote equality or fairness.[4] Scholars in cultural studies do not have a monopoly over such claims, which permeate the social body at large.[5] As Michele Lamont's pathbreaking works have established, actors have a moral competence—solidarity or denunciation of injustice—that cannot be easily subsumed under the terms "domination" or "power struggle."[6]

A view of society as driven by power struggles produces a sociological narrative devoid of tensions, inner contradictions, and a sense of "poignancy" of the social, a poignancy that could derive, for example, from the tension between the coercive power of institutions and their ability to procure security and stability. This poignancy of the social is apparent in the work of Lamont, who shows, for example, that different institutional contexts produce different types of racism that exclude and include others differently, along boundaries of class or of nation. Max Weber, perhaps more than any other sociologist, understood the vocation of sociology as that of identifying the incommensurability and plurality of the various spheres of action[7] and the price different social paths exact from us. This fine and paradoxical texture of social life is too often obliterated by an exclusive attention to power. I do not suggest that power does not exist or that it does not wipe out dignity and freedom (a cursory look at recent and distant history is sobering), or that we should not track down its crippling effects. Rather, my point is that our actions are contradictory and discontinuous and that they contain moments when people relinquish power and engage in other modes of interaction, regulated for example by compassion, love, or claims to justice.[8]

In the context of this study, this means that we should explain the meaning of suffering in ways that take into account, rather than obliterate, the moral competence of the guests, the viewers, and the host. This brings me to the final reason for advocating a more careful and nuanced use of the notion of power: cultural analysis must explain the meanings of action in ways that include and make sense of the actor's own categories and self-understandings. While our description of cultural meaning does not end there, it must start from those self-understandings, a method I have used in my analysis of the romantic formula in *Consuming the Romantic Utopia*. Self-understandings are not, of course, substitutes for explanations. Someone may not know that the language of suffering she uses comes from a particular cultural tradition or institutional arrangement. But that she attends to her life in terms of a "dysfunction" or "inner psychic struggle" must be taken at face value if we want to understand how cultural structures are sustained by the people who use them. Beginning cultural analysis with social actors' self-understandings helps us accomplish two things the power paradigm is less well equipped for: it establishes a more ethical relationship with the people we analyze, taking them as full partners in our attempts at understanding their practices; and it helps to build more parsimonious explanatory models of culture based on a greater economy of assumptions—where there is less distance between the observer's interpretation and the meaning a person bestows on her acts.

The topic of suffering is particularly apt for illustrating this strategy, for, as French sociologist Luc Boltanski has shown in his wide-ranging and innovative study, *Distant Suffering*,[9] in order for it to be a "receivable" image, the representation of suffering must fulfill a complex array of moral "requirements." To be believed and to "work," an image of suffering must generate compassion. But to do that, the image of a suffering person must "resolve" an inherent moral instability, due to a number of uncertainties linked to three aspects of the process of producing the image: the person showing us the suffering (for example, does the journalist who shows us a starving child have hidden interests?); the suffering person herself (that is, is it real, fake, or exaggerated suffering?); and ourselves as viewers of suffering (in other words, how am I supposed to react to the suffering of another human being given the fact that I am distant?). These three moral uncertainties make the representation of suffering the object of an *a priori* suspicion.[10]

Let me thus offer the following hypothesis, which in fact is the guiding idea of this chapter: when the image of suffering is fed daily by the same program and when this program has enabled a fantastic accumulation of wealth, only by using symbols and values central to the American definition of a moral person can it alleviate the suspicion and accusation of cynical exploitation. Although that accusation is sometimes leveled against Oprah, by and large, she has generated an astonishing trust and loyalty among her viewers and, especially during the last decade, among journalists and cultural critics as well. I will thus move away from the somewhat conventional critique that the use of the image of suffering by media in general and by talk shows in particular commodifies and trivializes suffering. Precisely because the representation of suffering is intrinsically unstable, that is, the object of an *a priori* suspicion, we should pause and wonder why and how Oprah has made it stable and convincing.

Oprah Winfrey has built an empire based on indignation and compassion precisely because she has known how to surmount the suspicion to which the image of suffering is normally subject. Her cultural virtuosity is thus first and foremost a moral virtuosity: she has been able to manipulate the boundaries of our moral repertoire so as to avert suspicion and the accusation of exploitation. The question in this chapter is thus: How can we account for that stabilization of the image of suffering without having recourse to the presumption of the cynicism of the producers or the blindness of those Oprah enlists (both her viewers and her guests)? How can we explain the trust she generates without presuming her audience and her guests to be gullible fools or mistaken and irrational social beings? Oprah Winfrey has "solved" in a remarkable way the problem of the moral instability of the representation of suffering by making self-change the legitimating foundation of her enterprise and her show a platform that initiates a wide variety of philanthropic and transformative projects. In other words, her show has crossed the boundary of entertainment and become a moral enterprise because she has made the biography of suffering into a biography of change. The spectacle of change in turn taps into the core moral assumptions of selfhood at work in the American polity.

If, as argued in chapter 3, her show initially opened up and scrambled moral categories, the revamped Oprah has recentered this open-endedness on an ideal of self-transformation and self-creation, and deploys a vast apparatus to manage, change, and improve the self. That this was achieved by enlisting moral values is apparent in one simple fact: the history of *The Oprah Winfrey Show* is to a great extent the history of the response by Oprah Winfrey to her critics (and to the declining ratings of her show in 1994 especially) in moral terms. Oprah's swiftness to accept and endorse the moral critiques of her show, to address them in a way that altered the show's format and upgraded its moral tone, is a remarkable element in the history of her show. A quick comparison between Donahue and Winfrey will clarify this point. Responding to critics, Donahue claimed in 1993, "We get paid to draw a crowd. When we don't draw a crowd, we don't get paid."[11] Oprah's response was different in a self-explanatory way: "The time has come for this genre of talk shows to move on from dysfunctional whining and complaining and blaming. . . . I am tired, yes, I am. I'm tired of it."[12] Oprah is a remarkable player in the field of popular culture because she has cast her professional choices, persona, and style as *moral* ones and has practiced a form of public "moral accountability" with her audience. For example, she has devoted entire shows to guests and guests' letters criticizing her statements (such as that her weight loss was due to her personal determination and not to her private cook and trainer). She exposed in public her feeling that her show was contaminated by an ambient vulgarity and that it ought to change its moral standing. She also devised a rubric for her show with the self-explanatory title of "Our Most Forgettable Shows." Once she decided to upgrade her show, she amplified her role as moral entrepreneur, psychotherapist, and public confessor, engaged in philanthropic action, and created the Book Club, which provided both a genteel and a moral character.[13] Oprah has responded to her critics—both lay and professional—by repositioning her show as a moral enterprise and by acknowledging, rather than refuting, criticism, thus displaying an uncanny ability to use critiques as if they were marketing research devices and positioning herself as a moral entrepreneur.

The moral uplift *The Oprah Winfrey Show* has undergone since its creation is revealed in a number of genre shifts. Instead of featuring individual deviants, she has focused on relationship problems and offered quick-fix recipes to solve them, thus taking on a more decisively therapeutic vocation. Oprah has become highly focused in her determination to embark on a spiritual mission and to make her guests' lives "successful" and "healthy." Toward that end, she has consistently used a mix of New Age spirituality and popular psychology to promote self-help themes in which all viewers can engage. As Linda Rountree, senior vice president and media director at the advertising firm of Luckie and Co., put it, "I don't think she's evangelical in terms of a particular religious sect. . . . It's more of a self-help, self-confidence type thing without having necessarily religious overtones, per se." This is an accurate observation, for, akin to the New Age spirituality that transcends locality, Winfrey promotes a religion of the self "thin" and abstract enough to include viewers from all ethnicities, ages, genders, sexual orientations, and social classes.

Oprah has introduced a regular coterie of experts who have acquired the double role of professing scientific expertise and providing spiritual guidance. She has made some of them regular features of her show in specific topics and problems (e.g., Suze Orman for financial advice, Phil McGraw for self-efficacy). In other words, she has created a cast of experts, regular and familiar figures with whom viewers have come to know and develop a stable relationship, much like with a psychologist. This in turn suggests that Oprah has created a structure that offers greater continuity and familiarity to viewers.

Oprah's effort to uplift is also apparent in the philanthropic initiatives mediated by her show through the "Angel Network" and "Change Your Life Television." Her numerous altruistic and charitable actions have made her show a conduit for many projects to act on and transform both the social environment and the lives of private citizens. Oprah's Angel Network is an outlet for charity and for volunteer work: for example, collecting spare change to help send needy students to college, building houses for Habitat for Humanity, volunteering at local schools, cooking meals for homeless people, soliciting checks to support a variety of "causes," and simply inviting all of us to make significant emotional improvements in problematic lives.

These changes have repositioned Oprah in the cultural field. What sets her apart most clearly from other talk show hosts is the fact that she has elaborated a distinctive worldview, an account of how the world is and ought to be, and has simultaneously developed the rituals and the material infrastructure to infuse it with authority and to enlist viewers in promoting it during and after the show. She offers not only a particular worldview but also the symbolic and practical tools to achieve it. In that respect, she promotes a rationalization of action in the sense given by Max Weber: she creates values as well as the means to reach them, thus inviting guests and viewers to rationalize their acts and commitments according to the set of values she and her (regular or invited) experts provide. How this worldview unfolds and is enacted by her guests is examined below.

THE UNCHANGING IDEAL OF CHANGE

In her study of guests' motivations to appear on talk shows, Patricia Priest suggests that guests are motivated by the desire to spread a message, to legitimate their lifestyle, or to obtain celebrity.[14] These are probably the motivations of some of the guests who appear on any given show. But we need to supplement this description by adding another probable motivation, namely the hope that the show will effect a change in their life and relationships. Like suffering, self-help is one of the central meanings imparted by Oprah Winfrey to her show, and since 1995 it has become an integral aspect of its design and format. Concomitant and adjacent to the image of a suffering self, victim of others' negligence or malevolence, is the image of a powerful self that can surmount dysfunctions, predicaments, and impairments, whether self-generated or caused by external agents. Change provides the strongest moral legitimation for the show. For example, when Tipper Gore, who suffered from depression, was invited on *The Oprah Winfrey Show*, she declared, "My intention in doing what I did [revealing her depression to the newspaper USA Today] . . . is to help other people who have depression and perhaps who are depressed now and might be listening to this show and not know it."[15]

The exposure of suffering has one main narrative and moral purpose: to bring about a narrative closure in the form of change. For example, in a

1998 retrospective of her shows of the previous year, Oprah Winfrey aired her "favorite guests."[16] Such retrospective shows present the "ideal type" guests and stories, offering a condensed version of the models of selfhood Oprah Winfrey would like to convey. One of these ideal typical shows featured a woman who had survived the concentration camps during the Holocaust. Her story is framed as follows: the guest is introduced as having experienced unspeakable atrocities in German concentration camps; then we are shown a letter she wrote more than forty years earlier to her then-suitor (and subsequent husband), in which she told him of her terrible suffering. Her husband-to-be's response—also a forty-year-old letter read on the show—was a pledge to make her forget that suffering. In a climactic sequence, Oprah declares that through her husband's love, the victim has been able to surmount her pain and agony and live a normal and good life.

This fragment contains the quintessential elements of the moral uplift *The Oprah Winfrey Show* promotes: by displaying the forty-year-old letter, Oprah can draw a straight narrative line between sequences in the story of the woman's suffering self: her martyrdom in the camps (opening), uncertainty about her life to come (complication), the husband-to-be's pledge to make her overcome her suffering (remedial), and the resolution, in which promises have been fulfilled and goals met (closure). By introducing an object -the letter—intended to be a private communication between two lovers, Oprah is able to subtly replace the "war narrative" with a domestic narrative, changing a collective tragedy into an intimate one. The reading of the letter on the air enables us both to penetrate into the couple's intimacy and to have tangible proof both of the woman's past traumatic experience and of her present recovery, thus creating a narrative that telescopes past trauma and present recovery, large-scale disasters with intimate triumph.

A similar story was the main item in the first issue of O *Magazine*. Considering the fact that the first issues of a magazine are essential to position the publication in its market, we can assume that this "star interview" was carefully chosen and invested with a particular importance, as it was to determine the magazine's market niche. For the November 2000 issue Oprah interviewed Elie Wiesel, one of the most potent symbols of survival of the twentieth century. Wiesel's story also is constructed and framed as a story of fortitude in the face of extreme assault on the self.

[WINFREY]: Does having seen the worst of humanity make you more grateful for ordinary occurences?

[ELIE WIESEL]: For me, every hour is grace. And I feel gratitude in my heart each time I can meet someone and look at his or her smile.

Elie Wiesel was an ideal typical guest for Oprah Winfrey's launching of her magazine because he was the "super-victim" of the twentieth century. In fact, long before Winfrey, Elie Wiesel had told the world how he had been a victim of extreme atrocities, and, like Oprah, in the very process of telling that story, made himself a prolific member of the culture industry. Because he experienced atrocities and yet forgave them, Wiesel positioned himself beyond moral suspicion.

Holocaust stories exist in other quarters of our culture; it is therefore worthwhile to compare them to the ways Oprah frames her "own" Holocaust stories. According to Holocaust scholar Lawrence Langer, the traditional Holocaust literature has been characterized by a "language shorn of a spiritual bond." As he puts it, the "Holocaust and subsequent large-scale atrocities exist in an *orbit void of the usual consoling vocabulary*: martyrdom, the dignity of dying, guilty conscience, moral rigor, remorse, even villainy, which in literary tragedy so clearly distinguishes the victim from his or her persecutor"[17] (emphasis added). These observations highlight the specificity of Oprah's Holocaust narrative, which, in stark contrast to Langer's accounts, is replete with "consoling vocabulary." When interviewed by Oprah Winfrey, a victim of the Nazi Holocaust becomes the bearer of a story of self-overcoming, improvement, and triumph. Combining the moral glory of self-change with the gruesome depictions of suffering helps recycle misery into a narrative in which the self becomes a double hero: on account of what it has suffered from a hostile world and because it can claim ultimate victory over that world and its own self, by overcoming itself.

In the quintessential Oprah story, suffering comes to a closure not through, for example, the fatalistic acceptance of destiny or the admission of the human penchant for evil but through change. Misanthropy, renunciation of the world, and the acceptance of failure are not moral or narrative options. Rather, closure is reached when the self is able to transcend itself either through will, determination, and self-knowledge or through the display of altruistic dispositions. Such self-overcoming is accomplished sometimes through the implementation of moral virtues like altruism, love, and self-sacrifice; sometimes through therapeutic techniques of self-examination, confession, and dialogue; and sometimes through a combination of these. Both the spiritual and the therapeutic discourse insist on transformation and on making the self "work" toward an improved and pain-free state. For example, here Oprah interviews a medical doctor who has contracted the HIV virus:

[WINFREY:] Why do you think it happened to you? You must have asked yourself and God that question.

[DR. LIPSCHITZ:] Judy [his wife] always says that there is a reason. We may not know it yet.

[WINFREY:] Mmmm . . .

[DR. LIPSCHITZ:] . . . but perhaps, if people like ourselves can speak out and help other people, and have the people of our country see that we can unite to fight a common goal—everyone out here today can be a victim of this disease. . . .

[MS. STEIN, WIFE OF ANDY, ANOTHER GUEST WITH A SIMILAR PROBLEM]: You know what this disease has done to me? It has empowered me—it truly has.

[DR. LIPSCHITZ:] . . . and—and we need—

[STEIN:] . . . to stand up and fight. . . .

[DR. LIPSCHITZ:] And we need to not give a million dollars here or a little—we need to say, "Listen, let's get this disease under control now."

Suffering, fear, and anxiety normally attached to the prospect of one's own death become here their opposite—empowerement—thus making this tragic story into a narrative of glorious self-overcoming.

THE SHOW AS AN AGENT OF CHANGE

In the examples of the Auschwitz survivor and the HIV-positive doctor, the change was performed before and outside the show and constitutes the hidden justification for the show. But in fact, the most frequent—and interesting—image of change occurs during and in close association with the show. On *The Oprah Winfrey Show*, the self is treated as a highly malleable entity that can be changed and transformed in the course of a single episode. Oprah Winfrey has been able to upgrade the use of suffering into a morally receivable image, as a segment in a larger narrative of self-change performed on her show. More exactly, change is performatively induced by the telling and showing of suffering, a motif already present before Oprah upgraded her show. For example, in 1992, Oprah invited people who had been scarred for life by classmates' mockery. The guests provided a (heartbreaking) testimony of the ways in which they had been hurt during their childhood and had carried that hurt throughout their lives. The narrative closure of the guests' stories converges with the emotional climax and the moral justification of the show: it is attained when the "victims" of malicious mockery were confronted with the "perpetrators." The perpetrators expressed guilt and remorse, which in turn produced, on live television, the healing of the guests' still-open wounds and a newfound capacity to better live their normal lives.

The spectacle of physical and emotional change procures the narrative resolution to the conflict presented, in the formal sense that the story comes to an end and in the moral sense that reparation is brought to the injured person. This reparation is in turn the moral justification for the show, because it helps heal wounds and repair damaged relationships. This particular episode does not have the moral force of the Holocaust excerpt, but it serves the same purpose of performing the transformation of self and relationships. Thus the theme of change takes on many forms and covers different arenas: physical change (make-up, clothing styles, hairstyle), diet, furniture, health, financial status, education, marriage, work performance, and mental health.[18] All of these have become objects of advice and domains in which one is instructed to transform one's life. For example, in a 2000 show on "Men Whose Hair Is Too Long," Oprah brought to the stage women who told the audience of their desire to have their sons, lovers, brothers, or husbands change a "hairy part" of their body (mustache, hair, beard). The men were exposed to the public, taken to a back room, and then brought out again with a change supposed to effect a spectacular transformation and improve their physical appearance. Here again, we may observe Oprah's style in action: the "hairy parts" are exposed as a transactional object in a domestic, intimate relationship that is constructed as contentious. The haircut or mustache shave provides a double change, in the man's physical appearance and in his intimate relationship to a close other. The show's pleasure derives from the instantaneous transformation—physical or psychic—undergone by the guests and their relationships, which in turn promotes closer bonds.

CONATIVE LANGUAGE

Oprah Winfrey does not confine her injunction to change to the participants present in the studio but extends it to the viewers of the show as well. She uses conative devices to address them in their own domestic environment and to call on them to effect change in their lives. For example, on a show on abused women and the ways in which they can escape, Oprah addresses the viewers: "When we come back, planning your escape. . . . I said to the producer, Susan, 'Today what we want is to help people out; to answer the question, How do you begin to get out?' . . . . So today we're going to give you an escape plan for getting away from an abusive man."[19] This mode of address is typical of Oprah Winfrey: by referring to the show's production team, she produces a personal and trustworthy relationship between herself and her viewers. She can thus address her audience directly at home, in an ordinary conversational manner, thereby creating a relationship based on trust and care. She provides them with the moral justification for leaving their abusive husbands as well as the practical strategies to do so, thus inserting herself in the concrete predicaments of women's lives.

In her analysis of the soap opera, Modleski has argued that "the family is, for many women, their only support, and soap operas offer the assurance of its immortality."[20] Oprah Winfrey, on the contrary, assures women of the highly transient and precarious character of the family, and claims that the only "immortality" they can count on is that of their own self, that is, a self that is healthy and self-reliant. This ideal is key to Oprah's worldview and to the ways she forges her relationship with her guests and viewers. Expressing her views about the self, Oprah has developed a well-defined, albeit not original, worldview. One of the key ideas she promotes is that "Everyone has the power for greatness. . . . Starting today, you can decide to have a life of significance by how you give of yourself to others."[21] Considering that Winfrey locates the self in the psyche, it is not surprising that she endows the self with the power to make or unmake itself. This discourse of self-help is shrouded in spirituality—the search for "meaning" and "purpose" in one's life.

Many of the meanings articulated by Winfrey can be found in the New Age movement, characterized by the view that spirituality is to be constructed by an individual rather than handed down through a tradition. This spirituality synthesizes opposites: it links us to a greater whole and yet simultaneously demands that we be connected to our "deeper self." As Paul Heelas put it in his study of the New Age movement: "a major factor in the appeal of the New Age . . . is that it does not require any great leap of faith. Basically, all that one has to do is *participate*, in order, that is, to *experience* one's barriers, one's potential."[22] Similarly, Oprah enjoins us to experience our own self in a richer way, from which transformation of self and others will ensue. I now analyze some techniques she uses to promote such self-transformations.

THERAPY FOR FREE

In addition to confrontation between guests, direct alteration of guests' physical appearance, and conative language, Oprah uses techniques of therapeutic interviewing to induce a psychological change on the show. For example:

[MS. LANE:] Can't be much longer. I'm thirty-four years old, and I know that I am a good woman. It's just I'm an emotional woman, and I know that someday someone, instead of manipulating the love I have, will appreciate the love I have. Therefore, that's why I know one day I'll wake up.

[WINFREY:] So you know this. You know that he manipulates you, he uses you, he lies to you. He says " I'm going to be there," and he's not there.

[MS. LANE:] Right.

[WINFREY:] And you're waiting and waiting and waiting. And then he walks in the door and what? You forget it?

[MS. LANE:] Everything kind of goes to the back, you know? Everything goes to the back. . . .

[WINFREY:] What does he do when he comes in to make you forget all of the anguish and the pain?

[MS. LANE:] It's just the presence, his presence. It's just him. He doesn't have to say a word to me when he comes in, it's just him, the person, it's just him.

[WINFREY:] You feel redeemed.

[MS. LANE:] Not so much redeemed, just relieved, just glad he's there.

[WINFREY:] Yeah.

[MS. LANE:] Not redeemed.

[WINFREY:] And when he's there, do you enjoy the time that you have? Or do you live in fear that "he's going to leave soon and I'm going to have to go through this anguish again?"

In this example, Oprah's therapeutic interviewing technique invites a process of self-examination through mirroring (repeating the interviewee's words) and a subtle challenging of the guest's self-perceptions. As the example above illustrates, Oprah Winfrey frequently probes her guests to clarify what their emotions are, encourages them to make distinctions between various emotions and to spell out the assumptions that guide their actions, and engages them in a general process of self-examination. The show foregrounds the self-images of the guests and the audience by inviting them to reflect on their emotions and values.

[WINFREY:] OK. I really want you to do this, because many times when people say things on television like "Ask yourself this question," you never do. But I want you to ask yourself this question: Does the image that you have of yourself match the image that other people have of you? . . . .

[WOMAN #1:] I think that I am very sweet; I am very goal-oriented; and I know what I want and I'm going to do whatever it takes to get there. But I'm a little bit on the argumentative side.

. . . .

[WINFREY:] And what she just said, is that the way you see her?

[MS. TAMMY SHUSTER (FRIEND OF WOMAN #1)]: No, not at all. I just want her to be friends with me after the show.

[WINFREY:] Because you don't see her that way.

[MS. SHUSTER:] I see her as a paranoid person. She's manipulative, scheming. And she can be very mean.[23]

Using the basic therapeutic premise that our perceptions of reality shape that reality, the show preaches change through self-examination, even when that self-examination is forced upon a guest by another guest, as is the case here. Oprah's basic technique is also used by her invited experts. For example, as one of the star guests—a former abused and addicted guest converted into being an expert, Iyanla—put it: "So your perceptions about him create your projections about him."[24] In a show on a mother and son invited to discuss their conflicts, Phil McGraw induces a transformation of their relationship by having them talk together and fight, and instructing the mother to examine her pattern of talk based on the premise that a change in self-awareness and self-perception brings about interpersonal change. The woman's recognition and understanding that she uses "controlling speech patterns" with her son and her resolution to mend her ways in turn provide the spectacle of a self-performing change.

Therapists would typically dismiss the potential for self-change contained in such an interaction. Quoting a study conducted by Frederick Thorne in the *Journal of Community Psychology*, George Mair suggests that "evaluation of the advice provided by the guest 'experts' suggests that some advice is invalid, unrealistic and not always suited to particular groups of women . . . considerable harm might be done by widely disseminating unproven or inapplicable concepts which may have sensational appeal but are not solidly grounded in scientific fact."[25] I am not convinced by these claims. More exactly, if they are correct, they are not less true for run-of-the-mill psychologists than they are for talk shows. Experts' advice outside talk shows can also be "invalid," not "grounded in scientific fact," and unsuited to particular groups of women. Therefore, the critique, if it is to be voiced, ought to be addressed to the practice of psychological counseling as a whole. Moreover, I argue that pop psychology is closer to professional psychology than is assumed by its certified practicioners. Family therapy, for example, aims at establishing dialogue in which self-awareness derives from confrontation with partners' and children's mutual perceptions. Conversely and symmetrically, I argue that, like therapists, Oprah

Winfrey solicits incessant reflexive self-observation from both her guests and her viewers, by foregrounding emotions and identity: "We're always on this show trying to get you to think about yourself and think about ways that you can change yourself if you don't like who you are. Here's some questions you can ask yourself at home right now to get some insight into your own personality."[26] Echoing the therapeutic injunction that we examine our thoughts and emotions, Oprah encourages her viewers to become reflexive by answering a set of prewritten questions. "Just about an hour ago these people sitting right here took a very revealing personality test to get a better idea of what makes them tick. We're going to give a similar test to all of you at home that you can take right now. In just a few minutes, you can try and find out more about your personality and why you like yourself so much, your relationships and your career, and your family too."[27] We find a similar injunction in O Magazine. For example, in an advice column written by Phil McGraw, estranged wives and husbands are advised to do "an assignment" before they go to bed. "You and your husband should each get out a piece of paper and a pen and make a 40-item blessing list. Don't collaborate on the lists, but share them with each other after you're finished."[28] This technique aims at enhancing reflexive self-awareness of what a couple appreciates in their lives in order to repair their relationship.

Similar to endless books, articles, and workshops of therapeutic inspiration, the talk show increases reflexive self-awareness for the purpose of explicitly changing one's emotional makeup and actions.[29] Like so many other aspects of popular culture geared to women,[30] Oprah Winfrey uses and promotes a rational management of emotions, offering analytical frames to name emotions, find their causes, and integrate them in a process of self-observation and understanding.[31] This is because the boundary between professional psychologists and popular culture is far less porous than it appears. Indeed, throughout the twentieth century psychologists were mobilized en masse to pronounce themselves, legislate over, and adjudicate in a variety of social spheres, from work relations to the family, in order to promote mental health, with the result that their worldview and techniques have largely penetrated the broad public through the mass media as well.[32] The cultural authority of psychologists has been exercised through the medical model of "mental health" and "healthy relationships," which in turn mobilizes definitions of "competent" and worthy selves.

"Emotional health" is a powerful cultural motif, because it plays the function of "signified" as described by Derrida: it is a meaning that forever slips away from its numerous signifiers. "Health" can be anything and everything: having many sexual partners or marrying one's high school sweet-heart; being satisfied with one's work or striving for more success; being modest or being assertive; conforming to social norms or breaking them. This implies that emotional health is not a stable cultural category. As Oprah Winfrey's infinite variations on this theme show, it is a shifting signi-fied whose power derives from the fact that it cannot be fixed to a clear con-tent. It is opposed to whatever does not "feel" quite right in one's life, and striving for health is what makes a self a worthy one. The self that ought to repair itself must satisfy two conditions: what ought to be repaired is one's close relationships, but they must be repaired in a self-reliant way. The ethos of self-help so central to Oprah's worldview thus mobilizes and conflates two cultural repertoires, one of emotional health and one of self-reliance, the latter being, in the American context, a code word for a morally and so-cially competent self.

Such a radically voluntarist view of the self is based partly on the fact that Americans have always held a strong ethos of self-help, derived from the stern Protestant sense of loneliness—the outcome of the inevitability of the divine decree—and from the fact that the American state did not initially provide strong institutional support, thus leaving individuals to their own re-sources. As already suggested in chapter 2, Oprah Winfrey has femininized the meaning of self-help, mimicking Horatio Alger with a vengeance: the raw material she calls us to work on and improve is not our moral make-up or actions but the inner psychological core of the self. To illustrate the twist Oprah brings to the nineteenth-century self-help tradition, we may compare her with Samuel Smiles's famous and widely popular book *Self-Help*, writ-ten in 1859. The book offers a series of biographies of men who had risen from obscurity to fame and wealth and makes a powerful case for Victorian notions of individual responsibility. With the characteristic optimism of nineteenth-century faith in progress, Smiles evokes the "spirit of self-help in the energetic action of individuals who, rising above the heads of the mass, knew to distinguish themselves from others." Their lives, he writes, inspire high thinking and are examples of resolute industry, integrity, and "truly noble and manly character." The power of self-help, Smiles argues, is the power of each to accomplish for himself, and is truly democratic, as it en-ables even the "humblest of men to work out for themselves an honorable competency and a solid reputation."[33] Oprah's self-help ethos is also part and parcel of a democratic impulse to inspire members of the lower rungs of society to believe they can reach higher standing through their hard work and determination.

But Oprah's self-help ethos also contains new and unprecedented elements. Where Smiles's self-help ethos aims at helping the self to enter the capitalist market (by instilling work habits), Oprah's discourse of improvement aims mostly at empowering a self that has already been debilitated by capitalism (due to the combined effects of unemployment, stress, role overload, the destruction of communities, and anomie). Moreover, Oprah's self-help ethos does not concern the area of work or of worldly success proper. Instead, its purpose is to restore the self to functionality in *all* areas of life— from work to intimate relations, sexuality, and self-esteem (with a special emphasis, however, on domestic relations). While the nineteenth-century version of the self-help ethos concentrates on goals, endurance, and moral qualities to perform well in the realm of work, Oprah's system calls upon the self to changing itself in multiple areas of life in the name of an ideal of "mental health." While the nineteenth-century self-ethos enjoins men to develop clearly defined moral traits (discipline, industriousness, etc.) ultimately serviceable to the community, the contemporary self-help ethos is mostly addressed to women and is more diffuse, as it calls on women to forge close yet "healthy" relationships. Finally, while Smiles's ethos of self-help conjures up moral character and virtues such as honesty, strength of will, and resolve, Oprah Winfrey uses mostly the language of therapy and New Age psychology. The wounded and failed self is such a central motif of Oprah Winfrey and of therapeutic culture in general because it enables the generation of a discourse and a dynamic of emotional "empowerment" under the guidance and authority of experts and spiritual guides. The ethos of self-help that was grounded in a strong Puritan tradition of individual self-improvement has been co-opted by the discourse of therapists, whose authority lies in their claim to improve mental or physical health, and spiritual guides not identified with any particular established religion.

There is another important difference between the nineteenth-century and the contemporary versions of self-change: the former is masculine in orientation, but the latter has its roots in "feminine culture." "Women are overrepresented among clients of the therapy industry as consumers of counseling, medication, self-help literature, and support groups."[34] Among other reasons, this is because for the past two centuries, women have been made to bear the brunt of "emotional work" in society, both inside and outside the domestic sphere.[35] Hochschild, Illouz, Stearns and Stearns, and Cancian have all variously documented how throughout the twentieth century, the control and reflexive management of emotions have become intrinsic to women's identity in the workplace and inside the home.[36]

In her study of the self-help movement, Wendy Simonds has argued that women turn to self-help literature for "inspiration," "comfort," "explanation," and "validation."[37] But a more immediately relevant aspect of the self-help movement is that it provides techniques of self-management and self-control and promises to reconcile the conflicting discourses shaping women's identity. Winfrey's self-help ethos has been enthusiastically embraced by women because it contains and synthesizes the two main but contradictory cultural repertoires currently available to them: that of freedom and self-reliance, and that of intimacy and nurturance. It affirms that, through self-observation and emotional control, the self can achieve a form of emotional independence that can in turn be conducive to stronger and better attachments. This dual dimension of the self-help ethos is played out in *The Oprah Winfrey Show*, simultaneously affirming autonomy and repairing damaged bonds.

TEXTUAL AND EMOTIONAL COMMUNITIES

One of the most interesting techniques Oprah has used to rewrite life narratives as self-help narratives and to instill techniques of self-observation is her massive reliance, from the start of her show, on pop psychology manuals. She uses them as frameworks both to "rewrite" autobiographical narratives and to generate transient narrative communities constituted by the very text around which they gather. Oprah has created a television genre in which, through the creation of an ephemeral community organized around a written text—advice book or novel—the self can rewrite its narrative and perform changes with and for others.

To provide an example of the way in which texts and narrative communities reciprocally constitute each other, I will dwell on an early show about Robin Norwood's best-selling self-help manual *Women Who Love Too Much*. Relying on the barest elements of dynamic psychotherapy, Norwood's famous book claims that women who are unhappy with ungiving men "love them too much," and are basically reenacting an unhappy childhood during which they were not "loved enough." These emotionally abused women seek relationships that will help them heal that initial lack of love, and thus become "addicted": to want a relationship that does not deliver perfect love and equality is nothing less than "addictive." Robin Norwood uses here the tautological reasoning characteristic of the recovery movement and offers a simple but powerful cultural matrix that at once describes and explains many unhappy romantic stories and provides the women involved with a clear alternative autobiographical narrative ("get off the addiction"). To use and twist the words of historian of medieval literacy Brian Stock,[38] what Oprah Winfrey has created here is an amalgam of textual and emotional community in which a given text—Robin Norwood's book—serves as a framework around which women organize and focus their emotional biography and identify with an imagined community of women with similar biographical narratives. Not only is her show a symbolic device through which women's stories are reorganized, but Oprah Winfrey frequently uses a written text—usually derived from the realm of popular psychology—to rewrite women's narratives and to create an imagined community. For example, introducing Robin Norwood and her book, Oprah says: "Well, we're talking today to women who have loved too much, and if you're a woman who is watching this show, undoubtedly at some point in your life you have experienced it, too. Perhaps maybe not to the extent that you all have, but everyone has been through it." This framing creates simultaneously a narrative structure and an imagined community, constituted by a particular story structure that can be appropriated and shared by individuals to make sense of and manage their biography. This imagined community is empowering because it provides a rational explanation for women's predicaments with men, and because it transforms individual failure in intimate relationships into a collective problem. Emotions are "the glue" binding members together; more specifically, the group comes into existence through a particular shared way of narrating emotions.

A decade later, in a show on "Working with Emotional Intelligence," Oprah uses a very similar method: she invites the author of a popular psychological book, Daniel Goleman, and uses his text to enunciate an emotional syntax that can in turn be used to reorganize the life stories of the women invited. For example:

[SHARMAYNE:] I attended a training class. And someone had given me the book . . . *Emotional Intelligence*. And I read that, and started to institute changes in my life . . . and things changed around for me, not only personally, but my business is much better and I'm working on a promotion. And I've worked very hard to get to this point. . . .

[WINFREY:] That's fabulous. That is fabulous. That is fabulous. Your whole life is better.

. . . .

[MR. GOLEMAN:] Sharmayne has turned herself around. She became aware of what the problem was when it was happening, and she's really made that effort to do it different.

[WINFREY:] Which is one of the keys to being emotionally intelligent, is self-awareness. Yes.

[MR. GOLEMAN:] Self-awareness is the first step.[39]

The narrative has the same structure as the previous one, but its key theme has changed: it is not "addiction" to men but lack of "emotional intelligence" that serves as a peg around which the therapeutic narrative can "hang" in such a way that it both describes a problem of the self—which becomes a "story"—and directs the self to move along a specific narrative "path" (get off the addiction; become emotionally intelligent). The therapeutic narrative simultaneously constitutes a community of sufferers and helps individuals write and author their own particular biography. These communities are simultaneously textual—organized around a particular book—and oral—maintained by the public act of telling stories about the self.

Oprah's techniques to generate virtual communities of suffering and sufferers resonate with the pervasive support group movement. Support groups participate in the reigning therapeutic ethos, which stipulates that the self can empower itself by talking about its predicaments and by exposing its failings to the nonjudgmental gaze of another.[40] Guests participate in the show by taking literally Oprah's claim that she wants to help them. Not only do guests take at face value the reality of Oprah's self-proclaimed intent to empower them, but they also "carry it away" with them to change their own lives.

SPECULAR THERAPY

In exercising its newfound vocation to promote emotional health, *The Oprah Winfrey Show* has penetrated viewers' lives and homes in an unprecedented intrusive way. In its early stages, the show brought the domestic sphere to television; in its later stages, it has taken itself to the home, becoming a sort of appendix to domestic life. *The Oprah Winfrey Show* illustrates the way television has become an extension of identity; the guests' emotional life is processed and transformed in the nexus of technology, mass-mediated narratives, and capital. One of the most original techniques to induce change consists in "grafting" television onto the self, that is, making television itself an active agent conducive to change. This is achieved by creating a process through which the very visual character of television generates reflexivity. This is one example among many:

[WINFREY:] Eddie Reynolds wrote that watching one of our last Iyanla shows was like coming out of a blinding fog for him. That's why we do TV. Here's more from Eddie's message.

[EDDIE:] Dear Oprah, I would just like to thank you and the producers for today's show. It opened my eyes to a lot of issues that I didn't know I was dealing with. I've been in an intense relationship for over three years, and because of your show, I've determined that it's time for the relationship to terminate. Thanks for enlightening me. You may have saved me from quite a calamity. It is better to eat soup alone than to eat steak with someone and be miserable. It's time for me to make a—some major changes in my life.

. . . .

[Going back to the studio. where Eddie Reynolds is sitting]

[IYANLA:] OK. What did you do?

[EDDIE:] The show I taped, went back and watched it again at 2:30 in the morning and took notes and studied and replayed it and studied and replayed and . . . I've never looked at a mirror the same way since that last show. The part about she was a reflection of who I am, that scared me and it made me really turn and look within at what I was producing and how it was affecting her, which was in turn affecting me. And the part about men feeling like they wanted to be number one—you said—crucial.

[IYANLA:] Yeah.

[EDDIE:] The part about value, another crucial point.

[AFTER A DISCUSSION ON THE CHANGES THAT HAPPENED, IYANLA SUMMARIZES IT AS FOLLOWS:] You found out work you needed to do.[41]

This show is remarkable in a few respects: for one, the person who interviews Eddie Reynolds is Iyanla Vanzant, a former drug addict and abused woman who has transformed her failures into cultural commodities—bestselling books—through the same narrative of self-overcoming that Oprah incessantly promotes. Here, Oprah mirrors and multiplies herself into an institution capable of producing and certifying replicas and transmitting to others her own authority and techniques. Also important is the fact that the narrative of recovery enables the recycling of the *same* guest numerous times, to keep track of self-change through a narrative in the making, that is, a narrative that unfolds progressively through the different shows in which the same guest appears. The guest thus develops the very narrative virtuosity with which Oprah has transformed her biography into an ongoing spectacle. Importantly, what enables Reynolds's biography to unfold for us is the intertwining of technology and autobiographical discourse. In the dialogue quoted above, four layers of text are superimposed on one another: the first show to which Eddie Reynolds was invited to discuss his failing relationship with his girlfriend; the show transported to his home in the form of a videotape, used as a "mirror" in which Eddie could watch himself that generated self-observation that in turn generated a process of inner change; the letter that he wrote to the Oprah show after watching to thank them for their help, a third text that in turn generated a new invitation and a new show; and the fourth text, building and commenting on the three previous texts, addressing, tracing back, and ultimately generating a process of change again staged for us on the show. I suggest that this show is to TV what sequels are to movies: a recycling of a story in which the different episodes featuring the same hero create the effect of a life narrative developing and unfolding in real time.

The intertwining of "real" biographical time with studio time has been accompanied by the penetration of the camera and the studio into the domestic space of the guests. For example, in a follow-up show on "Women and Anger"—that is, a sequel to a previous show on the same topic with the same guests—we watch a segment of the show in which women appeared because of a recurrent problem of "anger." In this second show, we also understand that between the two shows, the television crew went to the women's homes and filmed their outbursts of anger in a naturalistic way, that is, in their daily and familial setting. Here again, the intertwining and superimposition of different texts is constructed in such a way that it unfolds through "real" time , that is, through the process of having viewers watch guests watch themselves at different points in time; this creates narrative thickness and continuity through specular duplication. The show thus becomes the interface between the "real" space and time of everyday life and the space and time of the TV studio. The same guests who appear in their domestic chaos and anger have become their own viewers, and in that process of observing themselves in their "real" domestic settings are transformed, live in the TV studio. To alleviate any doubt about the effectiveness of such specular therapy, the same guests are invited to appear in second and sometimes third shows to bear witness to the long-lasting changes they have experienced. To put an additional seal of guarantee on the therapeutic and transformative power of the show, Oprah frequently reads viewers' letters stating that watching other people struggle with their anger transformed their own lives. This suggests that the show's transformative power reverberates in the guests and in their viewers through a process of specularity that intertwines real time and studio time (more exactly, subsumes the former to the latter), domestic space and television. Viewers become healed, and therefore take on the status of guests, while guests watch themselves, acquiring the status of viewers. This illustrates a point made in chapter 3 to the effect that *The Oprah Winfrey Show* is characterized by its ability to interchange the positions of the various participants in the structure of the talk show. This is because the narrative of self-change is convertible into a new position in the structure of roles that make up the talk show.

To be sure, Oprah Winfrey did not invent the intrusion of television in the daily and domestic settings of ordinary people, nor its attempt to mimic the "time" of real life. Following a trend that was started in British documentary media in the late 1970s, television espouses "real" biographical time, that is, follows people in their daily space and is constrained by the real time of their lives. However, while these documentary films tried to document daily life as unobtrusively as possible, Oprah and her show have taken the status of an obtrusive instrument of change. The very persona of Oprah Winfrey as well as her show mark, I believe, a radical transformation of television, which has become, in Donna Harraway's famous term, a "cyborg,"[42] a technological appendix to self and identity. The self staged by Oprah Winfrey is cyborgic in the sense that it is half human and half technology. Television—and the multiple technologies mobilized by Oprah Winfrey—have been "grafted" onto modern selves and identity, simultaneously expressing, performing, and changing the self. Cyborgic entities "are substantially the same as the carriers of culture in other eras."[43] Oprah's cyborgic self is performed through elements present in other quarters of culture, namely the therapeutic discourse and the discourse of New Age. At the same time that her vast cultural structure refracts identity in a multiplicity of different technologies and sites, it processes the self in a strong narrative of self-help. Contrary to postmodernists, who claim that we have become "nomadic subjects," who cross several different discourses and about whom meaning is indeterminate, Oprah energetically recenters the self in a narrative of self-change and improvement.

THE BOOK CLUB: HYPERLINK TO SELF-CHANGE

The Book Club novels, *The Oprah Winfrey Show*, the Web site, and *O Magazine* all intertwine in a cultural matrix that stages and induces change performatively. These elements are used by Oprah Winfrey as tools to merge texts and experience. This intertwining of texts and experience is an effect of the fact that Oprah Winfrey's cultural enterprise is encoded and framed in the powerful cultural text and cultural performance of self-change. This "performance," as I show in the following pages, is present in relation to the books of the Book Club as well. Readers are solicited to actively incorporate the novels in their lives, precisely through the moral open-endedness of their plots and characters.

An analysis of the Web site comments on the novels indicates that readers react strongly to the stories as moral dilemmas. Let us take the example of *The Pilot's Wife*, the story of a woman whose husband is killed in the crash of a plane he was piloting. Because the insurance company undertakes a massive investigation, she discovers that her husband secretly led another life with another woman in London, his most frequent flight destination. Typical readers' reactions, as expressed on the Oprah Winfrey Web site, were: "it teaches you how much you can't trust the person you live with; it shows you we never really know anybody," and, in contrast, "it reminded me how much of a great husband I have." Readers discuss characters' moral worth and decisions in a way that resonates directly with their own lives. Did Kathryn fail to pick up on important clues about her husband's double life? Did the pilot love his first wife or his second (secret) wife more? What meaning does this retrospective discovery bestow on her marriage? In other words, these readers use the books to ask and probe questions that are essentially moral. Thus the books are readily applicable to readers' own lives.

To take another example, reactions to *The Deep End of the Ocean* revolved typically around the question of whether Beth, the mother of the kidnapped son who lets her family drift into disaster, could be excused from blame:

> I cried for the first 35 pages or so—I was pregnant with my second child at the time, and I have a little boy named Sam, who's the same age as Ben [in the novel]. So I took this book very personally, and couldn't help but wonder what I would do in that situation. I would like to think I would be strong and be there for my other children, but I have a strong suspicion that I would react much the same as she did. (Wobbie6, April 15, 1999, 6:05)

This is a glaring example of the ways in which readers identify strongly not only with the characters but also, and mostly, with the moral problems their actions raise. Here is another:

> This book was so thought-provoking, I couldn't stop thinking about how I would have reacted when I found Ben [the kidnapped child] and he didn't want to be

part of our family. There was no right answer, and no way to make everyone happy. I almost wish there was a sequel, written a few years later so I would know how it turned out. (Mary Hanke, September 16, 1999)

As these quotes clearly suggest, the novels draw readers in precisely because their narrative structure bears a resemblance to the structure of Oprah Winfrey's talk show, which stage a multiplicity of points of view with no overarching moral standpoint. This structured ambiguity allows readers to incorporate these stories in their everyday life and make them "work" through a moral interrogation of the situations they pose. The dense entanglement of life, language, texts, media technologies, and biographical narratives is made possible by the moral ambiguity of the cultural forms Oprah promotes. Here again, as examined in the preceding chapter, the moral code structuring the narrative is intertwined with a therapeutic code.

The community of readers is a community of sufferers in which the interpretation of and the relation to the texts is cast as therapeutic: novels are used to mirror and reflect the private stories of misfortune of guests and readers and to transform one's experience. Here is a reaction to the novel *White Oleander*:

> As a person who was part of the foster care system (in Canada), I was able to relate to the issues that Astrid [the novel's heroine] had to deal with. My foster mother also seemed to only be doing it for the money, which sadly is all too often the case. We should not forget however that there are many loving foster families who genuinely care for the children and do help them, and people should remember not to paint all foster parents with the same brush. Janet Fitch did a remarkable job with this book, and I look forward to reading more of her work in the future. (E Matheson, January 27, 2000)

White Oleander is the story of an adolescent whose mother killed her lover and was sent to jail; as a consequence, the daughter herself wanders from one foster family to another. These adventures enable the protagonist, Astrid, to sample the ills and evils of American society, at its bottom and at its top, and to observe the state of decomposition of the American family. "This book [*White Oleander*] awakened me to reading again. Had an unexpected impact on my personal growth—painful, but very positive. Simply beautifully written. I hated for it to end. Where can I learn more about the author and her plans for future novels?" (Cgush, August 5, 1999). This reader, like many others, suggests that the novels touch upon deep aspects of womens' selfhood. In conjunction with the show, the novel is used to reflect on daily life and to transform it. This is effective because of the ways middle-class women approach this kind of fiction: as yet another arena in which to reflect and fashion identity.

> I was so inspired by this book [*White Oleander*] that I have convinced my husband that we should get involved and become foster parents. we have applied and are waiting for response. i was told that there is a tremendous need in our area. p.s. found a stray dog while i was reading this book. . . . . what did i name her? ASTRID [the name of the novel's heroine]. (Trosales, August 10, 1999)

The mode of appropriation of texts makes intensive use of what literary scholar Louise Rosenblatt has identified as "efferent transactions," that is, "readings that are motivated mainly by a search for something to 'carry away.'" Some readers read fiction even of the least didactic kind "efferently"—that is, in the search either for some practical guidance or for some special wisdom, what Wayne Booth calls some useful "'carry-over' into non-fictional life."[44] Oprah's viewers, readers, and users achieve such carryover because they approach the show in general and the Book Club in particular with moral dilemmas and questions about the values that ought to guide them and with an ethos of self-help, i.e., the belief that they should shape their lives with the bits and pieces of cultural experience they garner along the way.

If these readers display the same "intense fervor and expansive pleasure" Janice Radway has found to characterize "middle-brow" literature,[45] it is because these narratives mimic closely biographical narratives of the quest for self, identity, and self-help staged and encoded by the show. These books address readers "in highly concrete, deeply resonant ways as persons moving through life in embodied form."[46] Such uses of novels stand at the opposite of the "ideology of the solitary reader,"[47] which stipulates that the activity of reading is detached from the rest of society and consists in the meeting of an author's unique mind with that of the self-enclosed mind of the reader. Oprah's uses of books point to reading as an essentially social activity, in the sense that books are read with others, but more radically in the sense that reading makes people reflect about and want to transform their close bonds. Oprah Winfrey uses both novels and self-help manuals as tools to improve and guide the process of self-identity and the process of forming relationships. The therapeutic narrative is intertwined with a moral narrative questioning the values that ought to guide us, and in that respect is deeply resonant with the cultural codes of the show.

This use of the novels also stands at the opposite of the formalist approach, which, according to Bourdieu, characterizes the upper middle-class approach to reading, art, and culture. For Bourdieu, working-class culture is "participatory" in the sense that cultural users identify with the emotional and moral content. But here, women not only identify with the emotional content of novels but also literally appropriate and rework the text through *and in* their lives to understand themselves and to make changes. Ironically (for a middlebrow genre), we may say that the Book Club takes literature more seriously than the formalist "highbrow" reading, for these readers-viewers-users not only show an intellectual enjoyment of the novels' formal devices but also display a pragmatic way of using these novels' narratives as tools to reflect on their lives and to make them their own. The use of these middlebrow books corresponds to the vocation philosopher of art Arthur Danto assigns to (highbrow) literature:

> Each work of literature shows in this sense an aspect we would not know were ours without benefit of that mirror: each discovers . . . an unguessed dimension of the self. It [literature] is a mirror less in passively returning an image than in transforming the self-consciousness of the reader who in virtue of identifying with the image recognizes what he is. Literature is in this sense transfigurative, and in a way cuts across the distinction between fiction and truth. There are metaphors of every life in Herodotus and Gibbon.[48]

More than any literary institution I am aware of, Oprah has worked toward "cutting across the distinction between fiction and truth." I suggest, therefore, that her massive use of and reliance on books to reflect about and shape selfhood has created through her show a series of communities simultaneously organized around emotions and texts.

The Book Club discussions are always constructed through the careful intermingling and overlapping of one book and a guest's life story. To take a few among the many examples available: the novel *Here on Earth* is about a woman who is married to a good and loving man. But upon visiting her childhood town, she falls in love all over again with a man she had loved as an adolescent. Their passionate relationship turns out to be dark and abusive. When bringing this novel to the studio, Oprah Winfrey constructs the show so that the story line of the novel can be appropriated by her readers-viewers through the different points of view and perspectives in the book, thus mimicking its open-ended moral structure.

[WINFREY:] Did you see yourself [in the story]?
[LORELIE:] Well, what I mostly saw was Richard. My husband is Richard [the good husband].

. . . .

[WINFREY:] For thirty-six-year-old Cynthia, *Here on Earth* reminded her of why she left her husband of ten years, a comfortable lifestyle and a beautiful home, in search of a deeper love.
[CYNTHIA:] Even the situation I'm going through now with the breakup—it hurts, but it still was worth the high highs. . . . I have great memories.

. . . .

[WINFREY:] Melissa is a thirty-two-year-old stay-at-home mother who related to the search for passion. Melissa wrote, "As a wife, I wanted so desperately to hold on the passion I felt while we were dating."

. . . .

[WINFREY:] Our youngest guest was 25-year-old Amanda, who related to the teen daughter in the book.
[AMANDA:] Well, my particular situation was very similar with my mother, my mother being March and me going, "What are you doing?"

. . . .

[WINFREY:] But it was 46-year-old Michele who poured her heart into one long letter. She wrote that seeing herself in the pages of this novel moved her to tears. (April 9, 1998)

Oprah constructs the interaction with the novel in such a way that readers are intensely attentive to the ways stories relate to their own lives and to their practical dilemmas. She has created a group whose various members mimic the various positions and experiences of the characters of the novels. Readers not only identify very strongly with the stories and their protagonists but use them as narratives to frame their own lives as well. Oprah Winfrey weaves together the different plot lines of these women's lives with the novel in such a way that they mirror and mimic different characters and their differing points of view on the moral action of the main protagonist. We move swiftly through a moral hypertext whose effectiveness derives from the close mirroring and blurring of life and texts, enabled by readers' projecting themselves into a moral position in the novel's narrative. Oprah can go back and forth between the "real" guest and the fictional character, because if both occupy the same moral position—that is, the same position in a relationship defined by the same dysfunction—they are easily interchangeable.

By interweaving so carefully readers' letters, the novels she chooses, the guests' life stories, their interpretations of the stories, and the ways these interpretations reflect on her guests' biographical experience, Oprah creates a dense cultural structure in which technology, biography, and emotions overlap, intersect, and produce a hypertext of identity. The self is refracted in multiple textual and technological sites that echo with each other (a letter, the show, the novel, a sequel show) and connect to other selves who are similar in that they occupy the same position in a dysfunctional relationship.

Let me give another example taken from movies, which Oprah also frequently features. In a show about a movie starring Susan Sarandon (who plays the role of a domineering mother), Oprah invites not only the two lead actresses (the mother and the daughter) but also "ordinary" women with their daughters to discuss their relationships. We have thus two parallel sets of relationships: the mother-daughter relationship of the movie as discussed by Sarandon, and the real mother-daughter relationships as discussed by the "ordinary" guests. The guests' speech interweaves reactions to the movie and autobiographical accounts of their own relationships. The show is structured according to the same democratic and naturalistic impulse to translate a fictional creation (literary or cinematic) into the "real" problems of ordinary people. The presentation of a cultural item—movie or book—is justified if it mimicks and reflects a "real life" relationship and story and lends itself to a moral dilemma. In addition, faithful to her incessant blurring of "real" (private) life and television, Oprah makes the viewers penetrate Sarandon's own mothering style by having her husband in real life, Tim Robbins, appear on a screen and describe Sarandon "as a mother," thus using the talk show formula to create three parallel textual structures: one in which a movie presents a story played by actresses invited on the show; one in which ordinary people's lives mirror a fictional story; and one in which the actress is "brought down" to the status of an ordinary mother. We have here the superimposition of several texts: the movie of a mother-daughter, the interview with Sarandon during The Oprah Winfrey Show; the guests' interpretation of the movie they saw prior to the taping; their own mother-daughter biographical stories; and finally Sarandon's own relation to her children, as described by herself and by her husband, made present in the studio through a giant screen. This dense textual structure offers an eerie intermingling of "real" and fictional biography, which sustain each other because they are all about a similar way of narrating the self.

Viewers, guests, host, and Web users flip through various media technologies to interrogate and shape their self, which, worked through Oprah's technological and textual apparatus, is "multiple" and fragmented. At the same time that the self works toward change, it is reverberated through multiple cameras, media technologies, social spheres, and fictional characters. This complex mirroring and processing of the self resembles the multiplicity of selves freely played out and accessed on the Internet, described by Sherry Kurtle, who has argued that "the culture of simulation may help us achieve a vision of a multiple but integrated identity whose flexibility, resilience, and capacity for joy comes from having access to our many selves."[49]

HEALING THE SELF

Many have interpreted the prominence of therapy, and especially the quick-fix kind, in our times as the mark of a culture of "false consolation,"[50] as the "collapse of moral hierarchies,"[51] the triumph of "surveillance,"[52] or "consumerism."[53] But these critiques are oblivious to the fact that most, if not all, cultures contain public rituals through which the self is performed and changed. In this perspective, the spectacle of change staged by Oprah is better understood as bearing an affinity with ritual systems of healing. This in turn suggests a connection between the performance of suffering addressed in the previous chapter and the performance of self-change. The pain staged by Oprah is translated into a ritualized performance of healing, and the relationship between *The Oprah Winfrey Show* and her guests is often that between healer and sufferer.

In his classical study of the healing process, psychiatrist Jerome Frank has argued that the "sufferer's distress has a large emotional component, produced by environmental or bodily stresses, internal conflicts and confusion, and a sense of estrangement or isolation from his usual sources of group support. . . . The persuader and his group represent a comprehensive and pervasive worldview, which incorporates supremely powerful supra personal forces."[54] Many of the emotional transactions between Oprah and her guests take on the character of such a healing process: the guests clear up their emotional confusion, renarrate their experience through powerful symbols, and are provided support from the healer and from the group. The change takes place within the framework of a group, imagined or present in the television studio.

As in traditional religious healing processes, in talk shows this process occurs through a combination of catharsis, insight, imagination, and use of memories.[55] For example, on a December 1999 show, Phil McGraw invited a woman who carried an inconsolable grief about her dead daughter. Through persuasion, Phil McGraw induces the woman to imagine her daughter, enter in a dialogue with her, and for the love of her, "let her go." Phil McGraw invites her to engage in a mental exercise in which the spirit of the dead daughter is invoked and "sent" back to her "proper" place in an orderly fashion. This is akin to traditional rituals of excorcism, in which an evil spirit is expelled from the body of the possessed person:[56] indeed, shortly after his injunction, we actually see the woman undergo a bodily transformation as her agitation turns into calm and she claims that she now understands something she did not understand before. The ritual ends when she proclaims that she is now free of her grief.[57] After abundant tears and persuasion, the woman transforms her grief and lets "her daughter go," agreeing to accept her daughter's death.

This story is similar to medical anthropologist Arthur Kleinman's story about the Chinese man who cures a chronic physical symptom when he identifies that his disease derives from the fact that he has not given the proper funerary rituals to his dead mother.[58] Once "proper funerary rituals" are identified as the problem, the pain and depression stop, thus suggesting that the healing process occurs through a complex mix of charismatic power, imagination, and ability to find a name and a cause for one's ailments and to renarrate it. Kleinman further argues that while the West has developed a dyadic healing system (therapist-client), most healing systems throughout the world are not dyadic but rather involve the family, friends, and one's social group. It follows that in most cultures healing is not private, but a public occurrence. Finally, as Kleinman usefully reminds us, in many societies, healing is not long term but a one-time event, which can be repeated when new problems arise. This, I suggest, explains something that has baffled many: the fact that people willingly expose their predicaments in public. But that is the point: healing occurs precisely because it takes place in public. In light of this, I argue that Oprah uses techniques of symbolic healing systems and that her charismatic power is like traditional charismatic power, the power to cure others, and especially diseased social relationships.

In his analysis of universal aspects of symbolic healing, the anthropologist James Dow suggests that a sign of a healer is that he must himself have been healed. And indeed, as I showed in chapter 2, one of Oprah Winfrey's most spectacular achievements is her fashioning of her biography into the story of a healing in the making. By connecting her weight to her emotional problems, Oprah has been able to be—so to speak—twice a charismatic healer: first on account of her physical transformation, and second on account of her successive and incremental emotional transformations.

The second aspect of symbolic healing consists, as Claude Levi-Strauss has argued in a seminal article, in providing "a historical account of the events that preceded it. Everything occurs as though the shaman were trying to induce the sick woman . . . to relive the initial situation through pain, in a very precise and intense way, and to become psychologically aware of its smallest details."[59] This is indeed the narrative technique and framing used by Oprah and analyzed in the previous chapter: making a guest retrace her steps and relive her usually difficult experience. It is characteristic of trauma to be relived in an intense way. The third aspect of the healing process consists in trying to make "incoherent and arbitrary pains"[60] coherent and comprehensible by using mythical symbols. Oprah Winfrey's symbolism mixes the suffering with the powerful mythology of self-change. Finally, what is even more interesting for this discussion is that ritual healing is, as James Dow aptly suggests, most often about "diseased relationships," broken social bonds, which are transformed into either bodily or emotional disturbances. This interpretation is highly congruent with my own interpretation of the talk show genre, which stages and addresses the contentiousness of modern social relationships through the cultural idiom of trauma and suffering. As in traditional communities, healing is geared toward curing the diseased relationship between the self and others. I infer from this that the change effected on the show is not fictitious but real.

The multiple forms of change accomplished by and on the show are the result of multiple powerful symbolic processes. Foremost is the presence of social figures defined as authoritative—the experts and the host—who offer interpretations of the world and solutions to the guests' predicaments. Authoritative figures are likely to constrain the guests toward producing, on stage, a change. Much research, from Milgram's famous experiments on conformity and authority down to the sociology of experts and scientific authority, has shown that experts have the power to constrain ordinary actors' interpretation of reality. In modern societies, it is the experts who have been invested with the authority to heal. Their power is redoubled by the presence of a healer who has, in this particular case, a great deal of charismatic power. She has healed herself and can show to others tangible proofs of her power to change herself. Another significant fact is that speech proffered in and for a group of listeners creates a powerful emotional dynamic that ritualizes the oral delivery of the life narrative. This ritualization in turn endows the public telling of a story with "emotional effervescence," which, according to

Emile Durkheim, is is the "energy" of the group, expressed and communicated to the individual performer. The global organizational context of television and its ability to construct an imagined community of viewers nationwide and even worldwide endows the self with the even greater power of a vast—if imagined—community. The storyteller acquires the symbolic status of a totem, expressing the group of sufferers at the same time that it constitutes them. The symbolic processes culminate when the very structure of the therapeutic narrative constrains the self to bring closure to its autobiographical story through self-change. In this way, "self-change" is paradoxical: it makes the story of the self reach completion and closure, yet it calls on to the self to be in perpetual movement.

THE EMPIRE OF CHANGE

I have stressed the affinity between Oprah's religion of change and traditional healing systems. However, it is important to stress that Oprah Winfrey's industry of healing is unique in that it is sustained by a vast technological apparatus and constitutes, at least for Oprah, an ongoing source of capital. Moreover, Oprah's sphere of influence is not confined to the level of the individual biography, but rather moves easily to the level of the national and affects institutions and organizations with the same swiftness that it transforms particular lives. What sets Oprah Winfrey apart is not the commodification of biography—practiced by all talk show hosts—but rather the ways in which her show has penetrated and transformed a wide variety of social spheres, ranging from individuals' self-esteem and benevolent acts to the meat industry and congressional legislation on child abuse. She commands the power to change the lives of homeless people as well as of entire industrial branches (e.g., the meat and publishing industries). Her show is such an original case for the power of television because it is continuous with a wide variety of social arenas. In the same way that she makes the biographical material of her guests' lives material for the show, Oprah engages and influences matters of politics and business, thus illustrating the ways in which television has become entangled with other social realms and exerts a deep influence on them. For example, a journal of home furnishings reports that " Zrike—the licensee of Porter's glass, ceramic, and wooden accessories, dinnerware and serving ware—has also experienced a flurry of activity since the program aired"[61] (Oprah featured them on her show). When in 1996, Oprah asked out loud on her show why Frito-Lay was not producing low-fat baked potato chips with ridges, the company rushed to start developing them. And: "Business has been booming for Rhonda Lashen's company since her appearance on the 'Oprah Winfrey show.' And with her entry into the electronic commerce arena this week, she expects anything but a slowdown."[62] These examples and many others show that Winfrey commands great economic power in making and unmaking businesses and careers.

But the most striking effect of Oprah Winfrey's economic power is the ways in which she has mixed, to the point of confusion, civil society and marketing, benevolence and market strategy. This can be illustrated by the example of the FBL, Families for a Better Life, an organization she created in 1993–1994. She raised money from government and corporate sponsors to get 100 families off of welfare and to reintegrate them into the work force and normal family life. To give another example of the perplexing mixture between charity, television, and the market: Starbucks joined Oprah's Book Club and offered to carry and sell the eighth selection of the book, Mary McGarry Morris's *Songs in Ordinary Time*, at 1,200 Starbucks stores. Schulz (Starbucks' chairman) announced that he planned to donate the proceeds from Oprah's Book Club sales to literacy causes in America.[63] Profit and benevolence freely mix here in the sense that benevolence helps increase sales and is converted into the surplus value of advertising and image, which she in turn uses to generate further benevolent action. Oprah promotes altruism and charity at three levels: the macroscopic, the individual, and televisual communities, that is, ad hoc communities created by television. For example, the Angel Network rubric helps the poor, makes scholarship awards, organizes charity auctions of Oprah Winfrey hand-me-downs, encourages people to offer birthday gifts to handicapped children, etc. Winfrey's philanthropy has become legendary and is very well publicized.

In her study of philanthropic giving, Ostrower distinguishes between charity and philanthropy.[64] While the former is geared to the poor, the latter can be and most often is geared to rich institutions. Philanthropy is the form of giving of the rich to the rich. Oprah displays both forms of giving, with the qualifier that, contrary to traditional philanthropy, which is geared to upper middle-class institutions (Ivy League universities, museums, etc.), Oprah gives her money to institutions that represent the poor or middle-class black people.

Television's economic power is usually understood to derive from its ability to command a high degree of visibility. While Oprah undoubtedly commands an almost unprecedented degree of visibility, I would like to suggest that her impact on culture is of a different, and perhaps qualitatively new, nature: she generates and induces coordinated action in civil society by initiating nationwide and local charitable actions and self-empowerment efforts. She has been able to summon viewers to action by simultaneously setting herself as an example, grafting television onto the home, mixing benevolence and profits, and creating communities through the conjunction of television, the publishing industry, and the Web. In that sense, her philanthropy has a "social" rather than "cultural" (in the narrow sense of the word) character. This seems an apt illustration for Bruno Latour's claim that the social has been recast "so that it longer excludes non-human actants, and a consequent conceptualisation of technological formations and co-productions of technological determinism therefore becomes redundant, as the very entities of the technological and the social are themselves deconstructed."[65]

CONCLUSION

Oprah Winfrey's use of the self-help ethos points in two different directions. On one level, Oprah offers a politics of biography that is highly congruent with the decomposed subject of late capitalism. As a commentator put it wryly, "capital has fallen in love with difference."[66] Distinctions and hierarchies have been recoded in an infinite play of "differance"—differences that are dispersed, disseminated, and embedded in social structure. This is the distinctive mark of the postmodern subject forever in search of identity in the singularity of her story. But it is also congruent with a far sterner image of capitalism, represented by such characters as Margaret Thatcher, whose dictum was "that there is no such thing as society, only individuals and their families." Oprah Winfrey likewise privileges individual choice as "the essence—as Mrs. Thatcher put it during the 1987 election campaign—of morality."[67]

However, Oprah's enterprise has incessantly preached and promoted solidarity, philanthropy, and altruism both by her own example and by creating organizational structures to mobilize others to transform their close and distant environment. She seems to foster a dispersed form of action in civil society that cannot be reduced to yet another form of false or compromised consciousness within the established order. The desire to change and improve society and relieve suffering is a precondition of the moral life and cannot be dismissed when it is undertaken under the aegis of commercial television. Winfrey poses a problem to cultural analysis precisely because she has been able to tap into the moral core of the American polity[68] through her relentless affirmation of self-improvement, self-control, solidarity, liberation, and equality. Even if her stress on individual choice and self-made lives feeds into capitalist ideology, it cannot be equated with it. Oprah Winfrey and her ethos of self-help have captured the fundamental ethical substance of the American polity, and this provides a strong legitimation to her show.

SUFFERING AND SELF-HELP AS
GLOBAL FORMS OF IDENTITY

And the writing down of events, the editing so to speak of experience, gave rise to unprecedented parallels between literature and life: for, as texts informed experience, so men and women began to live texts.
— Brian Stock, *The Implications of Literacy: Written Language and Models of Interpretation in the Eleventh and Twelfth Centuries*

The Oprah Winfrey Show is distributed in a dizzying array of countries: Afghanistan, Bahrain, Botswana, Chad, China, Slovenia, Singapore, Thailand, and Yemen are only a few haphazardly picked examples. In the span of a decade, Oprah Winfrey and her show have become global cultural forms. Indeed, a wide variety of confessional talk shows have sprung up throughout the world, suggesting that *The Oprah Winfrey Show* is only one aspect of a more general phenomenon: globalization of the talk show genre. In this chapter, I offer a few reflections on the relation that Oprah's moral project to stage and change suffering bears to the globalization of culture. What makes the story of suffering and of self-change so easily cross-cultural? In what sense can we characterize *The Oprah Winfrey Show* as a global cultural form?

In musing about these questions, I will move to another level of analysis. Although this chapter discusses the therapeutic biography, which has been addressed in the previous two chapters, here my concern is to show that Winfrey and her guests use a "deep" cultural structure, embodied in institutional frameworks that have become transnational. This structure explains simultaneously the mechanism by which autobiographical discourse is routinized in the television format, and how this format paradoxically organizes and processes a wide variety of personal and particular narratives.

SUFFERING AND THE EMERGENCE
OF A GLOBAL PUBLIC SPHERE

Sociologists of globalization frequently take the position that global media are defined by their capacity to diffuse definitions of the good life and happiness. For example, in an article titled "Sociology and World Market Sociology," Bob Connell suggests that

> we get global systems of mass communication dominated by commercial fantasy—Hollywood, TV soaps, consumer advertising, celebrity gossip, the major content of mass culture. . . . We now live in a world where the normal content of mass communication is lies, distortions, and calculated fantasies. I don't think it is any wonder that the last 20 years have seen a steady decline in political party membership, a deepening public disillusion with politicians and the collapse of citizenship.[1]

Indeed, according to many, global media recruit us worldwide through the same utopia of consumption, which distributes worldwide the same icons—of youth, beauty, glamour, abundance, and happiness. Arjun Appadurai has best theorized the possibilities that such utopias hold for global consciousness. As he suggests, transnational culture has opened new spaces for the imagination, thus making fantasy an intrinsic part of global social and cultural practices: "Ordinary lives today are more often powered not by the givenness of things but by the possibilities that the media (either directly or indirectly) suggest are available."[2] In this view, global consciousness is characterized by the play of the imagination, the open-ended conception of one's life, and deterritorialized fantasies provided by global advertising, the film industry, and the publishing industry.

Yet the image of suffering has been intrinsic to the emergence of a global public sphere and of a global consciousness, and Oprah Winfrey arrived at a time and in a space in which suffering was already a chief cultural vector connecting people across and beyond national allegiances. No less than utopia, dystopia has been central to the formation of global imagination. From the evening news to soap operas via the talk show, global media are ridden with spectacles of private and public misery. Icons of agony—no less than icons of glamour—are the regular staple on which the global imagination feeds. In the following sections, I conceptualize more clearly the relationship between the image of suffering as Oprah Winfrey has constructed it and the globalization of her show.

It is interesting to observe that the image of suffering has been historically intimately connected to the emergence of a public sphere. One historical example will enable me to generate comparisons and observations on Oprah's uses of suffering in a global context. The first occurrence of a global awareness of suffering was the public reaction to the 1755 earthquake that shook Lisbon, Portugal. The news of the disaster quickly reached the French *philosophes* and provoked a surge of compassion rarely encountered before because tens of thousands of people had perished. For the first time in the history of ideas, philosophers had the opportunity to debate the role of Providence in human affairs. Voltaire, who responded most swiftly, also offered the most unsettling view on the relationship between Providence and suffering. In *Poeme sur le Desastre de Lisbonne*, he wrote:

> Misled philosophers who shout "all is well," come here, run and contemplate these horrible ruins, the wrecks, these carcasses, the pitiful ashes, the women, the children piled on each other under the broken marble, dismembered, one hundred thousand unfortunate people devoured by the earth, people covered with blood, torn apart, and yet still throbbing with life; buried under their own roof, they end without any help, in horror and agony.[3]

Voltaire's highly realistic style prefigures the naturalism of television cameras "in the field," and his denunciation makes explicit what has become an implicit moral assumption of our culture: natural disasters punish people who have done nothing to deserve their fate, thus rendering their suffering intolerable to our reason and morality.

Voltaire further drives home his point and clarifies what, for him, was unacceptable about the event:

> which crime, which mistake have committed these children, crushed on their mother's breast in their own blood? Was Lisbon, which is not anymore, more corrupt than London or Paris full of delights? What? Lisbon is broken and we dance in Paris? [my translation]

Voltaire's intervention marked the first time that a philosopher addressed directly his community of fellow philosophers *and* the general public about a contemporary but distant disaster and, more important, did so by stating the unacceptability of suffering.[4] Voltaire's bold conceptual move thus consisted in refusing to view suffering either as the punishment for a hidden sin or as the incomprehensible but just decree of an unfathomable God.[5] He claimed that suffering ought to be submitted to the realm of human intelligibility and reason, to the ordinary criteria of justice, wherever it takes place. In so doing, Voltaire parted company not only with traditional theodicy (suffering is always just, but its causes are inaccessible to human reason) but also with the eighteenth-century literary cult of suffering that had made tears synonymous with virtue and the spectacle of heroines' misery into a sweet, sentimental scene supposed to elicit gentle compassion.[6] Indeed, Voltaire's discourse is proffered in a global rather than a domestic setting, and the confrontation with the suffering of distant others does not soften, uplift, or make us feel more virtuous.

On the contrary, once suffering is disentangled from theology and from sentimental literature, it can become what it is here: a scandal. And it is a scandal both because the innocent meaninglessly suffer and because they suffer when others are merry and happy. The engagement of the philosopher with the suffering of distant others takes place in the present and goes with the compression of spatial and national boundaries: what happens in Lisbon is scandalous from the standpoint of what happens in London and Paris and vice versa; we should feel uncomfortable dancing in Paris when thousands are buried alive in Lisbon. To denounce suffering from a global standpoint thus paradoxically implies an awareness of the incommensurability of conditions around the globe. Moreover, even if Voltaire made an ordinary use of synecdoche, it is interesting that he refers to cities rather than to countries, perhaps suggesting a subtle solidarity among cities beyond their respective national frameworks. By placing the Lisbon disaster into the perspective of the moral intelligibility that guides the world, Voltaire manages a double tour de force: he creates a protoglobal public sphere—that is, a space of discussion about the moral coherence of the world as a whole—and places the question of the immanent rationality of the world squarely at the center of the relationship that links Lisbon, Paris, and London. Lisbon is destroyed while Paris continues to dance: by constructing this incongruence as a *moral problem*, Voltaire is able both to make it a scandal and to mark this scandal as one of the central world images of global consciousness.[7] The less justifiable the disparity of conditions around the globe became (through questioning the good sense and justice of God), the more a world consciousness of (and solidarity with) misfortune was enabled.

In that sense, Voltaire's involvement with the Lisbon disaster is paradigmatic of what would become a central axis of the global public sphere: that the calamities of some become the problem of others, across territorial and national boundaries. They become a problem for us when the notions of commonly shared "humanity," "rationality," and "justice" are applied uniformly to all places and peoples. The exposition—and commodification—of suffering in the public space implies and presupposes a commonly shared humanity with distant others. Moreover, those people are not apprehended through abstract reason but through imagination, compassion, and the temporary bracketing of one's own religious, national, and ethnic allegiances. The imagination used and invoked by Voltaire combines sentiment and cognition, pathos and logos, and invites one to reflect on the order and principles that organize the world through the simultaneous use of philosophical debate and emotions such as empathy, compassion, and guilt.

This particular form of global public sphere contained from the start two languages, each aiming at a different kind of universality. One expressed the rational desire that there be a correspondence between one's moral failings and one's fate, and that the absence of such correspondence be accounted for and accountable.[8] The other language appealed to what many eighteenth-century philosophers thought of as a universal capacity of the imagination, compassion and sympathy.[9] The public sphere as Voltaire constructs it here plays on both dimensions, inviting one to join in a rational discussion on the intelligibility of the world as well as to identify with and have compassion for distant victims on the basis of a shared humanity.

Voltaire's relation to suffering and the role of that suffering in establishing a relationship across national boundaries was necessary for the development of a cultural form such as Oprah Winfrey. Oprah's exposition of suffering differs from Voltaire's in the then incipient global public sphere in a few respects, which may help us gain insight into the ways in which Oprah Winfrey's cultural form is deployed across the space of global media institutions.

First, the children crushed under their own roofs on their mothers' breasts have been replaced by (potentially) beautiful childhood crushed by neglectful or abusive parents; the destruction of a city has been replaced by the destruction of families and psyches. Where Voltaire discussed the large-scale visible, objective physical destruction of human lives, Oprah makes us witnesses to the psychic suffering of a single person, a suffering that is by definition intimate, subjective, and situated in the private sphere. Second, Voltaire's clever philosophical and rhetorical construction juxtaposes the moral closeness of Lisbon and Paris with the irreducible phenomenological distance separating Lisbon from Paris; the problem of theodicy is precisely to account for that distance. Talk shows, on the other hand, are structured on the principle of immediate presence and intimacy and on the mirroring of the experience and life stories of guests, studio audience, viewer, and host. Indeed, everything in the talk show is designed to suppress the distance between the happy and the unhappy and to make all of us into "victims," whether already consummated or victims *in potenza*. Third, while in Voltaire's public sphere the suffering person is indirectly apprehended — through the mediation of somebody else's speech and eye — on the talk show the suffering person assumes a direct agency, witnessing directly for her own story, drawing us in via the radical subjectivity of her speech and feelings. Fourth, whereas Voltaire's speech is "referential" — talking about a real disaster that took place in a real geographical location — on talk shows speech is essentially performative. The "event" reported on and staged by the show is the public revelation of the dark secrets of family life, because to speak is already to heal. As I have made clear, *The Oprah Winfrey Show* is a deeply therapeutic genre in that it is predicated on a shared belief that revealing and talking about emotions "liberates" and generates change. Fifth, while Voltaire's victims are just that — absurd victims of an absurd disaster — Oprah's victims are endowed with a meaning. The suffering person is summoned to make her pain a compelling narrative of identity, to work on it and make it into a meaningful life project. Concurrently, the victim has become sacred and suffering has now a special and definite glow. Finally, and perhaps most importantly, while Voltaire refers to the theological chaos that makes the innocent suffer meaninglessly, Oprah Winfrey discusses almost exclusively the worldly chaos that saturates families and identity. Where Voltaire asked what is the meaning and moral coherence of a world in which suffering is haphazardly distributed, Oprah's show mostly asks how identity and psychic coherence should be built when families, love, and marriage no longer provide a reliable source for the formation of identity. As argued in earlier chapters, *The Oprah Winfrey Show* is about a certain form of social suffering that originates in the family and that is articulated from the experience and viewpoint of women inside the family.

There is a certain irony here. While western photojournalism and the evening news regularly import nonwestern images of war, famine, and natural disasters, the Oprah Winfrey talk show represents the first television genre that *exports* American forms of suffering to the rest of the world, a suffering that differs significantly from the imported kind in that it is individual, is located in the private sphere, has a psychic character, and concerns the self. Imported suffering is mostly visual; this kind of American export is mostly narrative. The import is a daily and perhaps by now routinized reminder of the inequality in the distribution of collective resources across the globe; the export is resolutely democratic in that it includes all and invites all of us to join in the community of sufferers. Suffering as constructed by Oprah Winfrey has no color, no class, and almost no cultural specificity. Yet this seemingly "universal" idiom of suffering rests on a very particular cultural structure, that of the therapeutic discourse.

In what sense, then, can we say that Oprah Winfrey is a global cultural form? At a simple level, to say that a cultural object is global is to say that it can be found all over the world, a condition easily met by *The Oprah Winfrey Show*. The show is also global in the more diffuse sense that it addresses the problems and predicaments of the global condition of selfhood, in which the cultural reproduction of identity is severely challenged with the result that the self alone must carry out that work. There is yet a third sense in which the show can be said to be global: Oprah Winfrey uses the difficulties of the self to reproduce the self in the cultural idiom and narrative structure of the therapeutic discourse, which have spread and solidified throughout the western world.

THE NARRATIVE STANDARDIZATION OF PAIN

I argue that what has enabled *The Oprah Winfrey Show* to develop as an economic empire and as a global tentacular media structure is the fact that Oprah has increasingly segmented, individualized, and standardized its biographical formula. As marketing strategies increasingly target particular groups and even individuals (as is the case in Nike's advertising strategy to have one's own logo printed on the shoe), Oprah Winfrey has reached a mass market through her ability to mobilize individuals and biographies. The transformation of the medium of television into an active tool for examining and shaping the self has been made possible by the extraordinary customization of the show, which over time has become more and more able to respond to and process a wide variety of individual biographies.

At the same time that Oprah's show became refracted and fragmented into a multiplicity of rubrics, experts, and categories of problems, it forcefully engaged in the task—elevated to a moral mission—of transforming the personal life of an increasing number of viewers. The show no longer has one cultural location but rather has become a cultural structure carried over to different sites. To that extent, it is a striking illustration of Castell's claim that "the unifying cultural power of mass television (from which only a tiny cultural elite had escaped in the past) is now replaced by a socially stratified differentiation, leading to the coexistence of customized mass media culture and an interactive electronic communication network of self-selected communes."[10] Oprah Winfrey became a global empire, yet she simultaneously increasingly segmented and specialized her show. Thus Oprah has revolutionized the use of television by making it a technology far more contiguous with the individual home than perhaps has ever been the case.

Through her Web site, *The Oprah Winfrey Show* has become more interactive, soliciting ever more viewers to tell their stories on the talk show, as well as more segmented, compartmentalizing the talk show and the site according to different kinds of stories and expert advice (e.g., financial consultant Suze Orman, "The Angel Network," and the "Heal Your Spirit" rubric). The Book Club follows this trend. Its novels represent a segmentation of types of suffering that, when brought to the show, are attached to individual stories, which in turn generate intense Web site activity on the part of individuals who will share with others their own stories, usually a minor variation of the story of the novel. The Web site enables the exchange of autobiographical discourse and constitutes a highly individualized platform for asking for and receiving advice. Biography has been made a cultural category that is the object of intense exchanges ("tell me your story, I will tell you mine"), negotiations ("are you right to be angry at your 14-year-old daughter?") and advice ("you can fix your dysfunctional relationship by changing your frame of mind")by the standardized and institutionalized discourse of therapy.

The role assumed by television in general and *The Oprah Winfrey Show* in particular can be understood in the context of the presence of psychology and psychologists in American society. After the Second World War, American culture underwent a significant transformation as psychologists joined key social institutions—the state, education, marriage, the corporation, and the army—in which they helped better control conflicts and engineer harmonious social relationships.[11] The result was a vast reservoir of commercially produced therapeutic guidance to cope with the increasingly contested and self-managed character of selfhood. Oprah Winfrey, both as a persona and as a television program, is an outcome of and vehicle for this therapeutic revolution. Therapeutic culture—understood here as a complex, fuzzy, and multistranded array of theories, languages, and organizations, the vocation of which was to manage the psyche—increasingly came to shape and even dictate the language in which selfhood, pain, and healing were formulated.

Oprah's reliance on therapeutic knowledge is apparent in three main ways. The first is her extensive use of written therapeutic texts, ranging from Dr. John Gray's *Men Are from Mars, Women Are from Venus* to Daniel Goleman's *Emotional Intelligence*.[12] However different from one another these texts are, they have in common the vocation of analyzing the predicaments of the self by relying on various bodies of knowledge produced for the most part by certified psychologists. *The Oprah Winfrey Show* is a major conduit both to promote and advertise therapeutic advice literature and to implement it. The therapeutic outlook, in its popular and professional forms, is organized around telling stories about the emotional self and changing that self in the act of the telling. Therapeutic culture is a hybrid of electronic and written texts, expert knowledge, and the oral narration of personal stories, organized around such key emotions as guilt, love, and fear. This system is the dominant cultural form of *The Oprah Winfrey Show* and is apparent in Oprah's extensive use of experts to discuss and manage her guests' emotions and, more importantly, to change their lives.

Second, Oprah Winfrey draws on the basic therapeutic creed that we are perfectible and that identity can and perhaps ought to be shaped by willful self-management and introspection. This creed is congruent with a structural feature of the consumer market: both therapeutic and consumer activities are set into motion by a state of perpetual dissatisfaction and a Sisyphean desire to fashion and improve one's own self. *The Oprah Winfrey Show* solicits the viewer-consumer within this fine and dual dynamic of dissatisfaction and self-improvement.

Finally, therapeutic culture makes a highly reflexive use of language—the medium through which one changes oneself and fashions one's relations to others. The cultural project of Oprah Winfrey is not only to perform the autobiographical narration of suffering but also to rewrite autobiographical narratives through the discourse and techniques of therapy.

I offer the following claim: the various stories elicited, staged, and reconstructed by *The Oprah Winfrey Show* are undergirded by a deep cultural structure that runs through and unifies Oprah's various cultural sites. Oprah's own biography, the Book Club novels, *O Magazine*, the Web site, and last but not least, the television show all have a common narrative matrix, which I have dubbed "therapeutic." It is a matrix because it can generate a variety of stories based on a common narrative structure. Through the therapeutic matrix, women are invited to make sense of their unhappy relationships in a narrative frame that names dysfunctions ("you are addicted to men," "you are codependent," "you have a failure compulsion," "you are not emotionally intelligent") or describes them ("you feel you have to be nice to be loved," "you feel worthless without another person," "you suffer from the feeling of not deserving what you have"). The narrative also explains the dysfunctions ("you are addicted to men because you were abused in your childhood," "you choose unworthy men because you have never felt loved") and instructs change through powerful metaphors and narrative goals ("get off the addiction," "start loving yourself"). These narratives all have the goal of explaining a wide variety of "failed stories of self," with the result, I argue, that they process a wide gamut of biographical discourses in routinized and predictable narrative patterns. One pattern, with four main features, emerges as dominant:

1. It guides the selection of states or events significant to one's life; the events most likely to be selected in these narratives are emotional states defined as problematic (e.g., "lack of self-confidence," "anxiety," "worthlessness") or problematic behaviors (e.g., "avoidance of intimacy").
2. It explains the source of the dysfunction at the same time that it names it ("social anxiety is a lack of self-esteem," "addiction to men comes from a feeling of not having been loved").
3. It can be applied to various domains and thus can duplicate itself ("I lack self-confidence with all men who have authority over me, such as my boss, my father, and my teacher").
4. It works by setting up goals ("not to crave men's attention," "choose the right man," "become more assertive in public"). The goal of the narrative is properly what makes the self "work." By striving toward a different version of itself, the self strives to bring closure to its narrative of suffering.

What makes the therapeutic narrative so powerful is thus a great paradox: in the therapeutic worldview, suffering is the outcome of improperly understood and improperly managed conflicts or beliefs. Any form of maladjustment, dysfunction, or failure can be read backward, as pointing to an impairment in the self (which can, however, always be corrected if one works enough on it). In that sense, therapeutic narratives codify and encourage a view of the self as dysfunctional. However, because the therapeutic narrative is based on the assumption that our suffering is due to emotional confusion, perceptual mistakes, or distortions, and that these can be corrected in the act of telling our story, the telling marks—ironically—the beginning of the end of the story being told.[13]

The structure of this therapeutic narrative pervades not only Oprah's autobiography and her narrative framing of her guests' stories but also many of the novels selected for her Book Club, which in turn suggests that this narrative pervades American culture at large. Let us take the example of the first book selected for the Book Club, *The Deep End of the Ocean*. The novel is the story of a family that disintegrates after the young son is kidnapped. Late in the narrative, ten years after the terrible event, the kidnapped son is found again. Yet, far from auguring the happy reunion of the family and the end of the story, the miraculous discovery of the kidnapped child generates further narrative complications. When the son is found, he chooses not to return to his biological family; the family he loves is the one that kidnapped him. What keeps the narrative going and working is the fact that the psychic disintegration and agony of Beth, the mother, are paired with moral dilemmas and a questioning of what constitutes a "real" family. The plot shifts from the mother's psychic agony to that of the kidnapped son's brother, Vincent, who like the other family members is consumed by guilt. What brings the novel to an end, however, is the final liberation of Vincent's "secret" through a therapeutic session: as a child, Vincent was asked by his mother to watch over his little brother. But when they got into a skirmish, Vincent let his brother's hand go and told him to "get lost." Thus the closure of this novel is not, as in the classical novel, worldly success, matrimony, or a compensation for an injury or loss. Rather, it is self-understanding and the liberation of one's own guilt. These are inscribed in a cultural code in which introspective self-knowledge (gained after long therapy) brings about one's own and intimate others' liberation. The novel is about the disintegration and recomposition of the self and of the family through the process of understanding one's own psyche.

To take another Book Club example: *We Were the Mulvaneys* by Joyce Carol Oates creates narrative tension from the fact that the daughter, who is also a fervent Christian, is the one who feels guilty for having been raped by a male acquaintance and refuses to reveal his identity, thus disabling her family from punishing her attacker and throwing the family in a spiral of shame and self-punitive behavior. Here again, the narrative is based on the cultural code that repressed or hidden feelings (of guilt and shame) are the main agents destroying this family, thus leaving the characters struggling to understand and cope with this tangled emotional dynamic.

To take still another example: Wally Lamb's novel *I Know This Much Is True* offers a thick and complicated plot of a man who feels excruciating guilt about his twin brother's schizophrenia. His guilt reaches a denouement only at the end of a long course of therapy that brings self-knowledge (a realization of his guilt) and liberates him from his obscure dependence on his twin. Here again, the cultural code that makes the narrative possible is therapeutic: it is an emotional secret to be "liberated" that keeps the narrative moving.

The same could be said, in fact, of the majority of the novels read for this study. If the detective novel is a masculine genre in which the hero is set on discovering a factual truth from clues and fragments "left behind," the genre of novels chosen by Oprah is its feminine and therapeutic counterpart: the plots are about discovering an "inner" psychological truth that is revealed only after a painstaking process in which, in many cases, the heroine's family disintegrates and is subsequently reconstituted. In other words, these novels offer a literary version of long-term therapy: their narrative structure is built around an individual struggling with a family that is disintegrating, who reconnects with the family by liberating an emotional "secret."

These novels, like Oprah's guests' narrative framing of their lives, rest on the deep cultural structure of the therapeutic self. Because Oprah uses the therapeutic narrative as her main cultural device to stage and frame her guests' lives, the show simultaneously processes a wide variety of singular biographies, mobilizes the industry of experts, and makes the self "work" in a variety of global technologies. The therapeutic narrative structure is a powerful cultural device that unites specific individual experience with the abstract and global language of therapy; moreover, it is particularly well suited to television as a daily provider of stories because it is able to name a wide variety of ills, which in turn provide an endless stream of stories. Anything and everything can become the departure point of the therapeutic narrative and thus the topic for a show—eating too much or not enough, having too many sexual partners or not enough, being emotional or not emotional enough. In the context of television, therapeutic narratives are highly profitable because they require no economic investment, can be applied to a wide variety of life stories, and generate novelty and surprise while being easily processed in a standardized and routinized speech format. Moreover, they name a wide variety of predicaments and build explanatory frameworks, as well as provide the tools and techniques, to overcome the guests' predicaments. But perhaps their most significant characteristic is the fact that therapeutic narratives link the host, the participants of the show, the viewers, and the Web site visitors in a common cultural matrix that standardizes biography.

Let me explain this with examples. In the rubric called The Angel Network on the Oprah Web site, a woman calling herself ladydi13 (December 29, 1999) addresses, like many other users, one of Oprah's regular experts, Phil McGraw:

> My birth father left us when I was just five years old. He was an alcoholic and my mother had a violent marriage . . . parts of which are burned in my brain. . . . The man she married turned out to be a pedophile and I was ripe for the picking when he adopted us four kids. . . . Being a child of alcoholics, it was not uncommon for me to choose one for a husband who looked like my father. . . . I was never able to have a good relationship with a man. . . . I still am not healed of all the trauma. . . . I can't afford Dr. Phil's books or tapes but am going to scrounge the libraries. God bless him and make more like him. We injured spirits need his kind of guidance.

What enables her to make a swift connection between "being a child of alcoholics" and her choice of a husband is the therapeutic assumption—translated in a narrative format—that we are the determined products of our childhood. In accordance with the therapeutic way of constructing the self, she conceives of herself as a victim of wounds inflicted in the family by a family member. She links this event to a later event (she chose a man like her father), thereby building a more complex therapeutic narrative. Her biography is centered on her psychic wounds, but in telling the story she already claims that the goal of her life is to move toward healing. And this woman, like many others, generates around her further support, stories, and advice from other viewers—visitors to the Web site—because they share the same therapeutic narrative. Moreover, the advice they provide is strikingly similar in content and structure to that provided by Dr. McGraw. In the therapeutic narrative, we have all become sufferers as well as experts and one another's therapists, because therapeutic language has standardized life trajectories and autobiographical discourse.

Compare this story to one that appeared in the March 2001 issue of *O Magazine*. The author of an article on meditation introduces her topic as follows:

> My father left when I was four. My mother died when I was nine. My father returned briefly when I was 11, until a suicide attempt spun him away into the

mental health system, from which he was never again free. Savage, uprooting turns and incomprehensible losses as I moved from household to household left me feeling abandoned over and over again—abandoned by life itself. Though caring people raised me, no one was able to speak openly about all that had happened. With very little stable love coming toward me, I developed the feeling that I didn't deserve much in life. I held my immense grief, anger, and confusion inside, fortifying my isolation and my innermost conviction that I was unworthy of love.[14]

The readily apparent therapeutic narrative structure of this story is similar to the story quoted above as well as to the format of the stories endlessly told by Oprah Winfrey about herself, and to the format with which her guests frame their lives. Being abandoned and unloved, her "self" becomes the narrative subject and object of dysfunctions, which then become the "narrative peg" of her autobiography, that is, what motivates and constitutes it.

Finally, this story structure is also readily apparent in books selected by Oprah. For example, a novel that achieved great success in Oprah's Book Club, White Oleander, tells of a young adolescent abandoned by her mother (who went to jail) who subsequently moves from one foster family to another, whose members abuse her. The story can be summarized as consisting of abandonment, abuse, psychic suffering, self-hatred, and the heroine's slow and difficult process of learning to love herself through inner self-understanding and through overcoming her wounded self.

The point here is a double one: Oprah's own biography and the biographies of her seemingly endless pool of guests have become commodities offered daily through a powerful narrative matrix at work in various cultural locations, on the Web site, in O Magazine, in the Book Club novels, in the self-help manuals presented on the show, and in the show's staging and performance of the self. The narrative isomorphism among the various technologies and media Oprah uses indicates a great unity of style and intent. The therapeutic narrative is a stable cultural form pervading and organizing her cultural enterprise. We arrive here at a cultural paradox that is, I believe, key to understanding the extraordinary success of Oprah Winfrey. At the same time that she has offered a wide variety of stories, telling singular forms of pain and staging individual voices, the stories have been processed within a standardized cultural form, which we may call, following an expression coined by John Tomlinson, "standardized intimacy."[15] The narrative of suffering constructs intimacy in a routine that decontextualizes the image of the storyteller.

Five cultural devices are particularly efficient to decontextualize the image of suffering:

1. The visual technique of camera and studio style in the talk show genre presents people and stories in the abstract and neutral context of the TV studio, devoid of spatial or cultural markers. Abundant close-ups and almost exclusive focus on the human face make the genre simultaneously intimate and highly decontextualized. As Daniel Keyes put it, "producers attempt to stage and capture traces of live spectacle while erasing most signs of locality and temporality in order that the programs can be syndicated nationally if not internationally."[16]

2. In Giddens's terms, on the talk shows, personal relationships and intimacy are "lifted out" of their spatio-temporal contexts to be processed by a visual and cultural form that is "abstract" in the sense given to that word by Marx or Simmel in reference to money circulation. In the same way that money converts a concrete value (e.g., shoes for walking) into an abstract one (these shoes cost $200 and are therefore equivalent to a plane ticket), the talk show converts the concrete and singular experience of a person into a decontextualized narrative of suffering, equivalent to other singular narratives. The victim of sexual abuse becomes equivalent to the victim of "emotional abuse," who becomes equivalent to the victim of emotional neglect. Unlike the many commentators who have claimed that talk shows make the public sphere into an intimate space, I argue that it is the other way around: *The Oprah Winfrey Show* makes intimacy highly decontextualized and abstract.

3. The temporality of the trauma narrative—which is the most outstanding cultural example of the therapeutic narrative—is structurally standardized. The psychology of trauma has identified what is specific in traumatic time, namely the fact that it "freezes" the self at a singular point in time, the point at which trust in the world collapsed. Traumatic time "stands still" in consciousness because it is cut off from the past as well as the present. It becomes a sort of inaugural moment in which a "new" self emerges, cut off from its history as well as from its projection in the future. Whether the trauma was provoked by sexual abuse, rape, betrayal, or an earthquake, the traumatized psyche revolves around a traumatic time that is homogenous because it is atemporal. It in turn generates a narrative of self that, although a "memory narrative," is also atemporal.

4. Trauma narratives are by definition abstract narratives of self: they frame the self in standardized analytical and narrative categories such as "lacking self-confidence," "anxious," "obsessive," and "self-destructive." Paradoxically, it is the cultural availability of such concepts—the standardization of emotional

life through models and norms of mental and psychological health—that can generate a wide variety of personal stories.

5. The therapeutic narrative leans on a highly standardized conception of the individual institutionalized in modern polities through the modern legal and state apparatus. As sociologist John Meyer[17] has extensively and persuasively shown, models of the individual are based on scripts that are abstracted from institutions, such as the welfare state and the market, which in turn have rationalized the individual through such notions as "rights," "mental health," and "self-interest." The discourse of therapy has been institutionalized in most western polities, and political discourse has in turn rationalized individuals' self-conceptions, as well as their biographical trajectories.

This rationalization is sustained by the fact that psychology has been institutionalized in an increasing number of countries through worldwide models of selfhood constructed and propagated through the state, academia and the professions, global media, and now the Internet.[18] Psychological knowledge is institutionalized in social services provided by the welfare state; it caters to families and standardizes parent-child relationships and couples' relationships through similar therapeutic models of "communication." Psychologists have also widely penetrated the corporate world through their presence in industrial relations.[19] The diffusion of therapeutic knowledge through publishing, state services, and clinical practice allows people to use the therapeutic narrative to explain their own and others' failings and misfortunes, as well as guide themselves in the complexity of the contemporary social world.

For example, on June 20, 1990, ABC aired an Oprah special, sarcastically summarized by her biographer George Mair as follows: "This program focused on what Oprah felt was the cause of most of the problems of the world. Because of lack of self-esteem, Oprah believed people abused others who were weaker; wars were fought; crimes were committed. . . . Oprah wanted to explain how important self-esteem is to everyone's happiness."[20] Oprah can apply self-esteem to any domain because she draws on a cultural script that is institutionalized in different spheres of life. Therapeutic narratives can be applied to virtually any realm of human action and generate a potentially infinite variety of stories because the therapeutic narrative structure can process almost any breakdown of the biographical course. Moreover, they activate a large array of experts, who can in turn intervene—through television and the publishing industry—to "diagnose" and "heal" psychic problems. Therapeutic biographies are thus particularly efficient symbolic forms because they mobilize a vast array of experts and media industries, but in an individualized cultural form. To that extent, we may call them techno-therapeutic biographies.

Therapeutic narratives are particularly well suited to the economy of what Douglas Kellner has dubbed "techno-capitalism,"[21] based on the interface of high-velocity capital, information technology, and expert knowledge. They constitute a gold mine of topics (and profits) for television, because they require virtually no production costs and because they can be endlessly recycled through various technologies that process the decomposed subject of late modernity.

Techno-therapeutic narratives have a paradoxical cultural property: they help constitute autobiography as a particularized and individualized discourse, and yet they simultaneously standardize it. I suggest that the Oprah Winfrey cultural matrix is to life stories what the assembly line is to commodity production: a highly efficient way to manufacture and standardize products that can be customized to fit the particular needs of an individual consumer. These narratives have become global commodities through the worldwide diffusion of therapeutic knowledge and through standardized models of individuals institutionalized in the market and in the state.

The global reach of the Oprah Winfrey cultural enterprise is not "spaceless" and "contextless" because it "interconnects between various local cultures" or because it is "ecumenist."[22] *The Oprah Winfrey Show* does not aim at encompassing the world as such. Rather, it is global in the sense that it decontextualizes and homogenizes experience. As Anthony Smith put it: "Today's emerging global culture is tied to no place or period. It is a contextless, a true melange of disparate components drawn from everywhere and nowhere, borne upon the modern chariots of global telecommunications systems."[23] Within this melange, Oprah Winfrey offers a cultural matrix that reorders experience through a dynamic of distance and intimacy. This is also congruent with Arjun Appadurai's understanding of globality as simultaneously producing alienation and psychological distance between individuals and groups and fantasies of "electronic propinquity."[24]

To conclude: the therapeutic narrative is a cultural tool that emerges from the increasing difficulty of carrying on the work of cultural reproduction and from the fact that the self is now summoned to achieve this work through self-management techniques. The therapeutic narrative of suffering simultaneously reaches the singular level of the individual and the level of the state or even beyond through global media. Therapeutic narratives can segment individual biographies in this way because they are sustained by a vast apparatus of worldwide institutions that have standardized the individual biography. Oprah has invented a global cultural form that offers an example of "infra-globalization," or "globalization from within," that is, a cultural form that emerges from the very gaps and contradictions of "reflexive modernization."[25] The routinized narrative and speech pattern of the show is a "cultural structure in action" that emerges from the fissures and cracks of lives saturated with contradictions. As Beck suggests, because of the contradictions of late modernity between family and market, between the state and individualism, biography is made to do a massive work of self-management, which I have argued is sustained by standardized cultural resources. Oprah has created such a resource, a transnational community of sufferers, from the very contradictions and aporias of the contemporary American family, which are reaching family structures of numerous other societies. Oprah Winfrey offers a language and a forum to stage these contradictions and make sense of them in a decontextualized form.

A COMMUNITY OF SUFFERERS

Oprah Winfrey has integrated TV technology with magazine and novel reading and the use of the Web, thus making it difficult to distinguish between viewers and readers, passive or active users of cultural material, tellers and listeners of stories, experts and laypeople. She has created a gigantic structure in which various cultural sites, technologies, and roles are ultimately interchangeable through the mediation of therapeutic biographies: one can be simultaneously an expert and a victim, a guest and a member of the audience, a spectator and an actor of one's own life story.

As argued in the previous chapter, the standardized narrative of suffering has generated transient and media-based communities that we may call "communities of sufferers." These communities are at once textual, biographical, and emotional. But more interesting, they are created by the fact that storytellers act as their own or as one another's expert, and use the generality and abstractness of experts' discourse to frame or respond to stories. The globality of Oprah Winfrey is carried on the shoulders of the experts language, which disentangles the concrete and specific character of individuals' stories from idiosyncrasy and brings it to a higher level of abstraction and generality, thus helping to standardize the cultural material through which a community of sufferers gathers.

This is manifest in several ways. First, experts frame individual stories so that they are representative of a larger community of bearers of the same type of stories. Thus, one may say that *The Oprah Winfrey Show* constructs and stages story structures borne by particular individuals. Singular stories are converted by experts into general categories ("women who love too much," "can't get over your ex," "women with social anxiety problems"). The label of a dysfunction or problem functions as a rallying point for a virtual community of people united by the common story structure they bear. Second, the lawlike language of the experts frames singular stories in terms of the general mechanisms and rules they put into motion ("people with low self-esteem will choose abusive partners," "if you crave a relationship, you are showing that you are emotionally dependent"). This is an attempt to mimic the cause-and-effect language of science. Finally, because experts prescribe remedies like handing down laws, these remedies can encompass and transcend particularity and individuality ("look at yourself in the mirror and repeat ten times 'you are wonderful'"). Stories that have a similar narrative and normative goal ("to regain self-confidence," "to love my body," "to be able to say no") can therefore unite people around that common goal.

From a message board organized around the theme of depression, which was itself a theme of a show, here is an example of the ways in which those virtual therapeutic communities are assembled:

> Just sharing my experience with others like you makes me feel better as a person. To me, it's kinda like therapy. I just recently realized that there was such a thing as social anxiety. Before that, I just thought it was the way I was. Wow! It's so amazing how just realizing that I wasn't the only one dealing with it lifted me. (Heather24, March 7, 2001)

One of the many answers to this note reads:

> I really appreciate you writing about social anxiety disorder. It was so nice to hear from someone who understands. I was picked on constantly at school and when I read what you said about past events affecting you later in life I totally agree! I believe that is why I feel like I'm having these problems today. (Mary32, March 9, 2001)

These two messages show clearly how a therapeutic concept—"social anxiety"—that was the theme of a show is used to generate communities of sufferers. Like other therapeutic concepts, "social anxiety" is used as a retrospective narrative frame to understand the past through a dysfunction. This dysfunction can thus name and homogenize a variety of social experiences, which can in turn be shared and thereby constitute a community, however tenuous and transient.

Recent studies of such groups as Codependents Anonymous[26] and Alcoholics Anonymous have dwelled on the relationship between individualism and community provided by groups organized around a common narrative of dysfunction and recovery. But they have failed to understand what makes the interplay between the two possible: the standardization of biographical narratives. The biography of suffering and the therapeutic narrative that tells and presumably overcomes that suffering form the main vector through which readers and Web site visitors respond to and continue the "show after the show" on the Web. A review of many of the Oprah Winfrey Web site rubrics makes obvious that the expression of personal suffering, the story of disrupted biographies, and the search for social support are the core motivations around which Book Club readers, TV viewers, and site visitors gather into virtual communities of sufferers. For example, Oprah's Angel Network contains a subrubric called "In Need of Prayer," which is a large reservoir of sad stories about why people feel both powerless and in need of others' support. This rubric, in which each person asks for others' prayers, differs from others in that it is less oriented toward psychological advice.

An analysis of this rubric on the Oprah Web site during the year 2000 reveals two main sources of distress: medical and pecuniary. For example:

My husband and I are once again homeless, and this is causing a lot of stress for me, and on our marriage. For a short time we are allowed to live with a friend, but that won't last much longer. It has been hard to find jobs, because the phone has been shut off, and was turned on today. We have until March 5th, 2001 to find jobs, and a place to stay. (MysticWintermoon, Feb. 19, 2001)

Or:

My daughter a sigle [sic] mother of 6 needs your prayers. She works very hard and never misses a day of work but never seems to make enough money to stay a float. She has now became [sic] homeless because she doesn't make enough money to pay the 900 $ a month rent and all of the other bills so please pray. (grandma1, Feb. 14, 2001)

Indeed, many messages relate difficult and stressful social conditions and the absence of structures and networks of support, whether from the immediate community or from the state. A great number of the complaints and stories derive directly from the social problems connected to economic and cultural deprivation. However, what is interesting is that these messages generate few further messages; they do not compel other people to share their own stories or to provide counsel. The rubrics that have a marked therapeutic vocation are far more likely to generate virtual communities of people who circulate their stories and advice.

Oprah's biography, her show, her Book Club, O Magazine, and her Web site are striking illustrations of Manuel Castell's diagnosis that current mass media are characterized by "an integration of all messages into a common cognitive pattern."[27] Oprah Winfrey is a supreme example of this because she mixes entertainment, news, pedagogy, spirituality, New Age religion, expert knowledge, support group, literary reading group, and grassroots forms of protest and integrates them in a common cognitive pattern of therapeutic biography articulated around the management of biographical pain. The Oprah Winfrey empire functions as a gigantic matrix through which various textual technologies circulate the same narrative of suffering, organized around what I call transnational therapeutic and media-based biographies of trauma. Sexual abuse, divorce, overweight, or anorexia nervosa might be said to create new lines to shape biographies and organize communities inside countries and new connections with others across traditional national and territorial divisions, as evidenced by the wide variety of Internet sites on these disrupted biographies. Such communities of suffering can in turn become institutionalized, like such transnational organizations as Alcoholics Anonymous, Overeaters Anonymous, etc. Like The Oprah Winfrey Show, these organizations are based on the combined effects of suffering, biography, and standardized management of the self through therapy. This form of organization of social pain addresses the kinds of sufferings mapped and covered by the state as well as by traditional nongovernmental organizations.

I suggest that these transient communities, constituted by a common therapeutic narrative, can be thought of in terms of what David Held has called "communities of fate," which criss-cross traditional lines of political demarcation and bypass conventional class, ethnic, and national distinctions.[28] Communities of suffering at once reach below—they are biographical—and above the nation-state. Do these communities promote what Arjun Appadurai calls a "globalization from below" that does not derive from corporate power or media technology but rather from the emergence of a new form of world awareness and social movements deployed on a world scale? Indeed, do such communities of suffering correspond to a "global consciousness"?

Using many techniques to efface particularity and locality, leaning instead on an abstract and standardized language of the psyche and crossing all distance between viewer, host, and storyteller, *The Oprah Winfrey Show* compresses, like no other television program, the emotional and political space between viewers and the storyteller. The show thus creates a single, homogenous space in which autobiographies become interchangeable.

However, as pioneering sociologist of globalization Roland Robertson suggests, globalization is "both the compression of the world and the intensification of the consciousness of the world as a whole,"[29] a definition that describes aptly Voltaire's denunciation mentioned at the beginning of this chapter. But Oprah Winfrey, even if she provides powerful techniques, both visual and linguistic, to compress the world, still does not promote a consciousness of the world as such. Rather, her show promotes cultural standardization and homogenization without an awareness that the world "as a whole" is the context within which various forms of suffering and happiness are deployed. Oprah's cultural form is a *truncated global cultural form* in that it compresses the distance separating the show and its viewers throughout the world, yet does not promote an awareness of "the world as whole." Precisely because they suppress distance, such communities lack the moral force of Voltaire's point of view and make us unable to see the scandal of suffering, the simultaneity of suffering *and* happiness. Communities of psychic suffering may be global, but they do not promote a global consciousness, for their vocation is to disintegrate. To be a successful member of such communities means to ultimately leave them.

7

THE SOURCES AND RESOURCES OF
THE OPRAH WINFREY SHOW

Everything that [the Negro] touches becomes angular. . . . Anyone watching
Negro dancers will be struck by the same phenomenon. Every posture is
another angle.   —Zora Neale Hurston, *Characteristics of Negro Expression*

Suffering and self-change, the two meanings performed by *The Oprah
Winfrey Show*, offer two starting points for deciphering Oprah's vast cultural and textual enterprise. They are able to account simultaneously for the
structure of the show, the intentions of its author, the probable motivations
of its participants, and the broad frame of meaning within which it is received and interpreted. These intentions and motivations are contained
within a deep cultural structure that makes possible the packaging of
Oprah's biography and the routinization of her guests' speech within the
highly commodified sphere of global media. This cultural structure is present in the novels chosen for the Oprah Book Club as well, which confirms
that it is a narrative of selfhood central to contemporary American culture.

But cultural analysis cannot stop at clarifying the meaning of texts. It
must also inquire into the conditions that make certain actors more likely to
create new meanings, as well as the conditions that make their environment
receptive to those meanings. In chapter 3 I examined how Oprah modified
and reinvented the talk show genre. In this chapter, I examine more directly why Oprah has such a virtuoso command of the cultural codes of suffer-

ing and self-help and why these codes have resonated so powerfully with Americans. In which social experience is the performance of suffering and self-help grounded? How do such meanings reflect the social identity and habitus of Oprah Winfrey as an African American woman? How do these meanings play out important aspects of American selfhood?

I expand this inquiry beyond the social conditions that have shaped Oprah's biography by exploring the relationship between the meaning of *The Oprah Winfrey Show* and the broader environment of American society. Bourdieu's notion of habitus, "the ensemble of habits, ideas, and dispositions subjectively lived and communicated as personal identity and taste but objectively determined by position in the hierarchy of cultural and economic capital,"[1] is necessary for understanding how cultural socialization provides skills and resources for acting in the world. Habitus has been traditionally applied to such domains as appreciation of art and table manners and used to explain how people internalize and carry their position in the social structure in their own body, their tastes, and their ways of speaking. Habitus has a dynamic aspect as well, pointing both to the set of dispositions a person has inherited and to the ways they are augmented or left unused (and sometimes even diminished). To reconstruct Oprah's habitus is not only to find out her "habits, styles, and skills" but also to show how she "energetically seeks strategic advantage by using culturally encoded skills."[2]

But while habitus explains well how social structures become incorporated in tastes and in the body, it is less well equipped to account for the changes that can occur in the process of using such structures. In other words, while habitus has been unusually helpful in conceptualizing long-term strategies of action,[3] it does not explain the dynamics by which cultural resources and structures can change in the very process of being deployed. William Sewell Jr.'s discussion of the relationship between structure and agency is a needed complement here. Sewell has suggested that culture is the interplay of *resources*, which help maintain or gain (political or economic) power, and *schemas*, tools of thought (metaphors, binary oppositions, stories, assumptions) through which we grasp the world.[4] Schemas are abstractions and categorizations derived from one's social experience. Unlike the more elaborate "worldviews" or "ideologies," they are basic tools of thought rather than a bounded and coherent set of propositions. Moreover, according to Sewell, there is a reciprocal relationship between schemas and resources. Schemas are effects of resources, and resources are effects of schemas. To understand cultural action is to understand the seamless interplay between the two. Finally, and perhaps most interestingly, schemas are internalized rules that can be used as resources—that is, as sources of power—to transform the rules of the game. Thus, while both schemas and habitus try to find a meaningful point of articulation between social structure and actors' cultural equipment, Sewell's view of schemas makes more room for the possibility that, under given circumstances, the cultural codes from which actors draw become a source of power, which will in turn modify the initial cultural structure.

In this chapter, I focus on the cultural habitus that may help us describe and account for Oprah's cultural style. I also consider the mechanism by which the schemas that inform Oprah's style have been transformed into a powerful cultural enterprise. Oprah has used her show as a platform to stage the predicaments of the modern self, as played out in the contemporary American polity, by mobilizing schemas developed as cultural strategies by the African American community over the past two centuries to respond to their oppression. As argued in chapter 3, popular texts are likely to be popular precisely because they deal with difficult demographic, economic, and cultural conditions; address unresolved social contradictions; and help orient the self in the midst of these contradictions. Oprah Winfrey has brought to American culture symbolic tools and strategies that are an essential part of the accumulated experience of the African American community and its means of orienting a self in disarray, but she has applied them to the contemporary self, strategically using her own habitus to respond to the contradictions and predicaments of all women in contemporary American society. If habitus is the sedimented accumulation of the effects of power and social structure, these effects are also visible in the habitual ways and strategies with which a group responds to and copes with oppressive (or facilitating) social conditions through a moral orientation to the world. This twist on the notion of habitus is more in line with Swidler's "strategy for action"[5]—a way to move about in the world and to orient ourselves in the midst of challenging situations. Oprah Winfrey's use of culture as a strategic instrument of action invites us to rethink popular culture and to view it as a resource we can draw on for moral guidance in devising "strategies of action."

AFRICAN AMERICAN CULTURAL PATTERNS

I suggest that we enlarge our understanding of the kind of cultural dispositions included in the concept of habitus, viewing habitus as expressed not only in "taste" but also in the categories used to provide moral accounts of the world, to define problems for the self, and to devise solutions to cope with recurring problems. All of these constitute ways of coping with and making sense of social conditions through repeated and familiar symbolic patterns, which are no less a part of one's habitus than are aesthetic understandings. As I show in the following analysis, the symbolic patterns used on *The Oprah Winfrey Show* to define a problem and to devise strategies to address it are grounded in the cultural history of the African American community.

THE SOCIAL EXPERIENCE OF AFRICAN AMERICAN WOMEN

Disorganized Families As has often been remarked, Oprah captures and captivates the American woman's mind like no other popular entertainer. Interestingly, this fine-tuning to the predicaments faced by contemporary women has its roots in the particular social experience of African American women. It goes without saying that their social experience is as diverse as that of their white counterparts. However, considering the fact that Oprah herself was raised in some of the most difficult conditions African American women have to face, it is plausible to assume that she has mobilized some of the cultural resources characteristic of the black female underclass. It is this social experience that I try to recapture here in broad brushstrokes. This attempt runs the risk of essentializing and reifying the content of African American culture. However, it should be read as an effort to identify some cultural patterns that are salient in Oprah's habitus and prominent in her talk show as well.

Sociologist Julius Wilson has found that black women have higher separation and divorce rates than white women. In the 1980s, the period during which Oprah's show became national, the number of black single-mother households increased significantly.[6] This trend was accompanied by a startling increase in the proportion of never-married black women, a group that tends to be, in Wilson's analysis, far more vulnerable to poverty and lack of education because of entanglement in long-term cycles of poverty and dependency. In 1993, half of the families headed by black women lived at the poverty level, compared to only 12 percent of families headed by black married couples.[7] Moreover, globalization and the growth of the information technology economy has had the greatest effect on unskilled working-class jobs, to which the black working class has been limited. During the same period that *The Oprah Winfrey Show* ascended to a central place in American popular culture, the black family underwent strains resulting from severe economic pressures.[8] Massive reductions in welfare expenditures have helped throw households headed by single black women into a spiral of poverty and social problems.[9]

This in turn has accentuated the conflict between the sexes already prevalent in the African American community. As Patricia Hill Collins puts it, "Exploring the tensions between African-American men and women has been a long-standing theme in Black feminist thought."[10] A concrete manifestation of this battle of the sexes is the high frequency of negative stereotypes that black men and women have about each other.[11] Such social problems as battering are also prevalent among black women. According to an article published in the *Law Review*, battering is the leading cause of death among black women under the age of 44 and is the context within which most rapes, suicide attempts, and child homicides occur.[12]

I suggest that Oprah's predilection for the theme of disorganized families and the theme of injury and assault within and by the family is grounded in, and even a direct reflection of, black women's social experience of the family. In that respect, the show mirrors the real and deep social problems of black families, albeit in the euphemistic mode of entertainment. But what has made the spectacle of the "disorganized family" fascinating for the general public is the fact that this disorganization can now be found in all social classes and ethnic groups (for reasons other than poverty). As the white middle-class family becomes an increasingly contested terrain and men's power within it is challenged, the white family faces strains reminiscent of, albeit not identical with, the chaos of intimate relationships that characterizes the black family. With the demise of gender roles—or, at least, the possibility of questioning these roles—women are pitted against men and children against their parents. This suggests that the domestic experience of white women bears an increasing affinity with the long-standing experience of black women, even if it is obvious that the social forces shaping these experiences are different. If a black woman has put the spectacle of disorganized families at center stage on American television, it is because the problem of forming and maintaining stable family bonds was an essential part of the African American "cultural equipment" before it became one of the central cultural questions posed to members of white middle-class and lower middle-class families.

Similar schemas pertaining to the family are present in contemporary middle-class American culture. This is illustrated by the fact that most of the Book Club novels chosen by Oprah offer the image of a family in a state of decomposition. The family experience is presented as violent or oppressive; women are estranged from men; women cling to their children and to their friends and re-create social bonds that are not based on the legal bond of marriage.

More than any other cultural entrepreneur, Oprah Winfrey has systematized the representation of the family in a state of decomposition and has legitimized the multiple new forms of family that have emerged in the last thirty years. A cultural form that presents the dysfunctions of the family and simultaneously offers recipes to live with or change them is likely to affect viewers in two possible ways: it can relieve them of the sense that their families were abnormally problematic, thus providing a sense of normalcy, or it can provide a sense of (social and moral) superiority.

Everyday Life as a Problem If, as bell hooks puts it succinctly, "women are the group most victimized by sexist oppression,"[13] then black women have been and continue to be indubitably the most oppressed. We may characterize women's social experience in general as structurally confused and confusing, mixing normalcy and violence. This is particularly true for black women. As has frequently been observed, their daily existence is intertwined with their subjection and with routinized, visible and invisible forms of brutality caused by white racist and sexist oppression as well as by the black male, who is himself victim of the white racist oppression. As feminist black scholar Patricia Hill Collins says, "Black men's physical and emotional abuse of Black women is part of a large system of legitimated, routinized violence."[14] Black women have been thus twice victimized in that they have had no "backstage" to retreat to in order to resist. This implies that for black women, the experience of oppression is likely to be pervasive, invisible, and confusing, because it is located both in the domestic and the public spheres. This is borne out by the fact that rape and incest are "powerful themes in African-American women's writing."[15] Unsurprisingly, these themes not only dominate *The Oprah Winfrey Show* but also initially drew wide public attention to the show and to Oprah's persona.

What is debilitating about the simultaneous political and domestic forms of oppression is that both affect the very possibility of developing identity and trust in oneself. This has resulted in the fact that black women are more likely than white women to hate their own physical appearance, because African Americans' skin color, hair texture, and facial features have been systematically erased or denigrated by dominant standards of white beauty.[16] Since the body plays a fundamental role in self-perception, living in a culture in which black hair and skin color cannot count as "beautiful" constitutes a massive threat to identity and self-esteem. I suggest that the systematic assault by white culture on black physical appearance provides a useful clue by which to interpret Oprah's virtuosity in transforming her own physical appearance, as well as the ways she has obsessively promoted the theme of (physical or mental) *change* on her show.

Oprah Winfrey's obsessive promotion of the topic of appearance derives from cultural schemas pertaining to the social experience of black women whose bodies and appearance have been denigrated by the hegemonic white standards of beauty and by standards of thinness and "healthy bodies." This, in turn, sheds a new light on the apparent superficiality of many of her show themes (e.g., "Would you go out without your make-up?" or "What do you feel now that you have gained a few pounds?"). These subjects are not frivolous but rather express the preoccupation of black people with their appearance, which is not narcissistic self-contemplation but rather the result of oppression. Oprah's obsessive preoccupation with her own and others' physical change is anchored in a cultural habitus in which the black body is a "problem." Radical physical self-change—of the kind Oprah has performed—is a powerful cultural fantasy lurking in the background of black people's self-perceptions. Oprah's virtuosity at changing herself can be viewed as part and parcel of this cultural fantasy induced by oppression and made into reality by her access to wealth.

Ironically, black women's self-hatred vis-à-vis their bodies has become the condition of *all* women in late modernity, who, faced with the ideals of beauty relentlessly promoted by consumer culture via advertising, television, and films, have also developed high levels of bodily dissatisfaction and self-contempt.[17] This is evidenced by the extraordinary increase of the disease of anorexia nervosa in recent decades (a topic to which, incidentally, Oprah has devoted a great deal of attention). Indeed, contemporary white women now also experience the ideal of feminine beauty as oppressive.[18] Black women's negative perception of their body has become the dominant condition of all women, as the feminine standards of beauty promoted by advertising, televisual, and cinematic culture have contributed to increased body dissatisfaction.

The assault on black women's identity concerns not only their physical appearance but also other aspects of their social existence. Because of the combined effects of urban segregation, work discrimination, and poverty, the African American community contains a high concentration of social problems: chronic unemployment, poor and crowded housing conditions, mental disease and abuse. Because African Americans in general have been marginalized from the main circuits of economic and cultural production, and because women in particular have been systematically assaulted in their daily existence, psychological disorders have been found to affect black women in higher proportions than men. Black women's social experience contains and combines in a highly confusing and perplexing fashion normality and pathology, suffering and life-enhancing relationships, oppression and love services. As Andrea Dworkin puts it, "you cannot separate the so-called abuses of women from the so-called normal uses of women"[19]; this is even more accurate for black women. For lower middle-class and working-class women, everyday life cannot be taken for granted but rather is something to be painstakingly achieved against a hostile environment. In other words, the very possibility of black women's developing a self and an identity that can properly function in the spheres of work and the family has been jeopardized by their social and economic conditions. It is precisely this cultural condition that I have found, in chapter 3, to characterize the genre of Oprah Winfrey. As I have argued, everyday life is the site within which *The Oprah Winfrey Show* is deployed, and simultaneously, on *The Oprah Winfrey Show*, everyday life—carrying on the routine work of having stable relationships—is presented as an ideal to be achieved painstakingly.

Here again, I suggest that while white middle-class women's lives are incomparably more sheltered than those of black women of comparable or lower classes, they too have become increasingly characterized by the disintegration of their taken-for-granted character. White women also have become the prime victims of psychological disorders such as anxiety, depression, anorexia nervosa, and bulimia. In fact, two thirds of the adult population of community mental health centers, psychiatric hospitals, and outpatient clinics are women. In addition, 84 percent of all private psychotherapy patients are female.[20] Modern polities are saturated with many forms of suffering that derive from and are directly produced by the massive disruption of the lifeworld by capitalism but are not economic; rather, they are primarily psychic in that they concern the ability to form autonomous and worthy selves. Indeed, the main difference between industrial and postindustrial capitalism is that while the first produced massive economic distress, the second has provided affluence and produced massive forms of psychic distress, in which the very moral and spiritual resources of the self are severely undermined and threatened. Because women juggle many more contradictory roles than men, and because patriarchy still depletes women's social, economic, and moral resources, women have been far more likely than men to be the victims of psychic disorders.

More than any other cultural figure, Oprah has provided a platform acknowledging the difficulties of women—white and black—in forming their identity and in carrying on their work of cultural reproduction.

DECONSTRUCTING EVERYDAY LIFE

While during slavery and even up to the present, African Americans, especially women, have been made to cater directly to the needs of white families, their socioeconomic conditions prevented them from forming their own stable families, understood here as an institutional framework geared to economic survival and child rearing. Black women were thus prevented both from maintaining intact their tribal family structures and from imitating the patterns of the white family (better suited to the economy of the nineteenth and twentieth centuries). Yet, because black women worked in the household, they developed great familiarity with the mores and habits of white families. I therefore argue that African Americans have developed a habitus particularly apt at attending to the (arbitrary) rules that make up the (white) family institution. Indeed, as I have discussed in chapter 3, one central aspect of Oprah Winfrey's "style" is its deconstruction of everyday life and the family, which mobilizes a number of cultural schemas specific to the black family and central to Oprah's treatment of the family. As Patricia Hill Collins put it, African American women "have long been privy to some of the most intimate secrets of white society."[21] Because African American women worked in great proportion in domestic occupations, they have developed a cultural "expertise" in the art of observing family secrets, a position of exteriority and interiority dubbed by Collins as that of an "outsider within."

Similarly, the genre that Oprah Winfrey has created plays with the boundaries between private and public space by assuming a position of simultaneous interiority and exteriority in the family. Black women have been historically split between their own family and that of their white employers, with the result that they developed an intimate knowledge of the lives of the latter,[22] from an external point of view. The black writer June Jordan expresses this particular mental and cultural schema very well:

> I watched one Black woman after another trudge to the corner, where she then
> waited to catch the bus home. These were Black women still cleaning somebody
> else's house or Black women still caring for somebody else's sick or elderly, before

they came back to the frequently thankless chores of their own loneliness, their own families.[23]

The very fact that black women moved between different family settings is likely to have made them more attuned to the various norms and rules that undergird family arrangements and allowed them to occupy the position of "observer." This is precisely the position that Oprah has adopted. (Incidentally, Oprah's own mother occupied the role of "cleaning somebody else's house.")

There is a second reason black culture is particularly apt at offering a "deconstructive" stance vis-à-vis conventional family. As bell hooks suggests, the African American family has combined biological and nonbiological females as primary caretakers, a fact that makes "this form of parenting . . . revolutionary . . . because it takes place in opposition to the ideas that parents, especially mothers, should be the only childbearers."[24] In other words, already in the nineteenth century, the African American community experienced the decoupling of biological and social roles that has become the hallmark of the modern family. I argue that this is one of the sources of Oprah's capacity to deconstruct the family and to view it as the primary locus for the discussion of the self. Oprah herself has declared on many occasions: "many times your family isn't what you're born into. [It is] what you're able to create and that you find family in the people of the world who take you in."[25]

Another feature of the black family strikingly resonant with *The Oprah Winfrey Show* is that it has always been more "public" than the white family. As Patricia Hill Collins explains, the nineteenth-century black family did not exhibit the radical split equating private with home and public with work. This is because "in order to survive, the [black] family network [had to] share the costs of providing circulation of limited resources. African American families exhibit these fluid private/public boundaries because racial oppression has impoverished disproportionate numbers of black families."[26] The culture of privacy and the view of family as a haven, sheltered and even sealed away from the outside society, was not embedded in the organization of the black family. Oprah Winfrey's virtuosity in moving back and forth between the public and the private realms (as documented in chapter 5), is an intrinsic component of the African American cultural habitus.

Generally, the boundary between private and public is far more fluid in the African American community because, long before the feminist movement,

African American politics made a radical claim about the centrality of experience and the personal in politics. June Jordan illustrates the intertwining of the political and the personal for a black woman:

> My life seems to be an increasing revelation of the intimate face of universal struggle. You begin with your family and the kids on the block, and next you open your eyes to what you call your people and that leads you into land reform into Black English into Angola leads you back to your own bed where you lie by yourself wondering if you deserve to be peaceful or trusted or desired or left to the freedom of your own unfaltering heart . . . everything comes back to you.[27]

In its artful combination of the political and the domestic, this quote can be said to be the literary equivalent of *The Oprah Winfrey Show*. For black women, the family has not been the safe haven of privacy it has represented for white women. Rather, it has been the terrain of an experience that was, from the outset, political.

Poverty, the African pattern of rearing children, the location of black women's work in white women's households, the porous boundary between the political and the personal—all of these contribute to explaining why the boundary between private and public has been and continues to be far more fluid in the poorer segments of the African American community than in white middle-class culture. This explains how Oprah Winfrey has been able to so masterfully blur the boundary between the private and public spheres (from the home to television and from television back to the home).

To summarize: three aspects of the black family account for Oprah's extraordinary cultural skill in deconstructing the family: its simultaneous objective distance from and intimate knowledge of white domesticity, its combination of biological and nonbiological "constructed" definitions, and its permeability to the public sphere. All these elements are "mental schemas" characteristic of African American culture, which constitute part of Oprah's cultural habitus and which inform her show.

The hypermodern family is also characterized by the fact that it makes up the rules and norms as it goes along: parents and children, men and women are in a constant process of negotiation over tasks, chores, duties, and rights. The rules and norms must be continually "invented" or "improvised," with the result that the normative structure of the family lies open to the arguments and gaze of its members. To that extent, members of the contemporary family have developed what we may call an outsider's point of view on their own family. The discourse of therapy has contributed a great deal to institutionalizing this point of view, whereby people attend to the rules that make up their relationships with close others, thus standing simultaneously inside and outside their family. Moreover, the white family has been penetrated by the state and the market to such an extent that it has become the site of deployment of discourses borrowed from the public sphere (of autonomy, equality, fairness), again increasingly blurring the public and private divide.[28] Finally, as the technology of reproduction advances, the biological norms in which the family was grounded have been seriously shaken. Individuals can now overcome biological constraints to shape their own definition of a family, thus making it akin to the constructed and voluntary African American family. These transformations of the (white) family make it analogous to the black family in that both are the site of conflict, are contiguous with the public sphere, and are a composite of biologically and nonbiologically related sets of characters.

BLACK SUFFERING

More generally, I argue that the suffering self occupies a prominent role in the Oprah Winfrey cultural enterprise because suffering has been central to the very social experience and cultural schemas of the African American community. The long firsthand experience of slavery, poverty, and racism has had two results. First, the very ability to form identity has been an enduring problem of that community since long before it became the problem of modernity. Second, African American culture has developed "thick" cultural strategies to cope with suffering.

The great African American philosopher W.E.B. Du Bois provides a starting point for inquiring about the schemas pertaining to self and suffering at work in the African American community. As he famously puts it, the black person is plagued by a double consciousness, a sense of

> always looking at one's self through the eyes of others, of measuring one's soul by the tape of a world that looks on in amused contempt and pity. One ever feels his twoness — an American, a Negro; two souls, two thoughts, two unreconciled strivings; two warring ideals in one dark body, whose dogged strength alone keeps it from being torn asunder.[29]

Du Bois's remarks invite a number of observations: first, as he suggests, the problem of being able to form a coherent identity has been central to the social existence of African Americans at least since the Civil War. The split consciousness and experience of irreconcilable inner strife results from the fact that once African culture was cut off from the tribal social organization that made it meaningful, it became an unnatural home, a home that had lost its "taken-for-grantedness." Indeed, Du Bois's remarks underscore that African American identity has been characterized by a reflexivity caused by a double feeling of strangeness—in its own culture and in the culture that oppressed it. This state of strangeness to one's own self entails a sort of perpetual self-examination from an outside eye and point of view. To a certain extent, this reflexive distance from self and culture is a property of immigrant groups in general. But in the case of African Americans, it has been seriously aggravated by racism, violence, slavery, and chronic poverty. Members of the African American community have had to measure themselves with a "tape of self-contempt" because their culture, physical appearance, and very humanity have been massively, violently, and systematically denigrated by the host culture. We may thus say that the forced arrival of Africans on the American continent severely undermined what John Rawls calls the "social basis for self-respect" of that group and its possibility of forming identity by building organic connections to the social and moral environment.

This in turn explains why black culture and black theology have been particularly preoccupied with the theme of theodicy. While slave owners taught Christian mercy, justice, and righteousness, the slaves had to face daily brutality and exploitation, thus imbibing a deep-seated awareness of the contradiction between the teachings of the Gospels and the daily reality of their work.[30] As Holmes quotes,

> From the very beginning of the relationship between Black religion and Black Nationalism, there has been a perplexing question of the meaning of undeserved suffering in a cosmos governed by a good, loving, and omnipotent God. Because Blacks were in the peculiar position of being simultaneously evangelized—that is "taught" the Christian view on charity, justice and compassion—and brutally exploited they were forced to live and witness a brutal contradiction that is the heart of theodicy.[31]

Black culture thus developed an original position vis-à-vis suffering: the systematic denial of their freedom and humanity and the violence to which slaves were submitted made physical and psychic suffering an objective condition of their existencea mark of election carried like a necessary but elevating and even uplifting burden, black theology refused suffering and affirmed hope and redemption, which generated political action. Hope and a worldly struggle with suffering came to characterize the cultural patterns of black spirituality. African Americans' struggle with the problem of theodicy took the form of a concrete praxis that blurred the lines between theology and politics. For example, black churchmen were far more involved in the politics of black communities than were other churchmen.[32] Such nineteenth-century black theologians as Henry Highland Garnet and Henry McNeal Turner thought simultaneously about God's plans and about blacks' liberation.[33]

We can see here continuities between Oprah's cultural style and the cultural schemas of the African American community. Oprah's insistence that lives are made meaningful by grasping their moments of suffering and that identity is a restless work of salvation from the most difficult moments in life are anchored in the social experience of Africans in America. Oprah Winfrey displays a strong predisposition not only to pay attention to various forms of suffering but also to interrogate the moral meaning of suffering and to incorporate it into a project of self-transformation and redemption. This in turn suggests an affinity between her cultural sensitivity to suffering and the problem of theodicy that has preoccupied African American theology, resulting in a particular African American cultural pattern, mixing spirituality and politics. As stated in chapter 2, black politics emerged from church activities and mixed religious principles, brotherly love, and a universalist view of human suffering and of God's relations to his suffering people. The African American legacy that Oprah Winfrey declares she pursues does not approach politics as a separate and specialized realm of action; rather, it calls for a "spiritualized" politics that views individuals' spirituality and morality as a solution to the social or personal problems in which they are trapped. Oprah Winfrey's cultural formula offers a model—a symbolic recipe—for coping with crisis and psychic pain, and contains the same mix of politics and religiosity that has been the distinctive mark of black social activism.

This particular social experience has gained such visibility in popular culture because it resonates with and resembles the forms of suffering produced by modernity. Ironically, although capitalism has enabled affluence and material security, it has produced social pathologies and suffering reminiscent of those endured by the African American community. The institutions of modernity have assaulted and undermined the very basis of the formation of the self, as is apparent from the increasing rate of depression and mental diseases and the general decline in well-being. Yet as psychic misery, in its many forms, increases, people feel more entitled to happiness than they did previously; the experience of suffering becomes intolerable in the face of the promises of liberal polities. To that extent, there is an affinity between the experience of suffering that was inflicted on the African American community and the forms of suffering that have emerged from the very institutions supposed to deliver, if not happiness, at least well-being.

Let me make a further point. Oprah Winfrey has staged selfhood and its predicaments according to a pattern of representation that has its source in a genre central to African American culture, the slave narrative[34]—characterized by the "recounting, exposing, appealing, apostrophizing, and above all *remembering* [the slave's] ordeal in bondage."[35] In the very act of appropriating literacy, the slave narrative transgresses the boundaries of white culture and imposes the slave's voice as a "strident, moral voice."[36] The slave narrative thus simultaneously affirms the black subject—against all attempts to commodify her—and in the act of saying and telling, it procures the teller a voice.

I suggest that television has been mobilized by Oprah Winfrey much in the same way that literacy was appropriated by slaves: as a medium to transgress boundaries between white and black culture and, in that very process, through which to give groups and individuals full possession of a voice. The trauma narrative has a certain affinity with the slave narrative, for it emerged in the public sphere as an act of "remembering" one's ordeal, claiming agency, and owning one's own voice.

THE CHAOS OF MODERNITY

Oprah Winfrey's way of staging the suffering self is grounded in the cultural schemas of African American culture, which bear an (ironic) affinity with the predicament and contradictions of middle-class identity. This of course does not mean that the life of a slave is equivalent to the life of a white suburban housewife. It only means that social conditions that tend to disorganize the reproduction of identity can produce similar predicaments, especially for women. Having had a long acquaintance with the experience of suffering, African Americans have developed cultural schemas that addressed particular forms of experience that, while not equivalent to the "homelessness" of late modernity, yet are reminiscent of the forms such homelessness takes.[37]

Modern identity is saturated with multiple forms of suffering that derive from what Ulrich Beck has dubbed "individualization." According to him, contemporary polities are dominated by *individualization processes*, that is, the increasing segmentation of each life course by the market and the state. The traditional lifeworld has been destroyed by capitalism and recoded as individuals' choices. Individualization, Beck writes, "means, first, the dis-embedding and, second, the re-embedding of industrial society's ways of life by new ones, in which the individuals must produce, stage and cobble to-gether their biographies themselves."[38] Because the state and the market in-creasingly demand that we organize our lives as self-reliant and competitive actors, each individual has only himself or herself to turn to, to make up the rules and reasons for choices as he or she goes along. This implies that our most intimate bonds become simultaneously constructed and contentious. Actors cannot fall back on known rules and norms to organize their private lives; instead, they must endlessly improvise. As Beck and Beck-Gernsheim state, "it is no longer possible to pronounce in some binding way what fam-ily, marriage, parenthood, sexuality or love mean, what they should or could be; rather, these vary in substance, exceptions, norms and morality from in-dividual to individual and from relationship to relationship."[39] I suggest that as a cultural genre, the Oprah Winfrey talk show stages what is at the core of "reflexive modernization," a term that Beck, Giddens, and Lash[40] prefer to "postmodernism" and that means modernity is faced with the conse-quences of its own creation: destruction, losses, and new risks. Reflexive modernization reflects back on itself and contemplates the consequences of its destructiveness. Again, as Beck put it so well, in the "risk society," the do-it-yourself biography can very quickly become the breakdown biography: precisely because the management of the self is crucial for the workplace, marriage, and social networks, it is a far greater responsibility in the midst of chaotic conditions.

The Oprah Winfrey Show is a cultural genre of reflexive modernization par excellence. It reflects on the consequences that modernity has had for personal relationships and endlessly foregrounds a discussion of the norms that ought to guide us in our actions and emotions. In that respect, it is a supremely reflexive cultural institution, discussing and contemplating the losses entailed by modernity in the sphere of interpersonal relationships. The disputes, confrontations, and emotional outbursts that are basic to the format of talk shows are a cultural form in which the highly contested, fluid, and negotiated character of self and relationships is given a cultural form and reflexively examined.

Let me now offer the following suggestion: in the era of late moderniza-tion, the family as an institution has developed in a direction very similar to that of the black family, in that gender roles and divisions that formed the traditional foundations are disintegrating and traditional masculinity is threatened from within the hub of the family. Concurrently, women's relationships to each other and to their children have become of paramount importance to their social identity.[41] Because women have had to juggle far more new roles than men and have been in charge of attending to and maintaining relationships, they have been the main recipients of discourses and techniques concerned with managing the self. The "technologies of the self"—perhaps best illustrated by therapeutic discourse—provide strategies both to manage a multiplicity of roles and to construct relationships in an era of risks and uncertainty. Women have experienced modernity in a double mode: they have been massively dislocated from their traditional social and normative frameworks and because of this have had to construct female networks of support.

One may say that African Americans have been experiencing aspects of high modernity for a long time. Indeed, as the historian Lawrence Levine cursorily observes, antebellum black people had been engaged in what is traditionally identified as the quintessential attribute of modernity, namely "the simultaneous participation in a variety of social worlds."[42] Since the nineteenth century, blacks' identity has been far more fluid, more protean than their white contemporaries', acutely conscious of itself and therefore already reflexive. African Americans have thus had to face the problem of building their biographies from scratch since the end of the nineteenth century, and arrived at the twentieth century with the problem of generating from within their selves the resources to cope with an environment that strains people's capacities to form their identity.[43] Notwithstanding demographic patterns, the black family is in fact a magnified version of the modern or hypermodern family, in which women are increasingly self-reliant, struggle with and balance various roles, and must increasingly rely on other women for emotional support.

I would like to suggest now that Oprah's show is the meeting of two cultural structures—the structure that emerged from the conditions imposed on African Americans' social existence and the cultural structure of late modernity, in which the self and identity (of both black and white women) have been undermined and strained by the conditions of "risk society."[44] This is not to deny the important differences between the diffuse psychic "homelessness" of late modernity and the brutal exploitation to which black people have been submitted. My point rather is that the mental schemas developed as a response to African Americans' geographical and cultural dislocation can be used to make sense of and to address the predicaments of contemporary American selfhood. These two cultural structures informing *The Oprah Winfrey Show* explain why Oprah is able to capture the multiple forms of suffering inflicted on the self.

Let me now make a further point: Oprah not only addresses the predicament of contemporary selfhood but also transforms her schemas into cultural resources and deploys them through her show. As Sewell has suggested, in particular circumstances schemas can be turned into resources, that is, sources of power. Oprah Winfrey's habitus has wielded fantastic power because it resonates with the state of disarray in which late modern selfhood has been mired and because it offers symbolic tools and strategies to cope with the chaos of modernity. Because African Americans have long wrestled with the problem of fashioning their selves from bits and scraps of their cultural environment, they have developed symbolic strategies that can address the predicament of contemporary American women.

THE CULTURAL RESOURCES OF
THE OPRAH WINFREY SHOW

Reflecting on black culture, Gilles Gunn, following Kenneth Burke's *Philosophy of Literary Form*, suggests that we view critical and imaginative forms, including folk forms, as expressly, if not always obviously, constructed in answer to questions posed by the situations in which they first arose. But such forms are designed not as simple but rather as stylized answers, essentially strategic answers. That is, they are not merely responses to situations but responses intended to encompass critically the questions those situations pose. Burke therefore distinguishes between situations and strategies. Situations represent problematic experiences of a representative kind. Strategies, on the other hand, represent ways of dealing with such situations by sizing up the problems that compose them, analyzing them into their component parts, and defining them as a whole in a way that contains an implicit attitude toward them that, in essence, conveys an interpretive perspective.[45]

"Situations," in Burke's sense, refers to the ways in which the world resists and opposes our intentions and plans. "Strategies" refers to the patterned way of responding to, making sense of, overcoming, and accommodating the resistance of the world to our intentions. Obviously, schemas are the crucial determinant of strategies. To the extent that they not only make sense of situations but also are ways to actively cope with and transform them, Oprah has used the coping strategies that have been part and parcel of her African American habitus. Some of these coping strategies have been stylized on *The Oprah Winfrey Show*, and she has transformed them into cultural resources to address the condition of selfhood in late modernity.

1. The talk show has a strong improvisational quality and is an example of an oral genre based on conversation and dialogue. Oprah Winfrey gave a new impetus to the dialogical format of television by talking in an unscripted way and by making the conversational form the center of her show. Her extraordinary improvisational skill and ability to make a TV genre out of dialogue is one of her most outstanding characteristics. For example, as a 22-year-old assigned to read the news at a Baltimore TV station, she refused to read from the TelePrompTer, with the result that her speech was more informal and improvisational than was generally accepted at the time. This feature is directly derived from African American culture. Oratory—in which black people have excelled because of the rich lore they brought from Africa and because they were barred from literacy—pervades the entire cultural enterprise of Oprah Winfrey. As historian Lawrence Levine put it in his study, *Black Culture and Black Consciousness*,

> In their songs, as in their tales, aphorisms, proverbs, anecdotes, and jokes, Afro-American slaves, following the practices of the African cultures they had been forced to leave behind them, assigned a central role to the *spoken arts*, encouraged and rewarded *verbal improvisation*, maintained the *participatory nature* of their expressive culture, and utilized the *spoken arts to voice criticism as well as to uphold traditional values and group cohesion*.[46] (emphases added)

As is made apparent by this quote, African culture is characterized by orality and storytelling, at which Oprah Winfrey excels. Because African Americans were barred from literacy and came from Africa with a rich lore of stories, orality played a significant role both in maintaining African culture and memory and in resisting the repressive aspects of white culture. Songs and music, for example, were developed in a spirit of resilience and resistance. The storied form—which has been the privileged form of black culture—is a chief vehicle of group memory.

Oprah draws directly from what we may call a shorthand "black spirituality," which is very characteristically predicated on the oral and storied form, on responsiveness, on an open-ended, flowing, and flexible communication. This seems to be a typical African American cultural form. For example, commenting on the cultural achievements of Michael Jackson, black critic and scholar Michael Dyson says, "Jackson's concerts thrive on *call and response.* Jackson's live performances mediate *ritual structures of an antiphonal oral and verbal* exchange between artist and audience" (emphases added).[47] Similarly, Oprah Winfrey's genre is deeply antiphonal, structured between call and response and by the ritual interaction between audience and performers.

Patricia Hill Collins has argued that dialogue is central to "black epistemology," that is, to the ways in which black people know and apprehend the world: "The widespread use of the call and response discourse mode among African-Americans exemplifies the importance placed on dialogue. . . . The fundamental requirement of this interactive network is active participation of all individuals. For ideas to be tested and validated, everyone in the group must participate."[48] If, as novelist Gayle Jones says, in black culture "there is always the consciousness and importance of the hearer,"[49] it is no surprise that Oprah Winfrey has made dialogue such a central feature in addressing her viewers, framing the relationship between the guests and between the guests and experts, and between the viewers and the guests themselves.

The dialogical and oral structure of the talk show resonates with a powerful oral component of modern polities. Dialogue occupies a central place in contemporary polities because social relationships—both formal and intimate—have become deeply contentious. Consequently, contemporary polities have set regulatory mechanisms that are essentially dialogical. The liberal injunction to engage in a conversation about disagreements in order to reach understanding is the cultural motif at the heart of *The Oprah Winfrey Show.* The talk show provides a symbolic structure that puts organized dialogue at the center of interpersonal interactions.

2. African American culture is characterized by the intertwining of reason and emotion, and by the refusal to separate the two. The black style of preaching is infused by what scholar Lawrence Levine calls a "black emotional effervescence."[50] Black preachers and their sermons do not call for contemplation of otherworldly truths or goods; rather, "The preachers quickly touch their listeners' deep emotions, describing and elaborating biblical stories, and working toward an emotional climax of joyful weeping and shouting."[51] Oprah Winfrey was deeply imbued with the church culture of the South and acquired rhetorical skills grounded in that culture. Scholars have stressed the importance of tone and emotion in black preaching. In her ability to display emotions and to intertwine them within dialogue, Oprah draws from the emotional cultural style of African American spoken

arts. Here again, I argue that the integration of emotions with reason has be-come a central cultural feature of modern identity, it is exemplified by Oprah's artful mix of emotional discourse and expert advice. This form caught women's imagination and psyche because throughout the twentieth century, women have been increasingly defined both through their emo-tional lives and through the discourse of experts who have prescribed stan-dard rules for emotional control.[52] The emotional culture that emerged from the intervention of experts in private life was paradoxical in that it made emotions the site and center of identity, thus inviting women to re-flect a great deal on their emotions and to realize themselves by discovering the authenticity of their inner life.[53] Yet, to the extent that women have also entered the main institutions of male power—political, economic, and sci-entific—they have also increasingly defined their selves by adopting the ra-tional core of these institutions.

3. Along with this profoundly oral genre—using and mixing storytelling, dialogue, preaching, conversations, debate, and practical wisdom—*The Oprah Winfrey Show* displays a reverence for books that (as publishing in-dustry representatives have claimed) has had very few equivalents in Amer-ican culture. This reverence for books too is rooted in the African Ameri-can community. Like many oppressed groups, African Americans inherited a powerful reverence for books and learning because of the wide-spread nineteenth-century belief that literacy brought with it freedom. Ac-cording to Salvino, "early Americans constructed a view of literacy and ed-ucation as powerfully enabling—literacy as currency in the New World."[54] And, indeed, "black slaves transmitted among themselves the white belief in the power of literacy, as their post-Civil War enthusiasm for education attested."[55]

Oprah Winfrey has made several pronouncements on her love of books, and has declared numerous times that she drew much of her inspiration from black female writers such as Sojourner Truth and Maya Angelou. Ac-cording to a *Time* magazine article, "[Young] Oprah spent most of her time at the library and curled up at home reading such slave books as *Jubilee*, Margaret Walker's 1966 novel about a black woman during the antebellum, Civil War and Reconstruction years, and *God's Trombones*, the 1927 collec-tion of folk sermons in verse by James Weldon Johnson."[56] Indeed, many of her in-depth interviews highlight this love of literature. "Books showed me there were possibilities in life," she said, "that there were actually people like me living in a world I could not only aspire to but attain. Reading gave me hope. For me it was the open door."[57] Such an intense love of reading is a central attribute of black culture. Studying rap as a cultural form, scholar Eric Dyson suggests that "Rap expresses the ongoing preoccupation with literacy and orality that has characterized African-American communities since the inception of legally coerced illiteracy during slavery."[58]

Oprah's way of interweaving orality and literacy into a narrative in which both suffering and hope are inscribed is a distinct mark of black culture and is at the heart of the Book Club. Such a reverence for literacy resonates deeply with a society that makes the written word paramount not only in the ways knowledge is transmitted but also in defining moral competence. Literacy is one of the most basic skills for qualifying as a competent member of the American polity. Moreover, as Janice Radway shows in her analysis of the romance novel, middle- and lower middle-class women read to acquire "information," not only for entertainment. This is congruent with the middle-class ethos that one should edify and improve oneself through knowledge.

4. African American culture is deeply moral in the sense that it was and probably still is preoccupied by the question of good and evil, but, unlike the Christian view of morality, does not reify categories of good and evil. According to Levine, "The moralizing tales of the slave were by no means primarily caught up with explicit religious messages. The majority of them centered upon everyday human relationships."[59] Indeed, African American morality was modern *avant la lettre* in that it was more centered on human relations than on theology. For example, it does not view evil as an intrinsic human characteristic, and certainly never held a notion of sin as determining the character of one's soul. Moreover, moral reflection in African American culture is essentially narrative, not formulated of clear dos and don'ts. This allows a fluid and complex approach to moral problems: moral responses are grounded in concrete situations, not on general principles. As did many other oppressed groups, African American culture bestowed moral value upon deviants. For example, witness the central place occupied by Brer Rabbit and other tricksters. These characters do not follow the agreed-upon path and show that the best way to cope with the world is through flexible intellect and wisdom. This is consistent with two aspects of *The Oprah Winfrey Show*: Oprah's predilection for deviants and a wide variety of moral dilemmas, and her pronounced taste for situations and stories in which it is difficult to adjudicate. A moral inquiry based on storytelling and on the systematic examination of the principles that govern ordinary conduct offers an open-ended approach to morality. I suggest that this cultural feature is in line with postmodern ethics, which refuses to adjudicate between different positions. On the contrary, it wants to acknowledge the ambivalence contained in moral dilemmas.[60]

5. No less important to the African American cultural habitus is an ethos of solidarity that has few equivalents in American society at large. This ethos derives from the patterns of motherhood practiced by African American women. Because they tended to remain with the children and be their primary nurturers and because they were frequently separated from the children's fathers, nineteenth-century black women developed strong self-reliance, denser networks of relations with other women who helped them care for children, and strained relations with men. This in turn led to a pattern of intensive motherhood. The black family became a matrifocal family, in which the woman had a lot of power in decision making, struggling for economic survival as well as raising her children with the help of other women. Moreover, biological mothers often raised their children with the collaboration of other mothers; black women have been abundantly exposed to "mothers, grandmothers, and other women who have either been the sole provider for, or contributed to the survival of, the family."[61] This pattern of child rearing had its roots in African traditions but was reinforced by the systematic exploitation of the male workforce. Since the nineteenth century, black women have been far more independent from men, as well as far more connected to other women, than their white counterparts. Because care and nurturance were not attached to an ideology of separate private and public spheres or to fixed social roles, they became intrinsic components of women's social relationships.

Black women's ethic of caring, endlessly and repeatedly displayed by Oprah Winfrey, is manifest by the value given to the individual, the centrality of emotions, and the capacity for empathy. As Patricia Hill Collins cogently puts it, while white women have also been socialized to value emotions, expressiveness, and caring, black women have had many more institutional supports to validate this particular way of knowing the world, such as the church, extended families, and an African American tradition.

I argue that this accounts for Oprah's extraordinary understanding of the modern condition of women, who, because of processes of individualization pitting them against men, have become increasingly dependent on other women for guidance and nurturance. This cultural model is clearly apparent in Oprah's choices for her Book Club, which, as already suggested, emphasize women's relationships and make motherhood one of the most poignantly problematic features of womanhood. Moreover, Oprah's extraordinary capacity to create communities around books and to instigate forms of social solidarity that extend beyond her show derive from the African American patterns of organizing resources in communal patterns and emphasizing solidarity as an ethos instrumental to survival.

6. Finally and perhaps most importantly, black people have developed a strong ethos of self-help. As Du Bois's remarks quoted earlier suggest, the struggle with the demoralization entailed by racism has demanded a massive mobilization of spiritual and moral resources, which is the "strength" not to be "torn asunder." Long before moralistic advice literature, members of the African American community developed a strong self-help ethos as their only cultural resource with which to cope with the conditions of exploitation. A nineteenth-century poem from the black lore quoted by historian Lawrence Levine illustrates this:

Once or twice though you should fail
Try, try again;
If you would, at last, prevail
Try, try again;
. . .
All that other folks can do,
Why, with patience, should not you:
Only keep this rule in view
Try, try again.[62]

This ethos of self-reliance derives from several sources. One is the extraordinary resilience of the African American family. Refuting the widespread idea that the black family is on the whole incompetent to produce adaptive cohesiveness in the face of the society's demands, scholar James Floyd has argued that the resilience of a family should be evaluated according to its capacity to face and cope with crises over a period of several generations. He describes the ability to handle misfortune and change as an expression of family strength. The particular history and structure of the black family has generated a culture of endurance in the face of misfortune, as well as an ethos of self-reliance, that has no equivalent in the surrounding white culture.[63] Moreover, as black feminist scholars have suggested, because black women were denied male protection and assets, their mothers strongly emphasized skills that "could take them anywhere." Long before the feminist revolution became widespread, black women learned to develop self-reliance and strong patterns of solidarity with other women, thus creating one of the new ideals of feminine selfhood. More than any other television host, Oprah Winfrey incessantly affirms the utmost importance and centrality of friendship and of close relationships for the formation of the self as well as the value of resilience and self-help in the face of adversity.

Another source for the ethos of self-help that pervades African American culture is the traditional African stress on personal uniqueness. As Hill Collins puts it, "Rooted in a tradition of African humanism, each individual is thought to be a unique expression of a common spirit, power, or energy expressed by all life."[64] I thus argue that Oprah Winfrey has derived her insistence on endurance, self-help, and the perfectibility of the self from African American culture, in particular, from an interpretation of the world that helped make sense of and bear suffering:

> The ethos prevailing in the African cultures from which the slaves came would have had little use for concepts of the absurd. Life was not random or accidental or haphazard. Events were meaningful; they had causes which Man could divine, understand, and profit from. Human beings could "read" the phenomena surrounding and affecting them because Man was part of, not alien to, the Natural Order of things, attached to the Oneness that bound together all matter, animate and inanimate, all spirits, visible or not.[65]

This holistic vision of meaning is at the heart of black spirituality. In addition to the African lore that accorded a hidden meaning to every occurrence, a strand of thought developed within Christian African American culture that emphasized the idea of redemptive suffering, that"there is something of value in Black suffering,"[66] and that—as Oprah Winfrey on almost every possible occasion puts it—"there is a lesson" in every misfortune. These different components of black culture have thus contributed to making the theme of self-help prevalent in African American selfhood.

Oprah Winfrey's strong and even obsessive ethos of self-reliance shares with contemporary discourses of self-help a form of spirituality in which ordinary occurrences take on significance. The innermost corners of the psyche and the body have become the site for self-fashioning because everything—marriage, sex, identity—is up for grabs and because we are called upon endlessly to choose and fashion our social, mental, physiological, and even biological destiny. The normal biography becomes reflexive, a project to be achieved in every component and stage of life. For this reason, the self-made biography has turned to a variety of self-help discourses, which in turn draw on a variety of cultural sources: the Puritan tradition, the reigning ethos of economic liberalism, the psychotherapeutic worldview, and the New Age. The African American belief that all events have meaning and purpose became associated with the psychological worldview that suffering has meaning and that we can "profit" from it for self-knowledge and for psychological growth. This association provides us with an important key to understanding why the self-help ethos that pervades Oprah Winfrey has resonated so powerfully with American culture.

ANOTHER APPROACH TO POPULAR CULTURE

The cultural strategies deployed by Oprah Winfrey emanate from what Patricia Hill Collins calls "Black epistemology," a way of apprehending and knowing the world that derives from accumulated experience and cultural schemas to make sense of that experience. What defines such black epistemology is, according to Collins, an approach to the world based on wisdom rather than on formal knowledge. Wisdom is the knowledge that helps the subordinate survive gender, race, and class oppression.

The notion of wisdom is particularly relevant to sociologists because people use their own and others' accumulated experience as a guide through a constricting and constraining social structure. Bourdieu's notion of habitus allows no room for such an idea, because for him, experience can be accumulated only to either "make virtue out of necessity" or increase the various forms of capital at one's disposal. Yet, like the notion of habitus, the notion of wisdom contains and implies a tacit knowledge of the world derived from a habitual response to it and from it, basaed on concrete experience. Wisdom entails also a more dynamic relation to one's experience and the ability to reflect on it so as to learn how to act strategically. Moreover, unlike habitus, which reflects and reproduces the inequality of economic positions, wisdom is likely to be particularly developed among those who have had to face arbitrary and unpredictible forces. As Bloomfield and Dunn put it, practical wisdom "enables us to act and choose so as to move in harmony with the world."[67]

As I have suggested, *The Oprah Winfrey Show* is deeply grounded in the moral tradition of African American culture and, I now add, in its wisdom. Oprah's persona mixes attributes of traditional media celebrities as well as of the bearers of wisdom in traditional societies. Thus, her show conveys and performs what Bloomfield and Dunn have dubbed "the role of the poet in early societies," which is to enact and transmit wisdom, roughly defined as "everyday philosophy inherited from earlier generations. Practical wisdom rests on a sapiential view of the world, the view that the world makes sense, possesses order, rules, and patterns to which individuals if they wish happiness must conform, and that everything has its proper place and time."[68] Indeed, congruent with the view offered in chapters 3, 4, and 5—that Oprah Winfrey makes sense of the uncanny conditions of modern life and its attendant forms of suffering and provides symbolic tools to process them in a narrative of healing and self-change—we may say that wisdom enables us "to control by either action or understanding the arbitrary and the unusual."[69] According to Bloomfield and Dunn, wisdom is the early form of a rational mode of thought; it seeks to impart order, meaning, and predictability to the world. Therefore, popular culture—when and inasmuch as it connects itself to traditional wisdom—is a form of "rational thinking" that tries to bring order to chaos.

This view of wisdom is very illuminating because it suggests that popular culture is not only, as many postmodern accounts have suggested, cacophonous or carnivalesque. Rather, it provides meaningful reflections on reality and attempts to manage and transform that reality. I argue that our contemporary popular culture, like wisdom, often takes the form of convoluted ruminations about evil and about the art of making do with failing or failed lives.

This goes against both critics and advocates of popular culture. For, whether it is indicted as a mere industry of consciousness or redeemed as a site of production of "pleasure" and "resistance," popular culture is deemed radically antithetical to rational thought. In the end, both critics and advocates agree that it does not (or cannot) engage us in moral reflection. I suggest here that many elements of popular culture "ruminate about" the political and philosophical assumptions of contemporary polities and that the murkiness of popular culture is closer to the clarity of philosophers than media critics or apologists often suggest. Popular culture is cacophonic, but it also contains definite philosophical interrogations such as "What does it mean to be an autonomous self?" "What do we owe to each other?" and "Why do we suffer?" In other words, popular culture should not be taken seriously only when it engages us in pleasure, semiotic inventiveness, and play.[70] It should also be taken seriously because it articulates interrogations that are not the sole prerogative of professional philosophers.[71] To be sure, philosophical inquiry proceeds by formal reasoning and argumentation, while the stories of popular culture interrogate social reality and moral codes through "highly energized symbols," stories, morality plays, icons, and performances. But, as several philosophers have argued,[72] ordinary language, stories, plays, and metaphors are also powerful ways of interrogating philosophical meanings. Like literature and art, popular culture articulates some of the questions that are fundamental to modern and postmodern selves: What is the price of autonomy? What is and what ought to be the relation between individuals and institutions? What is the meaning of marriage and sexuality for men and women in the contemporary era?

Undoubtedly, this understanding of popular culture deviates from current paradigms. But it is congruent with the accounts of traditional premodern popular culture provided by such historians as Peter Burke, Nathalie Zemon-Davies, Robert Darnton, and even Lawrence Levine. Each, in different ways, has pointed to the ways in which popular culture is deeply moral in its preoccupation with questions of order, merit, and justice. Current sociologists have been oblivious to this aspect of popular culture, however, usually viewing its moral content as an ersatz middle-class "hegemony."

For example, Lawrence Levine's remarkable study of Shakespeare examines how the cultural location of Shakespeare moved historically from entertainment to highbrow canon. But Levine's analysis also indicates what made Shakespeare "popular" in the nineteenth century: his work resonated powerfully with the century's values and was incorporated into a moral discourse of right and wrong. That era's uses of Shakespearian tragedy emphasized melodrama, emotional expressiveness, and most of all, a moral outlook: "language and style in American productions of Shakespeare were not utilized randomly; they were used to inculcate values, to express ideas and attitudes. . . . From the beginning, Shakespeare's American admirers and promoters maintained that he was preeminently a moral playwright."[73] This is precisely what made this appropriation of Shakespeare "popular" and sets it apart from its later highbrow appropriation.

If morality is that which interrogates the meaning of conflicting commitments and inquires about the content of good lives, then we may say that Oprah Winfrey offers a supremely moral genre, and in that respect she revives what I believe is a core component of popular culture. As Michael Walzer put it so well in *The Company of Critics*, "the everyday world is a moral world, and we would do better to study its internal rules, maxims, conventions, and ideals, rather than to detach ourselves from it in search of a universal and transcendent standpoint."[74]

This is, to be sure, one of the ways in which literature and high art have been interpreted. Philosophers have been increasingly claiming that literature has much to teach us about the moral life. I suggest that we extend this claim to popular culture, even if it is obvious that popular culture too often offers a cramped and constrained space in which to engage in such discussions. Television, far from blunting this moral voice, uses it, and undoubtedly builds its own broad support from its ability to engage us in a form of moral interrogation.

TOWARD AN IMPURE CRITIQUE
OF POPULAR CULTURE

"This whole class," she said. "It's just bullshit every week. It's one critic after another wringing their hands about the state of criticism. Nobody can ever quite say what's wrong exactly. But they all know it's evil. They all know "corporate" is a dirty word. And if somebody's having fun or getting rich — disgusting! Evil! And it's always the death of this and the death of that. And the people who think they're free aren't 'really' free. And people who think they're happy aren't 'really' happy. And it's impossible to radically critique society anymore, although what's so radically wrong with society that we need such a radical critique, nobody can say exactly."

—Jonathan Franzen, *The Corrections*

I have spent most of this book trying to understand the meaning of the cultural enterprise of Oprah Winfrey. In this final chapter, I discuss the ways she has been criticized, and offer my own critique of her cultural and moral enterprise.

Critique and understanding are two notoriously antinomic intellectual postures. To understand is to reduce as much as possible the distance from the observed in order to grasp their point of view. In that sense, in understanding there is always the risk of endorsing the point of view we study, espousing the social world and its faults with the "happy consciousness" that reconciles us with it. On the other hand, to critique is to apply a point of view heterogeneous to the object under consideration. Critique thus contains the risk of remaining external and oblivious to the internal meaning and function of the object examined. Critical theorists such as Theodor Adorno, Max Horkheimer, and Leo Lowenthal have been famously indicted as elitists who hide their distaste for (and misunderstanding of) popular culture under a patronizing discourse of emancipation.[1] Thus, critique not only may fail to understand the meaning of social practices but also might — and often does — do violence to them as well.

At face value, the postmodern approach to culture represents a way out of this conundrum. Gamson's analysis of talk shows can be taken as an example of postmodern critique characterized by "systematic ambivalence," a refusal to endorse the point of view of an object or critique it. To quote him: "There is in fact *no choice here between manipulative spectacle and democratic forum*, only the puzzle of a situation in which one cannot exist without the other, and the challenge of seeing clearly what this means for a society at war with its own sexual diversity"[2] (emphasis added). In her analysis of the Book of the Month Club, A *Feeling for Books*, Janice Radway displays a similar ambivalence toward her object of study as she confesses to being both fascinated by the "middle brow" genre and critical of its implicit ideology.[3]

For the traditional critic—who views her role as that of defending a political and moral standpoint—this ambivalence is one of the most devastating and disempowering effects of postmodernism, the main cultural sensibility of late capitalism. In its incessant play of differences, late capitalism leaves us deeply perplexed and ambivalent, because it addresses contradictory desires, speaks to all, and uses a variety of points of view, thus undermining the very ability to wage a coherent and sustained critique.[4] These are indeed difficult times for critique, because postmodernism has cut the branch on which cultural critique used to sit in that liberal culture is premised on the respect for a variety of forms of life and cultural expression, which makes it more difficult to prefer and privilege one moral content over another.

In this chapter, I argue that we should resist the postmodern call to abandoning critique because sociology's vocation *is* critical, that is, deeply involved with the question of which social arrangements and meanings can enhance or cripple human creativity and freedom. However, the metanarratives that enabled the activity of critique have been seriously challenged—we cannot any longer engage in cultural critique "innocently," by presuming to know in advance what texts ought to say and how. We cannot presume that its categories—whatever they may be—can be transparently applied to a text. What may remain of critique given these constraints is what I examine now.

IN PRAISE OF IMPURE CRITIQUE

Traditional critique, from the left or from the right, is characterized by what I suggest calling a longing for purity. Indeed, if many critics accord a great deal of importance to culture, it is because they view it as the realm within which we can (and ought to) articulate ideals (of beauty, morality, and politics) and form valuable selves. These assumptions become obvious when we examine the various critiques that have been launched against talk shows in general and against Oprah Winfrey in particular.

Conservative critics believe culture ought to instill self-discipline and impulse control for the sake of civility and morality. It is therefore not surprising that these critics worry about the fact that talk shows celebrate "impulse over restraint, notoriety over achievement, rule-breaking over rule keeping and incendiary expression over civility."[5] William Bennett is one of the most forceful representatives of this view of culture, which has led him to claim that talk shows signal "cultural rot": they dangerously celebrate indecent exposure as virtue, herald the disappearance of guilt or embarrassment, and confuse normality and deviance.[6] In this brand of critique, culture should teach us the difficult art of moral discrimination and classification. When culture does not accomplish anymore this function, the entire civilization is threatened, because only when culture represents the "best" of our thoughts and values can society instill order, discipline, and commitment. Thus what cultural conservatives find particularly dangerous is not that some of the culture produced is "vulgar" but rather that it has become increasingly difficult to distinguish between valuable and vulgar creations. Conservative critique can thus be characterized by its implicit but forceful assumption that cultural classification (distinguishing between "good" and "bad," "high" and "low") shapes and strengthens moral judgment, and that its collapse indicates the demise of morality and virtue. It is because talk shows annul the possibility of classifying cultural objects that they signal what an editorial in USA Today called "a vulgar morass."[7]

The idea that culture has an "elevating" mission has also been endorsed in the liberal ideal of the public sphere. The public sphere should present issues that are significant, as opposed to trivial, and should do this by following rules and procedures of impartiality and fairness. Despite its principled commitment to freedom of speech, the liberal model of the public sphere is nonetheless predicated on the assumption that only problems that are of public interest are worthy of our attention, thus relying on an implicit hierarchy distinguishing between trivial and important issues (the former being often associated with the private sphere and with the feminine). A public sphere that confuses the trivial and the important becomes impoverished and, to use the words of a New Republic editorial, the mark of an "idiot culture."[8] Thus, liberal critics are as frequently unhappy about talk shows as conservatives, because in their view, talk shows seriously diminish the ability to discriminate between what matters for political discourse and what obfuscates it, which means that they also seriously impair the activity of judgment and discrimination.

Despite their variety in content and political allegiance, these critiques all have in common the view that culture ought to elevate us and enact moral and political values, such as "civility," "equality," and "fairness." I suggest calling such critiques "pure critique."[9] Pure critique informs liberal as well as conservative approaches to culture, and can be characterized by a number of common assumptions. The first concerns the relationship between "entertainment" and culture. For most critics, entertainment is not only distinct from cultural forms that have an educational, artistic, political, or moral purpose but also inferior to them.[10] While the latter elevate us through effort, thought, and an orientation toward the public good, the former is less valuable, as it makes too few demands on our intellect and moral behavior.[11] For example, evaluating the Oprah Winfrey Book Club, cultural commentator Martha Bayles suggests that although the club suffers from the blockbuster mentality and from the feeling that the culture either lacks a center or has surrendered its center to the wrong people, it nonetheless provides "something uplifting."[12] Because books are viewed as effortful, serious, and socially useful, they are more than simply entertaining.

Closely associated with this assumption is the claim that cultural material is noxious when it distorts reality. To take only one of the most famous examples, Gerbner and Gross's study of prime-time television has argued with an impressive amount of data that television entertainment distorts reality by overrepresenting policemen and criminals, thus giving an inaccurate image of the world as a "violent and mean" place.[13] Implicit in this research is the claim that cultural material ought to be truthful to demographic and sociological reality, so as to help us evaluate distortions and manipulations. This proposition is at the center of a great deal of research on the relationship between minorities and the media, the purpose of which is to examine whether media content reflects accurately their actual demographic proportions, and whether minority representations perpetuate racial, gender, and sexual stereotypes.

A third assumption is that culture ought to conform to moral standards beneficial to the public good, whether they are defined as respect for religious tradition, equality for all social groups, or an energetic public sphere. In this view, culture ought to reflect good political arrangements but also contribute to them. Culture then ought to foster virtues and values with the ultimate aim of producing worthwhile political and moral communities of meaning.

This is indeed the cardinal assumption of the activity of cultural critique, deeply buried in critical theory as well as in communitarian critiques of culture: that culture ought to represent values conducive to the "good society" (whether it is defined by more equality and freedom or by more religion and tradition). While conservatives and cultural critics of Marxian inspiration may quibble about the content of the good society, they ultimately agree that it ought to guide the production as well as the critique of culture.

Interestingly, most attempts to defend popular culture against its detractors have operated on similar assumptions, arguing that popular culture furthers political and moral ideals. For example, talk shows have been defended by the fact that they provide a new democratic forum.[14] Gamson's analysis illustrates this, as he has suggested that talk shows have significantly altered the politics of invisibility and symbolic annihilation of sexual minorities, thus contributing, albeit in an indirect way, to their political advancement. To give another example provided by a feminist writer, talk shows have also been praised for "making visible and palpable the changes and the sexual revolution of the sixties, which has become so stifled in the conservative climate of the 1980s.'"[15] Thus, both the indictment and the defense of talk shows are waged in reference to a certain vision of the political bond, an unflinching political narrative, be it liberal or conservative.

To be sure, the political point of view provides a convenient vantage point from which to observe culture and exert our authority as "professionals" of culture studies; moreover, if the central task of cultural critique is, to use Terry Eagleton's words, to be engaged with the "struggle against all forms of absolutism,"[16] pure cultural critique is unusually well equipped to achieve this task. However, such an approach has become increasingly problematic. I will try to explain briefly why.

In the first place, by making popular culture ancillary to the political sphere, we run the risk of turning our analysis into the counting of the many ways in which popular culture either emancipates or represses, delivers trash or treasure, a position that threatens to impoverish our analysis because, to use Barbara Johnson's cogent words, critique ought to leave "room for a surprise . . . for someone or something to surprise you and say 'Stand aside, I want to speak.'"[17] For texts to surprise us, we need to stop reducing them to their ability (or inability) to deliver a clear political or moral stand on the world.

The second drawback of pure critique is that it usually demands nothing less than a *total* point of view: when I claim that a given television program is noxious to the cause of women, I do so in terms of the economic, political, and domestic social spheres. In other words, this critique is achieved by assuming that one sphere (the cultural) both reflects and shapes other social spheres (the economic, the political, the domestic) and is functionally and dialectically related to them through a "higher" social logic. This view in turn assumes that different spheres are transparent to each other, that is, that one sphere mirrors the values and dynamics of others. The assumption that culture ought to be analyzed from the standpoint of all social spheres, that it is to society what a part is to the whole, is the cornerstone of critical theory.

In contrast, I suggest that there is no continuity or transparency between social spheres. This means that we cannot know *a priori* how symbols and values will "behave" in the social, political, and economic spheres. This is essentially because of the famous problem of unintended effects brilliantly analyzed by Max Weber: principles of action, ideas, and values that emerge in one sphere (e.g., the religious) can give rise to something quite different from what they originally intended in another sphere (e.g., the economic). To put it more simply: what can be backward in one sphere can be progressive for another and vice versa.[18]

Another problem in predicating cultural analysis on political critique is that culture and politics use language in different ways, so they will inevitably clash with each other. A politician is summoned to use language in a referential way, pointing toward a realm of praxis in which roads are built and wars fought and taking a clear stand vis-à-vis "reality" (for example, he must say clearly whether he favors raising or cutting taxes). In contrast, a poem or a movie is not summoned to refer to reality and cannot be held accountable for distorting it. In fact, a poem or a movie can do just that—say two contradictory things at the same time (e.g., praise individualism and community, love and duty), without violating norms of communication. Moreover, a politician is summoned to tell the truth and to make valid claims (he might lie or err, of course, but will always be held accountable for doing so). We may criticize a poem or a movie for being too realistic or not realistic enough, but it would hardly make any sense to criticize it for "lying" or for not understanding inflation or unemployment. By the same token, using political criteria to evaluate popular culture is not as straightforward as it seems, for the simple reason that popular texts are often self-consciously and deliberately ambiguous, ironic, reflexive, self-contradictory, and paradoxical. All of these are properties of television no less than of other cultural creations and exceed the field of politics, at least as it is traditionally understood.[19] While culture is indisputably an extension of our social relations in its systematic silences, closures, and oppositions, it cannot be wholly contained by and subsumed under the political.

There is a final (and much glossed) problem in subsuming culture under politics: it frequently condemns the critic to an Olympian distance, increasingly untenable in an era when cultural democracy reigns supreme. Adorno's rejection of jazz is only one of the most famous examples of such radical (and mistaken) detachment from the concrete experiences and meanings from which culture springs. Critique is most forceful when it is grounded in a deep understanding of the concrete cultural practices of ordinary actors. Unavoidably, this entails a "compromise" with purity. But this is all the more necessary because in the era of late capitalism, whether by choice or by necessity, the critic of contemporary culture is condemned to be located within the very commodified arena she criticizes. The nineteenth-century intellectual could criticize capitalism and yet be located somewhere outside its reach, but few contemporary critiques can be proffered out of the compass of capitalist institutions and organizations. This does not mean we should resign ourselves to accepting the domination of capitalism over all social spheres. But it implies that we should develop strategies of interpretation that are as cunning as the market forces we want to oppose. Powerful critiques derive from an intimate understanding of their object. It is not by accident that the best critiques to have emerged in the last decade have been those that have combined critique and understanding. Paul Willis and Janice Radway produce the best examples of what I suggest calling "impure critique,"[20] for both work at the juncture and articulation of critique and understanding. This is pertinent to my object of analysis because Oprah Winfrey works at the interface of moral leadership, entertainment, psychology, capitalist enterpreneurship, spiritual quest, comic performance, and literature. It is indeed difficult to hold on to a single political or moral point of view to approach her text. Thus my point is emphatically not to dispose of critique, but rather to engage in a critique that does not become the "counting of the ways" in which culture promotes (or fails to promote) a given political agenda (equality, emancipation, or visibility). This suggestion is consistent with the goals of critical theory itself as explained by David Held:

> The method or procedure (of critical theory) is immanent criticism. . . . Social theory, developed through immanent criticism, is concerned to investigate (aspects of) the social world "in the movement of its development." It starts with the conceptual principles and standards of an object, and unfolds their implications and consequences. Critique proceeds, so to speak, "from within" and hope to avoid, thereby, the charge that its concepts impose irrelevant criteria of evaluation of the object."[21]

Unfortunately, this understanding of critical theory has not been sufficiently heeded, as both critical theorists and their followers seem to have too often remained "outside" their object.

A model of "immanent critique" has been best developed by political philosopher Michael Walzer, who, in his thought-provoking *Spheres of Justice*,[22] claims that we should apply different principles of justice to different social spheres (say, the family or the market). This is because each sphere contains different kinds of goods (love or money), which must be distributed differently. Walzer has famously argued for different spheres of justice, that is, for the idea that different social spheres are animated by different principles that define what in them is valuable and how to distribute equitably the resources to reach those goods. In two later books, *The Company of Critics*[23] and *Criticism and Values*,[24] Walzer has extended his argument to the activity of critique and has argued that in order to criticize a cultural practice, the cultural critic ought to use the moral criteria at work within the community (or social sphere) she or he is examining. In a similar vein, the impure critique I suggest means developing criteria of evaluation that are as much as possible internal to the traditions, standards, and meanings of the object we analyze.[25]

This mode of engaging in critique is not new. In fact, it stands squarely at the center of psychoanalysis. As is well known, the aim of traditional analysis is to "liberate" the patient from her masked consciousness by questioning the very assumptions, images, and metaphors that structure her inner world.[26] But this liberation, if it happens, can occur only when both therapist and patient have gained a deep understanding of the world of meanings the patient inhabits. The interpretative method of the psychoanalyst is thus a mix of deep understanding, generated by and in collaboration with the patient's own self-understandings, and critique, a questioning of habits of thought and feeling induced by the patient's own speech. More exactly, this critique is generated through dialogue and the opening of alternative metaphors and fields of vision. Importantly, it is always based on the patient's own discourse. The fragile dialogue between the (psycho)analyst's authority and a person's self-understandings generates a process of self-examination and self-change. This process does not rest on an Olympian point of view and does not presume a total point of view. Cultural critique ought to be similar in structure: both the sociologist's and the (psycho)analyst's critical understanding ought to emerge from a subtle dialogue that challenges reality by understanding it from within its own set of meanings. Cultural critique is better if it refuses to censor and arbitrate good taste and instead tries to recover the claims and meanings of texts or actors.

CRITIQUE #1: TALK SHOWS VS.
THE IDEAL OF THE PUBLIC SPHERE

In the following sections, I review various critiques of talk shows and argue that precisely because they are "pure" critiques, they misunderstand their object, offer ritual reaffirmations of the moral or aesthetic categories of the critic, and frequently do not sustain careful analysis. Let me start with an example.

> [OPRAH:] We're talking today to juveniles under the age of 18 on death row. My next guest was convicted of three murders. He killed his mother, his stepfather, and a convenience store clerk. His defense argued that he was under the influence of Satan at the time of those killings and tried to save the youngster from the death penalty with no success. He is scheduled to be executed in July 1987. Please meet Sean Sellers [the young man on death row]. Sean, welcome to the show. Tell me what happened on the night you killed your parents.
>
> [SEAN:] Well, that would be pretty hard for me to talk about it right now, I said everything to Op—excuse me, to Sylvia Tomkin of *People* magazine. And the whole story is pretty much there. . . .
>
> [later in the interview]
>
> [OPRAH:] Were you in the courtroom when you heard the sentence? Where were you when you heard it?
>
> [SELLERS:] Yes, I was.
>
> [WINFREY:] What was your feeling when you realized that you had been sentenced to death?
>
> [SELLERS:] It was a very scary feeling you know, just scared mostly.

The classical model of the public sphere cannot admit five elements contained in this vignette: a) that fear—an emotion rather than an idea—occupies the space of public discourse; b) that the deviant lives in the same space as the "normal" and has the same "right" to speak; c) that this man's voice addresses us directly, without the mediation of an expert, solely authorized to speak for the deviant; d) that this young man appeals to our (emotional) identification with his fear, rather than engages us in a rational deliberation on his moral faults; and e) that entertainment is inextricably related to such a serious problem as the death penalty. In a classical model of the public sphere, we would have been more likely to hear a report denouncing the worrisome statistics of young males waiting on death row, psychologists quibbling about the age at which we can expect an adolescent to bear moral responsibility, or conservative leaders claiming that children must be protected from the dark forces of destruction encouraged by a permissive culture. In other words, we would have heard a mass of experts offering us intransitive speech about the juvenile inmates, that is, a speech about them but never to them or from them to us. In the traditional public sphere, experts talk to us about others but almost never let subjects—especially if they are destitute—address the audience directly. Oprah violates norms of the public sphere not because of the nature of the problems she raises per se but because of the mode of speech in which she casts these problems.

But why is intransitive speech such an essential part of our model of the public sphere? This model is predicated on the claim that it should be the realm the activity of reason, expressed in impartial speech. In traditional democratic theory, the public sphere is supposed to enable people to engage in rational discourse and discuss ideas in a neutral way, undisturbed by emotions and by particular allegiances; this task is best achieved by experts' intransitive speech. In the model of the public sphere that is at the heart of liberalism, the most important objective of a liberal society is to set up rules of debate—or in Bruce Ackerman's words, of "conversation"[27]—that guarantee the exchange of points of view of people who disagree with each other but can simultaneously assume a neutral point of view. The idea of the public sphere is based on the assumption that participants can both disagree with each other and speak from a detached standpoint aiming at the public good.[28]

Indubitably, *The Oprah Winfrey Show* deviates dramatically from this structure and in more than one respect represents a symbolic pollution of the "pure" categories of liberal political philosophy, reason, objectivity, and neutrality. Oprah Winfrey has brought to the public sphere the spectacle of tears, heartbreaking reunions, diseased bodies, broken families, addictions, self-destructive behavior, uncontrollable drives, anger, revenge, and illicit lust, and most of all has made the family into the subject and object of debate, thus abolishing the ideal of a public sphere guided by critical reason and impartial speech. It is precisely because they deviate from these norms of speech that talk shows are perceived as a threat to cultural norms and ideals. For example, in their article suggestively entitled "The Shameless World of Phil, Sally and Oprah: Television Talk Shows and the Deconstructing of Society,"[29] Abt and Seesholtz suggest that "television talk shows privatize our social concerns while collapsing boundaries between public and private spheres."[30] Against this view, I argue that what maintains this boundary in the public sphere is not any given kind of topic, but rather who can raise a problem and through what kind of language.

In contradistinction to a Habermasian account of the public sphere, I argue that the public sphere, from the start, admitted two forms of speech, one emotional, the other aiming at neutrality. The vocation of the public sphere was to make us aware of distant forms of injustice and suffering and to create a relationship to these objects through imagination, compassion, and our identification with a person in her subjectivity and particularity.[31] As already briefly discussed in chapter 6, the eighteenth-century public sphere not only was a Habermasian disembodied space of discussion for rational actors but also invited one to reflect on the order and principles that organize the world through the simultaneous use of philosophical debate and invocation of such emotions as empathy, compassion, and guilt.[32] Thus, the project of the public sphere contained from the start two languages, each aiming at a different kind of universality: the dispassionate language of reason and another language appealing to what many eighteenth-century philosophers thought of as a universal capacity of the imagination, compassion, and sympathy, which, by definition, are geared only to concrete, specific people.[33] In that sense, the faculty of imagination required by the public sphere is as emotional as it is cognitive, and is far from the required neutral discourse associated with procedural liberalism. This brings me to my first observation: Oprah Winfrey's intensive use of compassion and emotions is not heretical to the classical project of the public sphere but rather a direct outcome of the early ambivalence of the public sphere about the representation of suffering others.

I suggest a further point. The impassioned speech of Voltaire and Zola was receivable in the traditional public sphere because both were males situated at the top of the cultural hierarchy: when a denunciation is made by men and concerns male issues (the Jewish officer unjustly accused of having betrayed the French army), it belongs almost automatically to the public sphere. When a woman asks batterers why they engage in domestic violence, this form of speech is defined as sensationalist, because, I submit, it is proferred by a woman, concerns the domestic sphere, and equalizes perpetrator and victim in the subjectivity of their speech.

CRITIQUE #2: VOYEURISM

The second most frequent and vehement critique against talk shows is that, as the aforementioned example amply illustrates, they put viewers in a position of voyeurs, where they are made to watch—or worse, can enjoy watching—something that ought to remain, to use Hannah Arendt's beautiful expression, within "the shadowy realm of the interior."[34] While conservatives attribute this voyeurism to a culture of facile self-indulgence, liberals attribute it to the cynical and endless search for profit that animates the media industry. Another version of this is Jean Baudrillard's critique of the "ecstasy of communication." Baudrillard defines the obscene in contemporary culture as that which "is the visible, the all-too-visible, the more-visible-than-visible."[35] Obscenity for Baudrillard is overrepresentation, an attribute suitable to and characteristic of talk shows, which he opposes to an absence or economy of representation.

The accusation of voyeurism is imprecise and contains two different claims. "Voyeurism" expresses a transgression of the proper distance we should mark between our own and others' private space. Voyeurism undermines the dignity that ought to be bestowed on the public sphere and the private life by maintaining the proper distance between them. But it contains another moral problem: the voyeur not only trangresses the boundary between private and public but also takes pleasure in doing so. However, suffering poses a slightly different problem than sexual voyeurism. Although both sex and suffering have been intensely privatized, the spectacle of suffering, contrary to the spectacle of sex, cannot admit at any point the feeling of pleasure (in contrast, we can and must enjoy sex, as long as it is confined to the private sphere). To enjoy the spectacle of suffering is thus doubly immoral, because it is an infringement on a person's privacy and therefore dignity and because it is inappropriate—suffering should elicit another type of moral response, such as compassion or indignation.

However, the critique of voyeurism is oblivious to the fact that aggressive voyeurism has been present in cultural quarters that critics otherwise admire, as, for example, eighteenth-century sentimental literature. In her excellent study, historian Karen Halttunen has clarified that this literature was based on "a literary scenario which made ethics a matter of viewing the pain of another" and that "from the outset [it] lent itself to an aggressive kind of voyeurism. In this literature, pleasure mixed with pain, and pain with pleasure, in an eighteenth-century culture of sensibility intensely preoccupied with both."[36] Indeed, in such classical novels as Richardson's *Pamela* and Rousseau's *Julie ou La Nouvelle Heloise*, heroines' misery and abundant tears were a mark of their virtue; thus, this genre solicited the reader in a mode of viewing in which suffering was morally uplifting and emotionally reinvigorating. These observations are not meant to suggest that voyeurism is a morally appropriate response but that "high" culture itself contains many voyeuristic elements, in the sense that it combines the spectacle of suffering with aesthetic pleasure. However, in contradistinction to popular culture, the voyeurism of high culture is not—or is rarely—decried.

More: the mixture of pleasure (or entertainment) and the spectacle of misery has also been translated by high culture into aesthetic experience. For example, the tragedy—considered to be the most "highbrow" of all literary genres—notoriously solicits an artful mix of horror and pleasure. Pity and fear, the two components of tragedy according to Aristotle, can become catharsis only when we process them in an aesthetic form. In a similar vein, in a famous essay on aesthetics, Lessing discusses a masterpiece known as the group sculpture of Laocoon—a man and his two sons strangled by a snake. Lessing suggests that what makes this piece a remarkable aesthetic achievement is the fact that its artist knew how to balance Laocoon's pain and horror with the aesthetic desire to please the eye of the watcher.[37] The famous problem he explores in this essay is how to know how much suffering can be depicted in order for the viewer not to turn away his eyes from the work of art and to enjoy its beauty. Here again, high culture offers a confusing mix of pain and pleasure that is never perceived as voyeuristic because it is sublimated under the category of the aesthetic.

My final objection to the accusation of voyeurism has to do with the fact that it misses an important element of popular culture. The cultural mixture of pain and suffering is frequently an essential ingredient of traditional forms of healing. Discussing therapeutic performances, the anthropologists Carol Laderman and Marina Roseman state that "Techniques of aesthetic distancing often rely upon a willing suspension of disbelief, and combine experiences of pleasure and pain, as evidenced by the interweaving of awesome scenes with comic episodes that not only relieve tension but also provide critical comments about status, class, religion, politics, and relations between the sexes."[38] To criticize such a mixture in the name of the moral separation between the realms of pleasure and pain is to misunderstand its healing function. With regard to Oprah Winfrey, it is important to recall that black culture is characterized by a great attention to suffering combined with laughter, humor, and hope in the face of adversity, which suggests that the mixture of humor and suffering is a culturally bound form of therapeutic, tension-releasing laughter.

CRITIQUE #3: THE COMMODIFICATION OF SENTIMENTS

The third—and, to sociologists, perhaps the most familiar—critique of television in general is that it commodifies culture. This critique starts from the moral intuition that human suffering ought not be recycled into something else—be it an "interesting" image, a good story, or a media commodity. To go back to the example of the young man on death row: at the same time that we, the viewers, are taken into the eerie space of a prison cell and are told what will prove to be a ghastly murder story, we are thrown into the commercial reality of a television talk show: when asked to tell his story, the inmate answers that, in fact, he has already sold his story to a magazine, thus rendering visible the commercial environment underpinning the gruesome spectacle. Such guests' life stories are the flesh and blood that have helped constitute Oprah Winfrey's phenomenal wealth. Thus we, the viewers, are made accomplices in what seems to be an unprincipled commerce of misery, in which private misfortune is traded for advertisement slots.

Many scholars worry about the fact that the media make a cynical use of suffering. For example, anthropologist Arthur Kleinman says that "the globalization of suffering is one of the more troubling signs of the cultural transformations of the current era: troubling because experience is being used as a commodity, and through this cultural representation of suffering, experience is being remade, thinned out, and distorted."[39] Kleinman is troubled because the experience of suffering is transformed into something that is qualitatively different—entertainment and an aestheticization of suffering—and is incorporated in the predatory commercial engine of capitalism. Behind this critique lies the Kantian moral imperative that we not profit from others' experiences and that we keep separate commerce and sentiment, interests and passions. The argument about the commodification of suffering is all the more troubling because many talk shows guests are clearly socially and economically destitute.

This critique is especially pertinent in Oprah Winfrey's case because she has accumulated extraordinary wealth, more than any other television host. What is properly exploitative is that her primary commodity—her guests' stories—is "free," so to speak; that is, it requires very little production costs, thus enabling unprecedented profits. The argument of commodification views this as twice objectionable: the "authors" of the stories are unpaid, and the stories of misfortunes are recycled and integrated for large profits in a commercial entertainment circuit.

I suggest that this argument is not as straightforward as meets the eye. For one, the true inventor of the commodification of suffering and private life was Freud, not television or Oprah Winfrey. The classical therapeutic relation is premised on the fact that it is a monetary transaction. In fact, the therapeutic session works according the logic of the advertising slot on TV: what is sold is time. More: what makes the professional therapeutic encounter effective is precisely that it is contained within the rigid time frame of the therapeutic session—a time frame that is exchanged for money. The therapeutic session, no less than the talk show, fits the capitalistic logic of the commodification of time and services. Whether talk shows are truly "therapeutic" is beside the point. What interests me here is that while the upper-class commodification of private life is almost never questioned—because abundantly justified by experts and institutions—the commodification of lower-class private life is systematically decried and denounced.

Second, it is unclear whether the fact that the guests perform an "unpaid" narrative labor is a case of commodification. I argue that it is as morally problematic to pay for people's stories as it is not to. The current situation preserves one of the most central tenets of our normative fabric, namely that private life, emotions, and suffering ought to remain outside the logic of monetary exchange. This is, I believe, the reason the guests' biographies are traded following the economy of the gift and are not paid for with money. Oprah's guests are flown to Chicago and provided with hotel rooms in a form of equalitarian payment that does not make class distinctions among guests.[40] Thus, while there is no doubt that the fact that her guests are not paid has been a key element explaining Oprah's quick access to phenomenal wealth, from a normative standpoint, it maintains the boundary between commodity exchange and storytelling, in the sense that it does not attach a price tag to different life stories. In fact, in a memorable battle to obtain an exclusive interview with Monica Lewinski, Oprah Winfrey stood firm in her determination not to pay for Lewinski's appearance—contrary to the policy of other programs or networks. This suggests, quite ironically, that Oprah "de-commodifies" the media, because none of her guests, from the Nobel Prize winner to the most obscure unemployed person, is given a price tag derived from their position in the market of celebrity. Oprah Winfrey's uses of biography is based on a staunch refusal to attribute a pecuniary value to life stories and to rank her guests' stories accordingly. Her talk show is compelling precisely because of the implicit pact that stipulates that the guests are not motivated by pecuniary considerations but rather by emotional ones. This, of course, does not mean that the media organizations that produce the show are not predatory. But it means that there is a separation between the economic benefit they draw from the talk show and the normative principles that animate the relationship between the program and its guests.

There is a final argument to be considered here. Conventional wisdom has it that the more commercial a medium is, the more it appeals to the lowest common denominator, understood as our "basest" and "lowest" instincts. I suggest a different view inspired by philosopher Alexander Nehemas, who makes the following claim: the open-endedness, polysemy, and undecidability of television content derives precisely from the commercial desire to reach diverse audiences. Commercially driven ecumenism makes the text offer a multiplicity of points of view in an open-ended moral structure. This openness in turn enables people to engage in moral deliberations when attending the meaning of a television text.[41] This is congruent with the genre created by Oprah Winfrey: the moral ruminations and dilemmas she stages preserve the commercial ubiquity of her show. The amorality of the market promotes a cacophony of points of view that can, by an ironic twist of liberal polities, enlarge the scope of our moral imagination.

CRITIQUE #4: SUFFERING AGAINST JUSTICE

An additional critique of talk shows comes from the ranks of cultural critics for whom the use of compassion in the public sphere is problematic. This critique has been aptly formulated by Robert Hughes, who, in his book *The Culture of Complaint,* writes that "the vulgarity of confessional culture is stupefying. . . . There has always been a vulgarity of aggression, based on sex and violence; now American mass culture has a vulgarity of therapeutics, undreamed of twenty years ago."[42] Hughes, like many others, holds the view that the public sphere should restrain the expression of private feeling and that some important boundary between the two ought to be maintained. He proffers an additional and familiar critique: namely, that talk shows encourage and legitimize a culture of whining. He laments about what he calls "the all-pervasive claim to victimhood," which has infiltrated American culture. In this view, the representation of suffering makes us complacent and overindulgent. To suffer becomes an illegitimate form of pleasure, with the consequence that we do not take responsibility for our acts anymore. This view is echoed by legal scholar Alan Dershowitz, who believes Oprah has made jury members approach perpetrators and victims with the mentality of a social worker. Pursuing this line of thought, researchers Zillman and Bryant have argued that *The Oprah Winfrey Show* makes jurors become lenient, thus confusing "understanding" and justice.[43]

The same desire to separate legitimate political claims and victimhood has preoccupied feminists. For example, in her history of hysteria, Elaine Showalter distinguishes between the feminist denunciation of abuse, which was "about self-determination, action, and responsibility," and denunciation that is about "victimization and accusation."[44]

The idea that people secretly enjoy being victims because victimhood entitles them to undeserved rewards and privileges is one of the most frequent critiques of "victim culture" in general and of *The Oprah Winfrey Show* in particular. It derives partly from the fact that with the help of legislation, victims have increasingly made monetary claims on institutions, demanding reparations and damages for past and present suffering. Here again, the claim that victims enjoy telling their sad stories in public should be seriously qualified, for two reasons. First, one of the origins of the centrality of suffering in modern autobiographical narratives is to be found in psychoanalytical theory and practice. Indeed, writing about Freud, Peter Gay suggests that "this very suffering [of the patient] is an agent in the curative process." Precisely because of this, Freud declared in a congress at Budapest that: "We must see to it, cruel as it may sound, that the sufferings of the patient . . . do not come to an end prematurely."[45] To that extent, psychoanalysis may be said to have been the first secular cultural movement to bestow a positive value upon suffering in the process of identity making.

The second reason the critique of victim culture is not as straightforward as it seems has to do with the fact that in our culture, failure is hardly ever discussed, much less rewarded. As Richard Senett put it in his *Corrosion of Character*, "coming to terms with failure, giving it a shape and a place in one's life history, may haunt us internally but seldom is discussed with others."[46] I argue that until the era of talk shows, failure was, by and large, absent from public discourse. In this vein, Oprah Winfrey may play a useful role in breaking this public "spiral of silence" and making failure and suffering into acceptable public narratives of the self. The publicizing of victimhood has resulted in an increasing politization of the emotional and psychic "pain" used to make legal, financial, and political capital.

But perhaps the most interesting critique of the public uses of suffering comes from the writings of philosopher Hannah Arendt. In her less-read book, *On Revolution*,[47] she takes a stand against the uses of suffering in the public sphere because the spectacle of victims and sufferers entails a necessary asymmetry between ourselves and the oppressed. As Catherine Canovan, one of Arendt's most authoritative commentators, states, we should approach the oppressed and the exploited as equal partners in human dignity.[48] Arendt's call is for justice rather than sympathy, principle or "virtues" rather than emotion. The representation of suffering can not only distract us from cultivating the virtues that lead to genuine solidarity but also disguise itself as something far more pernicious. The problem is summarized by Canovan as follows:

Unlike compassion, which is a matter of direct fellow-feeling with a specific sufferer, pity is boundless. It can take in the entire imagined multitude of the unfortunate and feed upon it, battening upon suffering and turning it into a disguise for power-seeking and an excuse for cruelty . . . displaying personal feelings on the public stage is bound to distort them. . . . Those who, like Robespierre, were inspired by this kind of generalized pity, seemed to become immunised against compassion for the victims of their [own] policies. . . . Unfortunately, Arendt concludes, authentic human feelings cannot stand the glare of publicity without being perverted, so that "every effort to make goodness manifest in public ends with the appearance of crime and criminality on the political scene."[49]

However, here again Arendt's critique does not seem easily applicable to Oprah Winfrey, for two reasons. Arendt's suspicion of the public uses of suffering and of the mobilization of pity applies to the sphere of politics, in which sufferers are shown and sometimes paraded to make political claims and gains. Oprah's use of suffering differs in that it does not lean on the political sphere, but rather on transient communities that may or may not overlap with civil society but do not usually have a clear relationship to organized politics. Because the sufferer is always individualized and not, as in Arendt's scenario, a "mass," it can only rarely be used for political ends. Moreover, Arendt's view of the public sphere does not admit the possibility that morality can be based on compassion. I submit that Oprah offers another (female?) model of the public sphere, in which imaginative compassion and empathy with the plight of others are the main vectors to "encounter" distant others. This is a public sphere that displays all the characteristics of Carol Gilligan's "different voice,"[50] distinct from the detachment and "higher principles" to which traditional moralists have resorted to define the nature of moral reasoning. As Gilligan puts it, "Detachment is considered the hallmark of mature moral thinking within a justice perspective, signifying the ability to judge dispassionately, to weigh evidence in an evenhanded manner, balancing the claims of others and self. From a care perspective, detachment is *the* moral problem."[51] Moral emotions should be mobilized rather than pushed to the side, in order to foster moral attitude. As another feminist writer aptly says, "Such emotions as empathy, concerned for others, hopefulness, and indignation in the face of cruelty—all these may be crucial in developing appropriate moral positions."[52]

Let me therefore suggest that Oprah offers a model of public sphere in which the *voice*, not discourse, predominates. Literary scholar David B. Morris explains, "Voice matters precisely because suffering remains, to some degree, inaccessible. Voice is what gets silenced, repressed, preempted, denied, or at best translated into an alien dialect, much as clinicians translate a patient's pain into a series of units on a grid of audiovisual descriptors."[53] In other words, voice is opposed both to silence and to a form of speech predicated on the assumption that neutrality represents a higher form of morality. A public sphere of voice is necessarily more cacophonous, because it contains many voices and does not make a sustained argument. The inmate waiting for his death, the woman who has been abandoned by her fiancé on her wedding day, and the child who has been abused are all voices, in the sense that they express pain, violence, and injustice from the standpoint not of an abstract standard of justice but of their private and particular experience.

Seyla Benhabib provides additional arguments: "All struggles against oppression in the modern world begin by redefining what had previously been considered 'private,' non-public and non-political issues as matters of public concern, as issues of justice, as sites of power which need discursive legitimation."[54] The range of topics that can make up the public sphere must not be restricted, precisely because of the shifting definitions of what constitutes a "political struggle." To have a voice is essential to the democratic process. Even if there is no doubt that these voices have a higher pitch than we would like, they remain nonetheless voices we would not otherwise hear but that must be heard if we want to stretch the limits of our moral and institutional imagination.

CRITIQUE #5: SUFFERING AND ACCOUNTABILITY

In a famous lecture on Lessing,[55] Arendt makes a further point against the uses of compassion in the public sphere: they abolish what is, in Arendt's view, vital to the political bond, namely what she calls "in-betweenness," a distance within which discourse and dialogue about the world can flow. In contrast, because it is based on an immediate identification with the sufferer, compassion is not discursive. It is not about the world but about compressing as much as possible the distance between us and the world. Compassion does not discriminate between sufferers or forms of suffering; it exists only in the intensity and immediacy of its multiple identifications. Arendt suggests that because compassion reduces distance between people, it should be excluded from the realm of the public sphere. It follows that so, then, should psychic pain: since one is the only legislator of one's own trauma—because psychic pain is not observable or contestable—it cannot invite dialogue and debate.

Interestingly, although he is equally worried by the apolitical implications of compassion, anthropologist Arthur Kleinman has expressed an opposite critique: the problem of invoking compassion in the public sphere is that it rests on a real distance—between viewer and sufferer—converted into an illusion of closeness, which, I presume, Kleinman would like to see transformed into real closeness. If we watch pain from a distance, we do not feel responsible for others.[56] He suggests that television and media in general have made us the passive bystanders and witnesses of pain and cruelty, that they have routinized voyeurism, and that they do not offer a way of eliciting our moral local voice.

The spectacle of pain reduces distance and does not require a "reasonable" or "rational" discussion, only sympathetic understanding, because suffering overwhelms us with its presence and does not seem to require proofs or debate (while "poverty," for example, can and often does). Suffering—especially psychic suffering—comes into existence at the moment somebody claims to be suffering. Because of the assumptions we make about the radical privacy of our relationship to our body and psyche, we alone have the authority to pronounce on the intensity of our suffering. In that sense, suffering cannot invite dialogue or conversation. Moreover, what makes compassion incompatible with the imperative of justice is that when confronting a suffering person, we are asked to suspend judgment. The person makes a moral claim by the sheer fact and act of suffering, which neutralizes the possibility for others to contest the claim because our moral vocabulary is not equipped to describe hierarchies of suffering. It would indeed be morally distasteful to compare the plight of a poor single mother to that of a woman whose daughter has betrayed her by sleeping with the mother's recently wed husband. Even if we feel greater indignation at the spectacle of poverty than at the spectacle of a woman betrayed by her daughter, most of us will be reluctant to rank these two forms of suffering. As Oprah tellingly put it on her show (December 1, 1994), "One of my favorite Bible verses is 'Judge not that you be not judged,' because we really—we really—we don't know the whole life circumstances and her pain is her pain. We have no right to tell her what she should do with her pain or how she should be feeling." Compassion is not easily compatible with the imperative of justice, which relies on a hierarchical view of human suffering.

CRITIQUE #6: THE FLATTENING OF HIERARCHIES OF JUSTICE

One of the major reasons the image of the victim on talk shows is deeply problematic to our moral culture is that it flattens the moral point of view: it does not give us a privileged standpoint from which to judge others but rather makes everybody ultimately understandable in the subjectivity of their experiences. As George Mair, one of Oprah Winfrey's biographers, explains, "[the shows] lump human problems together and equalize them, which in fact trivializes them because 'Women Who Used to Be Men Marrying Men Who Used to Be Women' gets thrown in with 'Child Abuse.'"[57] This is echoed by Todd Gitlin's pessimistic assessment of contemporary American culture in general, which he sees as exemplified by Oprah Winfrey: "the academy has no monopoly on the decline of the claim to truth. Perspectivists crop up everywhere, from op-ed pages to the Grand Ole Oprah of the daytime talk shows in which Klansmen and Afrocentrists, anorexics and abusers, rapists and rape victims all get their hearings."[58] But here again I submit that if talk shows invite compassion and understanding and seem to contradict the idea of a hierarchy of evils that is at the heart of our notions of justice, this contradiction is a basic feature of our moral and even judicial system. As the hero (a lawyer) of an international best-seller by Bernard Schlink, *The Reader*, which was chosen for the Oprah Book Club, put it eloquently: "I wanted simultaneously to understand Hanna's crime [war crimes by a woman who had collaborated in the Nazi regime] and to condemn it. But it was too terrible for that. When I tried to understand it, I had the feeling I was failing to condemn it as it must be condemned. When I condemned it as it must be condemned, there was no room for understanding. But even as I wanted to understand Hanna, failing to understand her meant betraying her all over again. I could not resolve this."[59] It is not by accident that this novel was the first—and only—foreign novel chosen by Oprah's Book Club, for it explores the moral and cultural contradiction between imaginative compassion and justice, which is at the heart of the Oprah Winfrey talk show.

What is at stake in the cultural form proposed by Oprah Winfrey is the fact that imaginative compassion seems to neutralize the capacity to judge and therefore flattens moral hierarchies. This might indeed threaten our ability to proffer a sustained moral judgment. But this critique must be seriously qualified by the fact that the flattening of moral hierarchies exists in high culture as well. In fact, it was inaugurated there, in the form of the novel—which, according to Mikhail Bakhtin, is characterized by this flattening of aesthetic and moral hierarchies.[60] Bakhtin has famously argued that the novel differs from the tragedy because it does not hierarchize moral points of view. The "polyphony" of the novel is due to the fact that it gives equal weight to various voices, thus suggesting that "polyphony" was radical because amoral. To a great extent, the equalitarian multiplicity of forms of suffering that is the hallmark of *The Oprah Winfrey Show* is an ultimate radicalization of what he calls the "polyphony" of the novel, in which various and even conflicting voices and genres speak to each other without an overarching point of view.[61] I suggest in a similar vein that the talk show radicalizes the moral polyphony of the novel.

Let me make an additional point: this flattening of moral hierarchies does not necessarily represent a decay of our moral capacities. According to Zygmunt Bauman, postmodern ethics is characterized by the acknowledgment of the open-endedness of moral situations and by the fact that instead of searching for virtue or general rules, we now acknowledge ambivalence as a way to cope with contradictory moral requirements.[62] As the systematic ability to entertain multiple points of view and to refuse to adjudicate between them, it can thus be viewed as a prerogative of the moral attitude. In his study of the moral life displayed in Henry James's novels, Robert Pippin describes it in these terms, a situation he views as characterized by "indeterminacy" and "contingency." "The key issue in morality might not be the rational justifiability with which I treat others, but the proper acknowledgement of, and enactment of, a dependence on others without which the process of any justification . . . could not begin."[63] This acknowledgment entails the refusal to rule from "first principles," and to accept that dependencies create multiple loyalties that can conflict with one another and cannot be settled. Dialogue, perspective-taking, and the representation of suffering, far from being opposed to morality, can be the precondition for a more open-ended form of truth seeking.[64]

CRITIQUE #7: THE PSYCHOLOGIZATION OF SOCIAL PROBLEMS

For many commentators, the claim that *The Oprah Winfrey Show* heals and helps people change is a most superficial way of solving problems, for the show promotes a culture of false feeling, false contrition, and apology.[65] Moreover, the very psychological discourse onm which the show draws is suspect. In this respect, one critique of Oprah's show and of the cultural resources she has drawn upon is that they depoliticize issues that ought to be framed as economic or social problems. By calling on individuals to understand and remedy their problems in terms of their self-esteem, the psychological discourse defuses any possibility of real social change.

However, this is a narrow and limited view of both politics and culture. The realm of political relationships, as the anthropologist James Scott has showed so well,[66] is preceded by "infrapolitics," a realm of representations and meanings in which social relations and violent social conditions are addressed obliquely in order to maintain the dignity and integrity of the self without confronting power relations in a direct way. Indeed, Scott's studies have shown that oppressed groups use symbols in a veiled way, so as to simultaneously accommodate power structures and promote individuals' autonomy. This suggests clearly that the realm of infrapolitics does not and cannot—by definition—correspond to organized politics and be judged by the standards of articulate ideologies.

I suggest that Oprah Winfrey offers an infrapolitics of black women and of the family in a few respects. First: if as Pierre Bourdieu put it, the "most radical censorship is absence,"[67] Oprah's persona is significant, for she offers herself as an unprecedented model for black and white women. Indeed, "silence and invisibility are the hallmarks of African American women . . . typically the roles available for black women in American popular culture are mammy, jezebel, and welfare queen, considering variations and reconstructions of these images over time."[68] To the extent that Oprah symbolizes the very values that are promoted in the white middle class to account for success (hard work, self-help, endurance, altruism, moral self-improvement), she not only offers a powerful alternative to the stereotypical images of black women but also has become a symbol of power and moral strength for all women. That a black woman would become a model and a guide for mainstream white women is, to the best of my knowledge, unprecedented in American history.

Second: many commentators have accused Oprah Winfrey of psychologizing social problems, thereby defusing their political implications. They miss the fact that *The Oprah Winfrey Show* offers what we may call an infrapolitics of the family, a mode of representation in which the family is presented as dangerous for women, yet also as the only framework to organize their close relationships. Winfrey's infrapolitics concerns the violence perpetrated within the confines of the home and family.[69] For example, one of her main techniques of representation—queering the ordinary and normalizing the deviant—corresponds very closely to one of the main tactics of feminist thought. As feminist legal scholar Vicki Bell suggests in her analysis of the feminist treatment of the issue of incest: "In feminist analysis, incest signals not the chaos it did (and does) for sociological functionalism, but an order, the familiar and familial order of patriarchy, in both its strict and its feminist sense. . . . Importantly, feminists argue that incest cannot be regarded as *asocial* at all, but has to be analysed instead in direct relation to the social structures which are continually *produced and reproduced as 'normal'*"[70] (emphasis added). As I have argued, Oprah Winfrey's artful mix of the uncanny and normality explains the ways in which she has staged families in a state of decomposition. While this idea may appear stale today, especially after thirty years of active feminism, in the early 1980s this view of the family was not very visible in mainstream culture, because Americans entertained rosy myths about the family, viewing it as a haven of harmony impermeable to the corrosive influences of society.[71] Oprah Winfrey is part of the same feminist politics of representation noted by Vicki Bell, because, like no one else, she has juxtaposed the normality of family with its pathologies. This is congruent with a feminist infrapolitics because, as Martha Nussbaum and others have suggested, "liberalism assumed that the family reconciled the interests of its participants through love and has failed to interfere and intervene in the family, even when needed."[72] At the time Oprah Winfrey started staging the family this way, initiated by Reagan and continued by Clinton, poor women's conditions dramatically worsened, leaving them at the mercy of domestic violence. Legislators have done their best to ignore these problems, implementing policies that forced women to collect money from fathers, remaining oblivious to the fact that in a third of the cases women were escaping male violence. Legal scholars concur. "In the civil arena, all but two states have passed legislation recognizing the importance of domestic violence in custody disputes."[73] In other words, there are a rather wide range of coercive acts specific to battering relationships that have not been criminalized by the courts. Another scholar echoes this view and suggests that Battered Women Syndrome (BWS) has been only reluctantly acknowledged.[74]

In this context, I argue that Oprah has probably contributed to increased awareness of categories of social problems and criminal behavior that were reluctantly criminalized because they undermined the ideology of the family. As legal scholar Janice Drye states, "Whatever the causes for 'battering and violence in the home, whatever the effects on the victims and the children living in violent homes, the result is that too many people, including our judicial system, look the other way. Judicial discretion has not been sufficient to protect the interests of battered women and children. Judicial willingness to stretch to protect the parental rights of batterers, believing that a child needs both parents, regardless of the costs, conveys the message that society *is willing to excuse violence in the family more readily than violence that occurs in other contexts*"[75] (emphasis added). Indeed, if, as Drye suggests, most institutions have done their best to forget about domestic violence, Oprah has probably contributed more than any other institution to transform the representation of the family and to make the family into a social and legal problem.

From this discussion, it emerges that one of the chief contributions of Oprah Winfrey to American culture has been to draw our attention to the category of "psychological abuse," which is at the interface between individual and political problems. "Psychological abuse is the sustained, repetitive, inappropriate behavior which damages, or substantially reduces, the creative and developmental potential of crucially important mental faculties and mental processes of a child; these include intelligence, memory, recognition, perception, attention, language and moral development."[76] The notion of psychological abuse—which indeed has become overused—is a useful departure point to criticize such institutions as the family in the name of the forms of well-being and psychological development they are able to provide.[78] To summarize, I would suggest that Oprah has engaged in an infrapolitics of the family by altering the image of the family as a harmonious site and by systematically raising issues of fairness and commitment within it.

And yet, Oprah does not call on women to think of their position in the family in terms of a radical politics of selfhood that would reject the family as a basic framework for the formation of identity. As the selection of her novels for the Book Club and the therapeutic literature she uses attest, the family remains the main site of the formation of identity and aspiration, especially for women—the dominant institutional framework within which women look for love, social status, and identity. To that extent, Oprah offers a "compromised" formula: the family is where women's identity collapses, yet it is also where they strive to reconstruct their identity.

A CRITIQUE OF OPRAH'S MORAL IMAGINATION

The critiques evoked above are not convincing because they do not examine Oprah Winfrey's proclaimed intent and meaning, "to make sense of our lives," nor do they succeed in drawing significant and convincing distinctions between "valuable" and "less valuable" cultural expressions. Indeed, many of these critiques can be applied to segments of high culture, which in turn suggests that it is our entire culture—"high" and "low"—that should be disposed of. Instead, I suggest that we critique Oprah Winfrey on her own terms, that is, by taking into account the meaning she bestows on her cultural enterprise.

In this respect, one of the most powerful critiques of talk shows has been voiced by political philosopher Michael Sandel: "Since human beings are storytelling beings, we are bound to rebel against the drift to storylessness. But there is no guarantee that the rebellions will take salutary form. Some,

in their hunger for story, will be drawn to the vacant, vacrious fare of confessional talk shows, celebrity scandals, and sensational trials. . . . The hope
of our time rests instead with those who can summon the conviction and restraint to make sense of our condition and repair the civic life on which
democracy depends."[79] Does Oprah, as she claims to do, help us "make
sense of our condition"?

As I argued in chapters 2, 4, and 5, Oprah Winfrey has taken on the function of a healer and addresses the perplexing crises of meaning posed by the
experience of suffering, offering a narrative of self-help and techniques for
self-change. While she has been criticized for her parading of suffering and
lauded for her promotion of self-help, I argue that her cultural performance
of self-help is actually the most problematic aspect of her enterprise. I illustrate this with an example:

[WINFREY:] I try not to get in crisis before asking it, but whenever any kind of difficulty comes into my life, a sense of anxiety, frustration, I immediately stop and
ask it and myself, "What are you here to teach me?"

. . . .

[UNIDENTIFIED WOMAN #8:] I've got two kids that—my daughter was two; she got
cancer. And we made it through all that. We filed bankruptcy, did all that. I had
a son. He's got a heart condition. We've been through three open-heart surgeries.
Now I find out that he has something wrong with his brain and now I'm dealing
with all that again.

. . . .

[DR. CARTER-SCOTT:] And what I want you to do is close your eyes and I want you
to breathe deeply and I want you to ask, "What is the lesson I'm to learn?"
[WOMAN #8:] That's what I want to know. I mean . . . I don't know what the les-
son is yet.
[DR. CARTER-SCOTT:] You're scared to hear. Close your—breathe. You're not
breathing right now. Breathe. And ask the question, "What is the lesson I am to
learn from these experiences that I am being presented with? What is the lesson
for me?"
[WOMAN #8:] To be a stronger person.
[DR. CARTER-SCOTT:] OK. You're getting stronger every time you deal with one of
these adverse situations. What else?
[WOMAN #8:] I really—I don't know.
[DR. CARTER-SCOTT:] Oh well, that's a good one.
Now wait a second. OK. Now wait a second, God does not give you challenges
like this if you are weak. . . . You wouldn't be given this set of lessons unless you
were up for the challenge.[80]

This guest is a modern equivalent of Job, because like him, and like many of the heroes of the novels selected for the Oprah Winfrey Book Club, she is the victim of incomprehensibly difficult blows of fate. This woman expresses her inability to comprehend, accept, and come to terms with the arbitrariness of disease and loss. Her voice is disturbing because she does not and cannot provide any "consoling" vocabulary to make sense of and redeem her sufferings. Oprah's response is a systematic refusal to let the voice of this suffering person become disturbing. Her constant, and almost mechanical, response to suffering is that we ought to recycle it into an uplifting experience—which becomes overtly absurd when applied to a life whose very foundations have been shattered.

The remainder of the show makes this even clearer: another guest, Dr. Carter-Scott, author of the best-seller *If Life Is a Game, Then These Are the Rules*, displays the same mechanic desire to uplift suffering.

[GUEST:] I realized we were homeless, and not only were we homeless but my neighbors with three small children were homeless and there were maybe 10 or 15 families that were. And it really broke my world open. We lost all stability in a matter of hours. And so I have a choice to be a victim or to be a survivor. And every single day, I choose to be a survivor and I choose to make—help to let this make me stronger.

[WINFREY:] Terrific.

[DR. CARTER-SCOTT:] It's absolutely terrific. And that's the path that we are to face, whether we want to be the victim or we want to be victorious. And it's that path— that bridge—you cross that's what this whole series of shows are about.[81]

The anthropologist Schiefflin's idea of "a failed performance"[82] means that the healer fails to be convincing and persuasive and that the problem with which the healer was approached has not been adequately resolved. What makes this healing performance into a failed one is the fact that all forms of suffering are directed to melt into the same thin air of "survival," self-help, and victorious voluntarism, thus flattening the heterogeneity of the sufferers' voices.

But the use of self-help to address certain forms of suffering can also prove inadequate because the therapeutic injunction to self-change transforms suffering into a positive event. An example taken from Oprah's Web site, a summary of the January 7, 2000 show entitled "Depression Can Be a Good Thing," will illustrate my point. "Sarah Ban Breathnach remembers her spirit through the smallest and the simplest of things. Her greatest successes have been the fruit of depression. She shares how acknowledging and being grateful for your depression can bring relief." Here, suffering is described as a positive value because it is a "signal" that something must change. As the Web site makes clear: "Depression is pain. Any time that we have pain it is a signal from our body or our spirit that something's wrong. Depression can also be divine discontent—you don't like anything in your life and your spirit is trying to get your attention to say something's wrong." If pain is a signal, then it points toward self-change, which in turn means that pain has a positive value. This echoes one of Oprah's mantras, incessantly repeated in her show, Web site, and magazine: "There are no mistakes, only lessons."[83] Or still to take another example: "In 1987, after Oprah went public with her story of sexual abuse, she insisted: 'It was not a horrible thing in my life. There was a lesson in it.'"

Why does the stubborn recycling of pain into a victorious narrative of self-transformation and self-learning signal a resounding moral failure of Oprah Winfrey, that is, her failure to provide an acceptable account of "our condition"? In the first place, her position—that all suffering can, if appropriately processed, uplift—makes suffering into a useful experience for the person. In this scheme, it becomes a good experience, something that can in fact teach us faster and better than happiness itself how to be responsible and strong human beings. If suffering is indeed such a powerful source of "lessons" and moral knowledge, it should, logically, guide educational practices—a view that conflicts with too many premises of our moral world. Second, her position entertains "false consciousness," not in the sense given to this word by Marx and Engels, but rather in the sense given by historian of science Ian Hacking: a form of consciousness through which "people . . . have formed importantly false beliefs about their character and their past."[84] Oprah's ethos of self-help is false in that it confuses two experiences that are and ought to be logically and emotionally kept separate, that of suffering and that of positive learning, change, and improvement. By making all experiences of suffering into occasions to improve oneself, Oprah ends up— absurdly—making suffering into a desirable experience. She thus collapses and mixes two opposite moral and emotional experiences, producing confusion that undermines the very message she wants to promote to women, namely that they ought to separate "healthy" from "pathological" relationships, and dare affirm their self with others. By making suffering into a positive value (because it generates self-help), Oprah perpetuates the very emotional and moral confusion that characterizes the condition of women and in fact encourages them to see in suffering the possibility to rewrite their life narratives and thus to claim moral strength and autonomy. This form of narrative makes suffering the main plot of their autobiographies, as well as their main source of moral worth.

Recycling narratives of suffering into narratives of self-improvement is problematic in yet another respect: it erases the scandal of suffering. As philosopher Emmanuel Levinas puts it, "All evil refers to suffering. . . . Thus the least one can say about suffering is that in its own phenomenality, intrinsically, it is useless, 'for nothing.'"[85] Such a view is foreign to Oprah Winfrey, and it is precisely what prevents her from connecting suffering to the moral standpoint that gives force to Voltaire's point of view (discussed in chapter 6): that much of human suffering is undeserved and unexplained and that this is what makes it a scandal, a problem to our reason and morality.

Indeed, Oprah Winfrey often resembles Cunegonde, Voltaire's satirical heroine in *Candide*. Cunegonde lives through rape, war, and betrayal and witnesses horrific acts of barbarity, yet keeps intact her belief that all is well in a world ridden with evil. Like her, Oprah Winfrey shows us the way to make the best out of the worst of misfortunes, for, in her view, the self can always rescue itself from its (past) misfortunes.

But there is an even more worrisome problem. If, as Oprah Winfrey suggests, failed lives point to failed selves, and if strong selves can always transcend failure by the alchemy of their own will and of therapy, then people have only themselves to blame for their misery. When they are unable to recycle suffering into a positive narrative of self-transformation, they are likely to feel guilt or inadequacy. Then, not only is the self burdened with its own difficult experiences, but it also must now produce a meaningful narrative that overcomes those experiences. If it cannot do that, it is suspect of secretly relishing or desiring its own suffering.

As I stated in chapter 7, Oprah Winfrey's emphasis on self-help has its source in the African American belief that everything has a purpose, in the ethos of self-reliance black women developed, and in the ambient do-it-yourself cultural imperative dictated by the market. I believe that the self-reliance ethos, which was essential for black people to survive, was morally coherent and justified by the fact that black people *objectively* lacked outside sources of support and had only themselves to rely on. The ethos of self-help was their only resource available in a coercive environment in which "blaming" institutions would not have any currency or efficacy. However, when it takes the general and mechanical form of a psychic injunction to recycle misfortunes into psychic benefit, this self-help ethos becomes an attribute of "false consciousness" and impoverishes the very moral imagination and action Oprah wants to promote.

Moral imagination is characterized by the ability to understand and identify with a variety of life situations and predicaments and the capacity to understand the paradoxical texture of human action, that is, to grasp the conflicting nature of human commitments and values. However, Oprah Winfrey's obsession with self-help impoverishes her moral imagination in two important ways. First, it undercuts the very compassionate temperament she wants to promote, an essential attribute of African American culture that is essential to moral imagination in general. By making us the eternal and ever-working architects of our emotional destiny, Oprah Winfrey reduces our tolerance for failed lives. In her book *The Fragility of Goodness*, Martha Nussbaum discusses this very problem in the context of Aristotle's view of pity.[86] Aristotle's opponents held the view that "if a person's character is good, the person cannot be harmed in any serious way." And Nussbaum adds very rightly that in this view "there is no room, conceptually, for pity."[87] Similarly, we may say that if we can always learn and benefit from suffering, there never is real and intolerable suffering;, nor is there a conceptual possibility that a person can be harmed in an irreparable way or be held responsible for that fact. Thus, Oprah Winfrey undercuts the very moral force of her public display of suffering.

The second point has to do with what we may call, again following a notion coined by Martha Nussbaum in *Love's Knowledge*, the depth and complexity of the moral imagination. Nussbaum offers a powerful definition of "moral knowledge" (in reference to Henry James's work) as neither an intellectual grasp of propositions nor "an intellectual grasp of facts; it is perception. It is taking in what is there, with imagination and feeling."[88] As the self-help ethos reduces all forms of moral dilemmas and suffering to the same emotional imperative to convert them into learning and improvement, it flattens them and makes them all equivalent, thereby erasing the particularity of each story. It also blinds us to the dilemmas that make the moral life precisely so compelling.

Ultimately, Winfrey's democracy of suffering is unappealing, but not because it is voyeuristic, emotional, or commodified—rather, because it negates the very phenomenality of the experience of suffering and attempts to mechanically substitute the glamour of vanquished suffering for the disquieting spectacle of intractable misery. It is therefore, and perhaps ironically so, the meaning of self-help that undercuts the exposition of suffering.

9

CONCLUSION: ORDINARY PEOPLE, EXTRAORDINARY TELEVISION

A basic error of the translator, Walter Benjamin tells us, is that he "preserves the state in which his own language happens to be instead of allowing his language to be powerfully affected by a foreign tongue."[1] In a similar vein, a possible error of the sociologist of culture would be to leave intact her original theoretical language without being affected by the object she analyzes. A cultural object as formidable as Oprah Winfrey challenges traditional categories of analysis and ought to help us transform them.

As I hope I have shown throughout this book, Oprah Winfrey's marked control of her program and authorial versatility invite us to rethink the role of agency in the process of creating popular culture. Indeed, popular culture has usually been viewed in terms of either anonymous structural cultural patterns or economic and organizational constraints. "Agency" is usually the prerogative of media audiences, with the result that the agency of the creators of media is often neglected. As a cultural object, Oprah Winfrey demands a revision of that conception and requires that we think more carefully about the role of intention, creativity, and even authorship in the production of televisual texts.

Moreover, as a whole, popular culture seems to have largely confirmed the postmodern idea that contemporary culture is cacophonic, depthless, and devoid of coherent narratives for the self.[2] Oprah Winfrey suggests a far more nuanced appreciation. Far from confirming Frederic Jameson's view that postmodern culture lacks emotionality or intensity because cultural products are disconnected from the people who produced them, Oprah Winfrey suggests that both the meaning and the emotional intensity of her products are closely intertwined with her narrative authority. Moreover, not without a certain dose of irony, her tentacular, multifaceted, and even cacophonous cultural enterprise has mobilized the self as an autonomous and coherent center of volition and decision. Through the twin cultural codes of pain and self-help, Oprah offers nothing less than a narrative work to restore the coherence and unity of contemporary life.

Yet Oprah Winfrey also represents some quintessentially postmodern aspects of culture, decidedly different from television material of the 1970s. As discussed in chapter 5 and 6, the autobiographical stories that populate her show are marked by the "timelessness" that has been the hallmark of postmodern culture.[3] These stories are not played out in a concrete time or space, but are presented in the "abstract" and "congealed" time of the television studio and of the trauma experience.

Moreover, Oprah Winfrey is a paradigmatic example of the radical de-differentiation of postmodern culture.[4] This de-differentiation is manifest in two ways: first, producer, audience, and cultural product merge to form one single spectacle, thus abolishing the distinctions on which traditional cultural production (and hermeneutics) has been based. Moreover, as I have striven to make clear throughout this study, Oprah Winfrey's long cultural arm reaches into domains that have traditionally belonged to different social and cultural spheres: "highbrow" novels and popular best-sellers; literacy and daytime television; a profit-driven empire and a vast organization of charity and benevolent voluntarism; television, cinematic, and publishing ventures combined with political action under the broad aegis of spiritual and moral leadership. Oprah Winfrey is a postmodern cultural persona, moving across different spheres and combining them through the power of television.

Oprah's cultural form represents a new way of connecting media and social practices. According to Georg Simmel, one of the ways in which cultural forms differ is in how they build distance and proximity. As one of the best commentators on Simmel puts it: "One of the respects in which worlds, and various forms within the same world, differ from one another is how near and how far they bring objects to the individual."⁵ Oprah Winfrey—and the plethora of talk shows that have imitated her—signals a new way of organizing distance and proximity between television and its audience, between the individual teller of a singular life story and the mass of its anonymous listeners, between intimacy and the public sphere.

If during the eighteenth century, the role of literature was to mediate between private life and the public sphere,⁶ the role of *The Oprah Winfrey Show* is to recenter the scattered and fragmented subjectivity of late capitalism. The discourse of therapy is the main vector through which the self is recentered. In that respect, it is the major cultural formation mediating between the disintegrating realm of sexual identity and fmaily relations, and the highly competitive realm of economic production.

The various technologies and cultural forms Oprah deploys point to the dense entanglement of the self with the texts and institutions of therapy. But this entanglement does not obliterate moral agency. To the contrary, Oprah Winfrey's empire is sustained by the fact that she herself is engrossed with moral meanings and regularly mobilizes biographies to enact those meanings—that is, she reflexively articulates values and norms to create commitment to and solidarity with others. If we are to understand how actors use and invoke culture concretely and pragmatically, we must take seriously the moral claims they raise and try to redeem in their social relationships. Oprah Winfrey is an outstanding example of the moral dimension of culture. The construction of her biography as a therapeutic project has been semiotically mobilized as a spiritual project of growth and improvement. Moreover, her talk show has assumed a moral vocation of being a platform for social suffering and for helping people assume a new responsibility for their lives, thus mobilizing one of the most central master codes of personhood available in American culture. The talk show itself is what we may call a moral cultural form, which in its very formal structure stages ethical debate and self-change.

In analyzing Oprah Winfrey's cultural enterprise, I have used two interpretive strategies likely to be criticized by those who hold that meaning is undecidable and plural. Other scholars in cultural studies have emphasized the irreducible plurality and contextuality of meaning, but I have worked in an opposite direction: I have tried to emphasize the stability and unity to be found in the cacophony of messages and stories voiced in Oprah's vast cultural organization by using her "intentions" as a key to enter her text and by conceiving of her talk show as a strategic response to problems related to the social existence of women. Where some interpretations might be criticized for being overdone and for relying on somewhat arbitrary categories, my interpretation might be criticized for having preferred caution, face-value validity, and simplicity to depth and thickness. I have opted for this strategy because, faced with a text as intricate as that of Oprah Winfrey, my first concern was to find nonarbitrary points of entry in order to unravel its semiotic structure and the relation this structure might bear to contemporary American society. The cultural analyst's interpretation of the meaning of a text is not exhausted by the intentions that precede and constitute it, but must resonate with what the users and creators of a text think they are saying. Thus intentions—when retrievable—provide a very convenient way to start probing the meaning of a text as well as the relation that the text bears to its social environment. Intentions are then the trace left by social constraints and contexts on individuals enacting meaning. Indeed, I have claimed that Oprah Winfrey offers to the American audience a powerful personification of elements and components of African American culture based on responses to the conditions of slavery, racism, and oppression. The social experience of African American women and the skills and resources they have developed have caught the American imagination because these skills have become useful symbolic tools to address the conditions of selfhood in late modernity.

Let me now offer the following claim: the cultural resources mobilized by Oprah Winfrey—most notably dialogue, self-help, and solidarity—echo with transformations of the personal and political spheres in which "recognition" has come to play a central role. From the 1960s onward, the politics of recognition has been the crucial dimension along which political struggles have been waged both in Europe and in the United States. As Charles Taylor (*The Politics of Recognition*), Axel Honneth, and Nancy Fraser (*Justice Interruptus*) have claimed, the politics of recognition implies that both individuals and groups of people demand that their identity be recognized and validated by others (e.g., the state ruling majority, cultural media). Because capitalism destroys traditional communal sources of identity, undermines the institutional framework of the family in which the work of forming identity is carried out, and yet at the same time demands from the self a massive work of self-presentation, improvisation, and role management, it also makes the problem of recognition the main problem of self and of relations witho others. Oprah Winfrey's cultural genre expresses, in the idiom of popular culture, the new centrality of a politics of recognition in which the very content of selfhood, its identity and dignity are at stake.

In this context, Oprah Winfrey uses culture as a form of therapy, that is, as a set of resources to make sense of our suffering and to build a coherent self reflexively. She puts culture quite literally in action, showing that it is the ensemble of resources we should pull together to build selves: experts, scientific knowledge, life stories, compassion, indignation, therapy, and the Internet. In the Oprah Winfrey cultural enterprise, these become cultural tools mobilized to make culture into a form of therapy, to bestow meaning on people's failed lives, and to change those lives.

To suggest that culture is a form of therapy does not mean we should attribute to it psychological power or that we should understand its effect in psychological terms. Rather, we should understand psychology as an increasingly inherent and structural component of modern culture. Psychology has become an impersonation, a dramatization of the breaches of our lives, as well as a cultural resource individuals and organizations mobilize to regain coherence. Oprah Winfrey is thus a powerful illustration of the fact that culture is not the background of action, nor its thick context. Rather, it is the very resource that is continually shaped, used, and invoked by actors to mold and change their lives. Oprah is such an interesting case for the student of modern culture because she points to the ways in which culture is increasingly used reflexively, as a "tool kit" to resolve problems and shape the self.

I have suggested that in this respect, popular culture, like other segments of culture, contains an ethical dimension that confronts us with the intractability of moral questions: Are all lives equally well lived? What makes a life better than others? How shall we fashion ourselves vis-à-vis the suffering that others inflict on us? While sociology has produced many illuminating studies of the ways in which popular culture justifies or shapes social inequalities, it has remained strangely silent on an old and perhaps more profound role of culture: to make sense of suffering; to explain death and disease; to help us confront loss and disappointment; to reconcile us to the fragility of our lives. Max Weber pointed to what I think is a powerful secret affinity between culture and religion: the ability to make sense of suffering. The need for an interpretation of suffering, or in Weber's words, of "the distribution of fortunes among men," was the original impulse of religious worldviews.[7] With the rationalization of social life, the need to perceive consistency between one's fate and one's merit increases.

Sociologists of culture might be willing to concede that the need to account for suffering was cardinal in religious worldviews, but would view it as at best marginal to the cacophonic and commodified realm of mass culture. Indeed, endless critiques of mass culture tell us that it desensitizes us to violence, turns the spectacle of suffering into sheer entertainment, and makes us morally callous. More specifically, most sociologists of culture would argue that considering the pervasiveness, cultural impact, and economic power of the culture industries, it is far more urgent to understand how they generate the forms of suffering of our society than to focus on their dubious capacity to heal.

I do not know whether Oprah's "healing" of the many wounds that are paraded on her show is effective. This study does not provide tools to evaluate that question. Instead, my argument has been that Oprah Winfrey has known to put into ritual form the deep longing for a symbolic system that helps explain, work on, and exorcise the demons of failed relationships and selfhood. To the extent that she has connected herself in a remarkable way with that fundamental dimension of culture, she marks a serious advance of the penetration of television in everyday life and of its capacity to append itself to the ordinary work of having a self.

NOTES

1. INTRODUCTION: OPRAH WINFREY AND THE SOCIOLOGY OF CULTURE

1. In 2001, her fortune was estimated to be $800 million.
2. Randolph 1995:22–28.
3. Clementson 2001:44–45.
4. Quoted in Lowe 1998:xi.
5. Ibid., 1.
6. To give one example among many: in 1998 she was named by *Entertainment Weekly* magazine the most powerful person in the entertainment industry. "She topped Steven Spielberg, Rupert Murdoch, George Lucas and the dual listing of Time Warner honchos Gerald Levin and Ted Turner in the Top. 5" ("Oprah Winfrey Named Most Powerful Person in Entertainment Industry," *Jet* 94 (24): 11. In 1998, she was voted the second most admired woman in America, after Hillary Rodham Clinton (Lowe 1998).
7. She is thought to reach 33 million viewers a day throughout the globe. In February 1999, she was rated second in the Nielsen ratings, after Jerry Springer (6.7 Nielsen number).
8. Quoted in G. Mair 156.
9. Quoted in Jane Rosenzweig, "Consuming Passions," *The American Prospect* http://www.prospect.org.org/archives/v11–2/rosenweig.htm1
10. See Bourdieu 1979; Beisel 1993, 1997.
11. Jonathan Franzen's reported disdain for the Oprah Book Club in 2001 is a very good example making apparent and tangible cultural boundaries.
12. See in particular Weber's "Social Psychology of World Religions" in Gerth and Mills 1958.
13. Beck and Beck-Gernsheim 1995.
14. Heaton and Wilson 1995.
15. Livingstone and Lunt 1994.
16. Shattuc 1997.
17. Durkheim 1915 (1969):205–239; Bellah 1985, 1991.

18. This approach contains various strands of thought, ranging from critical theory to Bourdieu (e.g., 1988) via Foucault (1965) and Althusser, *For Mark* (New York: Pantheon, 1969).

19. Proponents of institutional analysis of meaning count historians of the book as Roger Chartier (*Forms and Meanings: Texts, Performances, and Audiences from Codex to Computer* [Philadelphia: University of Pennsylvania Press, 1995]) or Robert Darnton (1979), as well as sociologists as Paul DiMaggio (1982) or Wendy Griswold (1991).

20. Marcus 1998:37.

21. Quoted in Schudson 1998.

22. Schudson 1992.

23. Greenblatt 1999.

24. Ibid.

25. Liebes and Katz 1990:8.

26. See D. Morley, *The Nationwide Audience: Structure and Decoding* (London: British Film Institute, 1980); Radway 1991; and Liebes and Katz 1990 for some of the most famous examples.

27. Ibid., 9.

28. The study of reception does not resolve the problem of interpretation and of its circularity in another respect. The danger of projecting our own interpretive grid lurks as powerfully when we analyze viewers' "interviews" as when we analyze texts. After all, the interview is a *text* produced by the researcher and the interviewee, and here also, the sociologist can simply "discover" what she knew or presumed to know all along. As Martin Allor put it, "As do other public intellectuals (advertising copywriters, pollsters, program producers, regulators), we work to produce figures of audience—figures that work to ground the claims of our research; figures that often work to condense contradictory assumptions about the social field and that often occlude the political implications of our work" (1996:209).

29. Illouz 1997b.

30. We must not be tempted to yield to the "affective fallacy," the fallacy that we can know the meaning of a text from its effects; but not to succumb to the affective fallacy does not mean that we cannot try to gain some understanding about the world of experience that is always at the threshold of the text. This is where textual analysis must always be historical and sociological in the sense that if we can reconstruct networks or structures of meaning (classifications, oppositions, etc.), we can fully grasp their relevance for a particular social condition only if we use historical and sociological evidence.

31. Quoted in Stock 1990:103.

32. It has often been said that texts include their readers, and that the inscribed reader thus may offer us some information on the probable audience of a cultural product. I believe this claim to be valid only in very specific cases (i.e., as when Oprah clearly addresses women) or in the case of a well-differentiated audience. But this is a far more difficult assumption to validate in the case of

texts that are produced by economic imperatives. While such economically driven texts manage to be in close touch with their audiences' expectations (through market research, letters to the host, Web site feedback), their all-inclusive character makes them a poor indicator of the inscribed reader.

33. See Griswold 1991.

34. See Radway 1991 or Kellner 1995. for examples of a dual hermeneutic and critical approach to popular culture.

35. Walzer 1988.

36. Nussbaum 1990:233.

37. Beck and Beck-Gernsheim 1995.

38. See Miller and McHoul 1998.

2. THE SUCCESS OF A SELF-FAILED WOMAN

1. Rogers St. Johns 1926:35.

2. Whitaker 1987:38.

3. Decker 1997:113.

4. Lowe 1998:xiv.

5. The field of art has concentrated on "authors" and "biographies" for a long time, to the point that literature had to disentangle from the "intentional fallacy" that the meaning of the text is to be found in the intentions of its authors. Media analysis has also been conducted from the standpoint of the strategies and constraints that shape media producers, but in general the assumption is that they operate within the constraints of an organization. By and large, most analyses of media have not engaged in the analysis of singular *biographies*—perhaps operating on the implicit assumption that biography belongs to the defunct analysis of high art according to the great names. Yet Oprah has authored television, much in the same way that French *cineastes* of the 1960s claimed the singular authorship of their works. Winfrey is a businesswoman, a gatekeeper, a host, an actor, and a persona.

6. Benjamin 1973 ("The Task of the Translator"):77.

7. Abu-Lughod 1999:113, emphasis added.

8. The Cambridge School in political philosophy has developed this point remarkably. For very illuminating discussions of the notion of intention see Skinner 1978 and Pocock's "Introduction" in *Virtue, Commerce and History* (1976).

9. As Umberto Eco put it (*Interpretation and Overinterpretation* [Cambridge: Cambridge University Press, 1992]), intention is always bound by "the state of the lexical system." While "intentions" are provided by actors and are the "key" the cultural analyst can use to attend to salient meanings, the *map* of the lexical system can be drawn only by the cultural analyst, for it demands a systematic investigation of the ways in which intentions relate to and are shaped by cultural structures.

10. In that vein, art historian Michael Baxandall has suggested that we study meaning by establishing "a brief," which he defines as a set of situational constraints

likely to have shaped an artist's design and intention. These constraints are, for example, those exerted by a genre and medium of expression, the economic imperatives attached to a given genre and the cultural outlook of the group of origin of the artist.

11. Geertz 1973:96–97.
12. Jameson 1981.
13. Swidler 1995:29.
14. Randolph 1995:22–28.
15. Such emphasis on intention derives from Bourdieu's view of culture as practice, that is, as deep "habits, styles, and skills (the 'habitus') that allow human beings to continually produce innovative actions that are nonetheless meaningful to others around them." For Bourdieu, active human beings continually re-create culture. "They . . . energetically seek strategic advantage by using culturally encoded skills" (Swidler 1995:29).
16. Mair 1998:29.
17. Morgan 1986:C17.
18. Stodghill 1998:80.
19. Morris 2000:447.
20. Lowe 1998:15.
21. Anne Saidman, *Oprah Winfrey: Media Success Story* (Minneapolis: Lerner Publications Company, 1990), 17.
22. Richman 1987:48.
23. Reynolds 1993:86, emphasis added.
24. Ibid.
25. Ibid.
26. Lowe 1998:10, emphasis added.
27. Mair 1998:17.
28. Richman 1987:48.
29. Clementson 2001:44–45.
30. Lowe 1998:8.
31. Ibid., 14.
32. Richard Dyer, quoted in Gamson 1994:199.
33. "Masters of Enterprise," *Publishers Weekly* 1999:61.
34. Tuchman, Darnton.
35. Gamson 1998.
36. See example of Theda Bara discussed by Gamson 1994; see Illouz 1997a.
37. Patricia Sellers, "The Business of Being Oprah," *Fortune*, April 1, 2002, 50–64.
38. Marshall 1997.
39. Or an Afro-American "token" of the American Dream, as Cloud (1992) suggests.
40. "Blowing Our Cover," *O Magazine* 2001:24.
41. Ibid., 171.
42. "Blowing Our Cover," *O Magazine* (March 2001):171–175.
43. Transcript, June 2, 1999.
44. Mair 1998:229.

45. Richman 1987:48.
46. "What I Know for Sure," O Magazine 2001:290.
47. Randolph 1995:26.
48. Ibid.
49. Randolph 1993:130.
50. Ibid.
51. Morrison 1994.
52. Morgan 1986:C17.
53. Williams 1999.
54. Waters and King 1984:51.
55. Harrison 1989:28, 54.
56. Saidman 1990:48.
57. Mair 1998:146.
58. Rogers 1993: 94–97.
59. Randolph 1993:130.
60. Greene and Winfrey 1996:15–17.
61. Raffel 1999:106.
62. McGraw 1999.
63. Ibid., 8.
64. Kanner 1994:46.
65. Powell 1998:112–115.
66. McGraw 1999:2.
67. Lowenthal 1944:109–140.
68. Weber 1958:246.
69. M. Weber, "The Sociology of Charismatic Authority," in Weber, Gerth, and Mills 1946:245–252; 249.
70. Germov and Williams 1999:118.
71. Seid 1994, quoted in Sobal and Maurer:119
72. Ibid., 120.
73. For an excellent discussion of "energy" as a sociological concept, see Collins 1990b.
74. Handelman 1985:353.
75. Grathoff 1970.
76. Ibid.
77. Handelman 1990:244.
78. Ibid., 245.
79. Swidler 2001:82–83.

3. EVERYDAY LIFE AS THE UNCANNY: *THE OPRAH WINFREY SHOW* AS A NEW CULTURAL GENRE

1. In certain cities, *Donohue* was as popular as, and sometimes even more popular than, *The Oprah Winfrey Show*.
2. Burke 1973:300.

3. As Chris Barker put it in his study *Global Television*: "Genre structures the narrative process and contains it. . . . Genre thus represents systemizations and repetitions of problems, and solutions in narratives" (1997:74).
4. Nussbaum 1986.
5. Ibid., 27.
6. Gamson 1998; Lowney 1999.
7. Illouz 1999; Simon-Vandenbergen 2000.
8. Lowney 1999:13.
9. In 1990, the Nielsen ratings showed *Oprah* as fifth of all syndicated shows, and *Donahue* tenth. See Mair 1998.
10. Mair 1998:215.
11. Ibid.
12. Benjamin 1973:84.
13. See Carpignano, Andersen, Aronowitz, and Difazio 1991.
14. Transcript, April 9, 1988.
15. Wuthnow 1989:67–72.
16. Danto 1985:78–82.
17. Austin 1962.
18. Frye 1957.
19. Speech codes are "the innumerable speech acts—asking, telling, promising, begging, urging, praising—that typify the intricate cultural and linguistic codes underlying even the most simple utterance" (Morris 1996:33).
20. Burke and Gusfield 1989:53.
21. Quoted in Mair 1998:327.
22. Patricia Sellers, "The Business of Being Oprah," *Fortune* (April 1, 2002):50–64.
23. See Bourdon 2000.
24. A text is popular if it reaches a wide number of people; if it crosses various social strata; and if it generates loyalty among its users.
25. Darnton 1985.
26. Ibid.
27. Hays 1996.
28. This is true of high art as well. For example: In his classic study of French tragedies Lucien Goldmann (1964) suggested that the tragic structure of feeling—a very popular genre in the seventeenth century—derived from the contradictory social location of the robe nobility.
29. Geertz 1973:219.
30. Horton and Wohl 1956:212–228.
31. See Jakobson 1956.
32. Transcript, September 15, 1998.
33. Nightingale 1990.
34. These data are quoted in Peck 1995:76.
35. Ang 1990.
36. Taylor 1989.
37. Giddens 1990, 1991.

38. S. Cavell, "The Ordinary as the Uneventful," in Cavell and Mulhall 1996.
39. Watt 1957; Taylor 1989.
40. Keyes 1999:1.
41. Mattelart 1997.
42. Ang 1990:29.
43. Gay 1998.
44. Transcript, June 21, 1995.
45. I use "polluting" in Mary Douglas's meaning in *Purity and Danger*.
46. Transcript, October 29, 1986.
47. Transcript, November 6, 1986.
48. Transcript, April 2, 1996.
49. Freud 1919.
50. Carson 1995:132–133.
51. Seidman 1997:25.
52. Modelski 1997:373.
53. Ibid., 372.
54. Stallybrass and White 1986:199.
55. Ibid.
56. Handelman 1979:185.
57. Beck and Beck-Gernsheim 1996.
58. Z. Bauman, quoted in Beck and Beck-Gernsheim 1996:26.
59. Nelson and Robinson 1994.
60. This corroborates Carbaugh's persuasive study of talk shows where he found that "choice" is one of the central codes of selfhood in talk shows (1988).

4. PAIN AND CIRCUSES

1. Derrida 1978; Volosinov 1986; Lyotard 1984.
2. This is a modest attempt to find a systematic way to link texts with their culture, and to understand which meanings they perform. Thus Greenblatt's work (1980), however brilliant, never quite helps us understand how we can choose one meaning over another to decipher broader cultural texts; see Montrose in Greenblatt and Gunn for an excellent discussion of this problem.
3. In that sense, I differ greatly from Hirsch's claims in *Validity in Interpretation* (1967).
4. Cleage 1997:1.
5. Ehrenreich 1995:92.
6. Zoglin 1988:64.
7. Dershowitz 1994:5–6.
8. Abt and Seesholtz 1994:177.
9. Quoted in Moore 1996:17.
10. See Bourdieu 1979.
11. Clementson 2001:44–45.
12. Rapping 1996:37.

13. Transcript, September 28, 1994.
14. Transcript, August 19, 1997.
15. Transcript, March 3, 1997.
16. Transcript, January 13, 1997.
17. Transcript, August 28, 1996.
18. Transcript, July 13, 1995.
19. Transcript, March 11, 1994.
20. Transcript, September 26, 1995.
21. Transcript, March 18, 1996.
22. Transcript, May 31, 1996.
23. Transcript, October 3, 1996.
24. Transcript, June 26, 1998.
25. Transcript, June 12, 1996.
26. Transcript, March 31, 1993.
27. Transcript, March 27, 1995.
28. Transcript, June 30, 1993.
29. Transcript, April 1, 1994.
30. Transcript, October 10, 1994.
31. Transcript, May 23, 1995.
32. Transcript, November 10, 1986.
33. Transcript, September 23, 1986.
34. Transcript, July 2, 1998.
35. Transcript, June 20, 1994.
36. Transcript, July 9, 1998.
37. Transcript, August 26, 1993.
38. Transcript, August 20, 1996.
39. Transcript, September 6, 1996.
40. Transcript, December 1, 1994.
41. Transcript, March 28, 1995.
42. Transcript, April 4, 1995.
43. Transcript, April 3, 1995.
44. Transcript, July 14, 1994.
45. Transcript, August 2, 1994.
46. Transcript, January 31, 1994.
47. Transcript, March 15, 1999.
48. Transcript, September 25, 1986.
49. Transcript, October 10, 1986.
50. Transcript, October 13, 1986.
51. Transcript, May 6, 1999.
52. Transcript, January 22, 1999.
53. Transcript, June 26, 1996.
54. Transcript, June 21, 1995.
55. Transcript, June 20, 1997.
56. Transcript, June 21, 1994.

57. Transcript, April 6, 1995.
58. Transcript, October 30, 1995.
59. Transcript, November 17, 1986.
60. Transcript, October 8, 1986.
61. Transcript, November 7, 1986.
62. Transcript, November 6, 1986.
63. Transcript, October 29, 1986.
64. Ehrenreich 1995:92.
65. The term is borrowed from Charles Taylor, and has been used extensively by Boltansky and Thevenot (1987).
66. Taylor 1985:103.
67. See Scannel 1991.
68. Goffman 1974; Snow et al. 1986. Note that neither Goffman nor Snow have focused on the emotional dimension of framing.
69. This discussion of narrative is inspired by and draws from Kidron's (1999) excellent study.
70. Gergen 1992:132.
71. Quoted in Kidron 1999:6; see Ortner 1990.
72. Ibid.
73. Transcript, December 1, 1994.
74. Transcript, December 2, 1986.
75. Transcript, December 27, 1994.
76. Transcript, March 28, 1995.
77. Foucault 1986.
78. Foucault 1999.
79. For examples see Nye 1993; W.I. Miller, *Humiliation: And Other Essays on Honor, Social Discomfort and Violence* (Ithaca: Cornell University Press, 1993); Abu-Lughod 1986; Demos 1988.
80. Transcript, October 30, 1995.
81. Transcript October 3, 1996.
82. See Boltanski and Thevenot 1991.
83. Ruddick 1995:212.
84. See Bellah 1985; Beck and Beck-Gernsheim 1995; Okin 1989.
85. Transcript March 27, 1995.
86. Shklar 1984.
87. Transcript, April 2, 1996.
88. Steiner 1961:9.
89. Transcript, June 21, 1995.
90. Williams 1981.
91. Transcript, June 21, 1995.
92. Transcript, April 2, 1996.
93. See Rapping 1996; Young 1995; Hacking 1995.
94. Transcript, August 10, 1993.
95. Stodghill 1998:80–82.

96. This discussion was inspired by Boltanski (1999).
97. Boltanski 1999; Arendt 1963:chapter2, "The Social Question."
98. Jacquelyn Mitchard and Wally Lamb were obscure before Oprah made them best-selling authors.
99. I have read and analyzed the following books: *Breath, Eyes, Memory* (Edwige Danticat); *Black and Blue* (Anna Quindlen); *The Deep End of the Ocean* (Jacquelyn Mitchard); *Beloved* (Toni Morrison); *Paradise* (Toni Morrison); *Song of Solomon* (Toni Morrison); *Here on Earth* (Alice Hoffman); *The Pilot's Wife* (Anita Shreve); *Jewel* (Bret Lott); *Midwives* (Chris Bohjalian); *The Reader* (Bernhard Schlink); *I Know This Much Is True* (Wally Lamb); *What Looks Like Crazy on an Ordinary Day* (Pearl Cleage); *White Oleander* (Janet Fitch); *Stones from the River* (Ursula Hegi); *Where the Heart Is* (Billie Letts); *River, Cross My Heart* (Breena Clarke), *The Corrections* (Jonathan Franzen).
100. Hillis Miller 1982:1.
101. Oates 2001:69.
102. Modelski 1997 and Radway 1991.
103. Danticat 1994:234.
104. Transcript, September 25, 1998.
105. Transcript, May 22, 1998.
106. Transcript, April 9, 1998.
107. Transcript, May 22, 1998.
108. Quoted in Downs 1996:14.
109. Showalter 1997; Hacking 1995.
110. Moore 1972:xvi.
111. Kleinman 1988:56.
112. Ibid., 57.
113. Ibid., 61.
114. Showalter 1997; Hacking 1995.
115. Kaminer 1992.
116. S. Langer, *Philosophy in a New Key*, 287; quoted in Geertz 1973:99.
117. Ibid.
118. Geertz 1973:102.
119. Lasch 1977; Beck and Beck-Gernsheim 1995.
120. Geertz 1973:87–125.
121. Stromberg 1993:160.
122. Hoover and Lundby 1997:7.
123. Schofield-Clark and Hoover 1997:17.
124. This is somewhat reminiscent of what Swidler calls "unsettled lives." In *Talk of Love* (2001), Swidler argues that when a life is disrupted (by a divorce, a disease, or unemployment), one will engage in intense cultural activity, precisely to find cultural resources to shape one's strategies for action.
125. Lamb 1998:215.
126. Willis 1990.
127. See Morris 2000.

128. Amato and Monge 1990:155.
129. Craib 1994.
130. Schweder 1988:488.
131. Lamb 1996:89.
132. Das 1997:71.
133. Ibid.

5. THE HYPERTEXT OF IDENTITY

1. Foucault himself carefully avoided assuming such a role, but his imitators have by and large willingly taken on the role of "unmasking" the violence of modern institutions.
2. Philippe Corcuff, private communication.
3. The expression is Luc Boltanski's, informal communication.
4. This approach to culture has been best exemplified by the works of Robert Bellah (1985, 1991) but received new impetus through the path-breaking works of Michele Lamont in the United States and of Luc Boltanski and Laurent Thevenot (Boltanski and Thevenot 1987, 1989, 1991; Boltanski 1999) in France, as well as in the collaborative works of the two teams (Lamont and Thevenot 2000).
5. Boltanski and Thevenot 1987, 1989, 1991.
6. Lamont 2000.
7. Weber 1960.
8. Boltanski 1999, 1990.
9. Boltanski 1999.
10. Jose Brunner, "Identifications, Suspicions and the History of Traumatic Disorders," *Harvard Review of Psychiatry* 10 (2002): 179–184.
11. Quoted in Mair 1998:217.
12. Ibid., 351.
13. For example, a single appearance of Toni Morrison on the Oprah Winfrey show has generated three times as many sales of her books as the Nobel Prize.
14. Priest 1995.
15. Transcript, June 2, 1999.
16. Star World Channel, December 28, 1998.
17. Langer 1996:54.
18. Star World Channel, March 26, 2001.
19. Transcript, September 26, 1995.
20. Modelski 1997:371.
21. "What I Know for Sure," *O Magazine* October 2001:310.
22. Heelas 1996:173.
23. Transcript, March 11, 1994.
24. Transcript, April 14, 1999.
25. Quoted in Mair 1998:326.
26. Transcript, June 14, 1994. Emphasis added.

27. Ibid.

28. *O Magazine* April 2001:56.

29. Illouz 1997b.

30. See Illouz 1991.

31. Ibid.

32. See Cushman 1995; Illouz 1997b.

33. Tierny and Scott 1984:294.

34. Peck 1995.

35. In the domestic sphere, women are more likely than men to pay attention to and monitor the emotional exchanges with their partners and with their children. Moreover, being likely to work in the service professions, women need to monitor themselves more closely and intensely than men in the workplace.

36. Hochschild 1983; Illouz 1991; Stearns 1994; Cancian 1990.

37. Simonds 1992:7.

38. Stock 1990.

39. Transcript, October 6, 1998.

40. This is congruent with Leslie Irvine's findings about the organization of CoDA, Codependent Anonymous. To quote her: "Among the people I met in CoDA, the self is alive and well. They wanted no part of ad hoc identities, but longed for a coherent sense of who they are, instead" (1999:162).

41. Transcript, April 14, 1999.

42. Haraway 1991.

43. Hakken 1999:71.

44. Booth 1988:13.

45. Radway 1997:6.

46. Ibid., 14.

47. Long 1994.

48. Danto 1985:79.

49. Turkle 1995:268.

50. See Burke 1973.

51. Rieff 1966.

52. Rose 1996.

53. Cushman 1995.

54. Frank 1961:94–95.

55. Kleinman 1980; Csordas 1996:91–114.

56. Y. Bilu, "The Taming of the Deviants and Beyond: An Analysis of Dibbuk Possession and Exorcism in Judaism," *Psychoanalytical Study of Society* 11:1–32.

57. Getting Real, *Middle East Television*, December 16, 2000.

58. Arthur Kleinman, *Culture and Depression: Studies in the Anthropology and Cross-Cultural Psychiatry of Affect and Disorder* (Berkeley: University of California Press, 1980).

59. Levi-Strauss 1963.

60. Ibid.

61. Sample 1999.

62. Newpoff 1999.
63. Spillman 1997.
64. Ostrower 1995.
65. Crang, Crang, and May 1999:46.
66. Rutherford 1990:11.
67. Weeks 1990:92.
68. See Alexander 1984.

6. SUFFERING AND SELF-HELP AS GLOBAL FORMS OF IDENTITY

1. Connell 2000:292.
2. Appadurai 1996:78.
3. Redman 1949:560; the translation in the text is my own, not the book's.
4. London's great fire in the previous century had not spurred the same sense of theological disquiet.
5. Neiman 2002; Baczko 1997.
6. Richardson and Sabor 1985; see Boltanski 1999.
7. While Christianity might have played an important role in the development of the consciousness of the world as a whole, global consciousness was never better served and achieved than when traditional theological accounts of Providence collapsed. See Robertson 1992.
8. This was the rationalization Max Weber had found to be key to the major world religions and that he saw the West as developing to an even greater degree. See Weber, Gerth, and Mills 1946:[page number]; Weber, "The Psychology of World Religions" in ibid.; Neiman forthcoming.
9. Hutcheson 1963; Smith 1817.
10. Castells 1996:371.
11. Cushman 1995; Herman 1995; Baritz 1960.
12. Gray 1992; Goleman 1995.
13. In his analysis of the codependent movement, Joseph Gemin explains it in terms similar to my argument: "Incorporating a metaphor of boundary-as-place may help in explaining the vast number of religion-oriented books on codependency: the metaphor helps to *anchor* identity, paradoxically, by allowing the self to be conceptualized as "lost," which in turn motivates the codependent's moral quest to be "found" (Gemin 1997:261).
14. Salzberg 2001:212.
15. Tomlinson 1999.
16. Keyes 1999:2.
17. Meyer, Boli, Thomas, and Ramirez 1997.
18. Ibid.
19. Baritz 1960.
20. Mair 1998:204.
21. Kellner 1995.

22. The expressions are Hannerz's in *Transnational Connections* (1996).
23. A. Smith in Featherstone 1990:177.
24. Appadurai 1996.
25. Beck 2000.
26. Rice 1998; Irvine 1999.
27. Castells 1996:371.
28. Held and McGrew 2000.
29. Robertson 1992:8.

7. THE SOURCES AND RESOURCES OF *THE OPRAH WINFREY SHOW*

1. Bourdieu 1979:83.
2. Ibid.
3. Swidler 2001.
4. Sewell 1992.
5. Swidler 2001.
6. "The unprecedented increases in the proportion of births out of wedlock are a major contributor to the rise of female-headed families in the black community" (Wilson 1987:).
7. Hemmons 1996:75.
8. Job has a major impact on marriage because female tend not to marry males with inadequate incomes (ibid., 20).
9. In 1990, households headed by African American females had a median income far lower than corresponding households headed by white or black males or by white females. See Hemmons 1996.
10. Patricia Hill Collins', "Black Men and the Love and Trouble Tradition," in Ostrov Weisser, ed., *Women and Romance: A Reader* (New York: NYU Press, 2001).
11. Dickson 1993:480.
12. Stark 1994–95.
13. hooks 1997:484.
14. Collins 1990a:187.
15. Showalter 1997:151.
16. Abdullah 1998.
17. Wolf 1991; Germov and Wiliams 1996; Chrisler 1996.
18. Abdullah 1998.
19. Nussbaum 1999:245.
20. Data quoted in Peck (1995), 77. See also Hare-Mustin 1983.
21. Collins 1986:14.
22. Collins 1995:125.
23. June Jordan, 1985, *On Call*, quoted in Collins 1995:117.
24. Quoted in Collins 1995:123.
25. Transcript, January 19, 1999.

26. Collins 1990a:47.
27. This is an excerpt from her essay *Civil Wars*, quoted in Stuart 1990:37.
28. Illouz 1997b.
29. Du Bois 1968:45.
30. See Smith 1972.
31. Kirk-Duggan 1992:82.
32. This was due to the fact that with political association forbidden, the church became the center for addressing the social grievances and developing the political vision of black communities.
33. See Holmes 1997.
34. See Gates 1988.
35. Stepto 1991:3.
36. Ibid.
37. Berger, Berger, and Kellner 1973.
38. Beck, Giddens, and Lash 1994:13–14, emphases added.
39. Beck and Beck-Gernsheim 1995:5.
40. Beck, Giddens, and Lash 1994.
41. Beck and Beck-Gernsheim-Beck 1995, 1996.
42. Levine 1988:139.
43. Staples 1997.
44. Beck 1992.
45. Gilles Gunn 1987.
46. Levine 1993: 6, emphasis added.
47. Dyson 1993b:41.
48. Collins 1986:28.
49. Quoted in Hill Collins 1986.
50. Levine 1971.
51. Niles 1984.
52. Illouz 1997a; Hochschild 1983; Hays 1996.
53. Cancian 1990.
54. Salvino 1989:144.
55. Ibid., 149.
56. Stodghill 1998:80.
57. Lowe 1998:21.
58. Dyson 1993a:12.
59. Levine 1977:93.
60. Bauman 1993; Caputo 1993.
61. Dickson 1993:480.
62. Quoted in Levine 1977:143.
63. James Floyd, "The Role of Crisis Theory in Black Family Research," paper presented at the Society for the Study of Social Problems, 1988.
64. Collins 1989.
65. Levine 1977:58.
66. Pinn 1995:17.

67. Bloomfield and Dunn 1989:111.
68. Ibid.
69. Ibid.
70. Kellner 1995; Ross 1989; Radway 1991; Fiske 1989.
71. See Simon 1999.
72. Among them are Stanley Cavell, Martha Nussbaum, Alexander Nehemas, Richard Rorty, and Robert Pippin.
73. Levine 1988:39.
74. Walzer 1988:ix.

8. TOWARD AN IMPURE CRITIQUE OF POPULAR CULTURE

1. Ross 1989.
2. Gamson 1998:19.
3. Radway 1997.
4. See Lears 1981; Marchand 1985; Illouz 1997a.
5. Leo 1996:73.
6. Saltzman 1996:63.
7. Kreyche 1996:82.
8. "The Idiot Culture," *New Republic* 206 (23) (June 8, 1992): 22.
9. Richard Rorty uses a similar concept in his *Achieving Our Country* (1998), but the coining of this expression is independent from Rorty's.
10. This dates back to Aristotle's classification of the genres in which comedies were ranked as lower than the tragedy. "A virtuous life requires exertion, and does not consist in amusement. And we say that serious things are better than laughable things and those connected with amusement and that the activity of the better of any two things . . . is the more serious" (*The Nichomaean Ethics*, in Singer 1994:186). These assumptions are reminiscent of the opposition between carnival culture and the "official" culture, which, according to Mikhail Bakhtin, was enforced by the Church around the fifteenth century and was characterized by its contempt for laughter and its elevation of seriousness, gravity, and reverence. This culture of seriousness was evident in the repeated attacks against the bawdy and buffoon character of popular culture from the Renaissance to the nineteenth century.
11. See Burke 1973; Beisel 1993; Peiss 1986; Ginzburg 1980.
12. Martha Bayles, "Imus, Oprah and the Literacy Elite," *New York Times Book Review*, August 29, 1999, 35.
13. Gerbner et al. 1980.
14. Livingstone and Lunt 1994.
15. See William 1996:19.
16. Eagleton 1984:123–124.
17. Salusinszky and Derrida 1987:159.
18. To give one example among many: at the turn of the century, capitalists worried about meeting increasing consumer demands hired women at wages that were

far lower than those of their male counterparts. This blunt economic inequality Provide a great impetus for the feminist movement. See Hobsbawm 1987.

19. This is Nussbaum's view in her argument with Dworkin and McKinnon. See "Objectification" in Nussbaum 1999.

20. Willis 1977; Radway 1991.

21. Held 1980:183–184.

22. Walzer 1983.

23. Walzer 1988.

24. Walzer 1987.

25. Nussbaum 1997.

26. Abramson and Pinkerton 1995; Brunner 1995.

27. Ackerman 1980.

28. In Seyla Benhabib's (1992) summary of Ackerman's thought, liberalism is not based on "some general feature of the moral life, but upon the distinctive way liberalism conceives of the problem of public order," that is, how different groups, about whom we know only that they do not share the same conception of the good, can "resolve the problem of coexistence in a reasonable way."

29. Abt and Seesholtz 1994.

30. Ibid., 177.

31. Boltanski 1999.

32. For a development of this idea, see Illouz, "From Lisbon Disaster to Oprah Winfrey: Suffering as Global Identity" in Beck and Sznaider forthcoming.

33. Hutcheson 1742; Smith 1817.

34. Arendt 1958.

35. Baudrillard and Lotringer 1988:22.

36. Halttunen 1995:307. Such a new pleasure in the spectacle of the suffering of others is due to complex sociopsychological mechanisms: eighteenth-century people in England enjoyed unprecedented levels of wealth and the end of civil wars, and the spectacle of suffering might have provided a pleasure derived from the comparison with their own good fortune.

37. Lessing 1973.

38. Laderman and Roseman 1996:7.

39. Kleinman, Das, and Lock 1996:2.

40. In this respect, Oprah differs significantly from such shows as the European *Loft Story*, which pays its guests to live in a house for many months, and provides a monetary award to the winners of the six-month contest.

41. Nehemas 1991.

42. Hughes 1993:7–9.

43. Hill and Zillman 1999.

44. Showalter 1997:150.

45. Gay 1988:303–304.

46. Senett 1998:118.

47. Arendt 1963.

48. Canovan 1992:171.

49. Ibid., 170–171.
50. Gilligan 1982.
51. Gilligan 1995:43.
52. Held 1995a:157.
53. Morris 1996.
54. Benhabib 1992:100.
55. Arendt 1968.
56. Kleinman 1995:184.
57. Mair 1998:324.
58. Gitlin 1995:92.
59. Bernhard Schlink, *The Reader*, 157.
60. Bakhtin 1978.
61. Bakhtin and Holquist 1981.
62. Bauman 1993.
63. Pippin 2000:11–12.
64. In this vein, the dialogical moral structure of the Oprah talk show is reminiscent of the Truth and Reconciliation Committee of South Africa. According to the main architects of the committee: "truth is viewed to emerge from a dialogical process . . . a process involving a multi-faceted, always incomplete work of (re)construction. Truth is something, ironically, we will have to build on the back of lies, of truth and deceit." This dialogical structure, which is at the heart of African American epistemology, constitutes the "moral nerve" of Oprah Winfrey's enterprise.
65. Onstad 1998:23.
66. Scott 1990.
67. Bourdieu and Wacquant 1992:257.
68. Moseley-Braun 1996:120.
69. This is a theme that has been much developed by movies such as *The Sweet Hereafter* and *American Beauty*.
70. Bell 1993:3.
71. Coontz 1992.
72. Nussbaum 1999.
73. Stark 1995:58.
74. Raeder 1996.
75. Drye 1998/99.
76. Shull 1999:1666.
77. One of the many examples available of the ways in which courts do not recognize the category of psychological harm. In 1993, in Texas, a woman was secretly videotaped having sex with her boyfriend, after which the tape was circulated by the people who had videotaped her. As a result she was mocked by her classmates and her performance suffered; she felt deeply injured and sought psychological counsel. When the case was brought to the Supreme Court of Texas, it refused to recognize the harm that was done to her in psychological terms (Appleberry 1995).

78. See Kleinman, Das, and Lock 1996. Of course the notion of psychological health or harm is very loosely defined, but it carries with it the possibility of thinking about social arrangements in a very different way. Thus, for example, the World Bank economists have developed a meter of suffering called DALY (disabilty adjusted life years), which measures the cost of suffering from illnesses globally. In this index the cost of mental health problems—such as suicide, mental illness, trauma due to violence, abuse—is not included in the computations so that the state is in fact not deemed responsible for that burden.

79. Sandel 1996:351.

80. Transcript, September 15, 1998.

81. Ibid.

82. Schiefflin 1995.

83. Ibid.

84. Hacking 1995:258.

85. Levinas 1988:162.

86. Nussbaum 1986.

87. Ibid., 384–385.

88. Nussbaum 1990:152.

9. CONCLUSION: ORDINARY PEOPLE, EXTRAORDINARY TELEVISION

1. Benjamin 1973:81.

2. F. Jameson, "Postmodernism: Or the Cultural Logic if Late Capitalism," *New Left Review* 146:53–92; Lyotard 1984.

3. See Jameson (1984).

4. See in particular Scott Lash, *The Sociology of Postmodernism* (London: Sage, 1990).

5. Levine 1971:xxxiv.

6. See Eagleton 1984:116.

7. Weber, Gerth, and Mills 1946:275.

BIBLIOGRAPHY

Abdullah, A. 1998. "Mammy-ism: A Diagnosis of Psychological Misorientation for Women of African Descent." *Journal of Black Psychology* 24 (2): 196–210.

Abramson, P. R. and S. D. Pinkerton. 1995. *Sexual Nature, Sexual Culture*. Chicago: University of Chicago Press.

Abt, V. and M. Seesholtz. 1994. "The Shameless World of Phil, Sally, and Oprah: Television Talk Shows and the Deconstructing of Society." *Journal of Popular Culture* 28:171–191.

Abu-Lughod, L. 1986. "Honor and the Virtues of Autonomy." In *Veiled Sentiments: Honor and Poetry in a Bedouin Society*, 78–117. Berkeley: University of California Press.

——. 1999. "The Interpretation of Culture(s) After Television." In S. Ortner, ed., *The Fate of "Culture": Geertz and Beyond*. Berkeley: University of California Press.

Ackerman, B. A. 1980. *Social Justice in the Liberal State*. New Haven: Yale University Press.

Adams, V. 1998. "Suffering the Winds of Lhasa: Politicized Bodies, Human Rights, Cultural Difference and Humanism in Tibet." *Medical Anthropology Quarterly* 12 (1): 74–102.

Alexander, J. C. 1984. "Three Models of Culture and Society Relations: Toward an Analysis of Watergate." *Sociological Theory* 2:290–314.

Allen, E. Jr. 1992. "Ever Feeling One's Twoness: 'Double Ideals' and 'Double Consciousness' in the Souls of Black Folk." *Critique of Anthropology* 12 (3): 261–275.

Allor, M. 1996. "The Politics of Producing Audiences." In J. Hay, Lawrence Groosberg, and Ellen Wartella, eds., *The Audience and Its landscape*. Boulder: Westview, 209–219.

Amato, J. A. and D. Monge. 1990. *Victims and Values: A History and a Theory of Suffering*. New York: Greenwood.

Ang, I. 1990. "Melodramatic Identifications: Television Fiction and Women's Fantasy." In M. E. Brown, ed., *Television and Women's Culture: The Politics of the Popular*. London: Sage, 75–88.

Appadurai, A. 1996. *Modernity at Large: Cultural Dimensions of Globalization*. Minneapolis: University of Minnesota Press.

Appleberry, M. 1995. "Notes and Comments: Negligent Infliction of Emotional Distress: A Focus on Relationships." *American Journal of Law & Medicine* 21 (2–3): 301–322.

Arendt, H. 1958. *The Human Condition.* Chicago: University of Chicago Press.

——. 1963. *On Revolution.* New York: Viking.

——. 1968. *Men in Dark Times.* New York: Harcourt Brace & World.

Asad, T. 1996. "On Torture, or Cruel, Inhuman, and Degrading Treatment." *Social Research* 63 (4): 1081–1109.

Austin, J. L. 1962. *How to Do Things with Words.* Cambridge: Harvard University Press.

Baczko, B. 1997. *Job, mon ami: promesses du bonheur et fatalité du mal.* Paris: Gallimard.

Bakhtin, M. M. 1978. *Esthetique et theorie du roman.* Paris: Gallimard.

Bakhtin, M. M. and M. Holquist. 1981. *The Dialogic Imagination: Four Essays.* Austin: University of Texas Press.

Baritz, L. 1960. *The Servants of Power: A History of the Use of Social Science in American Industry.* Middletown, Conn.: Wesleyan University Press.

Barker, C. 1997. *Global Television: An Introduction.* Oxford, U.K.; Malden, Mass.: Blackwell.

Baudrillard, J. and S. Lotringer. 1988. *The Ecstasy of Communication.* Brooklyn, N.Y.: Autonomedia.

Bauman, Z. 1993. *Postmodern Ethics.* Oxford, U.K.; Cambridge, Mass.: Blackwell.

Baxandall, M. 1985. *Patterns of Intention: On the Historicla Explanation of Pictures.* New Haven: Yale University Press.

Beck, U. 1992. *Risk Society: Towards a New Modernity.* London; Newbury Park, Calif.: Sage.

——. 1997a. "Democratization of the Family." *Childhood* 4 (2): 151–168.

——. 1997b. "The Social Morals of an Individual Life." *Cultural Values* 1 (1): 118–126.

——. 2000. *What Is Globalization?* Cambridge, U.K.; Malden, Mass.: Polity Press; Blackwell.

Beck, U. and E. Beck-Gernsheim. 1995. *The Normal Chaos of Love.* Cambridge, U.K.; Cambridge, Mass.: Polity Press; Blackwell.

——. 1996. "Individualization and Precarious Freedoms: Perspectives and Controversies of a Subject-Orientated Sociology." In P. Heelas, S. Lash, and Paul Morris, eds., *Detraditionalization,* 23–48. Cambridge, Mass.: Basil Blackwell.

Beck, U., A. Giddens, and S. Lash. 1994. *Reflexive Modernization: Politics, Tradition and Aesthetics in the Modern Social Order.* Stanford: Stanford University Press.

Beck, U. and N. Sznaider. Forthcoming. *Global America.*

Beisel, N. 1993. "Morals Versus Art: Censorship, the Politics of Interpretation, and the Victorian Nude." *American Sociological Review* 58:145–162.

Beisel, N. K. 1997. *Imperiled Innocents: Anthony Comstock and Family Reproduction in Victorian America.* Princeton: Princeton University Press.

Bell, V. 1993. *Interrogating Incest: Feminism, Foucault, and the Law.* London; New York: Routledge.

Bellah, R. N. 1985. *Habits of the Heart: Individualism and Commitment in American Life*. Berkeley: University of California Press.

———. 1991. *The Good Society*. New York: Knopf.

Benhabib, S. 1992. *Situating the Self: Gender, Community, and Postmodernism in Contemporary Ethics*. New York: Routledge.

Benjamin, W. 1973. *Illuminations*. London: Fontana/Collins.

Berger, P. L., B. Berger, and H. Kellner. 1973. *The Homeless Mind: Modernization and Consciousness*. New York: Random House.

Bloomfield, M. W. and C. W. Dunn. 1989. *The Role of the Poet in Early Societies*. Cambridge, U.K.; Wolfeboro, N.H.: D. S. Brewer.

Boltanski, L. 1990. *L'amour et la Justice comme Competences: trois essais de sociologie de l'action*. Paris: Editions Metailie.

———. 1999. *Distant Suffering: Morality, Media and Politics*. Cambridge, New York: Cambridge University Press.

Boltanski, L. and L. Thevenot. 1987. *Les Economies de la grandeur*. Paris: Presses universitaires de France.

———. 1989. *Justesse et justice dans le travail*. Paris: Presses universitaires de France.

———. 1991. *De la justification: les economies de la grandeur*. Paris: Gallimard.

Booth, W. 1988. *The Company We Keep: An Ethics of Fiction*. Berkeley: University of California Press.

Boruah, B. J. 1988. *Fiction and Emotion: A Study in Aesthetics and the Philosophy of Mind*. Oxford: Clarendon.

Bourdieu, P. 1979. *La distinction: critique sociale du jugement*. Paris: Editions de Minuit.

———. 1988. *Homo Academicus*. Stanford: Stanford University Press.

———. 1996. *Sur la television; suivi de L'emprise du journalisme*. Paris: Liber.

Bourdieu, P. and L. J. D. Wacquant. 1992. *An Invitation to Reflexive Sociology*. Chicago: University of Chicago Press.

Bourdon, J. 2000. "Live Television Is Still Alive: On Television as an Unfulfilled Promise." *Media, Culture, and Society* 22 (5): 531–556.

Brunner, J. 1995. *Freud and the Politics of Psychoanalysis*. Oxford, U.K.; Cambridge, Mass.: Blackwell.

Burke, K. 1973. *The Philosophy of Literary Form*. Berkeley: University of California Press.

Burke, K. and J. R. Gusfield. 1989. *On Symbols and Society*. Chicago: University of Chicago Press.

Cancian, F. 1990. *Love in America: Gender and Self-Development*. Cambridge, U.K.; New York: Cambridge University Press.

Canovan, M. 1992. *Hannah Arendt: A Reinterpretation of Her Political Thought*. Cambridge, U.K.; New York: Cambridge University Press.

Caputo, J. D. 1993. *Against Ethics: Contributions to a Poetics of Obligation with Constant Reference to Deconstruction*. Bloomington: Indiana University Press.

Carbaugh, D. 1988. *Talking American: Cultural Discourses on Donahue*. Norwood, N.J.: Ablex.

Carpignano, P., R. Andersen, S. Aronowitz, and W. Difazio. 1991. "Chatter in the Age of Electronic Reproduction: Talk Television and the 'Public Mind.' " *Social Text* 26:33–55.

Carson, A. 1995. *Glass, Irony, and God*. New York: New Directions.

Castells, M. 1996. *The Rise of the Network Society*. Cambridge: Blackwell.

Cavell, S. and S. Mulhall. 1996. *The Cavell Reader*. Cambridge, Mass.: Blackwell.

Chartier, R. 1995. *Forms and Meanings: Texts, Performances, and Audiences from Codex to Computer*. Philadelphia: University of Pennsylvania Press.

Chrisler, J. C. 1996. "Politics and Women's Weight." *Feminism and Psychology* 6 (2): 181–184.

Cloud, D. L. 1988. *Control and Consolation in American Culture and Politics: Rhetoric of Therapy*. Thousand Oaks, Calif.: Sage.

——. 1992. "The Limits of Interpretation: Ambivalence and the Stereotype in *Spenser: For Hire*." *Critical Studies in Mass Communication* 9:311–324.

Cochrane, J. R., J. W. DeGruchy, and S. Martin. 1999. *Facing the Truth*. Athens: Ohio University Press.

Collins, P. H. 1986. "Learning from the Outsider Within: The Sociological Significance of Black Feminist Thought." *Social Problems* 33 (6): 14–31.

——. 1989. "The Social Construction of Black Feminist Thought." *Signs* 14 (4): 745–773.

——. 1990. *Black Feminist Thought: Knowledge, Consciousness and the Politics of Empowerment*. New York, London: Routledge.

Collins, R. 1990. "Stratification, Emotions, and the Transient Emotions." In T. D. Kemper, ed., *Research Agenda in the Sociology of Emotions*, 27–57. Albany: SUNY Press, 27–57.

——. 1995. "Black Women and Motherhood." In V. Held, ed., *Justice and Care: Essential Readings in Feminist Ethics*. Boulder: Westview.

Connell, R. 2000. "Sociology and World Market Sociology." *Contemporary Sociology* 29 (1): 291–296.

Conrad, P. and J. W. Schneider. 1992. *Deviance and Medicalization: From Badness to Sickness*. Philadelphia: Temple University Press.

Coontz, S. 1988. *The Social Origins of Private Life: A History of American Families, 1600–1900*. London; New York: Verso.

——. 1992. *The Way We Never Were: American Families and the Nostalgia Trap*. New York: Basic.

Craib, I. 1994. *The Importance of Disappointment*. London; New York: Routledge.

Crang, M., P. Crang, and J. May. 1999. *Virtual Geographies: Bodies, Space, and Relations*. London; New York: Routledge.

Csordas, T. J. 1983. "The Rhetoric of Transformation in Ritual Healing." *Culture, Medicine and Psychiatry* 7:333–375.

——. 1994. *The Sacred Self: A Cultural Phenomenology of Charismatic Healing*. Berkeley: University of California Press.

——. 1996. "Imaginal Performance and Memory in Ritual Healing." In C. Laderman and M. Roseman, eds., *The Performance of Healing*. New York: Routledge.

Cushman, P. 1995. "Self-Liberation Through Consumerism: Post–World War II Object Relations Theory, Self Psychology, and the Empty Self." In *Constructing the Self, Constructing America*, 210–278. Reading, Mass: Addison-Wesley.

Danticat, E. 1994. *Breath, Eyes, Memory.* London: Abacus.

Danto, A. C. 1985. "Philosophy as/and/of Literature." In J. Rajchman and C. West, eds., *Post-Analytic Philosophy.* New York: Columbia University Press.

Darnton, R. 1979. *The Business of Enlightenment: A Publishing History of the Encyclopedia, 1775–1800.* Cambridge: Belknap.

——. 1985. "Workers Revolt: The Great Cat Massacre of the Rue Saint Severin." In *The Great Cat Massacre and Other Episodes in French Cultural History*, 75–104. New York: Vintage.

Das, V. 1997. *Suffering, Theodicies, Disciplinary Practices, Appropriations.* London: Blackwell (UNESCO).

Decker, J. L. 1997. *Made in America: Self-Styled Success from Horatio Alger to Oprah Winfrey.* Minneapolis: University of Minnesota Press.

Demos, J. 1988. "Shame and Guilt in Early New England." In C. Z. Stearns and P. N. Stearns, *Emotion and Social Change*, 69–86. New York: Holmes and Meier.

Derrida, J. 1978. *Writing and Difference.* Chicago: University of Chicago Press.

Dershowitz, A. 1994. *The Abuse Excuse: And Other Cop-outs, Sob Stories, and Evasions of Responsibility.* Boston: Little, Brown.

Dickson, L. 1993. "The Future of Marriage and Family in Black America." *Journal of Black Studies* 23 (4): 472–491.

DiMaggio, P. 1982. "Cultural Entrepreneurship in Nineneenth-Century Boston: The Creation of an Organizational Base for High Culture in America." *Media, Culture and Society* 4:33–50.

Douglas, M. 1966. *Purity and Danger: An Analysis of Concepts of Pollution and Taboo.* New York: Praeger.

Downs, D. A. 1996. *More Than Victims: Battered Women, the Syndrome Society, and the Law.* Chicago: University of Chicago Press.

Dreyfus, H. L., P. Rabinow, and M. Foucault. 1984. *Foucault: Beyond Structuralism and Hermeneutics.* Paris: Gallimard.

Drye, J. A. 1998/99. "The Silent Victims of Domestic Violence: Children Forgotten by the Judicial System." *Gonzaga Law Review* 34 (2): 229.

Du Bois, W.E.B. 1968. *The Souls of Black Folks: Essays and Sketches.* New York: Allograph Press.

Durkheim, E. 1915 (1969). "Origins of These Beliefs (End)—Origin of the Idea of the Totemic Principle or Mana." In *The Elementary Forms of Religious Life*, 205–239. New York: Free Press.

Dyson, M. E. 1993a. *Reflecting Black: African-American Cultural Criticism.* Minneapolis: University of Minnesota Press.

——. 1993b. "Michael Jackson's Postmodern Spirituality." In *Reflecting Black: African-American Cultural Criticism*, 35–60. Minneapolis: University of Minnesota Press.

Eagleton, T. (1984) *The Function of Criticism: From the Spectator to Post-Structuralism.* London: Verso.

Elise, S. (1995) "Teenaged Mothers: A Sense of Self." In B. J. Dickerson, ed., *African American Single Mothers: Understanding Their Lives and Families*, 53–79. Thousand Oaks, Calif.; London; New Delhi: Sage.

Featherstone, M. (1990) *Global Culture: Nationalism, Globalization, and Modernity: A Theory, Culture & Society Special Issue*. London; Newbury Park: Sage.

Fiske, J. 1989. *Understanding Popular Culture*. Boston: Unwin Hyman.

Foucault, M. 1965. *Madness and Civilization: A History of Insanity in the Age of Reason*. New York: Pantheon.

——. 1986. *The Care of the Self*. New York: Vintage.

——. 1999. *Les anormaux: cours au College de France (1974–1975)*. Paris: Gallimard, Seuil.

Frank, J. 1961. *Persuasion and Healing*. Baltimore: Johns Hopkins University Press.

Frank, T. 1997. *The Conquest of Cool: Business Culture, Counterculture, and the Rise of Hip Consumerism*. Chicago: University of Chicago Press.

Freud, S. 1919. *The Uncanny*. The Standard Edition of the Complete Psychological Works of Sigmund Freud, Vol. 17, 219–256. London: Hogarth Press and the Institute of Psycho-Analysis.

Frye, N. 1957. *Anatomy of Criticism: Four Essays*. Princeton: Princeton University Press.

Gamson, J. 1994. *Claims to Fame: Celebrity in Contemporary America*. Berkeley: University of California Press.

——. 1998. *Freaks Talk Back: Tabloid Talk Shows and Sexual Nonconformity*. Chicago: University of Chicago Press.

Garsten, C. and C. Grey. 1997. "How to Become Oneself: Discourse of Subjectivity in Post-Bureaucratic Organizations." *Organization* 4 (2): 211–228.

Gates, H. L. 1988. *The Signifying Monkey: A Theory of Afro-American Literary Criticism*. New York: Oxford University Press.

Gay, P. 1973. *The Enlightenment; a Comprehensive Anthology*. New York: Simon and Schuster.

——. 1988. *Freud: A Life of Our Time*. New York: Norton.

Geertz, C. 1973. "Ideology as Cultural System." In *The Interpretation of Cultures*, 219. New York: Basic.

Gemin, J. 1997. "Manufacturing Codependency: Self-Help as Discursive Formation." *Critical Studies in Mass Communication* 14 (3): 249–266.

George, S. M. and B. J. Dickerson. 1995. "The Role of the Grandmother in Poor Single-Mother Families and Households." In B. J. Dickerson, ed., *African American Single Mothers: Understanding Their Lives and Families*, 146–163. Thousand Oaks, Calif.; London; New Delhi: Sage.

Gerbner, G., L. Gross, M. Morgan, and N. Signorielli. 1980. "The 'Mainstreaming' of America: Violence Profile No. 11." *Journal of Communication* 30 (3): 10–29.

Gergen, M. 1992. "Life Stories: Pieces of a Dream." In G. C. Rosenwald and R. L. Ochberg, eds., *Storied Lives: The Cultural Politics of Self Understanding*. New Haven: Yale University Press.

Germov, J. and L. Williams. 1996. "The Sexual Division of Dieting: Women's Voices." *Sociological Review* 44 (4): 630–647.

——. 1999. "Dieting Women: Self-Surveillance and the Body Panopticon." In J. Sobal and D. Maurer, eds., *Weighty Issues: Fatness and Thinness as Social Problems*. Hawthorne, N.Y.: Aldine de Gruyter.

Giddens, A. 1990. *The Consequences of Modernity*. Stanford: Stanford University Press.

——. 1991. *Modernity and Self-Identity: Self and Society in the Late Modern Age*. Stanford: Stanford University Press.

Gilligan, C. 1982. *In a Different Voice: Psychological Theory and Women's Development*. Cambridge: Harvard University Press.

——. 1995. "Moral Orientation and Development." In V. Held, ed., *Justice and Care: Essential Readings in Feminist Ethics*, 31–46. Boulder: Westview.

Ginzburg, C. 1980. *The Cheese and the Worms: The Cosmos of a Sixteenth-Century Miller*. Baltimore: Johns Hopkins University Press.

Gitlin, Todd. 1995. *The Twilight of Common Dreams: Why America Is Wracked by Culture Wars*. New York: Henry Holt.

Gledhill, C. 1991. *Stardom: Industry of Desire*. London; New York: Routledge.

Goffman, E. 1974. *Frame Analysis: An Essay on the Organization of Experience*. New York: Harper & Row.

Goldmann, L. 1964. "The Whole and the Parts." In *The Hidden God*, 3–21. London: Routledge.

Goleman, D. 1995. *Emotional Intelligence*. New York: Bantam.

Gottdiener, M. 1997. *The Theming of America: Dreams, Visions, and Commercial Spaces*. Boulder: Westview.

Grathoff, R. 1970. *The Structure of Social Inconsistencies: A Contribution to a Unified Theory of Play, Game and Social Action*. The Hague: Martinus Nijhoff.

Gray, J. 1992. *Men Are from Mars, Women Are from Venus: A Practical Guide for Improving Communication and Getting What You Want in Your Relationships*. New York: HarperCollins.

Greenberg, G. 1994. *The Self on the Shelf: Recovery Books and the Good Life*. Albany: State University of New York Press.

Greenblatt, S. 1980. *Renaissance Self-Fashioning: From More to Shakespeare*. Chicago: University of Chicago Press.

——. 1999. "The Touch of the Real." In S. Ortner, ed., *The Fate of "Culture": Geertz and Beyond*. Berkeley: University of California Press.

Greene, B. and O. Winfrey. 1996. *Make the Connection: Ten Steps to a Better Body—and a Better Life*. New York: Hyperion.

Griswold, Wendy. 1991. "American Character and the American Novel." *American Journal of Sociology* 86:740–765.

Gunn, Giles B. 1987. *The Culture of Criticism and the Criticism of Culture*. New York and Oxford: Oxford University Press.

Haag, L. L. 1993. "Oprah Winfrey: The Construction of Intimacy in the Talk Show Setting." *Journal of Popular Culture* 26 (4): 115–121.

Habermas, J. 1971. *Knowledge and Human Interests*. Boston: Beacon.

Hacking, I. 1995. *Rewriting the Soul: Multiple Personality and the Sciences of Memory*. Princeton: Princeton University Press.

Hagstrum, J. H. 1980. *Sex and Sensibility: Ideal and Erotic Love from Milton to Mozart*. Chicago and London: University of Chicago Press.

Hakken, D. 1999. *Cyborgs@cyberspace?: An Ethnographer Looks to the Future*. New York: Routledge.

Halttunen, K. 1995. "Humanitarianism and the Pornography of Pain in Anglo-American Culture." *The American Historical Review* 100 (2): 303–334.

Handelman, D. 1979. "Is Naven Ludic: Paradox and the Communication of Identity." *Social Analysis* 1:177–188.

——. 1985. "Charisma, Liminality, and Symbolic Types." In Erik Cohen, Moshe Lissak, and Uri Alamagor, eds., *Comparative Social Dynamics*, 346–359. London: Westview.

——. 1990. *Models and Mirrors: Towards an Anthropology of Public Events*. Cambridge; New York: Cambridge University Press.

Hannerz, U. 1996. *Transnational Connections: Culture, People, Places*. London; New York: Routledge.

Haraway, D. 1991. "A Cyborg Manifesto: Science, Technology, and Socialist-Feminism in the Late Twentieth Century." In *Simians, Cyborgs and Women: The Reinvention of Nature*, 149–181. New York: Routledge.

Hare-Mustin, R. 1983. "An Appraisal of the Relationship Between Women and Psychotherapy." *American Psychologist* 38:593–601.

Hays, S. 1996. *The Cultural Contradictions of Motherhood*. New Haven: Yale University Press.

Heaton, J. A. and N. L. Wilson. 1995 *Tuning in Trouble: Talk TV's Destructive Impact on Mental Health*. San Francisco: Jossey-Bass.

Heelas, P. 1996. *The New Age Movement: The Celebration of the Self and the Sacralization of Modernity*. Malden, Mass.: Blackwell.

Held, D. 1980. *Introduction to Critical Theory: Horkheimer to Habermas*. Berkeley: University of California Press.

Held, D. and A. G. McGrew. 2000. *The Global Transformations Reader: An Introduction to the Globalization Debate*. Malden, Mass.: Polity Press.

Held, V. 1995a. "Feminist Inquiry and the Future." In *Justice and care: Essential Readings in Feminist Ethics*, 153–176. Boulder: Westview.

——. 1995b. *Justice and Care: Essential Readings in Feminist Ethics*. Boulder: Westview.

Hemmons, W. A. 1996. *Black Women in the New World Order: Social Justice and the African American Female*. Westport, Conn.: Praeger.

Herman, E. 1995. *The Romance of American Psychology: Political Culture in the Age of Experts, 1940–1970*. Berkeley: University of California Press.

Hill, J. R. and D. Zillman. 1999. "The Oprahization of America: Sympathetic Crime Talk and Leniency." *Journal of Broadcasting & Electronic Media* 43 (1): 67–82.

Hillis Miller, J. 1982. *Fiction and Repetition: Seven English Novels*. Cambridge: Harvard University Press.

Hirsch, E. D. 1967. *Validity in Interpretation*. New Haven: Yale University Press.

Hobsbawm, E. J. 1987. *The Age of Empire, 1875–1914*. New York: Pantheon.

Hochschild, A. 1983. *The Managed Heart: Commercialization of Human Feeling.* Berkeley: University of California Press.

Holland, P. 1997. *The Television Handbook.* London; New York: Routledge.

Holmes, J. A. 1997. *Black Nationalism and Theodicy: A Comparison of the Thought of Henry Highland Garnet, Alexander Crummell, and Henry McNeal Turner.* Th.D. thesis, Boston University.

Holstein, J. A. and G. Miller. 1990. "Rethinking Victimization: An Interactionist Approach to Victimology." *Symbolic Interaction* 13:103–122.

Honkasalo, M. L. and J. Lindquist. 1997. "An Interview with Arthur Kleinman." *Ethnos* 62 (3–4): 107–126.

hooks, b. 1997. "Sisterhood: Political Solidarity Between Women." In D. T. Meyers, ed., *Feminist Social Thought: A Reader.* New York: Routledge.

Hoover, S. M. and K. Lundby. 1997. *Rethinking Media, Religion, and Culture.* Thousand Oaks, Calif.: Sage.

Horton, D. and R. R. Wohl. 1956. "Mass Communication and Para-Social Interaction: Observation on Intimacy at a Distance." *Psychiatry* 19 (3): 212–228.

Hoyer, W. D. and D. J. MacInnis. 2001. *Consumer Behavior.* Boston: Houghton Mifflin.

Hughes, M. and D. H. Demo. 1989. "Self-Perceptions of Black Americans: Self-Esteem and Personal Efficacy." *American Journal of Sociology* 95 (1): 132–159.

Hughes, R. 1993. *Culture of Complaint: The Fraying of America.* New York: Oxford University Press.

Hutcheson, F. 1742. *An essay on the nature and conduct of the passions and affections; with illustrations on the moral sense.* Gainesville, Fla.: Scholars' Facsimiles & Reprints.

Hutcheson, M. A. 1963. *Law and Authority in Eighteenth-Century Deerfield: Civil Authority, the Church, and Community Sentiment.* Deerfield, Mass.: Heritage Foundation [Fellowship Program].

Illouz, E. 1991. "Reason Within Passion: Love in Women's Magazines." *Critical Studies in Mass Communication* 8 (3): 231–248.

——. 1997a. *Consuming the Romantic Utopia: Love and the Cultural Contradictions of Capitalism.* Berkeley: University of California Press.

——. 1997b. "Who Will Care for the Caretaker's Daughter?: Toward a Sociology of Happiness in the Era of Reflexive Modernization." *Theory, Culture and Society* 14 (4): 31–66.

——. 1999. "That Shadowy Realm of the Interior: Oprah Winfrey and Hamlet's Glass." *International Journal of Cultural Studies* 2(1): 109–131.

Irvine, L. J. 1995. "Codependency and Recovery: Gender, Self and Emotions in Popular Self-Help." *Symbolic Interaction* 18:145–163.

——. 1999. *Codependent Forevermore: The Invention of Self in a Twelve-Step Group.* Chicago: University of Chicago Press.

Jakobson, R. and M. Halle. 1956. *Fundamentals of Language.* The Hague: Mouton.

Jameson, F. 1981. *The Political Unconscious: Narrative as a Socially Symbolic Act.* Ithaca: Cornell University Press.

——. 1991. *Postmodernism, or, The Cultural Logic of Late Capitalism*. Durham: Duke University Press.

Jay, M. 1994. "Experience Without a Subject: Walter Benjamin and the Novel." In M. S. Roth, ed., *Rediscovering History: Culture, Politics, and the Psyche*. Stanford: Stanford University Press.

Jordan, J. 1985. *On Call: Political Essays*. Boston: South End Press.

Kaminer, W. 1992. *I'm Dysfunctional, You're Dysfunctional: The Recovery Movement and Other Self-Help Fashions*. Reading, Mass.: Addison-Wesley.

Kellner, D. 1995. *Media Culture: Cultural Studies, Identity, and Politics Between the Modern and the Postmodern*. London; New York: Routledge.

Keyes, D. 1999. "The Imaginary Community of the *Live* Studio Audience of Television." *Studies in Popular Culture* 21 (3): 65–78.

Kidron, C. 1999. *Amcha's Second-Generation Holocaust Survivors: A Recursive Journey Into the Past to Construct Wounded Carriers of Memory*. M.A. thesis, Hebrew University of Jerusalem.

Kirk-Duggan, C. A. 1992. *Theodicy and the Redacted African-American Spirituals of the 1960s Civil Rights Movement*. Ph.D. diss., Baylor University.

Kleinman, A. 1980. *Patients and Healers in the Context of Culture: An Exploration of the Borderland Between Anthropology, Medicine, and Psychiatry*. Berkeley: University of California Press.

——. 1988. *Rethinking Psychiatry: From Cultural Category to Personal Experience*. New York; London: Free Press; Collier Macmillan.

——. 1995. "Pitch, Picture, Power: The Globalization of Local Suffering and the Transformation of Social Experience." *Ethnos* 60 (3–4): 181–191.

Kleinman, A., V. Das, and M. Lock. 1996. *Social Suffering*. Berkeley; Los Angeles; London: University of California Press.

Kleinman, A. and J. Kleinman. 1991. "Suffering and Its Professional Transformations: Toward an Ethnography of Interpersonal Experience. *Culture, Medicine and Psychiatry* 15 (3): 275–301.

Laderman, C. and M. Roseman, eds. 1996. *The Performance of Healing*. Routledge.

Lamb, S. 1996. *The Trouble with Blame: Victims, Perpetrators, and Responsibility*. Cambridge: Harvard University Press.

Lambert, F. 1992. " 'I saw the book talk': Slave Readings of the First Great Awakening." *The Journal of Negro History* 77 (4): 185.

Lamont, M. 2000. *Money, Morals and Manners: The Dignity of Working-Class Men*. Cambridge: Harvard University Press.

Lamont, M. and L. Thevenot. 2000. *Rethinking Comparative Cultural Sociology: Repertoires of Evaluation in France and the United States*. Cambridge, U.K.; New York: Cambridge University Press.

Langer, L. 1996. "Social Suffering and Holocaust Atrocities." In A. Kleinman, V. Das, and M. Lock, eds., *Social Suffering*, 47–65. Berkeley; Los Angeles; London: University of California Press.

Lasch, C. 1977. *Haven in a Heartless World: The Family Besieged*. New York: Basic.

Lears, T. J. J. 1981. *No Place of Grace: Antimodernism and the Transformation of American Culture, 1880–1920*. New York: Pantheon.

———. 1989. "American Advertising and the Reconstruction of the Body, 1880–1930." In K. Grover, ed., *Fitness in American Culture: Images of Health, Sport, and the Body, 1830–1940*. Amherst: University of Massachusetts Press.

Leslie, R. A. 1995. "Women's Life-Affirming Morals and the Cultural Unity of African Peoples." In B. J. Dickerson, ed., *African American Single Mothers: Understanding Their Lives and Families*, 37–52. Thousand Oaks, Calif.; London; New Delhi: Sage.

———. 1997. "Brer Rabbit, a Play of the Human Spirit: Recreating Black Culture Through Brer Rabbit Stories." *International Journal of Sociology and Social Policy* 17 (6): 59–83.

Lessing, G. H. 1973. *Laocoon*. In P. Gay, *The Enlightenment: A Comprehensive Anthology*. New York: Simon & Schuster.

Levinas, E. 1988. "Useless Suffering." In R. Bernasconi and D. Wood, eds., *The Provocation of Levinas: Rethinking the Other*, 156–167. London; New York: Routledge.

Levine, D. N. 1971. *On Individuality and Social Forms: Selected Writings [of] Georg Simmel*. Chicago; London: University of Chicago Press.

Levine, L. 1988. *Highbrow/Lowbrow: The Emergence of Cultural Hierarchy in America*. Cambridge: Harvard University Press.

———. 1993. *Black Culture and Black Consciousness: Afro-American Folk Thought from Slavery to Freedom*. New York: Oxford University Press.

Levi-Strauss, C. 1963. "The Effectiveness of Symbols." In *Structural Anthropology*, 183–201. New York: Anchor.

Lichterman, P. 1992. "Self-Help Reading as a Thin Culture." *Media, Culture and Society* 14:421–447.

Liebes, T. and E. Katz. 1990. *The Export of Meaning: Cross-Cultural Readings of Dallas*. New York: Oxford University Press.

Lifton, R. J. 1993. *The Protean Self: Human Resilience in an Age of Fragmentation*. New York: Basic.

Livingstone, S. M. and P. K. Lunt. 1994. *Talk on Television: Audience Participation and Public Debate*. London; New York: Routledge.

Long, E. 1994. "Textual Interpretation as Collective Action." In J. Cruz and J. Lewis, eds., *Viewing, Reading, Listening*, 181–211. Boulder: Westview.

Lowe, J. 1998/2001. *Oprah Winfrey Speaks: Insight from the World's Most Influential Voice*. New York; Chichester: Wiley.

Lowenthal, L. 1944/1961. "The Triumph of Mass Idols." In *Literature, Popular Culture, and Society*. Englewood Cliffs, N.J.: Prentice-Hall.

Lowney, K. S. 1999. *Baring Our Souls: TV Talk Shows and the Religion of Recovery*. New York: Aldine de Gruyter.

Lyotard, J. F. 1984. *The Postmodern Condition: A Report on Knowledge*. Minneapolis: University of Minnesota Press.

Marchand, R. 1985. *Advertising the American Dream: Making Way for Modernity, 1920–1940.* Berkeley: University of California Press.

Marcus, G. E. 1998. *Ethnography Through Thick and Thin.* Princeton: Princeton University Press.

Marris, P. and S. Thornham. 1996. *Media Studies: A Reader.* Edinburgh: Edinburgh University Press.

Marshall, D. P. 1997. *Celebrity and Power: Fame in Contemporary Culture.* Minneapolis: University of Minnesota Press.

Mattelart, M. 1997. "Everyday Life." In C. Brunsdon, J. D'Acci, and L. Spigel, eds., *Feminist Television Criticism,* 23–35. Oxford: Clarendon.

McGraw, P. 1999. *Life Strategies: Doing What Works, Doing What Matters.* London: Vermilion.

McKinley, N. M. 1999. "Ideal Weight/Ideal Women: Society Constructs the Female." In J. Sobal and D. Maurer, eds., *Weighty Issues: Fatness and Thinness as Social Problems.* Hawthorne, N.Y.: Aldine de Gruyter.

Meyer, J., J. Boli, G. Thomas, and F. Ramirez. 1997. "World Society and the Nation State." In *The American Journal of Sociology* 103 (1): 144–181.

Miller, D. 1998. *Shopping, Place, and Identity.* New York: Routledge.

Miller, G. 1997. *Becoming Miracle Workers: Language and Meaning in Brief Therapy.* New York: Aldin de Gruyter.

Miller, T. and A. W. McHoul. 1998. *Popular Culture and Everyday Life.* London; Thousand Oaks, Calif.: Sage.

Miller, W. I. 1993. "Emotions, Honor, and the Affective Life of the Heroic." In *Humiliation: And Other Essays on Honor, Social Discomfort, and Violence,* 93–130. Ithaca: Cornell University Press.

Modelski, T. 1997. "The Search for Tomorrow in Today's Soap Operas." In P. Marris and S. Thornham, eds., *Media Studies: A Reader,* 371–390. Edinburgh: Edinburgh University Press.

Montrose, L. 1992. "New Historicisms." In S. Greenblatt and G. B. Gunn, eds., *Redrawing the Boundaries: The Transformation of English and American Literary Studies,* 392–418. New York: Modern Language Association of America.

Moore, B. 1972. *Reflections on the Causes of Human Misery and Upon Certain Proposals to Eliminate Them.* Boston: Beacon.

Morris, A. 2000. "Charting Futures for Sociology: Social Organization." *Contemporary Sociology* 29 (3): 445–454.

Morris, D. B. 1991. *The Culture of Pain.* Berkeley: University of California Press.

——. 1996. "Voice, Genre, and Moral Community." In A. Kleinman, V. Das, and M. Lock, eds., *Social Suffering,* 25–46. Berkeley; Los Angeles; London: University of California Press.

Morrison, T. 1994. *The Nobel Lecture in Literature* (audio recording). New York: Random House Audio Publishing.

Moseley-Braun, C. 1996. "Black Women's Political Images in the Media." In V. T. Berry and C. Manning-Miller, eds., *Mediated Messages and African American Culture.* Thousand Oaks, Calif.: Sage.

Munson, W. 1993. *All Talk: The Talk Show in Media Culture.* Philadelphia: Temple University Press.

Nehemas, A. 1991. "Serious Watching." In D. R. Hiley, J. Bohman, and R. Shusterman, eds., *The Interpretive Turn: Philosophy, Science, Culture.* Ithaca: Cornell University Press.

Neiman, S. 2001. *Evil in Modern Thought: An Alternative History of Philosophy.* Princeton: Princeton University Press.

Nelson, A. and B. Robinson. 1994. *Gigolos and Madames Bountiful: Illusions of Gender, Power, and Intimacy.* Toronto; Buffalo: University of Toronto Press.

Nichter, M. 1981. "Idioms of Distress: Alternatives in the Expression of Psychological Distress: A Case Study from South India." *Culture, Medicine and Psychiatry* 5 (4): 379–408.

Nightingale, V. 1990. "Women as Audiences." In M. E. Brown, ed., *Television and Women's Culture: The Politics of the Popular.* London: Sage.

Niles, L. 1984. "Rhetorical Characteristics of Traditional Black Preaching." *Journal of Black Studies* 15 (1): 41–52.

Nussbaum, M. C. 1986. *The Fragility of Goodness: Luck and Ethics in Greek Tragedy and Philosophy.* Cambridge, U.K.; New York: Cambridge University Press.

——. 1990. *Love's Knowledge: Essays on Philosophy and Literature.* New York: Oxford University Press.

——. 1997. *Cultivating Humanity: A Classical Defense of Reform in Liberal Education.* Cambridge: Harvard University Press.

——. 1999. *Sex and Social Justice.* New York: Oxford University Press.

Nye, R. 1993. "Honor and Male Identity in the Old Regime." In *Masculinity and the Male Codes of Honor in Modern France,* 15–30. Oxford: Oxford University Press.

Okin, S. M. 1989. *Justice, Gender, and the Family.* New York: Basic.

Ortner, S. 1990. "Patterns of History: Cultural Schemas in the Foundings of Sherpa Religious Institutions." In Emiko Ohnuki Tierney, ed., *Culture Through Time: Anthropological Approaches.* Stanford: Stanford University Press.

Ortony, A., G. L. Clore, and A. Collins. 1988. *The Cognitive Structure of Emotions.* Cambridge: Cambridge University Press.

Orwin, C. 1996. "Distant Compassion: CNN and Borrioboola-Gha. (effects of television news coverage of suffering)." *The National Interest* 43:42–49.

Ostrower, F. 1995. *Why the Wealthy Give: The Culture of Elite Philanthropy.* Princeton: Princeton University Press.

Peck, J. 1995. "TV Talk Shows as Therapeutic Discourse: The Ideological Labor of the Televised Talking Cure." *Communications Theory* 5 (1) (Feb. 1995): 58–81.

Peiss, K. 1986. "Cheap Theaters and the Nickel Dumps" and "Reforming Working Women's Recreation." In *Cheap Amusements,* 139–162, 163–184. Philadelphia: Temple University Press.

Pfister, J. and N. Schnog, eds. 1997. *Inventing the Psychological: Toward a Cultural History of Emotional Life in America.* New Haven: Yale University Press.

Pinn, A. B. 1995. *Why, Lord?: Suffering and Evil in Black Theology.* New York: Continuum.

Pippin, R. 2000. *Henry James and Modern Moral Life*. Cambridge: Cambridge University Press.

Pocock, J. G. A. 1976. *Virtue, Commerce, and History: Essays on Political Thought and History, Chiefly in the Eighteenth Century*. Cambridge, U.K.; New York: Cambridge University Press.

Priest, P. J. 1995. *Public Intimacies: Talk Show Participants and Tell-All TV*. Cresskill, N.J.: Hampton Press.

Radway, J. 1991. *Reading the Romance: Women, Patriarchy, and Popular Literature*. Chapel Hill: University of North Carolina Press.

——. 1997. *A Feeling for Books: The Book-of-the-Month Club, Literary Taste, and Middle-Class Desire*. Chapel Hill: University of North Carolina Press.

Raeder, M. S. 1996. "The Double-Edged Sword: Admissibility of Battered Woman Syndrome by and Against Batterers in Cases Implicating Domestic Violence." *University of Colorado Law Review* 67 (4): 789–791.

Rapping, E. 1996. *The Culture of Recovery: Making Sense of the Self-Help Movement in Women's Lives*. Boston: Beacon.

Raviv, A., A. Raviv, and R. Yunovitz. 1989. "Radio Psychology and Psychotherapy: Comparison of Client Attitudes and Expectations." *Professional Psychology: Research and Practice* 20 (2): 67–72.

Redman, B. R. 1949. "The Lisbon Earthquake." In *The Portable Voltaire*, 556–569. New York: Viking.

Rice, J. S. 1998. *A Disease of One's Own: Psychotherapy, Addiction, and the Emergence of Co-Dependency*. New Brunswick, N.J.: Transaction.

Richardson, S. and P. Sabor. 1980. *Pamela, or, Virtue Rewarded*. Harmondsworth, Middlesex, England; New York: Viking Penguin; Penguin.

Rieff, P. 1966. *The Triumph of the Therapeutic*. New York: Harper & Row.

Rimke, H. M. 2000. "Governing Citizens Through Self-Help Literature." *Cultural Studies* 14 (1): 61–78.

Robertson, R. 1992. *Globalization: Social Theory and Global Culture*. London: Sage.

Rojek, C. 1985. *Capitalism and Leisure Theory*. London; New York: Tavistock.

Rorty, R. 1998. *Achieving Our Country: Leftist Thought in Twentieth-Century America*. Cambridge: Harvard University Press.

——. 1999. "Globalization, the Politics of Identity and Social Hope." In *Philosophy and Social Hope*, 229–242. London: Penguin.

Rose, B. 1996. *Television and the Performing Arts: A Handbook and Reference Guide to American Cultural Programming*. New York: Greenwood.

Rose, N. 1996. *Inventing Our Selves: Psychology, Power, and Personhood*. Cambridge, U.K.; New York: Cambridge University Press.

Rosenblatt, L. M. 1978. *The Reader, the Text, the Poem: The Transactional Theory of the Literary Work*. Carbondale and Edwardsville: Southern Illinois University Press.

Rosenthal, G. 1993. "Reconstruction of Life Stories: Principles of Selection in Generating Stories for Narrative Biographical Interviews." In R. Josselson and A.

Lieblich, eds., *The Narrative Study of Lives*, 1:59–91. Newbury Park, London, New Delhi: Sage.

Ross, A. 1989. *No Respect: Intellectuals and Popular Culture*. New York: Routledge.

Ruddick, S. 1995. "Injustice in Families: Assault and Domination." In V. Held, ed., *Justice and Care: Essential Readings in Feminist Ethics*, 203–223. Boulder: Westview.

Rutherford, J. 1990. "A Place Called Home: Identity and the Cultural Politics of Difference." In *Identity: Community, Culture, Difference*. London: Lawrence & Wishart.

Ryan, J. and W. Wentworth. 1999. *Media and Society: The Production of Culture in the Mass Media*. Boston: Allyn and Bacon.

Saidman, A. 1990. *Oprah Winfrey: Media Success Story*. Minneapolis: Lerner Publications.

Salusinszky, I. and J. Derrida. 1987. *Criticism in Society: Interviews with Jacques Derrida, Northrop Frye, Harold Bloom, Geoffrey Hartman, Frank Kermode, Edward Said, Barbara Johnson, Frank Lentricchia, and J. Hillis Miller*. New York: Methuen.

Salvino, D. N. 1989. "The Word in Black and White: Ideologies of Race and Literacy in Antebellum America." In C. A. Davidson, ed., *Reading in America: Literature and Social History*. Baltimore: Johns Hopkins University Press.

Sandel, M. J. 1996. *Democracy's Discontent: American in Search of a Public Philosophy*. Cambridge: Belknap Press of Harvard University Press.

Sanders, C. J. 1996. "Hope and Empathy: Toward an Ethic of Black Empowerment" (Inaugural Lecture). *The Journal of Religious Thought* 52 (2): 1–17.

Scannel, P. 1991. *Broadcast Talk*. London: Sage.

Schiefflin, E. 1995. "On Failure and Performance: Throwing the Medium Out of the Seance." In C. Laderman and M. Roseman, eds, *The Performance of Healing*. New York: Routledge.

Schofield-Clark, L. and S. M. Hoover. 1997. "At the Intersection of Media, Culture, and Religion." In S. M. Hoover and K. Lundby, eds., *Rethinking Media, Religion, and Culture*. Thousand Oaks, Calif.: Sage.

Schwartz, B. 2000. "Self-Determination: The Tyranny of Freedom." *American Psychologist* 55 (1): 79–88.

Schweder, R. A. 1988. "Suffering in Style." *Culture, Medicine and Psychiatry* 12 (4): 479–497.

Schudson, M. 1992. *Watergate in American Memory: How We Remember, Forget, and Reconstruct the Past*. New York: Basic.

——. 1998. *The Good Citizen: A History of American Civic Life*. New York: Martin Kessler.

Scott, J. 1990. *Domination and the Arts of Resistance: Hidden Transcripts*. New Haven: Yale University Press.

——. 1998. *Seeing Like a State: How Certain Schemes to Improve the Human Condition Have Failed*. New Haven: Yale University Press.

Secord, P. F. and K. Ghee. 1986. "Implications of the Black Marriage Market for Marital Conflict." *Journal of Family Issues* 7 (1): 21–30.

Seidman, S. 1997. *Difference Troubles: Queering Social Theory and Sexual Politics.* Cambridge, U.K.; New York: Cambridge University Press.

Senett, R. 1998. *The Corrosion of Character: The Personal Consequences of Work in the New Capitalism.* New York and London: Norton.

Sewell, W. H. 1992. "A Theory of Structure: Duality, Agency, and Transformation." *American Journal of Sociology* 98 (1): 1–29.

Shattuck, J. 1997. *The Talking Cure: TV Talk Shows and Women.* New York: Routledge.

Sheehey, J. 1999. "The Mirror and the Veil: The Passing Novel and the Quest for American Racial Identity." *African American Review* 33 (3): 401.

Shklar, J. N. 1984. *Ordinary Vices.* Cambridge: Belknap Press of Harvard University Press.

Showalter, E. 1997. *Hystories: Hysterical Epidemics and Modern Media.* New York: Columbia University Press.

Shull, J. R. 1999. "Emotional and Psychological Child Abuse: Notes on Discourse, History, and Change." *Stanford Law Review* 51 (6): 1665–1701.

Shweder, R. A. and R. A. Levine. 1984. *Culture Theory: Essays on Mind, Self, and Emotion.* Cambridge, U.K.; New York: Cambridge University Press.

Simon, Richard Keller. 1999. *Trash Culture: Popular Culture and the Great Tradition.* Berkeley: University of California Press.

Simon-Vandenbergen, A. M. 2000. "Towards an Analysis of Interpersonal Meaning in Daytime Talk Shows." In F. Ungerer, ed., *English Media Texts- Past and Present: Language and Textual Structure,* 217–240. Amsterdam/Philadelphia: John Benjamins.

Simonds, W. 1992. *Women and Self-Help Culture: Reading Between the Lines.* New Brunswick, N.J.: Rutgers University Press.

Singer, P. 1994. *Ethics.* Oxford; New York: Oxford University Press.

Skinner, Q. 1978. *The Foundations of Modern Political Thought. Volume 2, The Age of Reformation.* Cambridge, U.K.; New York: Cambridge University Press.

Smith, A. 1817. *The theory of moral sentiment, or, An essay towards an analysis of the principles, by which men naturally judge concerning the conduct and character, first of their neighbours, and afterwards of themselves.* Boston: Wells and Lilly.

Smith, T. L. 1972. *Slavery and Theology: The Emergence of Black Christian Consciousness in Nineteenth-Century America.* Orland, Pa.: American Society of Church History.

Snow, D. A., E. Burke Rochford Jr., Seven K. Worden, and Robert D. Benford. 1986. "Frame Alignment Processes, Micromobilization, and Movement Participation." *American Sociological Review* 51:464–481.

Snow, N. E. 1991. "Compassion." *American Philosophical Quarterly* 28 (3): 195–205.

Sobal, J. and D. Maurer. 1999. *Weighty Issues: Fatness and Thinness as Social Problems.* Hawthorne, N.Y.: Aldine de Gruyter.

Solomon, R. 1976. *The Passions.* Garden City, N.Y.: Anchor Press/Doubleday.

Spacks, P. M. 1975. *The Female Imagination*. New York: Knopf.

Squire, C. 1997. "Empowering Women? The Oprah Winfrey Show." In C. Brunsdon, J. D'Acci, and L. Spigel, eds., *Feminist Television Criticism*, 98–113. Oxford: Clarendon.

Stallybrass, P. and A. White. 1986. *The Politics and Poetics of Transgression*. London: Methuen.

Staples, R. 1997. "An Overview of Race and Marital Status." In H. P. McAdoo, ed., *Black Families*. Thousand Oaks, Calif.: Sage.

Stark, E. 1994–95. "Re-Presenting Women Battering: From Battered Woman Syndrome to Coercive Control." *Albany Law Review* 58:973–1028.

Stearns, P. N. 1994. *American Cool: Constructing a Twentieth-Century Emotional Style*. New York: New York University Press.

Steiner, G. 1961. *The Death of Tragedy*. London: Faber and Faber.

Stepto, R. B. 1991. *From Behind the Veil: A Study of Afro-American Narrative*. Urbana: University of Illinois Press.

Stock, B. 1990. *Listening for the Text: On the Uses of the Past*. Baltimore: Johns Hopkins University Press.

Striegel-Moore, R. and L. Smolak. 1996. "The Role of Race in EAting Disorders." In Linda Smolak and Michael P. Levine, eds., *The Developmental Psychopathology of Eating Disorders: Implications for Research, Prevention, and Treatment*, 259–284. Mahwah, N.J.: Erlbaum Associates.

Stromberg, P. 1993. *Language and Self-Transformation: A Study of the Christian Conversion Narrative*. Cambridge: Cambridge University Press.

Stuart, A. 1990. "Feminism: Dead or Alive?" In J. Rutherford, ed., *Identity: Community, Culture, Difference*, 28–42. London: Lawrence & Wishart.

Swidler, A. 1995. "Cultural Power and Social Movements." In H. Johnston and B. Klandermans, eds., *Social Movements and Culture*. Minneapolis: University of Minnesota Press.

———. 2001. *Talk of Love*. Chicago: University of Chicago Press.

Sznaider, N. 1998. "The Sociology of Compassion: A Study in the Sociology of Morals." *Cultural Values* 2 (1): 117–139.

———. Forthcoming. *Global America*. Liverpool, U.K.: University of Liverpool Press.

Taylor, C. 1985. *Human Agency and Language*. Cambridge, U.K.; New York: Cambridge University Press.

———. 1989. *Sources of the Self: The Making of the Modern Identity*. Cambridge: Harvard University Press.

———. 1992. *The Malaise of Modernity*. Concord, Ont.: Anansi.

Taylor-Guthrie, D. 1993. "Sermons, Testifying, and Prayers: Looking Beneath the Wings in Leon Forrest's 'Two Wings to Veil My Face.' " *Callaloo* 16 (2): 419.

Thompson, B. W. 1992. " 'A WAY OUTA NO WAY': Eating Problems Among African-American, Latina, and White Women." *Gender & Society* 6 (4): 546–561.

Tierny, B. and J. W. Scott. 1984. *Western Societies: A Documentary History*. New York: Knopf.

Tomlinson, J. 1999. *Globalization and Culture*. Chicago: University of Chicago Press.

Trevino, A. J. 1992. "Alcoholics Annonymous as Durkheimian Religion." *Research in the Social Scientific Study of Religion* 4:183–208.

Turkle, S. 1995. *Life on the Screen: Identity in the Age of the Internet*. New York: Simon & Schuster.

Twitchell, J. B. 1992. *Carnival Culture: The Trashing of Taste in America*. New York: Columbia University Press.

Volosinov, V. N. 1986. *Marxism and the Philosophy of Language*. Cambridge: Harvard University Press.

Wacquant, L. 1998. "A Fleshpeddler at Work: Power, Pain and Profit in the Prizefighting Economy." *Theory and Society* 27:1–42.

Wain, M. 1998. *Freud's Answer: The Social Origins of Our Psychoanalytic Century*. Chicago: Ivan R. Dee.

Walzer, M. 1983. *Spheres of Justice: A Defense of Pluralism and Equality*. New York: Basic.

——. 1987. *Interpretation and Social Criticism*. Cambridge: Harvard University Press.

——. 1988. *The Company of Critics: Social Criticism and Political Commitment in the Twentieth Century*. New York: Basic.

Ward, S. 1996. "Filling the World with Self-Esteem: A Social History of Truth-Making." *Canadian Journal of Sociology* 21 (1): 1–23.

Watt, I. 1957. *The Rise of the Novel: Studies in Defoe, Richardson, and Fielding*. Berkeley: University of California Press.

Weber, M. 1946. "The Social Psychology of World Religions." In M. Weber, H. H. Gerth, and C. W. Mills, *From Max Weber: Essays in Sociology*, 267–301. New York: Oxford University Press.

——. 1958. *The Protestant Ethic and the Spirit of Capitalism*. New York: Scribners.

——. 1960. *Science as a Vocation*. Indianapolis: Bobbs-Merrill, College Division.

Weber, M., H. H. Gerth, and C. W. Mills. 1946. *From Max Weber: Essays in Sociology*. New York: Oxford University Press.

Weeks, J. 1981. *Sex, Politics, and Society: The Regulation of Sexuality Since 1800*. London; New York: Longman.

——. 1990. "The Value of Difference." In J. Rutherford, ed., *Identity: Community, Culture, Difference*, 88–100. London: Lawrence & Wishart.

Whiting, G. C. 1971. "Empathy: A Cognitive Skill for Decoding the Modernization Import of the Mass Media." *Public Opinion Quarterly* 35 (2): 211–219.

Williams, B. A. O. 1981. *Moral Luck: Philosophical Papers, 1973–1980*. Cambridge, U.K.; New York: Cambridge University Press.

Willis, P. 1977. *Learning to Labor: How Working-Class Kids Get Working-Class Jobs*. New York: Columbia University Press.

——. 1990. *Common Culture: Symbolic Work at Play in the Everyday Cultures of the Young*. Philadelphia: Open University Press.

Wilson, W. J. 1987. *The Truly Disadvantaged: The Inner City, the Underclass, and Public Policy*. Chicago: University of Chicago Press.

——. 1997. *When Work Disappears: The World of the New Urban Poor*. Chapter 4, "The Fading Inner-City Family," 87–110. New York: Knopf.

Wolff, J. 1995. *Resident Alien: Feminist Cultural Criticism*. New Haven: Yale University Press.

Wuthnow, R. 1989. *Communities of Discourse: Ideology and Social Structure in the Reformation, the Enlightenment, and European Socialism*. Cambridge: Harvard University Press.

———. 1994. *Sharing the Journey: Support Groups and America's New Quest for Community*. New York; Toronto: Free Press, Maxwell Macmillan; Maxwell Macmillan International.

Young, A. 1975. "Magic as 'Quasi-Profession': The Organization of Magic and Magical Healing Among Amhara." *Ethnology* 14:245–265.

———. 1982. "The Anthropologies of Illness and Sickness." *Annnual Review of Anthropology* 11:257–285.

———. 1995. *The Harmony of Illusions: Inventing Post-Traumatic Stress Disorder*. Princeton: Princeton University Press.

INTERNET RESOURCES

"End Near for Fed-Up Oprah?" http://www.mrshowbiz. go.com/news/Todays_Stories/990209/opraho20999html (February 9, 1999).

Jane Rosenzweig, "Consuming Passions." *The American Prospect*. http://www.prospect.org.org/archives/v11–2/rosenweig.htm1

NOVELS

Bohjalian, Christopher A. 1997. *Midwives: A Novel*. New York: Harmony.

Clarke, Breena. 1999. *River, Cross My Heart*. Boston: Little, Brown.

Cleage, Pearl. 1997. *What Looks Like Crazy on an Ordinary Day: A Novel*. New York: Avon.

Danticat, Edwidge. 1994. *Breath, Eyes, Memory*. New York: Soho.

Fitch, Janet. 1999. *White Oleander: A Novel*. Boston: Little, Brown.

Hegi, Ursula. 1994. *Stones from the River*. New York: Poseidon.

Hoffman, Alice. 1997. *Here on Earth*. New York: Putnam.

Lamb, Wally. 1998. *I Know This Much Is True*. New York: Regan.

Letts, Billie. 1995. *Where the Heart Is*. New York: Warner.

Lott, Bret. 1991. *Jewel: A Novel*. New York: Pocket.

Mair, G. 1998. *Oprah Winfrey: The Real Story*. Secaucus, N.J.: Carol Publications.

Mitchard, Jacquelyn. 1996. *The Deep End of the Ocean*. New York: Viking.

Morrison, Toni. *Song of Solomon*. 1977. New York: Knopf.

———. 1987. *Beloved: A Novel*. New York: Knopf.

———. 1998. *Paradise*. New York: Knopf.

Oates, Joyce Carol. 2001. *We Were the Mulvaneys*. London: Fourth Estate.

Quindlen, Anna. 1998. *Black and Blue*. Rockland, Mass.: Wheeler.

Schlink, Bernhard and Carol Brown Janeway. 1997. *The Reader*. New York: Pantheon.
Shreve, Anita. 1998. *The Pilot's Wife: A Novel*. Boston: Little, Brown.

ARTICLES FROM POPULAR MAGAZINES (PARTIAL BIBLIOGRAPHY)

Andersen, Chris. "Meet Oprah Winfrey." *Good Housekeeping* 203 (2) (Aug. 1986).
Angelou, Maya. "Oprah Winfrey (Women of the Year)."*Ms.* 17 (7) (Jan./Feb. 1989): 88.
"An Undone Deal." *People* 47 (9) (Mar. 10, 1997): 116.
Barthel, Joan. "Here Comes Oprah!" *Ms.* 15 (2) (Aug. 1986).
Bendel, Mary-Ann. "TV's Super-Women." *Ladies' Home Journal* 105 (3) (Mar. 1988): 124.
Benson, Harry. "Oprah: The Woman Who Almost Bailed." *Life* 18 (4) (Dec. 1995): 20.
"Blowing Our Cover." *O Magazine* (March 2001):171.
Blyth, Myrna. "Advice from Oprah." *Ladies' Home Journal* 112 (2) (Feb. 1995): 10.
Brashler, Bill. "Next On Oprah." *Ladies' Home Journal* 108 (8) (Aug. 1991): 94.
Brothers, Joyce. "What Kind of Wife Will Oprah Winfrey Make?" *Good Housekeeping* 219 (5) (Nov. 1994): 68.
Brozan, Nadine. "Chronicle." *New York Times, Late Edition (East Coast)*. June 20, 1997, B20.
Burfoot, Amy. "Talk of the Town." *Runner's World* 28 (11) (Nov. 1993): 19.
——. "Inside Story (Running the Marine Corps Marathon with Oprah Winfrey)." *Runner's World* 30 (1) (Jan. 1995): 68.
Chapelle, T. "The Reigning Queen of TV Talk." *Black Collegian* 21 (2) (Nov./Dec. 1990): 136.
Cleage, Pearl. "Walking in the Light." *Essence* 22 (2) (Jun. 1991).
Clementson, Lynette. "Queen of All Media: Oprah Winfrey's Empire Ranges from Film and TV to Books and O: The Oprah Magazine." *Newsweek*, January 8, 2001.
Colander, Pat. "Oprah Winfrey's Odyssey: Talk-Show Host to Mogul." *The New York Times*, March 12, 1989, B31.
Copeland, Irene. "The Big *Time*! 8 Who Got Where Only Men Got Before." *Cosmopolitan* 216 (5) (May 1994): 208–212.
Corliss, Richard. "Bewitching Beloved." *Time* 152 (14) (October 5, 1998).
Cunningham, Kim. "Guess Who's Coming to Visit?" *People Weekly* 39 (23) (June 14, 1993): 136.
Dickerson, Debra. "A Woman's Woman (Talk Show Host Oprah Winfrey)." *U.S. News and World Report* 123 (12) (Sept. 29, 1997): 10.
"Documenting Pain." *Time* 140 (11) (Sept. 14, 1992): 25.
Edwards, Audrey. "Stealing the Show." *Essence* 17 (6) (Oct. 1986).
Ehrenreich, Barbara. "In Defense of Talk Shows." *Time* 146 (23) (Dec. 4, 1995): 92.
Farley, Christopher John. "Oprah Springs Eternal." *Time* 142 (9) (Aug. 30, 1993): 15.
——. "Queen of All Media." *Time* 152 (14) (Oct. 5, 1998).

Farrell, Mary H. J., Kelly Katy, and Barbara K. Mills. "Oprah's Crusade." *People Weekly* 36 (21) (Dec. 2, 1991): 68–69.

Feldman, Gayle. "Making Book on Oprah." *New York Times Book Review*, Feb. 2, 1997, Sec. 7, 31.

"Fine Tuning!" *Essence* 16 (3) (July 1985).

Fisher, Luchina. "In Full Stride." *People* 42 (11) (Sep. 12, 1994): 84.

Flamm, Matthew. "Book 'em Oprah." *Entertainment Weekly* 350 (Oct. 25, 1996): 27.

Flint, Joe. "Oprah Still Kings' Queen." *Variety* 360 (10) (Oct. 9, 1995): 104.

Friday, Carolyn. "A Lightweight Take on the Big Boys." *Newsweek* 120 (8) (Aug. 24, 199): 55.

Friedman, Roger D. and Pat Wechsler. "Nightmare She-Bosses, Today on Oprah." *New York* 28 (4) (Jun. 23, 1995): 11.

"From Grand to Light Oprah." *Time* 132 (20) (Nov. 14, 1988): 85.

Gerosa, Melina. "What Makes Oprah Run." *Ladies' Home Journal* 111 (11) (Nov. 1994): 200.

———. "Oprah: Fit for Life." *Ladies' Home Journal* 113 (2) (Feb. 1996): 108.

Gillespie, Marcia Ann. "Winfrey Takes All: On Air or Off, Oprah Makes Money Talk." *Ms.* 17 (50) (Nov. 1988).

Goodman, Walter. "Three Queens of Talk Who Rule the Day." *The New York Times*, July 29, 1991, C11.

———. "Behind the Scenes at Talk Shows." *The New York Times Late Edition (East Coast)*, Mar. 24, 1997, B10.

Gray, Paul. "Winfrey's Winner: Oprah Recommends a Book on TV and — Bingo! — Her Viewers Turn It Into an Instant Best-Seller." *Time* 148 (25) (Dec. 2, 1996): 84.

Gross, Linda. "Oprah Winfrey Wonder Woman." *Ladies' Home Journal* 105 (12) (Dec. 1988): 40.

Harrison, Barbara Grizzuti. "The Importance of Being Oprah." *The New York Times Magazine*, June 11, 1989, F28.

Heaton, Jeanne Albronda and Nona Leigh Wilson. "Tuning Into Trouble." *Ms.* 6 (2) (Oct. 1995): 45.

"How He (SHE) Proposed." *Ebony* 50 (12) (Oct. 1995): 52.

Jacobs, A. J. "Oprah Winfrey." *Entertainment Weekly* 359/360 (Dec. 27, 1996): 36.

Jaggi, Maya. "The Power of One." *The Guardian Weekend*, Feb. 13, 1999.

Johnson, Marilyn and Dana Fineman. "Oprah Winfrey: A Life in Books." *Life* 9 (Sept. 1997): 44.

Kanner, Miriam. "Oprah at 40: What She's Learned the Hard Way." *Ladies' Home Journal* 111 (2) (Feb. 1994): 46.

Kennedy, Dana. "Oprah: Act Two." *Entertainment Weekly* 239 (Sept. 9, 1994): 20.

———. "A New Soap Oprah." *Entertainment Weekly* 248 (Nov. 11, 1994): 10.

Kest, Katharine. "What Oprah Really Wants." *Redbook* 185 (4) (Aug. 1995): 74.

King, Norman. "Oprah." *Good Housekeeping* 205 (2) (Aug. 1987).

Kinsella, B. "The Oprah Effect: How TV's Premier Talk Show Host Puts Books Over the Top." *Publishers Weekly* 244 (3) (Jan. 20, 1997): 276–278.

Kramer, Linda. "Marathon Woman." *People Weekly* 42 (19) (Nov. 7, 1994): 44.

Kreyche, Gerald F. "The Debasing of American Dulture (Parting Thoughts)." (Editorial). *USA Today* 124 (2612) (May 1996): 82.

"Lady with a Calling." *Time* 132 (6) (Aug. 8, 1988): 64.

Leo, John. "Foul Words, Foul Culture." *US News and World Report* 120 (16) (April 22, 1996): 73.

Levitt, Shelley. "Oprah's Mission." *People Weekly* 40 (22) (Nov. 29, 1993): 106–112.

Levitt, Shelley, Barbara K. Mills, and Allan Freedman. "Not Scared, Not Silent." *People Weekly* 38 (10) (Sept. 7, 1992): 48–49.

"Masters of Enterprise: Giants of American Business from John Jacob Astor and P. Morgan to Bill Gates and Oprah Winfrey." *Publishers Weekly* 246 (15) (April 12, 1999): 61.

Melcher, Richard A. "Next on Oprah: Burned-out Talk-Show Hosts?" *Business Week*, Oct. 2, 1995.

Miller Roseblum, Trudi. "Make the Connection by Bob Greene and Oprah Winfrey." *Billboard* 108 (43) (Oct. 26, 1996): 81.

Moore, Suzanne. "On Talk Shows the Democracy of Pain Reigns Supreme. We May Not All Be Famous, but We Have All Suffered." *New Statesman* 128 (4423) (1996): 17.

Moore, Trudy. "How the 'Oprah Winfrey Show' Helps People Live Better Lives." *Jet* 85 (24) (Apr. 18, 1994): 56.

Morgan, Thomas. "Troubled Girl's Evolution Into an Oscar Nominee." *The New York Times*, Mar. 4, 1986, C17.

Newpoff, Laura. "Of Fame, Fortune Cookies and Oprah: Fortunately Yours Foretastes Internet Growth Possibilities." *Business First-Columbus* 15 (28) (March 5, 1999): 1.

Nguyen, Lan N. "Touched by an Oprah (Talking with Toni Morrison)." *People* 46 (23) (Dec. 2, 1996): 36.

Nicholson, Gilbert. "Fox Quits on Oprah." *Birmingham Business Journal* 15 (45): 1.

Noel, Pamela. "Lights! Camera! Oprah!" *Ebony* 15 (6) (Apr. 1985).

Noglows, Paul. "Oprah: The Year of Living Dangerously." *Working Woman* 19 (5) (May 1994): 52–55.

Norment, Lynn. "The Truth About Women's Networks." *Ebony* 51 (8) (June 1996): 88–92.

Onstad, Katrina. "Who's Sorry Now?: The Craze for Public Contrition Has Made the Apology Almost Meaningless." *Saturday Night* 113 (10) (Dec. 1998): 23.

"Oprah & Anthony: Wheels of Misfortune." *People Weekly* 45 (21) (May 27, 1996: 45.

"Oprah Gives $1 Million to Spelman College's Science Fund." *Jet* 89 (3) (Nov. 27, 1995): 22.

"Oprah Goes Hollywood." *People Weekly* 29 (23) (June 13, 1988).

"Oprah: A Heavenly Body?" *U.S. News and World Report* 122 (12) (Mar. 31, 1997): 18.

"Oprah Named Favorite Air Flight Seatmate in Poll." *Jet* 84 (18) (Aug. 30, 1993): 34.

"Oprah: Profile in Curvage." *Newsweek* 112 (22) (Nov. 28, 1988): 95.

"Oprah Reveals on Her Show She Smoked Crack Cocaine in Her Twenties." *Jet* 87 (12) (Jan. 30, 1995): 51.

"Oprah Winfrey." *People Weekly* 40 (26) (Dec. 27, 1993): 52.

"Oprah Winfrey." (The 50 Most Beautiful People in the World) *People Weekly* 47 (18) (May 12, 1997): 115.

"Oprah Winfrey." *US News and World Report* 118 (3) (Jan. 23, 1995): 18.

"Oprah Winfrey: Best Dressed." (From Best and Worst Dressed People of 1995) *People Weekly* 44 (12) (Sept. 18, 1995): 76–77.

"Oprah Winfrey Kicks Off 11th Season with New Format and Theme Song." *Jet* 90 (20) (Sept. 30, 1996): 32.

"Oprah Winfrey Reveals She's Not Ready to Get Married." *Jet* 86 (20) (Sept. 19, 1994): 8.

"Oprah Winfrey: She Believes." *Vogue* 176 (25) (May 1986): 102.

"Oprah Winfrey Shock: The Big Fall Book That Vanished." *Publishers Weekly* 240 (25) (June 21, 1993): 13.

"Oprah Winfrey Stars in TV Movie *There Are No Children Here.*" *Jet* 85 (5) (Nov. 29, 1993): 56.

"Oprah Winfrey: Talk Show Host." *Time* 147 (25) (June 17, 1996): 65.

"Oprah Winfrey Talks Openly About Oprah." *Good Housekeeping* 213 (3) (Sept. 1991).

"Oprah Winfrey's Success Story." *Ladies' Home Journal* 104 (3) (Mar. 1987).

"Oprah's Going Glossy." *Newsweek* 43 (July 19, 1999).

"Oprah's Wonder Year." *Ladies' Home Journal* 107 (5) (May 1990): 157.

Patterson, Orlando. "The Victimization Trap." *The New York Times*, Nov. 30, 1993, A25.

Pearlman, Cindy. "Civil Servant: Oprah Winfrey Shows Up for Jury Duty in Chicago, IL." *Entertainment Weekly* 162 (Mar. 19, 1993): 12.

Powell, Joanna. "I Was Trying to Fill Something Deeper (Oprah Winfrey Describes How Her Weight Problem Was Resolved by Dealing with Past Events." *Good Housekeeping* 223 (4) (Oct. 1996): 80.

——. "Oprah's Awakening." *Good Housekeeping* 1 (113).

"President Clinton Signs 'Oprah Bill,' New Law to Protect Children." *Jet* 85 (10) (Jan. 10, 1994): 16.

"Rack Race." *People* 42 (1) (July 4, 1994): 42.

Raffel, Dawn. "Oprah's Secret: How to Get What You Really Want." *Redbook* 192 (4) (Feb. 1999): 106.

Randolph, Laura B. "Sisters of the Spirit: Networks Help Celebrities Deal with Fame and Pain." *Ebony* 45 (9) (July 1990): 36.

——. "Oprah Opens Up About Her Weight, Her Wedding and Why She Withheld The Book." *Ebony* 48 (12) (Oct. 1993): 130–137.

——. "Oprah! The Most Powerful Woman in Entertainment Talks About Her Fame, Her Father and Her Future in TV." *Ebony* 50 (9) (July 1995): 22–28.

——. "How He (She) Proposed." *Ebony* 50 (12) (Oct. 1995): 52.

——. "Words to Live By." *Ebony* 51 (10) (Sept. 1996): 28.

Reynolds, Gretchen. "Oprah Unbound." *Chicago* 42 (11) (Nov. 1993): 86.

——. "The Oprah Winfrey Plan: She Started Running, Lost 70 Pounds and Completed a Marathon. Here's How." *Runner's World* 30 (3) (Mar. 1995): 64.

Richman, Alan. "Oprah." *People Weekly* 27 (2) (Jan. 12, 1987): 48–58.

Rogers, Jackie. "Understanding Oprah." *Redbook* 181 (5) (Sept. 1993): 94.

Rogers St. Johns, A. "The Married Life of Doug and Mary." *Photoplay* (Dec. 1926):35.

Rosen, Marjorie and Luchina Fisher. "Oprah Overcomes." *People Weekly* 41 (1) (Jan. 10, 1994): 42–45.

Sachs, Andrea. "Drinking Yourself Skinny." *Time* 132 (25) (Dec. 19, 1988): 68.

Salzberg, Sharon. "Everything You Wanted to Know About Meditation but Were Too Tense to Ask." *O Magazine* March 2001:211–234.

Saltzman, Joe. "Why Ordinary Americans Like Daytime Talk Shows." *USA Today* 125 (2618) (Nov. 1996): 63.

Sample, Ann. "Licensee in Limelight." *The Weekly Newspaper for the Home Furnishing Network* 44 (1) (March 15, 1999).

Sanders, Charles L. "Oprah Winfrey's Sky-High Home." *Ebony* 43 (12) (Oct. 1988): 56.

Sanders, Richard (reported by Barbara Kleban Mills). "TV Host Oprah Winfrey, Chicago's Biggest Kick, Boots-up for Star-Making Role in *The Color Purple*." *People Weekly* 24 (16) (Dec. 16, 1985): 161.

Sanoff, Alving with Jeannye Thornton. "TV's Disappearing Color Line." *U.S. News and World Report* 103 (2) (July 1987): 57.

Santow, Dan. "Christmas at Oprah's." *Redbook* 184 (2) (Dec. 1994): 82.

Sanz, Cynthia and Luchina Fisher. "Cookin' for Oprah." *People Weekly* 41 (18) (May 16, 1994): 84–88.

Scott, Gregory Sophfronia. "Oprah! Oprah in the Court!" *Time* 143 (23) (June 6, 1994): 30–31.

Shapiro, Eben. "Oprah Makes Huge Bestseller of a Cookbook." *The Wall Street Journal* 223 (87) (May 4, 1994): B1.

Shapiro, Joseph P. "Scared Silent Myths." *US News and World Report* 113 (10) (Sept. 14, 1992): 21.

Shay, Richard. "Oprah Throws a Party: Biggest Birthday Bash Honors Poet Maya Angelou." *Ebony* 48 (8) (June 1993): 118.

Smith, Liz. "Oprah Exhales." *Good Housekeeping* 221 (4) (Oct. 1995): 120.

Spillman, Rob. "Drink the Latte! Buy the Book!" *Salon Magazine* (June 1997): www.salon.com/june97/media/media970620.html.

Stodghill, Ron. "Daring to Go There: Oprah Winfrey Examines African American History in *Beloved*." *Time* 152 (14) (Oct. 5, 1998).

Taraborreli, Randy J. "How Oprah Does It All." *Redbook* 187 (4) (Aug. 1996): 76.

——. "The Change That Has Made Oprah So Happy." *Redbook* 189 (1) (May 1997): 94.

Taylor, Susan. "An Intimate Talk with Oprah." *Essence* 18 (4) (Aug. 1987): 57.

"Team Oprah: Their Seven Rules for Success." *Ladies' Home Journal* 113 (2) (Feb. 1996): 110.

"The Book Club, According to Oprah." *Newsweek* 128 (15) (Oct. 7, 1996): 83.

"The Ten Most Beautiful Black Women in America." *Ebony* 17 (9) (July 1987): 136.

"The 25 Most Intriguing People of the Year: Oprah Winfrey." *People Weekly* 28 (26) (Dec. 28, 1987).

Tresniowski, Alex. "Oprah Buff: After Four Years with a New Fitness Philosophy, Oprah Is Happy at Last." *People Weekly* 46 (11) (Sept. 9, 1996): 80.

Tucker, Ken. "There Are No Children Here (Television Program Review)." *Entertainment Weekly* 198 (Nov. 26, 1993): 52.

"TV's Hall of Flukey Fame." *People Weekly* 26 (8) (Aug. 25, 1986): 69.

Waters, Harry F. and Patricia King. "Chicago's Grand New Oprah." *Newsweek* 104 (28) (Dec. 31, 1984): 51.

"What I Know for Sure." *O Magazine* (Oct. 2001):290.

"What She Did for Love." *People Weekly* 43 (4) (Jan. 30, 1995): 55.

William, Ellen. "Bring in the Noise." *The Nation* 262 (13) (April 1, 1996): 19.

Williams, Mary Elizabeth. "She's All Chat." *Salon Magazine* (May 4, 1999): www.archive.salon.com/people/bc/1999/05/04/oprah/.

Whitaker, Charles. "The Most Talked-About TV Talk Show Host." *Ebony* 42 (5) (March 1987).

——. "TV's New Daytime Darling." *The Saturday Evening Post* 259 (5) (Aug. 1987): 43.

Winfrey, Oprah. "Wind Beneath My Wings." *Essence* 20 (2) (June 1989.

"Winfrey Reruns." *People Weekly* 42 (12) (Sept. 19, 1994): 173 (3).

Zoglin, Richard. "Lady with a Calling." *Time* 132 (6) (Aug. 8, 1989): 62.

——. "People Sense the Realness." *Time* 128 (2) (Sep. 15, 1986): 99.

OPRAH TRANSCRIPTS IN ORDER OF DATES

1986

September 22. "Gossips and Their Victims."
September 23. "Men Who Rape and Treatment for Rapists."
September 25. "Marital Problems."
October 8. "Teen Mothers."
October 10. "Reuniting Families."
October 13. "Children of Divorce."
October 14. "Facing Death."
October 20. "Sex, Greed, Power and Corruption."
October 21. "Handicapped Spouses."
October 23. "Affirmative Action."
October 29. "Adult Children of Alcoholics."
November 6. "Profiling Prostitutes."
November 7. "Confronting Racial Prejudice."
November 10. "Sexual Abuse in Families."

November 12. "The Right to Kill Intruders."
November 13. "Homophobia."
November 17. "Pros and Cons of Welfare."
November 24. "Juveniles on Death Row."
December 2. "Women Who Love Too Much."
December 5. "Living with Pain."

1991

June 6. "The Marriage of Ricky Ray 14-Year-Old AIDS Victim."

1993

March 31. "Prison Rape Scandals."
June 30. "Unsolved Crimes on Oprah Stations."
August 10. "Trudi Chase—Multiple Personalities."
August 26. "Forced to Give the Kids Away."

1994

January 4. "The Marriage Lab."
January 26. "Divorced Couples Take the Parenting Test."
January 31. "Broken Engagements."
February 22. "Can You Get Away with Murder?"
March 11. "You Are Not Who You Think You Are."
March 24. "The Divorce Ceremony."
April 1. "Confrontation Between Convict and Victim."
June 6. "Inside a Man's Mind."
June 14. "Test Your Personality."
June 20. "Women Confront Men to Find Out Why They Were Dumped."
June 21. "The Day of Compassion."
July 11. "Parents Admit the Truth to Their Teens."
July 12. "Oprah Letter Writers Get Advice."
July 14. "People Who Sold Their Souls to the Devil."
August 2. "My Teenaged Daughter Is Driving Me Crazy."
August 12. "Teen Dating Violence."
August 30. "Fat Family Intervention."
September 28. "Tracey Gold: I Almost Starved to Death."
October 10. "My Wife Was Raped."
December 1. "How to Forgive When You Can't Forget."
December 6. "School for Husbands."
December 13. "Friendship on Trial."
December 27. "People Who Never Use Their Good Stuff."

1995:

January 31. "I Sent My Son to Jail."
March 1. "How Far Would You Go to Protect Your Child?"
March 15. "Should You Be Ashamed?"
March 27. "Lives Shattered by Crime."
March 28. "Can't Get Over Your Ex."
April 3. "I'm Afraid to Hug Your Child."
April 4. "Stuck in a Traditional Marriage."
April 6. "Social Workers: Guilty?"
April 17. "Should You Stay Together for the Kids?"
May 23. "Married to a Molester."
June 1. "A Salute to Every Woman."
June 21. "Day of Compassion 1995."
June 28. "Violent Young Children: Could You Be Their Next Victim? Part 1."
July 4. "So You Think You Want a Baby."
July 13. "Ten Stupid Things Women Do: Part 2."
August 24. "Do You Know Who Your Child Is Dating?"
September 26. "Road Map to Abuse."
October 30. "Oprah's Child Alert: Children and Guns Part 1."
December 20. "Children and Poverty."

1996

March 18. "Oprah's Child Alert: Domestic Violence Through the Eyes of a Child."
April 2. "Nobody Knows I'm Homeless."
May 31. "Child Alert: Pedophiles."
June 12. "Women Abused During Pregnancy."
June 26. "Deadly Diseases Where You Live."
August 20. "Runaway Parents Headed for Jail."
August 28. "Male Eating Disorders."
September 6. "Bride Who Couldn't Remember Her Husband."
October 3. "Athletes Who Abuse Women."
October 18. "Newborn Quintuplets Come Home"
October 29. "Are You Who You Think You Are?"

1997

January 3. "People Who Made It Big in '96."
January 13. "Anorexia Follow-Up."
January 16. "Resolutions That Matter."
March 3. "When You Just Can't Stop."
April 8. "Selena's Family."
May 8. "Amazing Heart Transplant Story."

June 20. "AIDS Day of Compassion."
August 19. "Too Ugly to Leave the House."

1998

March 3. "Heroes and Angels."
March 6. "Book Club—Toni Morrison."
April 3. "How Well Do You Cope?"
April 9. "Oprah's Book Club."
May 22. "Oprah's Book Club."
June 18. "Oprah's Book Club."
June 26. "Did She Feed Her Daughter to Death?"
July 2. "Broken Promises That Made Headlines."
July 9. "John Gray on Loving Again."
September 15. "The Rules for Being Human."
September 25. "Oprah's Book Club."
October 5. "Absent Fathers."
October 6. "Working with Emotional Intelligence."
October 16: "The Cast of *Beloved*."
October 21. "The Toughest Time of My Life."
October 23. "How to Apologize."
October 26. "Iyanla Vanzant."
October 28. "Oprah's Book Club: Things Every Woman Should Know."
October 29. "You Do a Great Job."
November 15. "Medical Intuitive Carolyne Myss, Part 2."
December 10. "Absent Fathers."

1999

January 4. "Iyanla."
January 11. "Suze Orman."
January 14. "Do You Really Know Your Family?"
January 19. "Oprah's Book Club Goes to Wal-Mart."
January 22. "Absent Fathers (3)."
January 28. "Personal Success with John Gray."
February 2. "Angel Network Kindness Chain (4)."
February 8. "1999 Follow-Up Show."
February 10. "A Husband with 24 Personalities."
February 26. "Our Most Forgettable Shows."
March 1. "Wives Who Abuse Their Husbands."
March 15. "Do You Really Know Your Family?"
March 19. "Oprah's 2000 Time Capsule."
March 26. "Oprah's 2000 Time Capsule (11)."
March 29. "Iyanla (9)."

April 8. "Children's Letters to Oprah."
April 13. "Take the Perfectionist Test."
April 14. "Iyanla (10)."
April 15. "Oprah's Angel Network."
April 21. "Tragedy in Denver."
April 23. "Letters to Gary Zukav."
April 27. "Difficult Conversations."
April 28. "Phil McGraw."
May 6. "Husbands with Double Lives."
June 2. "Tipper Gore on Depression."
June 16. "How to Build a Family Team."

OTHER TRANSCRIPTS

THE MONTEL WILLIAMS SHOW

September 15, 1995. "Montel, I Turned My Life Around."

SUBJECT INDEX

A Feeling for Books, 207
African American culture, 21, 22, 23,
    24, 46, 181, 188, 189, 192, 196, 197,
    199, 202, 203, 235, 239
African American habitus, 196
African American women, 181, 183,
    186, 200, 228, 239
Aischrologia, 69
Alcoholics Anonymous, 175
American culture, 3, 16, 21, 22, 23, 24,
    33, 46, 79, 163, 166, 178, 180, 181, 182,
    188, 189, 192, 196, 197, 198, 199, 202,
    203, 221, 226, 230, 235, 238, 239
American polity, 82, 124, 155, 180, 199
American popular culture, 181, 228
American society, 26, 80, 103, 111, 144,
    163, 179, 180, 200, 239
Angel Network, 12, 125, 153, 163, 168, 175
Apt and Seezsold, 81
Arbitrary connectedness, 79
Arts of memory, 98, 99
Audience, 3, 6, 9, 10, 11, 13, 20, 30, 37,
    40, 41, 47, 49, 50, 52, 53, 54, 55, 56,
    57, 58, 59, 61, 63, 64, 82, 94, 103, 104,
    120, 124, 130, 131, 132, 161, 173, 197,
    215, 221, 236, 237, 238, 239, 244n, 245n
Autobiographical discourse, 9, 18, 85,
    86, 140, 157, 163, 168

Battered Women Syndrome, 229
Biographical icon, 30

Biographical narratives, 18, 88, 89, 90,
    91, 102, 137, 138, 144, 145, 164, 175, 222
Biography, 2, 5, 6, 9, 17, 21, 23, 28, 32,
    33, 34, 36, 38, 39, 41, 43, 45, 46, 53,
    57, 59, 81, 82, 91, 99, 100, 101, 111, 113,
    124, 138, 139, 140, 148, 150, 152, 154,
    156, 163, 164, 166, 168, 169, 173, 175,
    176, 178, 179, 193, 202, 220, 238, 245n
Black and Blue, 104, 106, 107, 109,
    110, 252n
Black culture, 22, 23, 187, 190, 192, 195,
    196, 197, 198, 199, 202, 218
*Black Culture and Black
    Consciousness*, 196
Black epistemology, 197, 203
Book Club, 3, 12, 15, 58, 59, 80, 103,
    104, 105, 107, 108, 109, 110, 116, 125,
    142, 143, 145, 146, 153, 163, 164, 166,
    169, 175, 176, 178, 182, 199, 200, 209,
    226, 230, 232, 243n
Breath, Eyes, Memory, 106, 107,
    109, 252n

Calvin Klein, 38
Candide, 234
Change Your Life Television, 125
Characteristics of Negro Expression, 178
Charisma(tic), 45; of leader, 53; in
    leadership, 43, 44, 45; power, 44, 45,
    150, 151
Codependents Anonymous, 175

Communities of fate, 176
Company of Critics, The, 205, 213
Concrete intention, 19
Confessional talk show, 48, 156, 231
Consuming the Romantic Utopia, 122
Content analysis, 10
Corrosion of Character, 222
Courtroom sciences, 40
Criticism and Values, 213
Cultural classification, 208
Cultural critique, 13, 207, 210, 213
Cultural enterprise, 1, 15, 17, 18, 20, 21,
    22, 27, 79, 81, 103, 143, 169, 172, 180,
    189, 196, 206, 230, 237, 238, 240
Cultural entrepreneur, 20, 183
Cultural key scenarios, 85, 86
Cultural objects, 4, 5, 8, 208
Cultural specialists, 11, 12, 80
Cultural studies, 1, 4, 78, 121, 122, 238
Culture of Complaint, The, 221
Culture of privacy, 187
Culture of recovery, 98, 102
Cyborgic, 142

Deconstruction, 74
Deep End of the Ocean, The, 106, 107,
    143, 166, 252n
Defetishization, 31, 32, 54
Discourse of therapy, 163, 171, 188, 238
Disorganized family, 182
Distant Suffering, 123

Electronic propinquity, 172
Emotional health, 134, 135, 139
Emotional Intelligence, 139, 164
Emotional work, 136
Empowerment, 6, 7, 136, 154
Ethic of care, 44, 54
Ethical criticism, 15

Families for a Better Life, 153
Feminine culture, 136
Feminist movement, 187, 259n
Fortune, 59, 246n

Fragility of Goodness, The, 235
Framing, 85

Genre, 11, 12, 15, 25, 48, 49, 50, 52, 53,
    55, 56, 57, 60, 64, 66, 73, 74, 76, 77,
    82, 96, 104, 106, 108, 114, 124, 125,
    137, 146, 151, 156, 161, 167, 170, 178,
    185, 186, 192, 193, 196, 197, 198, 205,
    207, 217, 218, 221, 227, 239, 246n,
    248n, 258n
Global capitalism, 58
Global consciousness, 157, 159,
    177, 255n
Global empire, 163
Global imagination, 158, 158
Global media, 47, 157, 160, 171,
    172, 178
Globalization, 156, 157, 158, 177,
    181, 219; from within, 173; from
    below, 176
Grounded ethics, 117

Habermassian account, 216
Habitus, 21, 22, 24, 25, 26, 27, 28, 104,
    179, 180, 181, 184, 186, 187, 188, 195,
    196, 200, 203, 246n
Harpo Productions, 56
Heal Your Spirit, 12, 115, 163
Hegemony, 118, 120, 205
Heimlich, 68
Here on Earth, 106, 107, 110, 146, 252n
Highbrow, 11, 13, 15, 28, 103, 146, 205,
    218, 237
History of sexuality, 90
Holocaust, 100, 127, 128, 130
Hypermodern family, 188, 194

I Know This Much Is True, 104, 106,
    107, 109, 110, 117, 167, 252n
Ideology, 84, 120, 121, 145, 155, 200,
    207, 229
*If Life Is a Game, Then These Are the
    Rules*, 232
In potenza, 161

Infraglobalization, 173
Infrapolitics, 227, 228, 229, 230
Interpretation, 1, 7, 8, 9, 10, 12, 13, 18,
    19, 20, 21, 40, 44, 48, 51, 62, 64, 78,
    79, 80, 97, 110, 123, 144, 148, 151, 202,
    212, 238, 240, 244n

King Corporation, 47
Kmart, 59

Jewel, 106, 107, 252n
Journal of Community Psychology, 133
Julie au La Nouvelle Neloise, 217
Justice Interruptus, 239

Laocoon, 218
Late capitalism, 154, 207, 212, 238
Late modernity, 76, 114, 172, 173, 184,
    192, 195, 196, 239
Law Review, 182
Liberal culture, 117, 207
Life strategies, 41
Liminal, 45, 54
Love's Knowledge, 235
Luckie and Co., 125

Metatext, 78
Middle-brow literature, 145
Middle class, 11, 28, 67, 68, 74, 84, 98,
    104, 146, 153, 205, 228; America, 23;
    American culture, 182; culture, 64,
    74, 75, 188; ethos, 64, 67, 74, 199;
    family, 26, 69, 75, 182; identity, 64,
    192; taste, 4, 20, 64; women, 145,
    185, 199
Midwives, 105, 107, 109, 252n
Moral emotions, 91, 223
Moral sociology, 1

Narrative: in action, 90; complication,
    39, 166; spectacle, 39
New Age, 125, 142, 202; movement, 131;
    psychology, 136; religion, 176
New Republic, 208, 258n

Newsweek, 2, 3, 38, 81
Nike, 162

Magazine, 3, 9, 12, 31, 33, 127, 134,
    142, 164, 168, 169, 176, 246n, 247n,
    253n, 254n

Overeaters Anonymous, 176

Pamela, 217
Peyton Place, 65
Philosophy of Literary Form, 195
Pilot's Wife, The, 106, 107, 143, 252n
Poeme sur le Desastre de Lisbonne, 158
Politics of justice, 102
Politics of pity, 102
Politics of pleasure, 13
Polyphony, 226, 227
Pop psychology manuals, 137, 145
Popular culture, 1, 3, 4, 5, 7, 8, 13, 14,
    15, 62, 91, 117, 124, 134, 180, 181, 191,
    203, 204, 205, 206, 210, 211, 218, 228,
    236, 237, 239, 240, 245n, 258n
Postmodernism, 79, 193, 207
Poststructuralism, 79
Pragmatic holism, 8
Private sphere, 55, 77, 91, 94, 160, 161,
    208, 215, 217
Public sphere, 5, 6, 34, 49, 51, 58, 77,
    93, 157, 158, 159, 160, 161, 170, 183,
    188, 189, 192, 201, 208, 209, 214, 215,
    216, 217, 222, 223, 224, 225, 238
Pure critique, 209, 210, 214

Queering, 69, 70, 75, 228
Quindlen, Anna, 104, 252n

Radical autobiography, 37
Reception, 8, 9, 10, 11, 12, 78, 79, 244n
Reflexive modernity, 15, 48
Reflexive modernization, 173, 193
Rethinking Psychiatry, 112
Resistance, 1, 4, 19, 121, 195, 196, 204
Retrospective structure, 87

Risk society, 193, 194

Self-help, 33, 125, 126, 131, 135, 136, 142, 145, 155, 179, 201, 202, 228, 231, 232, 233, 234, 235, 237, 239; discourse, 202; ethos, 135, 136, 137, 145, 154, 201, 203, 234, 235; guides, 12; literature, 136, 137; manuals, 10, 137, 145, 169; movement, 137; narratives, 137
Shameless World of Phil, Sally and Oprah: Television Talk Shows and the Deconstructing of Society, The, 215
Slave narrative, 192
Soap opera, 66, 73, 131, 157
Social anxiety, 165, 174
Sociology and World Market Sociology, 157
Sociology of emotions, 91
Songs in Ordinary Time, 153
Spheres of Justice, 213
Standardized intimacy, 169
Starbucks, 153
Strategy for action, 180
Structure of the code, 18
Style, 21, 23, 27, 37, 39, 48, 49, 50, 51, 63, 78, 80, 101, 104, 105, 124, 130, 148, 158, 169, 170, 179, 180, 186, 191, 197, 205, 246n
Support group, 5, 54, 136, 139, 176
Surveillance, 120, 149
Symbolic pollution, 215, 245
Symbolic type, 45, 59, 60, 75
Symbolic violence, 7, 120

Techno-capitalism, 172

Techno-therapeutic, 172
Therapeutic: code, 87, 90, 91, 144; culture, 27, 136, 163, 164; dialogue, 77; knowledge, 164, 171, 172; language, 39, 41, 168; narrative, 36, 39, 40, 41, 42, 45, 88, 89, 90, 139, 145, 152, 165, 166, 167, 168, 169, 170, 171, 172, 175, 176
The New York Review of Books, 103
The Phil Donahue Show, 50, 51, 53, 56, 57, 58, 59
The Reader, 103, 104, 226, 252n, 260n
Time Magazine, 2, 22, 81, 198
Time Warner, 59, 243n
Trauma narrative, 97, 98, 100, 170, 192
Truncated global cultural form, 177

Unheimliche, 68, 69

Valley of the Dolls, The, 65
Victim culture, 222
Victims and Values, 118
Vogue, 39, 45, 285n
Voyeurism, 56, 81, 111, 217, 218

We Were the Mulvaneys, 104, 106, 109, 166
What Looks Like Crazy on an Ordinary Day, 80, 252n
White culture, 184, 192, 196, 201
White Oleander, 104, 106, 109, 144, 169, 252n
Women Who Love Too Much, 137, 174
Working-class culture, 146

Yesterday, I Cried, 100

NAME INDEX

Abt, V., 215, 249n, 259n

Abu-Lughod, Lila, 19, 245n, 251n

Ackerman, Bruce, 215, 259n

Adorno, Theodor, 206, 212

Alger, Horatio, 33, 65, 135

Amato, 117, 253n

Ang, Ian, 63, 249n

Angelou, Maya, 22, 25 , 198

Appadurai, Arjun, 157, 172, 176, 255n, 256n

Arendt, Hannah, 102, 216, 222, 223, 224, 252n, 259n, 260n

Astor, John Jacob, 28

Austin, John, 56 248n

Bahktin, M., 226, 258n ,260n

Baudrillard, Jean, 217, 259n

Bauman, Zygmunt, 227, 249n, 257n, 260n

Bayles, Martha, 209, 258n

Beck, U., 75, 76, 113, 173, 192, 193, 243n, 245n, 249n, 251n, 252n, 256n, 257n, 259n

Bell, Vicki, 228, 229, 260n

Benhabib, Seyla, 224, 259n, 260n

Benjamin, Walter, 19, 47, 50, 236, 245n, 248n, 261n

Bennett, William, 208

Boltanski, Luc, 102, 123, 251n, 252n, 253n, 255n, 259n

Booth, Wayne, 15, 145, 245n

Botero, 63

Bourdieu, Pierre, 146, 179, 203, 228, 243n, 244n, 246n, 249n, 256n, 260n

Breuer, 69

Bryant, 221

Burke, Kenneth, 57, 195, 247n, 248n

Cancian, F., 136, 254n, 257n

Canovan, Catherine, 222, 259n

Carson, Ann, 69, 249n

Carter-Scott, Dr., 232

Castell, Manuel, 163, 176, 255n, 256n

Cavell, Stanley, 14, 64, 249n, 258n

Chartier, Roger, 10, 244n

Chase, Trudi, 32, 99, 100

Chodorow, Nancy, 107

Clinton, Bill, 229

Connell, Bob, 157, 255n

Cunningham, Fay, 86

Danto, Arthur, 56

Darnton, Robert, 60, 61, 62, 205, 244n

Das, Veena, 119, 253n, 259n, 261n

Decker, J. L., 17, 245n

Derrida, Jacques, 74, 134, 249n, 258n

Dershowitz, Alan, 81, 221, 249n

Dickinson Emily, 120

Donahue, Phil, 47, 49, 51, 52, 53, 54, 55, 57, 59, 60, 62

Dow, James, 150, 151

Drye, Janice, 229, 260

Du Bois, W.E.B., 189, 190, 201, 257n
Durkheim, Emile, 152, 243n
Dworkin, Andrea, 185, 259n
Dyson, Michael, 197, 257n

Eagleton, Terry, 210, 258n, 261n
Ehrenreich, Barbara, 81, 84, 249n, 251n
Engels, Friedrich, 233

Fairbanks, Douglas, 16
Fitch, Janet, 104, 252
Floyd, James, 201, 257n
Foucault, Michel, 77, 90, 121, 244n,
    251n,253n
Frank, Jerome, 149, 254n
Frankfurt School, 14, 121
Franzen, Jonathan, 206, 243n
Fraser, Nancy, 239
Freud, Sigmund, 68, 69, 70, 114, 219,
    222, 249n
Frye, Northrop, 56, 248n

Gamson, Joushua, 6, 28, 49, 62, 207,
    210, 246n, 248n, 258n
Gates, Bill, 28
Gay, Peter, 66, 222, 249n, 259n
Geertz, Clifford, 21, 61, 91, 114, 115,
    246n 248n, 252n
Gerbner, G. L., 209, 258n
Gernsheim-Beck, 75, 257n
Giddens, Anthony, 64, 170, 193,
    248n, 257n
Gilligan, C., 223, 260n
Gitlin, Todd, 226, 260n
Goleman, Daniel, 138, 164, 255n
Gore, Tipper, 31, 47, 126, 291n
Gramsci, Antoniou, 121
Grathoff, Richard, 45, 247n
Greene, Bob, 41, 42, 247n
Gross, Morgan M., 209
Gunn, Gilles, 195, 249n, 257n

Hacking, Ian, 98, 233, 251n, 252n, 261n
Halttunen, Karen, 217, 259n

Handelman, Don, 45, 46, 75,
    247n, 249n
Harraway, Donna, 142
Hayes, Sharon, 61, 62
Heaton, J. A., 6, 243n
Heelas, Paul, 131, 253n
Held, David, 176, 212, 256n, 259n, 260n
Highland Garnet, Henry, 191
Hill Collins, Patricia, 182, 183, 186, 187,
    197, 200, 202, 203, 247n, 256n, 257n
Hochschild, A., 136, 254n, 257n
Holmes, 190, 257n
Honneth, Axel, 239
hooks, bell, 183, 187, 256n
Hoover, S. M., 115, 122n
Horkheimer, Max, 206
Hughes, Robert, 81, 221, 259n
Hurston, Zora Neale, 178

Illouz, Eva, 136, 254n, 257n

Jackson, Michael, 197
James, Henry, 227, 235
Jameson, Frederic, 21, 237, 246n, 261n
Johnson, Barbara, 210
Johnson, Magic (wife), 97, 98
Johnson, Weldon James, 23, 198
Jones, Gayle, 197
Jong, Erica, 105
Jordan, June, 186, 188, 256n

Katz, Elihou, 10, 244n
Kellner, D., 172, 245n, 255n, 257n, 258n
Keyes, Daniel, 64, 170, 249n, 255n
Kleinman, Arthur, 112, 113, 150, 219, 224,
    225, 252n, 254n, 259n, 260n, 261n
Kurtle, Sherry, 149

Laderman, Carol, 218, 259n
Lake, Ricky, 43, 53, 65
Lamb, Wally, 104, 167, 252n
Lamont, Michele, 122, 253n
Langer, Lawrence, 128, 252n, 253n
Lasch, Christopher, 111, 252n

Lash, Scott, 193, 257n, 261n
Latour, Bruno, 154
Lewinski, Monica, 59, 220
Levinas, Emmanuel, 234, 261n
Levine, Lawrence, 194, 196, 197, 199,
  201, 205, 257n, 258n, 261n
Levi-Strauss, Claude, 151, 254n
Liebes, Tamar, 10, 244n
Lowenthal, Leo, 43, 206, 247n
Lowney, K. S., 49, 50, 62, 248n
Lundby, K., 115, 252n

Machiavelli, 24
Madame C., 22
Madonna, 31, 54
Magritte, René, 67
Mair, George, 39, 59, 133, 171, 226,
  243n, 246n, 247n, 248n, 253n,
  255n, 260n
Mandela, Nelson, 47
Marcus, Georges, 8, 244n
Marx, Karl, 114, 170, 233
McGraw, Dr. Phil, 40, 41, 42, 125, 133,
  134, 149, 150, 168, 247n
McNeal Turner, Henry, 191
Meyer, J., 171, 255n
Milgram, S., 151
Miller, J. Hillis, 104
Mitchard, Jacquelyn, 107, 252n
Modleski, Tanya, 131
Morgan, David B., 223, 246n, 247n
Morris, Aldon, 23, 246n, 247n
Morris, McGarry, 153
Morrison, Toni, 37, 47, 103, 247n,
  252n, 243n

Nehemas, Alexander, 14, 221,
  258n, 259n
Norwood, Robin, 137, 138
Nussbaum, Martha, 14, 15, 49, 229,
  235, 245n, 248n, 256n, 258n, 259n,
  260n, 261n

Oates, Joyce Carol, 103, 104, 166, 252n

Orman, Suze, 125, 163

Pickford, Mary, 16
Pippin, Robert, 14, 227, 258n, 260n
Priest, Patricia, 126, 253n

Radway, Janice, 61, 62, 145, 199,
  207, 212, 244n, 245n, 252n, 254n,
  258n, 259n
Raphael, Sally Jessy, 53
Rapping, Elaine, 82, 249n, 251n
Rawls, John, 190
Reagan, Ronald, 229
Reynolds, Eddie, 140, 141, 246n
Reynolds, Gretchen, 24, 246n
Rich, Adrienne, 105
Richardson, S., 217, 255n
Ricoeur, Paul, 11, 85
Rivera, Geraldo, 82
Robbins, Tim, 148
Robertson, Roland, 177, 255n, 256n
Rolonda, 53
Rorty, Richard, 14, 258n
Roseman, Marina, 218, 259n
Rosenblatt, Louise, 145
Rountree, Linda, 125
Rousseau, Henri, 217
Ruddick, Sara, 93, 251n

Sabor, P., 217, 255n
Sandel, M., 230, 261
Sarandon, Susan, 148
Schiefflin, 232, 261n
Schlink, Bernhard, 103, 104, 226,
  252n, 260n
Schulz, 153
Schweder, Richard, 118, 253n
Scott, James, 227, 228, 254n, 260n
Seeholtz, M., 215, 249n, 259n
Seidman, Steven, 69, 249n
Senett, R., 222, 259n
Sewell Jr., William, 179, 180,
  195, 256n
Shklar, Judith, 94, 251n

Showalter, Elaine, 221, 252*n*, 256*n*, 259*n*
Simmel, G., 170, 237
Simonds, Wendy, 137, 254*n*
Smile, Samuel, 135, 136
Smith, Anthony, 172, 255*n*, 256*n*, 257*n*, 259*n*
Sontag, Susan, 77
Speber, Dan, 8
Springer, Jerry, 47, 53, 65
Stallybrass, Peter, 74, 249*n*
Stearns, C. Z., 136, 254*n*
Stearns, P. N., 136, 254*n*
Stedman, Graham, 29, 31, 43
Steiner, George, 96, 109, 251*n*
Stewart, Martha, 59
Stock, Brian, 138, 156, 244*n*, 254*n*
Stromberg, Peter, 115, 252*n*
Swidler, Ann, 46, 180, 246*n*, 247*n*, 252*n*, 256*n*

Taylor, Charles, 64, 84, 239, 248*n*, 249*n*, 251*n*
Thatcher, Margaret, 154
Thorne, Frederick, 133
Tomlinson, John, 169, 255*n*
Truth, Sojourner, 22, 199

Walker, J., 22

Walzer, Michael, 205, 213, 245*n*, 258*n*, 259*n*
Weber, Max, 4, 43, 44, 114, 122, 126, 211, 240, 243*n*, 247*n*, 253*n*, 255*n*, 261*n*
White, A., 74, 279*n*
Wiesel, Elie, 127, 128
Wilkins, Peggy, 88
Williams, Bernard, 96, 247*n*
Williams, Mary-Elizabeth, 37
Williams, Montel, 53, 291*n*
Willis, Paul, 117, 212, 253*n*, 259*n*
Wilson, Julius, 181, 256*n*
Wilson, N. L., 6, 243*n*
Winfrey, Oprah: father (Vernon Winfrey), 24, 26, 27, 29; grandmother, 22, 24, 25; mother, 22, 24, 25, 26, 29, 33, 37; rape, 25, 26, 32, 37
Wittgenstein, Ludwig, 14
Wuthnow, Robert, 54, 248*n*

Vanderbilt, Cornelius, 28
Vanzant, Iyanla, 100, 140
Voltaire, 93, 158, 159, 160, 161, 177, 216, 234

Zillman, D., 221
Zola, Emile, 93, 216
Zukav, Gary, 55, 291*n*